What can we do to help those who struggle to develop effective social skills?

Social Skills. Developing Effective Interpersonal Communication is a definitive guide to understanding and meeting the needs of those who have difficulty with social skills. Written in a clear and accessible manner, this book provides a theoretical framework to the teaching of social skills alongside a range of practical ideas for practitioners.

The book offers a four-step plan that can be adapted for use with young people or adults who are struggling with any aspect of their social skills. A simple model for assessing social skills is provided, as well as ways to measure the impact of intervention. Full of interesting examples and case studies, it includes discussion of how to teach social skills, how social skills develop through childhood, why they sometimes might not, and why social skills difficulties can have an impact on self-esteem and friendships. It includes a breakdown of social skills into the following areas:

- body language
- eye contact
- listening and paralanguage
- starting and ending conversations
- maintaining conversations
- assertiveness

Written by one of the most well-known speech and language therapists in this field and the creator of the internationally successful *Talkabout* resources, this book provides a key reference for the study of social skills. It will be essential reading for educators, therapists, parents and anyone supporting others in developing communication and social skills.

Alex Kelly is a speech and language therapist based near Southampton, UK. She runs two businesses, both based in Hampshire: Speaking Space Ltd offers speech and language therapy and occupational therapy to children and adults, training in all areas of communication, and a day service for adults with intellectual disabilities and autism. Alex Kelly Ltd offers training and consultancy in social skills. Alex is the author of the best-selling *Talkabout* books and lectures internationally on all aspects of social skills.

More Brilliant Professional Resources from Bestselling Author Alex Kelly!

TALKABOUT

Each practical workbook in this bestselling series provides a clear programme of activities designed to improve self-awareness, self-esteem and social skills.

Title	Focus	Age-range
Talkabout (2nd edition)	Developing Social Skills for all ages	7+
Talkabout for Children 1 (2nd edition)	Developing Self-Awareness and Self-Esteem	4–11
Talkabout for Children 2 (2nd edition)	Developing Social Skills	4–11
Talkabout for Children 3 (2nd edition)	Developing Friendship Skills	4–11
Talkabout for Teenagers (2nd edition)	Developing Social and Emotional Communication Skills	11–19
Talkabout for Adults	Developing Self-awareness and Self-esteem in adults	16+
Talkabout Sex and Relationships 1	Developing Intimate Relationship Skills	11+
Talkabout Sex and Relationships 2	Sex Education	11+

Check out www.routledge.com/Talkabout/book-series/SMT for these and other resources

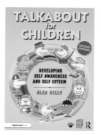

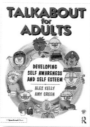

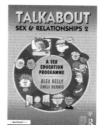

Social Skills

Developing Effective Interpersonal Communication

Alex Kelly

Routledge
Taylor & Francis Group

LONDON AND NEW YORK

First published 2019
by Routledge
2 Park Square, Milton Park, Abingdon, Oxon OX14 4RN

and by Routledge
52 Vanderbilt Avenue, New York, NY 10017

Routledge is an imprint of the Taylor & Francis Group, an informa business

British Library Cataloguing-in-Publication Data
A catalogue record for this book is available from the British Library

Library of Congress Cataloging-in-Publication Data
Names: Kelly, Alex, 1963- author.
Title: Social skills : developing effective interpersonal communication /
    Alex Kelly.
Description: Abingdon, Oxon ; New York, NY : Routledge, 2019. |
    Includes bibliographical references and index.
Identifiers: LCCN 2018024295 (print) | LCCN 2018030191 (ebook) |
    ISBN 9781315173405 (ebok) | ISBN 9781138332249 |
    ISBN 9781138332249(hardback) |
    ISBN 9781911186168(paperback) | ISBN 9781315173405(ebk)
Subjects: LCSH: Social skills—Study and teaching.
Classification: LCC HM691 (ebook) | LCC HM691 .K46 2019 (print) |
    DDC 302/.14—dc23
LC record available at https://lccn.loc.gov/2018024295

ISBN: 978-1-138-33224-9 (hbk)
ISBN: 978-1-911186-16-8 (pbk)
ISBN: 978-1-315-17340-5 (ebk)

Typeset in Sabon
by Apex CoVantage, LLC

*This book is dedicated to all the people who have inspired me to be the
speech and language therapist I am today: to all the amazing children and adults
who I have had the privilege to work with over the past 30 years and who continue to help me
to be a better therapist; to all my colleagues and friends at Speaking Space Ltd – I am
so proud of what we are achieving together; to my mum and dad for their love and support over
the years; to my boys Ed, Pete and George – you have grown up to be such lovely young men
and I am so proud of you all; and finally, the biggest thank you to Brian – I am living a happier,
more blessed life because of you and I love you.*

Contents

Contents

Contents

Tables and figures

Tables

Figures

Introduction to this book from the author

I am often asked to talk to people about social skills. As I walk out in front of them, I sometimes see someone looking back at me, maybe with their arms crossed, an eyebrow raised, lips pursed, 'saying' to me 'what has this got to do with me? . . . I teach design and technology/PE/science . . . what do I need to know about helping children to develop social skills?' And I know that in the next few hours I will have to convince them of why we all need to take this subject seriously. So, I might ask the audience, 'What do you want most out of life?' or 'What makes you happy?' and we will then consider if any of these things require them to be socially skilled or socially competent? How many of their 'happiness factors' involved a relationship with another person or a group of people? And I wonder if those people would think their social competence was important.

I might also ask them what they want most for their own children. As a parent, there are three things I want my children to have when they leave home. First, I want them to feel good about who they are – to be able to hold their head up and feel happy within their own skin. Second, I want them to have friends – a group of people to talk to, listen to, and share experiences with and people that will give them the knowledge that they are a valuable person because they are a friend. Third, I want them to get a job or meaningful employment – to give them something to get up for in the morning, a role in their community and a wage packet at the end of the month. These three things require my children to have a healthy self-esteem and also good social skills. I have yet to meet a parent who disagrees with me.

However, it is obvious that many children struggle to learn social skills. We need these skills to communicate effectively in order to express ourselves, to listen to others, to be taken seriously, to learn, to get a job and to make friends. So, shouldn't we be helping children to develop good social skills? Surely this is fundamental and central to everything? So we *must* take this subject seriously.

As I continue to talk to the group of people, I hope to see a slight shift in body posture. Maybe they will slowly nod their head or even smile at me. This is not a subject just for the health professionals and the special needs teachers. This is for all of us. This is my passion. If I could be the Queen or the President for the day, I would make a few changes to the world (I am obviously quite optimistic of their power and their ability to effect change in just one day!). Those small points aside, I would put social skills onto the curriculum of every school and then I would ensure the schools had the skills to teach children the art of effective communication. I would then sit back and wait to see the impact of a more socially skilled world. I wonder what would happen.

This book has been two years in the writing and 30 years in the making. I have tried to write something that is both informed by research and current practise but that is also practical. I want people to know more about social skills, but also to know how to develop effective social skills. So I have included what the literature says, but I have also told stories about the people I have worked with over the years. In this way, I hope I have captured the subject in enough detail and given readers the essentials to be able to practically do something with the knowledge.

The book is roughly divided into three parts. The first part of the book looks at what we mean by social skills. There are seven chapters that explore our body language, our conversation skills and our assertiveness. These chapters will give you a deeper appreciation of this fascinating subject and the rules for each skill. The second part of the book will give you a better understanding on aspects of social skills that are often relevant. There are four chapters that explore the areas of self-esteem and friendship skills – two areas that are inextricably linked to our social competence, the normal development of social skills and then the specific issues that may arise in autism. Then the final part of the book is all about how to practically develop effective social skills. There are six chapters that look at the following: how to assess social skills so we know where to start; how to teach them including the different approaches and interventions, and how to teach them at school and at home; and, finally, how to show you have been effective.

On a more practical note, this book is written with my international colleagues in mind and so I use the term 'intellectual disability' rather than the term 'learning disability' which is used in the UK. I also tend to refer to children more than adults, even though this is a book that is relevant to all.

Finally, I just need to tell you that my job is pretty great. The feeling I get when I know that I have helped someone to be a better communicator or someone to feel happier about who they are, is a gift. So, this book is a summary of what I have learned over the 30 years I have been doing this. I hope you enjoy it. But more importantly, I hope it helps.

A few quotes about the author and her work

The teaching of social and emotional skills is a crucial part of our core curriculum at The Ashley School Academy Trust. Working with Alex Kelly and embedding the *Talkabout* programme has enabled all staff, regardless of role, to understand both the importance of the explicit teaching of social skills and the hierarchy of social skill development.

We have been working with Alex, and her team, since October 2013 revisiting our learning; developing champions for social skills; embedding the *Talkabout* Programme and as a result seeing our pupils gain confidence socially and achieve academically.

Working with Alex has been a privilege, to learn from her extensive knowledge and research and to develop together systems and processes that are right for our staff and pupils. Alex always shares her knowledge with enthusiasm and humour thus really engaging all our staff. Alex's approach, as we developed our own skills, has always been encouraging, flexible and evidence based. There is no doubt that without her skills and strengths our social skills curriculum would not be as effective as evidenced by both *Talkabout* evaluations and external reviews/inspections.

Social Skills: developing effective interpersonal communication combines sound theory with authentic experience and credible evidence and will help put social skills at the forefront of the school curriculum developing pupils' ability to communicate effectively in the 21st Century world.

Sally Garrett, Head Teacher, The Ashley School Academy Trust, England

I first met Alex Kelly back in 2010 when she delivered a keynote speech at a conference in Wales, UK, on the importance of social competence. Listening to Alex was a 'light bulb' moment for me and I was keen to spread the word to schools across Wales, confident that if schools adopted this intervention, the impact on children could be huge. Over six years I was able to work with Alex to train staff from over 600 schools across Wales and I have collated pre and post data to evidence the improvements made by each child participating in this project. Every child improved in one or more area and furthermore, I received feedback from parents and teachers reporting on the positive impact of the intervention at home and at school.

Alex is held in high esteem with many professionals and always seems to "pitch" training days just right. Her presentations are always enjoyable but more importantly, understood by all who attend. You could almost feel the new-found enthusiasm of delegates going back to their work place, eager to start their social skills groups. All of the training days were a great success and all participants enjoyed a relaxed and happy atmosphere interacting well with each other and the speaker.

Jeannette Carr, Director of Afasic Cymru, Wales

The Alex Kelly books and DVDs are invaluable resources for myself as a speech therapist working with adults with an intellectual disability. I would highly recommend purchasing these books as some of your core essentials within any disability setting!

If you get the chance to attend training facilitated by Alex, please do! She is highly motivating, entertaining, interesting and an expert in the field of social skills. It was one of the best and most useful training sessions that I have attended as a therapist in 22 years.

Clare Byrne, SLT, Northern Ireland

After 20 years as a teacher, I have been on many courses and listened to many experts, but Alex is different – she is fun, vibrant, informative and funny. Within the first ten minutes, I knew that what we were doing would actually be able to be used in the classroom the next day and not end up on a 'wish list' at the bottom of the filing cabinet!

Kathryn Palmer, SENCo, England

The day I familiarised myself with Alex's research about social skills changed the way I deliver social skills at school. I previously wasn't sure what I should teach first and how I should teach each skill. Now, I am able to assess social skills and show the children's progress, and the knowledge of the hierarchy of social skills has solved the mystery of what I should teach first. Social skills are extremely important for children with special educational needs and thanks to Alex's hard work I have been able to prove the importance and effectiveness of teaching social skills. Not only has she changed the way I teach social skills but she has also helped children to achieve their full potential which has contributed to their quality of life.

Beata Bednarska, Teaching Assistant, England

Alex Kelly's *Talkabout* books have completely changed the way we think about Social Skills. It looks at the skills that underpin the ability to be social which can easily be missed with other social skills programs. The *Talkabout* books are easy to use and the children really enjoy the activities. Highly recommended.

Karen Slack, Teacher (ASD), England

I was very privileged to be able to participate in a course delivered by Alex in Ireland; she has a superb way of motivating a group, and being so enthusiastic about her work. Her social skills books, resources and activities are excellent for group work with children needing guidance in friendship, bullying, help with additional needs or just being different in any way. I find Alex has a way through her books to deliver information to children in a fun, easy to remember way, her ideas work so well.

Carmel Kilduff, Support Worker, Ireland

After attending a workshop delivered by Alex Kelly in 2013, I implemented the *Talkabout* program across our high school for students with disabilities. We assessed all of our students using the *Talkabout* assessment tool and teachers then facilitated small groups using the *Talkabout* resources. We have found that students' assessment results have improved since using *Talkabout* and teaching staff report that the resources are suited to our population and are easy to use. I like that the assessment gives someone a clear indication of progress and a starting point for therapy.

Claire Formby, Speech Pathologist, Australia

I had the pleasure of attending Alex's three-day social skills training in November 2017 and thought the whole course was fantastic. It was great to have the opportunity to see all the work you do at Speaking Space and get to meet so many of your service users – and it made me even more determined to get out there and get running some more social skills groups of my own!

Carla Morrell, Speech and Language Therapist, England

I found Alex Kelly's theories and activities concise and relevant to the population I work with – a true rarity to find appropriate activities for this demographic! I especially appreciate her social skills hierarchy – social skills are such an abstract concept that her classification of them into developmental stages is a huge advantage in delivering appropriate intervention.

Sally Glass, Speech Pathologist, Australia

I attended a two-day workshop presented by Alex Kelly in Melbourne a couple of years ago. It was absolutely inspiring and I learnt so much! Alex's way of teaching was so practical and helped me to become excited about using what I had learnt in my day-to-day work.

Julie Slater, Speech Pathologist, Australia

I have been using Alex's new Sex and Relationships *Talkabout* book, which is proving very useful in my work as an Occupational Therapist with young people with an intellectual disability!

Tiffany Amsdon, Occupational Therapist, England

Alex Kelly's training is inspiring and I left a one-day course feeling I had truly discovered a great resource for children with autism and/or self-esteem issues. Her *Talkabout* books, and the enjoyment some of our children derive from being part of the group, has very quickly had an impact on their self-awareness and self-confidence.

Amanda Farrell, Teacher, England

I have used *Talkabout* resources with children from Primary to Secondary age in mainstream schools as a Speech and Language Therapist. The activity sheets are well-presented and motivating (especially those in colour!). I listened and was enthused by Alex speaking about the hierarchy of social skills from body language to assertiveness. This knowledge has been invaluable to me to target social skill areas in the children I work with. Following the *Talkabout* format, the children develop their self-awareness and become better communicators.

Esther Parish, Speech and Language Therapist, England

After attending the training with Alex Kelly, the clarity of the social skills hierarchy and the simple structure of the therapy sessions made me determined to implement the groups within my own speech therapy department. We now run the social skills groups in schools which have been so valued they continue to run. I recommend her book nearly every day!

Victoria Williams, SLT, England

I have used Alex's *Talkabout* self-esteem and self-awareness book in our Primary School and the intervention has proved excellent. I have been running the scheme for eight weeks, and our children LOVE *Talkabout* (they are aged 7–11). We are already seeing fantastic improvements in all aspects of self-esteem and even more so self-awareness, particularly with our ASD children.

Luke Phillips, Teacher, Wales

Alex's understanding of social skills training provides a clear developmental hierarchy of skills that follow through to the training activities she has published. Her approach makes it easier for students to learn this complex set of skills.

Anthony Cooper, Speech Pathologist, Australia

Chapter 1

Social skills
An introduction

'Communication is truth; communication is happiness. To share is our duty; to go down boldly and bring to light those hidden thoughts which are the most diseased; to conceal nothing; to pretend nothing; if we are ignorant to say so; if we love our friends to let them know it.'

Virginia Woolf (1882–1941)

The art of communication

The art of communication is complicated and amazing. When one person communicates to another, something takes place that is found nowhere else in nature, which makes interpersonal communication probably humanity's greatest achievement. At a basic level communication involves at least two people, a message to communicate, the ability to communicate and then to check that this message has been successfully received. Effective communication requires that this is done accurately, in a timely manner, is appropriate to the context and that any communication breakdown is repaired. So, the skill of communicating not only involves articulating our own thoughts but also being able to use appropriate nonverbal behaviours, and then having an awareness of what the other person may be thinking or feeling as well as saying (or not saying). If we look at the root of the verb 'to communicate', it can be traced back to its Latin meaning 'to share' or 'to make common'. Maybe with this in mind, Hamilton (2014) defined communication as the process whereby people share ideas, thoughts and feelings in commonly comprehensible ways.

However, while mechanical means of communication have developed beyond our realms of imagination, people often struggle to communicate face-to-face. Smooth, reciprocal conversations can be difficult. Words are not spoken or misunderstood. Nonverbal messages are not seen or contradict what is said. Robert Bolton (1979) says 'in our society it is rare for people to share what really matters . . . and it is equally rare for people to listen intently enough to really understand what someone is saying'. So, what is the difference between someone who communicates effectively and someone who struggles to communicate face-to-face? What might we see?

Let's first consider the person who is struggling. We may picture the child who finds it hard to join in the conversation, averts their eyes and has a slouched body posture. We may think of the adult who pushes into conversations, monopolising the topic and stands too close to us. We remember the friend who looks at us while we are talking, but whose mind is clearly wandering while they formulate what they will say next. We may also think of the person who often seems to get it wrong and makes us behave or feel in a way that they say they didn't intend. And we think of those people who come across as annoying, boring, aloof, aggressive, awkward, isolated or inept, simply because of the way they communicate.

Now consider a person who communicates effectively, someone we would describe as socially skilled. We may think of the child who happily goes to school, meets friends, and talks to relatives in a cheerful and confident manner. We may think of the person who appears at ease with themselves, who makes friends easily, is generally accepted and well-liked by others and can meet the challenges of modern-day life head on. They appear to cope with different situations and different people by adapting their skills to be appropriate and effective communicators.

So how can we recognise and define social skills or social competence? What is it that defines why one person struggles and the other person does not? And why is it important? In this introductory chapter we will look at how we can define social skills or social competence and we will outline the differences between men and women and the effect this has on their social skills. I will then summarise why it is important to be socially skilled. I will argue that being socially skilled is something that has to be taken seriously, as our ability to communicate successfully with others is central to our quality of life and our self-esteem and that there is too much evidence that shows the positive difference we can make by improving someone's social skills. But first let us consider some definitions.

Defining social skills and social competence

Deciding how to define 'social skills' or 'social competence' has consumed vast amounts of energy in the academic field. Schneider (2016) quotes Louis Armstrong's comment about the difficulty of defining jazz: 'If you have to define it, you cannot possibly understand it'. I don't think it is that bad, but being socially skilled does have that subjective nature to it which can make it harder to define.

One issue is that different terms can be used synonymously to describe essentially the same thing – being able to communicate effectively. The terms 'social skills' and 'social competence', 'interpersonal skills' and 'communication skills' and sometimes a combination of these 'social communication skills', can all appear to describe the same thing in different contexts and different texts. This book is called *Social skills: developing effective interpersonal communication* – but do I mean 'social skills' or do I actually mean 'social competence' or 'interpersonal skills' or all of the above? Well I will, of course, argue that the title of the book is perfectly fine as long as we all understand what I mean by 'social skills' and being socially skilled. In addition, 'social skills' is certainly the term that is most commonly used by teachers and parents in the UK and so for me, this is the title that best fits the book. But let's start with trying to define the terms interpersonal communication or skills, social skills and social competence.

Hargie (2017) says that interpersonal skills in a global sense are the skills we employ when interacting with other people, but he goes on to define interpersonal communication as 'a process that is characterised by an ongoing verbal and nonverbal exchange of collaborative meaning' which requires skilled co-ordination, as each person regulates his or her actions in line with others. This is also described as the 'dance of dialogue' (Pickering, 2006) where individuals align their talk with one another, and construct shared meaning from the conversation: we need to pay attention to the moves of others and be flexible in how we respond.

Schlundt and McFall (1985) define social skills as 'the specific component processes that enable an individual to behave in a manner that will be judged as "competent". Skills are the abilities necessary for producing behavior that will accomplish the objectives of the task'. Robbins and Hunsaker (2014) also state that in order to gain competence in a skill, 'people need to understand the skill, get feedback on how well they are performing the skill, and use the skill often enough to integrate it into their behavioral repertoires'.

Most authors now recognise that social competence is a broader, more situation specific construct than skill. It must extend beyond observable behaviours to include internal processes related to the overt behaviour as well as the relationship between the person and the social environment. So, it is the person's ability to perform a certain behaviour or task in a certain context at a certain moment.

Schumaker and Hazel's (1984) definition of social skills includes both aspects. They say a social skill is 'any cognitive function or overt behaviour in which an individual engages while interacting with another person'. The cognitive functions include capacities such as empathy or understanding others' feelings, discriminating and making inferences about social cues, and predicting and evaluating the consequences of social behaviour. The overt behaviours include nonverbal behaviours such as eye contact and posture, and verbal behaviours such as starting up a conversation. They argue that social competence is therefore seen as having four sets of skills:

The four sets of skills for social competence

- Discriminating situations in which social behaviour is appropriate, for example is someone too busy to talk?
- Choosing the appropriate nonverbal and verbal skills to use, for example what greeting is appropriate here?
- Performing these skills effectively, for example the greeting is used with appropriate volume, facial expression etc.
- Accurately perceiving and responding to the other person's verbal and nonverbal cues, for example to stop speaking if they start, or to continue to speak if they look and smile.

In reviewing a number of the definitions available to us, I would argue that it is most helpful to consider the separate components of the definitions and to describe these under seven headings (adapted from Hargie, 2017).

Socially skilled behaviours are goal directed

Firstly, socially skilled behaviours are *goal-directed*. Part of Schlundt and McFall's definition of social skills is that skills are 'the abilities necessary for producing behavior that will accomplish the objectives of the task' (1985). This means that we use certain behaviours in order to achieve a desired outcome and therefore they are purposeful behaviours, as opposed to unintentional behaviours. An example of this is if I want you to speak, I will use certain behaviours to encourage you – I will look at you, I will nod my head, and use listening noises such as 'mmm'. These behaviours are therefore directed towards the goal of encouraging someone to communicate. So, the first part to our definition is:

> Socially skilled behaviours enable us to achieve a desired outcome from an interaction.

Socially skilled behaviours are interrelated

Socially skilled behaviours are also *interrelated* as we can see from the previous example. We will use several behaviours in a synchronised way to achieve a particular goal, for example, looking, nodding and smiling to show encouragement. It is often hard to isolate what someone has done to make us feel valued, threatened, ignored, and this is because we are always using several behaviours at once. This often means that we have to look for clusters of behaviours if we are to be able to read someone accurately and we will talk about this in much more detail in the body language chapter. This is also important to consider when teaching social skills as we will need to consider which behaviour will have an impact on the next. So, the second part to our definition is:

> Social skills are interrelated – one behaviour will lead to another.

Social skills are defined in terms of identifiable units of behaviour

Thirdly, social skills are defined in terms of *identifiable units of behaviour* which the person displays. So, by 'skill' we mean the *ability* that an individual has or the *behaviour* of an individual. Or as 'those identifiable, learned behaviors that individuals use in interpersonal situations to obtain or maintain reinforcement from their environment' Kelly (1982). We judge whether someone is socially skilled based on how they actually behave. These behaviours are essential for us to be able to identify so that we can assess and if necessary teach them and they can also be divided into nonverbal and verbal behaviours. We will consider these behaviours in more detail in following chapters, but for now we can also say that:

> Social skills include both nonverbal and verbal behaviours.

Social skills are behaviours which can be learned

The fourth element to this definition is that social skills are *behaviours which can be learned.* Our methods and style of communicating with others are primarily learned responses. They are learned through imitation, modelling and reinforcement, predominantly as a child is growing up. A child receives feedback, both positive and negative, and this is essential as they will use those behaviours which are encouraged more frequently and will display those behaviours that are discouraged or ignored less often. So, the fourth part to our definition is:

> Social skills are learned behaviours.

Social skills are appropriate to the situation

The fifth component of our definition is that social skills should be *appropriate to the situation*. Schlundt and McFall (1985) define social skills as 'the specific component processes that enable an individual to behave in a manner that will be judged as "competent"'. So, for someone to be truly socially skilled, they need to learn the social behaviours and then use them in a way that is acceptable to the other person and to the context. We need to adapt our behaviour to particular individuals and to specific social contexts. In this way, we may develop a style of communication in one context but will need to adapt our style in other contexts, for example when being interviewed. We need to learn that what is acceptable in one situation may not be acceptable in another. What is acceptable to say to one person may not be acceptable to another. So, we use context-appropriate behaviours which Dickson and McCartan (2005) refer to as 'contextual propriety'. So, our definition includes:

> Socially skilled behaviours should be altered to be appropriate to the context.

Social skills are under the cognitive control of the individual

Social skills should also be under the *cognitive control* of the individual. This means that a socially skilled person has learned *when* to use certain social behaviours as well as *what* and *how* to use them. So 'saying the right thing at the wrong time' may often seem to be as socially inadequate as not saying the right thing at all. So, this links in with our previous part to the definition – social skills need to change according to the context, and we need to decide *when* and *how* to use our behaviours. Hargie (2017) cites Zimmerman who identified four key stages in learning social skills:

- Observation: the person watches other people perform a skill and pays attention to other dimensions such as the motivational orientation and variations.
- Emulation: the person is able to execute a skill or behaviour similar to that observed. For example the style may be similar but the words different.
- Self-control: the person begins to master the skill.
- Self-regulation: the person learns to use the skill appropriately across different contexts and with different people.

So, our definition includes:

> Socially skilled people know when to talk, what to say and how to say it.

Socially skilled people can read their audience

Finally, socially skilled people can read their audience. Erving Goffman (1955) uses the term 'face work' to mean the ability to present oneself to others by putting on the appropriate face. Children who are able to do this are those who are the most socially skilled. They learn to 'read' their audience, to know what they are thinking, and to shape their responses so that others view them positively. Rubin says that face work is a central feature of social competence and defines it as 'the ability to achieve personal goals in social interactions while simultaneously maintaining positive relationships with others, over time and in a variety of situations' (2002). So, finally, we can include in our definition:

> Socially skilled people can 'read' their audience and shape their responses accordingly.

These seven components help us to define what we mean by being socially skilled and also help us to understand the distinction between what is meant by 'social skills' and 'social competence' (already inferred within our definition). Social skills typically refer to the discrete, goal directed behaviours which allow an individual to interact effectively with others in his or her environment (Sheridan and Walker, 1999) and social competence refers to the quality of their interactions as perceived by others around them. In short, the seven components to being socially skilled are as follows:

The seven components to defining socially skilled

- Socially skilled behaviours enable us to achieve a desired outcome from an interaction.
- Social skills are interrelated – one behaviour will lead to another.
- Social skills include both nonverbal and verbal behaviours.
- Social skills are learned behaviours.
- Socially skilled behaviours should be altered to be appropriate to the context.
- Socially skilled people know when to talk, what to say and how to say it.
- Socially skilled people can 'read' their audience and shape their responses accordingly.

So, in summary, we can conclude that a socially skilled person communicates with others using both their learned nonverbal and verbal behaviour in a way that is appropriate to the situation and listener, and that is effective, in that it has the desired outcome. They are able to read their audience and show the ability to say the right thing in the right way at the right time.

The difference between men and women (and our brains)

However, we also need to take into account some obvious differences that may influence us or affect us in our social competence. Is there a difference between the social skills of men and women? Most couples probably think so! So it may be a good time to talk briefly about the differences here and why this may affect social communication.

Some scientists believe that the main difference is related to how our brains work. We know that the right hemisphere, which is the creative side, controls the left side of the body, while the left hemisphere controls logic, reason, speech and the body's right side. The left brain is where language and vocabulary are stored and the right brain stores and controls visual information.

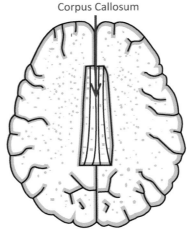

LEFT HEMISPHERE
Right side of the body

Mathematics
Verbal
Logical
Facts
Deduction
Analysis
Practical
Order
Words of a song
Lineal
See fine detail

Corpus Callosum

RIGHT HEMISPHERE
Left side of the body

Creative
Artistic
Visual
Intuition
Ideas
Imagination
Holistic
Tune of a song
Sees 'big picture'
Spatial
Multiprocessing

Figure 1.1 The functions of the brain
Adapted from Pease, 2001

In 2001, researchers from Harvard found that certain parts of the brain were differently sized in males and females, which may help balance out the overall size difference. The study found that parts of the frontal lobe, responsible for problem-solving and decision-making, and the limbic cortex, responsible for regulating emotions, were larger in women. In men, the parietal cortex, which is involved in space perception, and the amygdala, which regulates sexual and social behaviour, were larger (Hoag, 2008).

Baron-Cohen (2003) says that, indisputably, male and female minds are different. Men tend to be better at analysing systems (better systemisers), while women tend to be better at reading the emotions of other people (better empathisers). Baron-Cohen shows that this distinction arises from biology, not culture. Of course, not all scientists believe in this male/female difference but the main differences according to Baron-Cohen are described below:

The main differences between the male and female brain

- Cell numbers: men have 4% more brain cells than women, and about 100 grams more of brain tissue.
- Cellular connections: even though a man has more brain cells, it is reported that women have more dendritic connections between brain cells.
- Corpus callosum: it is reported that a woman's brain has a larger corpus callosum, which means women can transfer data between the right and left hemisphere faster than men. Men tend to be more left brained, while women have greater access to both sides.
- Language: for men, language is most often just in the dominant hemisphere (usually the left side), but a larger number of women seem to be able to use both sides for language. This gives them a distinct advantage in reading nonverbal cues and the emotion of a message.

- Limbic size: females, on average, have a larger deep limbic system than males. This means women are more in touch with their feelings; have an increased ability to bond and to be connected to others; and a more acute sense of smell. However, it also leaves a female somewhat more susceptible to depression, and suicide attempts.

So how does this all link to social skills? It is a well-known fact that boys find it harder to learn how to hold a conversation and are slower to develop language. This could be directly linked to a difference between the male and female brain. As we have said, the corpus callosum (the neural fibres which connect the left and right hemispheres) is larger in the female brain. This means that messages travel faster between the two hemispheres, so the language part of the brain (Broca's area) on the left side can communicate more easily with the right side, which is where interpretation of nonverbal behaviour mainly occurs. This is backed up by Simon Baron-Cohen (2003) who found that women use both sides of their brains in language tasks and men just use the left hemisphere with few connections bridging the two hemispheres. Boyce (2012) interprets this by saying that in a female brain 'the nonverbal processing area is able to communicate directly and at speed with the language centre in Broca's area . . . enabling the language area to access the nonverbal elements of communication'.

Of course, this explains a lot of the miscommunication that *can* arise between the sexes. We may interpret communication differently. Women can be more attuned to the nonverbal message whereas men seem to be more attuned to the words that are being said. John Gray (1992) says that 'men and women seldom mean the same things even when they use the same words'. So, a woman may say 'I'm fine' but she may use her nonverbal communication to say otherwise and she expects the other person to respond accordingly with maybe, 'Oh dear – I can see you are not fine. What's the matter? Can I help?' But the man may have heard that she is fine, which makes him feel better. On the other hand, if there is a problem, a man may say 'I'm fine' and he will mostly mean it. He may not express his feelings so readily and so his words need to be translated for the woman as meaning 'I'm fine because I am successfully dealing with my problem. I don't need any help. If I do I will ask'. A woman does not struggle to express her feelings verbally and she will often use superlatives, metaphors and generalisations to help, such as 'I feel like you *never* listen'. But she doesn't expect the word 'never' to be taken literally.

It would appear therefore, that in our quest to define social competence, it may be also helpful to consider the person's sex, or certainly the 'sex' of their brain. So, we may need to add to our definition that a socially skilled person will make adjustments to their communication according to the sex of the person to whom they are talking.

Why are social skills important?

But why is it so important to be socially skilled? Why do we need to worry?

Quality of life

First let us consider *quality of life* or *happiness*. It would appear from the many definitions of quality of life that it is partly linked to relationships and employment and these both have links with social competence. Some definitions refer to there being a number of 'domains of living'. Each domain contributes to our overall assessment of the quality of our life and the domains include: family and friends, work, neighbourhood or shelter, community, health, education, and spiritual. Myers and Diener (1995) define happiness as being related to 'knowing a person's traits, whether the person enjoys a supportive network of close relationships, whether the person's culture offers positive interpretation for most daily events, whether the person is engaged in work and leisure, and whether the person has faith which entails social support, purpose and hope'. So social relationships and work are important parts of this quote and we will discuss both in this next section of the chapter and the relevance they have to being socially skilled.

Relationships

When asked about happiness or quality of life, most people will mention friends, family or a lover or partner and as Ouvry (1998) states: 'social relationships are one of the most important aspects of most people's lives'. Schalock (2000) notes personal relationships have been found to mediate stress and so our quality of life is very dependent on our personal relationships and how rewarding they are.

Indeed, it is hard to imagine a world where we do not have many, or even any, relationships. So much of our self-identity and self-worth comes from being a mother, a husband, a lover, a friend, or a confidant. Who would we be, without our relationships? How would we feel about ourselves if we did not have any friends? How would we know if we were funny, a good listener, kind, or a good friend? It is hard, if not impossible, to imagine a life without friends and loved ones. And yet, this is the experience of a great number of people with social skills difficulties. They often live in a society that segregates or isolates them because of their difficulties and they often lack the skills or experience to make and maintain friendships when or if they do have the opportunity.

Few people *want* to live their lives completely on their own. People need people and effective communication is the lifeblood of any relationship. As Amado (1993) says:

> Some of the most noble activities in life include having friends and being a friend. Friendship should occupy a strong place in everyone's human development. They call up the best parts of people – sometimes the fun-loving side and sometimes the serious. The saddest thing a person can say about someone is, 'He doesn't have any friends'.

There are, of course, many kinds of relationship, and individuals have different social needs, which are met by different kinds of social life. But as Firth and Rapley (1990) state: 'for almost everyone, with or without a disability, the relationships with the people with whom they live, together with other social relationships, are a major contribution to the quality of their lives'.

Rubin (2002) describes friends as taking centre stage in a child's life and that 'they have the power to cause your child to feel truly happy or absolutely miserable'. So, if we agree that we need relationships to make us happy, we have to consider the skills that we need in order to form and maintain relationships. Can we go up to people and introduce ourselves? Do we listen and then comment appropriately? Do we use our body language to help people feel comfortable in our presence and use our voice to show them we care about them? People with social skills difficulties are often not able to do these things well and they are perceived as rude, awkward, shy, stand-offish, aggressive or inept and 'are often rejected by their peers'

(Warnes et al., 2005). And because of this, they struggle to make and maintain friendships. As Rubin (2002) says

> We are all social beings; we need to establish satisfactory and satisfying human connections. Figuring out how to get along with people, how to initiate friendships, how to walk away from relationships that are no longer pleasant and maintain the ones that are enjoyable and valuable – these are the challenges at the core of our emotional lives.

If we ask a child with social skills difficulties what school is like, in my experience, they will say 'no-one likes me' or 'people are mean to me' or 'I don't have many friends' or 'I get bullied'. The fact is that most people find it difficult to be friends with someone with poor social skills, so these children are often isolated and unhappy. We also know that friendships are essential for children to achieve a better chance at a good quality of life. This topic is discussed more in the chapter on friendships.

Friendships are essential for children

- Friends help each other to think things through more clearly and competently, thus improving problem solving skills.
- Children learn from one another about what is right and wrong, about loyalty, and what happens when we hurt someone's feelings or betray their trust, thus improving emotional intelligence.
- The better a child is able to form and maintain friendships, the more likely they are to be accepted and valued within their peer groups and the more likely they are to do well in school and later on in life, thus improving the chance for success and their self-esteem.

So, our social competence definitely contributes to our quality of life, as our lives are built on positive interactions and the relationships that we have with the people around us (Crawford and Goldstein, 2005). And as Bercow et al. said 'the ability to communicate effectively is the key life skill of the 21st century' (2008). So, we can summarise by saying:

> Social skills are central to helping a child to have friends and to be a friend, and this will contribute to their quality of life.

Success at school and work

When considering our happiness or our quality of life, we may also think about our job. We may not enjoy getting up for work on a cold Monday morning and we may currently dislike our boss and feel as if we live for the weekend, but being employed brings with it a sense of worth. We are a valued member of society. We have a role. We have a purpose. We have a goal. Anyone who has been unemployed for any period of time will relate to this and will recognise the importance of those social interactions at work as well as the money at the end of the month to make us feel good. But how did we get our job? Did we need our social skills to help us? Is it important to develop these skills at school and to have them at work?

School

Social competence has been repeatedly demonstrated to be a critical variable in predicting success in future life (Denham et al., 2001) – the people who get jobs and then get promoted are the people with good social skills. So, we can look at our school leavers and predict who will be able to get into college or get a job by considering one of the most accurate predictors: their social competence. Research has also demonstrated powerful connections between how well a child does socially and how successful they are in other areas of their life (Rubin 2002). Jean Gross (2008) also talks about the importance of children developing social skills early on in life. She states that there are three key 'protective factors' that increase the likelihood of 'positive life outcomes' by boosting children's resilience. They are: firstly, language, literacy and numeracy; secondly, good social competence; and thirdly, positive parenting. By developing all three early on, children are more likely to have a better quality of life.

We should also consider the research into academic competence. Schneider (2016) says that 'numerous findings have illustrated the positive effects of social interaction on cognitive development'. It has also been suggested that social competence is a more accurate predictor of achievement than measured intellectual capacity (Wentzel, cited by Schneider, 2016). As Elias et al. (1997) say: 'when schools attend systematically to students' social and emotional skills, the academic achievement of children increases, the incidence of problem behaviours decreases, and the quality of the relationships surrounding each child improves'. The findings of these research studies indicate that academic achievement is influenced by social competence and peer acceptance, which in turn is affected by levels of academic success – meaning there is a bidirectional relationship between social skills and academic success. This then also brings in the impact that friendships or peer relationships have on cognitive growth. So, children not only need social skills in order to make friends and be accepted by their peers, but then friendship skills enable them to learn more effectively. In addition, if we use social interaction with friends to help children learn, we see an improvement in academic achievement and social interaction with their friends. This is discussed more in the chapter on teaching social skills at school.

Work

As seen earlier, another aspect to our quality of life is whether we are engaged in work or meaningful employment, and social relationships are important here. Not only are work settings the second most important context for social relationships after the home (Stewart, 1985) but social relationships are important to working. Indeed Bolton (1979) says that eighty percent of people who fail at work do so for one reason: they do not relate well to other people, and when people with disabilities lose their jobs, it has been found that social factors are as important as any inability to carry out the tasks of the job (Ford et al., 1984). Jean Gross (2008) also says that good social and emotional skills are becoming increasingly important in the modern world: essential to learning, being valued by employers, and necessary in sticking to goals and staying out of trouble, something we will also talk about next.

So, our social competence definitely contributes to our ability to be successful. We need to develop social skills at school to help us achieve academically and socially; to help us to get into meaningful employment and stay in meaningful employment; and to develop social relationships at work. This will contribute to our quality of life and so we can also say that:

> Social skills are important to enable us to be successful.

Staying out of trouble

As we have just said, social skills are also important for staying out of trouble. A recent study showed that between 60% and 90% of young people who pass through young offender institutions have communication difficulties (Bryan et al., 2007) and this includes problems with social communication skills. This is an alarming statistic. This means that at least 60% of those children who ended up offending had some difficulties in understanding or expressing themselves. They may have had difficulties in reading the situation because of this and may have misinterpreted someone else's communication because of their difficulties. This is backed up by Mash and Barkley (1996) cited by Warnes et al. (2005) who say that 'social skills deficits are frequently associated with children exhibiting externalising disorders such as delinquency and conduct disorder'.

I wonder what would have happened if the children who ended up offending had been taught social skills within school? What if social skills were on the curriculum of every school and teachers were trained to teach these skills effectively? Would we see a difference in the years to come? I suspect we would. We have already seen what Elias et al. (1997) said when they concluded that 'when schools attend systematically to students' social and emotional skills, the academic achievement of children increases, *the incidence of problem behaviours decreases*, and the quality of the relationships surrounding each child improves'. Yet our education system at the moment does not seem to have much space for it, even though more children are being integrated into mainstream schools with additional needs. The Bercow report (2008) in fact showed that 7% of 5-year-olds entering school in 2007 had significant communication difficulties, including social communication skills.

So, our social competence also impacts on our ability to stay out of trouble because up to 90% of people who offend have difficulties with their social skills and if we teach social skills at school, we see a decrease in problem behaviours. So, we can summarise by saying:

> Social skills are important for staying out of trouble.

In summary

In summary, is it important to be socially skilled? Do we need to worry? Well it strikes me that we *do* need to worry. We live in a world where social skills are essential for our quality of life and our self-esteem. We need them to make friends, to do well at school and get a job, and to stay out of trouble. We are then more likely to feel good about ourselves.

So, what could be more rewarding than working with someone to improve their ability to interact successfully with others around them? To know how to help someone in a way that will have a direct impact on their quality of life? To understand what is getting in the way for a child and then knowing what we can do to help? For me, nothing. So please read on and hopefully the rest of the book will help you to answer those questions.

Key points from Chapter 1

Defining social skills and social competence

A definition of social skills should include the following factors:

- Socially skilled behaviours are goal directed – they enable us to achieve a desired outcome from an interaction.
- Social skills are interrelated – one behaviour will lead to another.
- Social skills are defined in terms of identifiable units of behaviour and include both nonverbal and verbal behaviours.
- Social skills are behaviours which can be learned.
- Social skills are appropriate to the situation and so should be altered to be appropriate to the context.
- Social skills are under the cognitive control of the individual and so socially skilled people know when to talk, what to say and how to say it.
- Socially skilled people can 'read' their audience and shape their responses accordingly.

The difference between men and women and our brains

Men and women have different brains and this has an impact on their ability to process nonverbal communication.

Why are social skills important?

Social skills impact on our *quality of life* and are important for three main reasons:

1. Relationships . . . social skills are central to helping a child to have friends and to be a friend and this will contribute to their quality of life.
2. Success . . . social skills are important to enable children to succeed at school and to get a job and be successful.
3. Staying out of trouble . . . at least 60% of young offenders have difficulties with their communication.

Chapter 2

Body language

'I speak two languages, Body and English.'

Mae West (1893–1980)

The importance of body language and how to read it

This is a truly fascinating subject. And the more we understand it, the better we will be at understanding people. I was watching a television programme the other day which helps people to find their ideal house to buy. It was near the end of the programme, when the presenter and potential 'buyer' were sitting over a cup of coffee talking about whether she (the buyer) wanted to put an offer in on a house. She said 'yes' and then when the presenter asked if she was sure, she displayed some interesting nonverbal behaviour. She smiled and said 'oh yes, definitely' (or words to that effect) but at the same time she shook her head revealing her true feeling. The offer for the house was accepted and then at the end of the programme, the narrator said that the buyer had decided to not go ahead with the purchase and was continuing her search. This was a really good example of emotional 'leakage'. Our body is telling the listener how we truly feel while our mouths are saying something else! To the keen observer of body language, the conclusion was inevitable. She didn't want the house.

One of the reasons why this subject is so fascinating is that our body language is totally unavoidable in the presence of other people – we may choose not to speak, or be unable to communicate verbally, but we still give so many messages about ourselves to others through our face and body. How we sit or stand, gesture or cross our arms, look or avert our eyes will contribute to how we are perceived by others. Indeed, it is rare for any of us, when talking to others, to believe in the words alone. We form constant predictions and inferences about what a person is thinking and feeling based on their nonverbal behaviour. When someone says 'I love you', we look in their eyes to judge their sincerity. When someone looks at us, then smiles and averts their gaze, we interpret this as flirting. Even young children will immediately look into our eyes if they are puzzled by something because they know they can find the answer in our face. Should they be scared, amused or worried?

We have been educated to believe that our words are of paramount importance. Of course, they are. But it is the 'silent' language of our nonverbal behaviour that will make people want to listen to us and believe us. It is our nonverbal behaviour that will make them want to stick around and get to know us better.

In 1971, Professor Albert Mehrabian conducted a ground-breaking study into the relative strengths of verbal and nonverbal messages in face-to-face encounters, from which he devised a communication model that has come to be regarded as a template for how we derive meaning from someone's message. His research showed there are three elements in any communication message: body language, voice (or paralanguage) and words. He showed that in situations of confusion or inconsistency: 55% of the meaning of the message comes from body language; 38% of the meaning comes from the nonverbal element of speech (voice); and 7% of the meaning comes from the actual words.

Mehrabian's communication model

- 55% of the meaning of the message comes from body language
- 38% of the meaning comes from the nonverbal element of speech (voice)
- 7% of the meaning comes from the actual words

This means that our nonverbal behaviour, which includes body language and the way we say things (paralinguistic skills), are rather essential to get right, as at certain times as much as *93% of our message is conveyed through nonverbal behaviours.*

Of course, many writers dispute Mehrabian's research or misinterpret it by concluding that words are not important as long as we look and sound right. This is not the case. Actually, what Mehrabian shows us is that if our 55% is not good, then people will not want to stick around to listen to the 45%. And even if they stick around because we look good, if our 38% then turns them off, then the words become meaningless. So, our objective is to get the person to *want* to listen to us. Think about first impressions . . . how quickly do we form them and on what? We tend to form initial impressions in the first seven seconds based on what we see, and in particular on their personal appearance, facial expression and posture. Then when they open their mouth and start talking to us, we are listening to *how* they speak rather than what they say. These are the things that will help us to decide whether we like them, trust them and want to get to know them. We listen beyond the words to get to the silent message that is being conveyed (often through the subconscious). And after the first three minutes of an encounter, we have usually formed a first and long-lasting impression based on the nonverbal behaviour of that person.

Think about this: have we ever met someone for the first time and even though they seemed to talk in a normal and friendly manner, we say 'I don't think he liked me' or 'I don't think I trust him'. That is because we are constantly reading the other person's body language without realising we are doing it.

This is backed up by other writers. Malcolm Gladwell (2006) writes about 'thin slicing' – the ability to process nonverbal information in the 'blink' of an eye and make a split-second judgement about what is going on. He says that the first judgement we make about someone is often the correct one, and that even though we may revise our opinions after some reflection, later on, we may agree that the first impression was accurate. Boyce (2012) goes further and says we use this 'thin-slicing' subconsciously to make moment-to-moment decisions about whether to say something, what to say, and how to say it, and that this high-level skill is based on the development of nonverbal communication skills.

So it would appear that the way people react and respond to us is down to three factors in the following order: how we look, how we sound and what we say. And this is also what Dale Carnegie said back in 1937 (although he added a fourth one): 'there are four ways, and only four ways, in which we have contact with the world. We are evaluated and classified by these four contacts: what we do, how we look, what we say, and how we say it'.

So, some of the time we get it right – we make a judgment and it turns out to be correct. But if we become masters at recognising these signals in others, we will also be able to know whether someone agrees with us, likes us, is interested in what we are saying and is telling the truth. Conversely, we will be able to see the opposite. This is because our nonverbal messages are powerfully communicating:

- Acceptance and rejection
- Liking and disliking
- Interest and boredom
- Truth and deception

Now, this is useful! Wouldn't it be good to be able to recognise how someone is *really* feeling about us and what we are talking about? Wouldn't it be handy to know if someone was lying to us or was trying to cover something up?

James Borg (2008), in his book *Body Language*, starts by saying 'body language is the window to a person's mind' and he says we can all learn to 'read minds' through empathy, sensitivity and perceptivity. Psychotherapist Alexander Lowen sums up the importance of body language by saying 'no words are so clear as the language of body expression once one has learned to read it' (cited in Bolton, 1979).

So how can we become better at this? How can we learn to be better at reading body language and using it ourselves? The key to reading body language is being able to understand a person's emotional condition while listening to what they are saying and also looking at the circumstances under which they are saying it. This allows us to separate fact from fiction and reality from fantasy.

Borg (2008) cites some research that was done back in the 1970s by Paul Elman and Wallace Friesen that states that our body language or body movements can be divided into five broad areas which are summarised in the following table. These areas are illustrators, emblems, affect displays or 'leakage', adaptors and regulators, and they all have different functions.

So what are we looking for when we are talking to someone? Well the first thing to be aware of is what Borg (2008) describes as the three Cs. No accurate reading of someone's behaviour comes about without considering *context*, *congruence* and *clusters*.

Context, congruence and clusters

Rule 1 Context

The first thing we need to consider is the context in which the behaviour is occurring. A woman is sitting outside at a bus stop in a thin jacket, on a cold winter's day. She has her arms and legs tightly crossed, chin down and a frown on her face. Is she defensive, unreceptive or angry? No, she's cold. However, if she used the same body language while in a meeting with

> ### Table 2.1 Area of body language

Area	Description
Illustrators	These are the gestures or body movements that accompany what we are saying to create a visual supporting message that describes or reinforces the verbal message. We often don't realise we are doing these and will continue to do them, even if we are on the phone.
Emblems	These are the gestures that *replace* words. An obvious one is the thumbs up to say we're alright. These are supposed to be easily understood by the listener but do vary across different contexts and cultures.
Affect displays or 'leakage'	These are the movements that tend to give away our emotions and are usually unconscious. They include facial expressions, hand gestures, and body posture and movement.
Adaptors	These are similar to affect displays, as adaptors are a *mood indicator* and are also difficult to control. They will reveal someone's true emotions and will also show whether someone is lying. Adaptors include switches in posture (alter-adaptors), actions that are directed towards the body such as touching the face (self-adaptors) and actions such as fiddling with jewellery (object-adaptors).
Regulators	These are movements that are related to our function of *speaking* or *listening* and are also indicators of our intentions – for example, head nods, eye contact, and shifting body position – and will help to manage the conversation.

us, we would be correct to interpret that she is feeling negative or is rejecting our ideas. So be careful not to quickly just analyse the behaviour. Step back and consider the context.

Rule 2 Congruence

The second thing to look for is whether the words match the actions. Since our nonverbal communication takes up more than 90% of the message, we need to see that the words match the actions – that they are congruent. This is what we saw in the woman in the television programme. She said she wanted to buy the house but her nonverbal messages revealed how she truly felt. So when a person's words and body language are in conflict, we should ignore what is said. Some writers call this 'synchrony' – so we look for synchrony between what is being said verbally and nonverbally, between the circumstances of the moment and what the person is saying, and between the events and the emotions. A lack of synchrony or a delay shows deceit or an alternative meaning behind the words.

Rule 3 Clusters

The third thing to look for is clusters of behaviours as it is a serious error to interpret a solitary gesture in isolation of other gestures or circumstances. For example, scratching the head can mean a number of things: sweating, uncertainty, dandruff, head lice, forgetfulness or lying – depending on the other gestures that are happening at the same time. Think of body language as any other spoken language, where each gesture is a single word and it is only when we put the words into a sentence that we get the real meaning. Gestures come in 'sentences' called clusters and like any language, we need at least three words before we can accurately understand the meaning.

Open versus closed body language

The second thing we are going to notice is whether someone's body language is open or closed. This gives us valuable information on whether the person is comfortable or whether they are in any kind of negative state such as anxious, frightened, nervous or hostile. In short, the more confident and comfortable we are, the more we spread out and the less secure we feel, the less space we take up.

Open body language

Open body language is welcoming, relaxed and attentive. It signifies a lack of barriers – our body is open and exposed and we are suggesting that we are vulnerable to others and we're comfortable about it. Our hands are in view, with exposed palms, and our legs and posture are free and easy and eye contact is good. Everything indicates a positive attitude.

Closed body language

Closed body language is a cluster of gestures, movements and posture that brings the body in on itself. We are trying to make our body appear smaller and to look for barriers to shield us from a threat. So, we will bring our limbs close in to our body which will give a closed effect and we will cross our arms and legs to create a barrier. We will typically avert our eyes and have tense shoulders. This indicates a negative attitude – we feel uncomfortable or threatened.

Power poses

'Humans and other animals express power through open, expansive postures, and they express powerlessness through closed, contractive postures' (Carney et al., 2010) and open body language can also have a direct effect on our confidence and feelings of assertiveness. In general, the high power poses are open and relaxed while the low power poses are closed and guarded. Recent research coming out of Harvard University, The University of Oregon, The University of Texas and many other places is revealing that powerful and effective leaders not only share similar mind-sets, but also similar hormone levels. More specifically, powerful leaders tend to have higher levels of testosterone and lower levels of cortisol which means increased feelings of confidence, decreased anxiety and an improved ability to deal with stress. This means that if we naturally have these hormone levels, then we are biologically primed to be more assertive, confident, and relaxed. At the same time, we will be less reactive to stress and more likely to handle pressure situations well. So the correct hormone levels can make us feel more confident and less stressed.

But can we trick our body into feeling more confident and assertive? Amy Cuddy and her research team studied the impact of high power and low power poses by conducting a research study on 42 students (Carney et al., 2010) and found that posing in high power nonverbal displays caused neuroendocrine and behavioural changes for both male and female participants. 'High power posers experienced elevations in testosterone, decreases in cortisol, and increased feelings of power and tolerance for risk; low power posers exhibited the opposite pattern'. In fact, the high power poses increased testosterone by 20 percent and decreased cortisol levels by 25 percent. So what this means is that by assuming a simple two minute high power pose (the most well-known is the 'The Wonder Woman' pose where we stand tall with our chest out and our hands on our hips) we will be more confident and assertive in our behaviour.

Emotional leakage

The third thing we are going to notice is all that emotional leakage – and this represents the key to mind reading! Borg (2008) describes mind reading as:

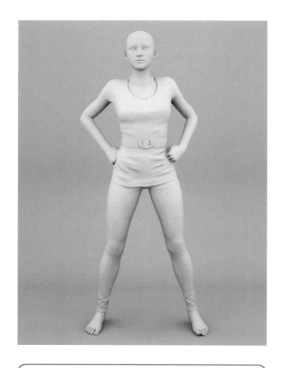

Figure 2.1 'Wonder Woman' pose

Mind reading

The mind produces a thought.

The thought produces a feeling.

That feeling 'leaks' out through body language.

We read the body language to ascertain a person's feeling – and hey presto, we're mind reading.

We are looking for the movements that tend to give away true emotions and these are usually subconscious. They include facial expressions, hand gestures, and body posture and movement and we can divide them into *displacement activities* and *self-comfort gestures*.

Displacement activities

These are the things we do to help displace anxiety or nervous energy. They are the little movements that are performed by us when we're experiencing any kind of inner conflict, torment or frustration of some sort. And they may just be small movements but they 'leak' out our true feelings and tell us an awful lot about what may be going on inside someone's head.

An interesting exercise is to spend some time watching people in a railway station or even better at an airport. We will be surrounded by examples of 'disguised activity' because most people don't want to reveal that they may be apprehensive or frightened of boarding a plane. We may see constant rechecking of tickets, making sure the wallet is still inside the pocket, picking up and putting down the luggage, gazing at mobile phones repeatedly. There will also be a lot of self-comfort gestures.

Self-comfort gestures

These are displacement activities that are internally directed - actions that are directed towards our own body. So we may see someone touching their face, tugging at their earlobes or clasping their hands together. We may even see people put their fingers in their mouth – this usually shows that the person is experiencing discomfort of some kind and any anxious situation makes us want to put something in our mouth. This comfort gesture takes us back to childhood, when as young children we looked to the mouth to placate us, from feeding to thumb sucking. So as with the displacement activities above, these self-comfort gestures provide comfort and will help to dissipate energy.

We all have our own personal displacement habits that come into play when we are experiencing conflict or tension. We may chew gum, bite nails, eat, drink, or fiddle with coins, jewellery or keys. These displacement gestures provide comfort, can pacify us and dissipate energy at the same time, but can be irritating to the onlooker and can also shout 'I am insecure' to the world. So, it is worth becoming more aware of our personal signals, and then we can try to get rid of these tell-tale signs in a situation where we don't want to be irritating or come across in a particular way.

As we have said earlier, we all use a mixture of facial expressions, hand gestures, body posture and movement to tell people how we are feeling and so in the next chapter we will look at our faces and eyes. In this chapter we are now going to consider our limbs and explore in more detail what they may be saying.

Our limbs . . . what are they saying?

Hands

We will begin with the hands because after the face (and we are going to tackle that in the next chapter) the hands are the most spontaneous and communicative part of our body and there is certainly a lot to say about them. We are certainly hard-wired to use our hands while speaking and that's because the number of nerve connections between the brain and the hands is greater than between other parts of the body. So we use our hands to greet people, illustrate a point and generally to express our feelings. In fact, it's generally accepted that we can get a message across more clearly if we use hand gestures. (Try describing a spiral staircase while sitting on your hands – it's not easy is it?!) It's not surprising then that the hands will communicate a lot to us and will influence how we are being perceived by others and also why they are responsible for so much leakage. I will briefly explain a few of the most common and interesting hand gestures or activities.

The hiding hands

As we have just said, the hands are a very expressive part of our body and as a listener we are constantly picking up signals from them, even though we are mostly not aware of this. So, if a person hides their hands, either under the desk or if lecturing, behind a lectern, then the perceived impression is a negative one. The speaker does not inspire confidence in us. So, the first thing to remember about the hands is to use them. Now let's look at how.

Palms of the hand

Throughout history, the *open palm* has been associated with truth, honesty, allegiance, submission, and being unarmed. One of the most valuable clues to working out whether someone is being open and honest is to look for palm behaviour. Just as a dog will reveal its throat to show submission, humans will reveal their palms. So, when someone wants to be open and honest, they will hold one or both palms out and we then interpret this as the person telling the truth. But it is also indicating that the person wants to be believed or accepted. When a person is trying to hide something, they will hide their palms, either behind their backs, in their pockets or in crossed arms. In fact, it is actually hard to tell a lie or fake a particular emotion with exposed palms. We may be able to physically do it, but the chances are we will still come across as insincere, because unless we are a highly practised con artist, there will be many other gestures and signs of honesty that will be absent and the negative gestures of lying will also appear and will be incongruent with the open palms. So, if we want to appear more open and credible, we need to practise using open palm gestures and interestingly, the more these become habitual, the easier it will be to be honest and credible. This in turn will encourage others to be more open with us too. It's a win-win.

A gesture with *palms down* is a different matter. This indicates dominance or authority. We are saying that there is no argument, no room for debate and we come across to others as controlling and possibly aggressive. However, if we are being questioned and not believed, we will place our palms down to show more confidence or assertion.

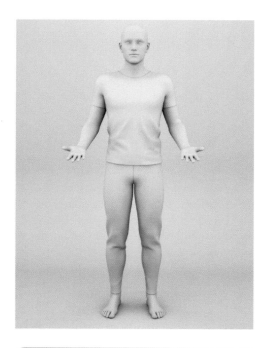

Figure 2.2 Palms up

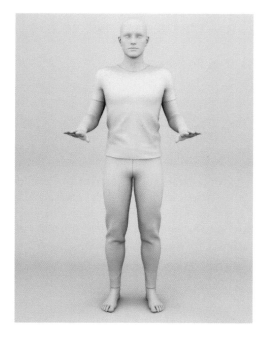

Figure 2.3 Palms down

The pointed index finger

One of the most irritating gestures is the pointed index finger, particularly if it beats time to the speaker's words. It's an aggressive gesture that doesn't make people feel good and can cause antagonism. We are basically saying 'do it or else' and listeners will see us as aggressive and rude. Interestingly in some countries such as the Philippines, pointing a finger at someone is an insult as this gesture is only used to point at animals. If you are someone who likes to point their finger, try altering it and squeezing your thumb against your index fingertip in an 'OK' signal. This avoids intimidation and you come across as focused and thoughtful.

In Allan and Barbara Pease's book on body language (2004) they describe an experiment where they asked eight lecturers to use each of these three hand gestures during a ten-minute lecture. They found that lecturers that mostly used the palm up position received 84% positive feedback, but this dropped to 52% when using the mainly palm down position and to 28% when mostly using the pointed finger gesture.

The hand clasp

People who hold hands with themselves while talking are usually telling us that they are in a state of conflict – they are suppressing a negative attitude which they cannot display. If the person is seated, their elbows may be on a table and the hands are then clenched in front of them or in front of their face. Research shows that the higher the position of the hands (i.e. in front of the face) the more negative tension exists (Borg 2008). If we clasp our hands in front of our crotch, then this usually signifies nervousness – we adopt a 'crotch covering' stance whether sitting or standing because we don't know what to do with our hands and this offers some protection to our vulnerable parts.

'Steepling' hands

The 'steepling' hand gesture has two forms – the raised steeple is where the elbows are rested on a table and the two palms come together and the fingertips of each hand gently touch each other and remain in that position – similar to praying.

Figure 2.4 Steepling hands 1

Figure 2.5 Steepling hands 2

If a person is listening then they may show the lowered steeple which can be resting on a surface or between the knees. This displays confidence and we see this used a lot by politicians being interviewed and from professional people such as hospital consultants and lawyers. This is a handy thing to know if we are feeling nervous or we are worried about our hands shaking. Try using the steeple and we will feel more confident.

Hands behind the back

Standing with our hands behind our back displays confidence because we are happy to expose the vulnerable front of our body. However, it is interesting to note what the hands are doing behind the back. If they are simply clasped together, this displays confidence. However, if one of the hands is gripping the other wrist or elbow, then we are seeing someone who is annoyed or frustrated or nervous.

Hands to face or head

When under stress or anxious, we will show a number of self-comfort gestures that involve the hands touching the face, hair or head. This is thought to go back to how we were often consoled in our childhood. For example, if we are anxious, we will smooth our hair on the top of the head or back of our neck with our hands. This is particularly common in men. The more extreme 'cradle' version of both hands going up to the head or back of the neck in a self-comforting gesture is communicating displeasure or anxiety and memories of parents supporting our head in their arms for a moment provides us with a sense of security.

A typical hand-to-face gesture is one where the hand supports the entire jaw with the elbow resting on the table. Sometimes this can indicate that the person is listening but it can also signify that they are bored. We will need to look for a cluster of behaviours that show us which one but generally the more we see of the hand covering the jaw / cheek, the more disinterested someone is. If the fist is supporting the chin and propping up the head, then this is a clear sign of boredom, but again, check for clusters and look at the eyes in particular. If the hand goes over the mouth, this is typically indicating that someone disapproves or disagrees and if the person is speaking at the same time, it may indicate they are lying.

The hand-to-head gestures are good indicators of stress, or 'emotional leakage' as we discussed earlier. The most common in order are: jaw support; chin support; hair touching; cheek support; mouth touch; and temple support. These are seen in both men and women but more men show temple support and more women show hair touching.

Hand to neck

The hands will instinctively go to the neck in instances of anxiety. Women tend to touch the front of their neck or fiddle with a necklace, and men are more likely to massage the back of their neck or enfold the area under the chin with their hand.

Arms

Arms are interesting as they are our own portable defence mechanism. Whenever we experience anxiety or distress, we withdraw our arms. They will go to our sides or we close them across our chest. As children we hid behind the furniture or our parents when we felt threatened, but by the age of six we had learnt to 'hide' in a more sophisticated way – we learnt to fold our arms tightly across our chests. We may have become less obvious about it now, but the message is still the same. It's a gesture that is seen worldwide and nearly always signifies that we disagree with something, we feel tense or insecure, or a negative thought has crossed our mind. At these times, as humans we want to withdraw our arms for protection and also for self-comfort. We will briefly consider a few common arm positions and what they mean.

The folded arms

As we have just said, the folded arms almost always signify some form of discomfort (unless it is cold!) and we will interpret this behaviour in others as a defensive or negative gesture. Of course, many people say to me that they regularly cross their arms because it is comfortable. And, actually, any gesture will feel comfortable if we have the corresponding attitude – that is we have a negative or defensive attitude. But I would normally point out to people who like to cross their arms that it is important to consider that the meaning of the message is also in the receiver as well as the sender. We may feel comfortable with our arms folded, but the reaction from others will be negative and people will find us unapproachable.

There are several ways we can fold our arms. The most common way is the general crossed arms – both arms are folded across the chest and one hand may be tucked between the arm and the chest. This says 'I am feeling defensive or negative about someone or something'. So if we are in a meeting and the person we are talking to suddenly does this, consider the fact that they may be telling us that they don't agree with us. If the gesture is accompanied by a change in facial expression to a slightly less open one, then we know they don't agree, even if they are saying something else. And as long as they have this 'closed' posture, their attitude is not going to change. If their fists are clenched as well, then this is also showing hostility.

Of course, we can always try to help them change their attitude by helping them to 'unlock' their gesture.... Try asking them to do something with their hands so that it makes them break the 'deadlock' of their arms. If we can encourage someone to unfold their arms and lean forward, we are moving them into a more open position and therefore a more positive attitude.

Figure 2.6 Arms crossed

Figure 2.7 Arms crossed with thumbs up

If the arm-cross involves the thumbs being in an upward position, then even though the person is showing discomfort or apprehension, they are also displaying a certain amount of confidence as well. We may see this in a junior person talking to his boss at work, who is conscious of his position but also feeling self-confident. However, if the hands are both gripping the upper arms or if the hands have been made into fists, then the negative attitudes have increased and we are maybe looking at extreme anxiety or even hostility. In this situation, it is important not to mirror these behaviours otherwise nothing will get sorted!

Another type of arm-cross is the double arm grip, where the person's hands tightly grip their upper arms. This can show extreme anxiety or they are anticipating an unpleasant event. It may also show extreme stubbornness.

The partial arm-cross

The partial arm-cross is where we put one arm across to hold the other arm. This is seen more in women and is a form of comfort when we are feeling anxious or lacking in self-confidence. It also provides a barrier and therefore makes us feel better. Men are more likely to hold hands with themselves, also known as 'the broken zipper position'. This position reveals a feeling of stress and may also reveal vulnerability or feeling dejected.

We may also see people disguise their anxiety by crossing their arm over their body to straighten a watchstrap, straighten a tie, check for the wallet in the jacket pocket, check an earring, and of course, the handbag over the arm is a great natural barrier. All of these help to make us feel protected and comforted and are examples of 'displacement activity'.

Figure 2.8 Partial arm cross

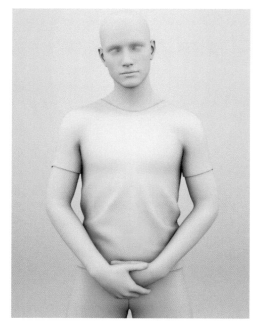

Figure 2.9 Broken zipper position

Feet

Feet can also give us a lot of information. We are all conditioned to turn towards things and people we like and so looking at which direction someone's feet are pointing will give us an indication of how they are feeling. Both feet pointing towards us is looking good, one pointing away may reveal they want to get going and both pointing away, well it's best to end it there. The reason why feet (and legs) are often regarded as the most honest parts of the body is because they are furthest from the brain and therefore there is less conscious thought involved. We therefore see *intention movements* without the person being aware of them. We point them towards the person we want to talk to and we adjust our feet to point to the exit to indicate when we want to leave.

Apart from pointing in certain directions, feet also move – they may tap or bounce or kick. This displacement of energy tells us that the person can't wait to leave or they are running out of patience. Pease (2004) tells us about a test where they asked managers to lie in a series of staged interviews. And whereas they all used fake facial expressions and tried to control their hands whilst lying, they were unaware of what their feet and legs were doing and they all showed increased foot movements. These results were backed up by the psychologist Paul Ekman who discovered that people increase their lower body movements when they lie. This may explain why some people prefer to talk to us from behind their desks!

Legs

Like the feet, the legs give us clues as to what the person's intentions are or where they would like to be. Our legs evolved to serve two purposes: to move forward to get food and to run away from danger. So, we move towards what we want and move away from what we don't and the way someone uses their legs reveals where they want to go – to stay or leave a conversation. Open or uncrossed leg positions generally show an open or dominant attitude and crossed positions reveal closed positions or uncertainty.

Standing positions

We can also consider how someone is standing and there are four main positions that we tend to adopt that are shown in the following table.

Table 2.2 Standing positions

Position	Description
At attention	This is the legs-together, standing to attention stance that says 'no comment' and we will often use this posture in more formal situations like talking to our boss.
Leg cross	Crossed legs show a closed, submissive or defensive attitude and can also make someone appear insecure. We may also see people standing with their arms crossed too and at a greater distance from the other person especially if they don't know each other well.

(Continued)

Table 2.2 (Continued)

Position	Description
The foot forward	Here the body weight is shifted to one hip and the front foot points forward to where they want to go (see the section on feet).
Legs apart	This is predominantly a male gesture and makes a clear statement of dominance because it highlights the genitals and is sometimes referred to as 'the crotch displayer'. Men may also stand around in groups, for example at a sporting event, giving their crotch a continual adjustment – this has nothing to do with itching but is used to highlight their masculinity and show solidarity as a team (if they are all doing it!).

Sitting positions

When sitting, there are similar things to look out for in terms of open or closed positions. There are three main seated positions with some variations is each:

1. The leg cross

One leg crossed neatly over the other one is a very common posture and can also reveal a negative attitude especially when combined with arm crossing.

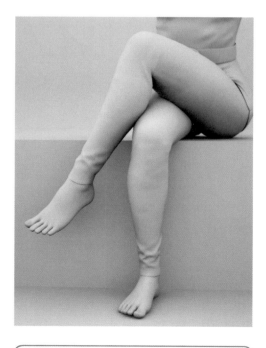

Figure 2.10 Leg cross

Figure 2.11 Leg twine

But of course, always look at the three Cs (context, congruence and clusters), as a woman may cross her legs due to clothing or seating. Of course, we respond better to people with an open posture, which means that if we do need to cross our legs, we need to make sure the rest of our posture is open. It has been found that people sitting with their arms and legs crossed tend to talk in shorter sentences, reject more proposals and can recall less detail of what was discussed than those who sit in an open position (Pease 2001). If the leg cross becomes a 'leg twine' – that is the foot of the crossed leg locks behind the other ankle – this reveals that the woman has a shy and timid attitude and that she has possibly retreated into her shell. I use 'she' as it is rarely seen in men.

2. The figure four

This version is seen more in men than women and is where one leg is crossed over with its ankle supported by the knee of the other leg. This is a seated version of the crotch display and shows an argumentative or competitive attitude and is seen as more dominant. A seated posture that is particularly irritating to women is where the above leg crossing is displayed along with the superior posture of hands behind the head. This says 'one day you could be as wonderful as me'. A similar posture to the above but with the legs open is equally irritating. This is an exposing posture that would signify arrogance or sexual dominance so men may use this to exert their 'maleness' in a situation. The figure four seated posture may also include a leg clamp – where the person locks their leg into a 'permanent' position using one or more hands as a clamp. This is a sign of a tough minded, stubborn person who will reject other people's opinions.

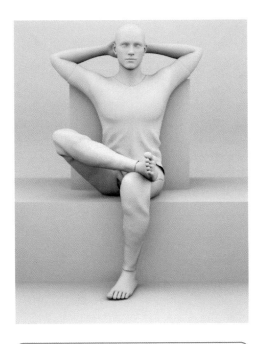

Figure 2.12 The figure four with hands behind head

3. The ankle lock

The ankle lock can look slightly different in men and women. Men are more likely to have their legs open and the ankle lock is often combined with fists resting on their knees or their hands gripping the arms of the chair. Women will keep their knees together and then their hands will rest side by side or on top of the other on their upper legs. In both cases, the feet are often withdrawn under the chair. Locking ankles shows that they are mentally 'biting their lip' and can also show they have a withdrawn attitude; they are holding back an emotion. So, in a dentist, 68% of people locked their ankles as soon as they sat in the dentist chair and 98% locked their ankles when the dentist administered an injection (Pease 2001). Of course, some women will use this posture due to the fact that they are wearing a short skirt. This then means that short skirts can give a woman the appearance that she is not approachable.

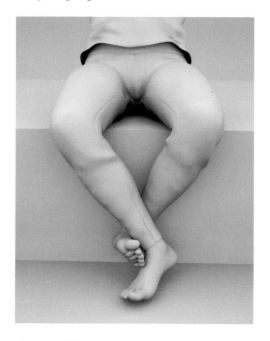

Figure 2.13 Ankle cross: male version

Figure 2.14 Ankle cross: female version

Proximity

Finally in this chapter, we are going to consider proximity or personal space. The concept of 'proxemics' was first introduced by an American anthropologist Edward Hall cited by Pease (2004), and his research led to a better understanding on our relationships with others and how we use space to create a 'bubble' around ourselves for protection. In general, we can identify four zones and children will have generally learnt these by the age of twelve (Pease 2004).

Table 2.3 The four zones of personal space

The four zones	The size or amount of space	A description
The intimate zone	This is between 6 and 18 inches or 15–45 centimetres.	Only people who are emotionally close to us are permitted into this space so this would include lovers, spouse, parents, children and close friends. If people we don't know well come into this space, we will immediately feel uncomfortable. There is also a 'close intimate zone' which is less than 6 inches (15cm) and this is reserved for the very few who we don't mind touching us.

The personal zone	This is between 18 inches and 4 feet or 46cm–1.22m.	This is the most important one for people to learn as it our 'one arm length' rule which is the ideal one in the western world for most personal interaction. We are able to shake hands at this length and are less likely to cause offence by invading someone's 'bubble'.
The social zone	This is between 4–12 feet or 1.22–3.6m.	We stand at this distance from people we don't know. This may include tradesmen doing work in our house or the new employee at work.
The public zone	This is over 12 feet or 3.6m.	When we have to address a large group of people, this is considered to be an acceptable distance from the front row.

There are several factors that will affect the distance rule. Like animals, the size of our bubble is dependent on the density of the population in the place where we grew up. So, we sometimes need to make adjustments when talking to people from different cultures. People from Japan and many southern Europeans, such as the Italians, have an intimate distance of 20–30cm which can make them appear 'pushy' or 'too familiar' to an American, northern European or Australian, and in turn the Europeans or Americans appear 'cold' or 'standoffish' to the Japanese and Italians.

Another factor is height – we will need to increase the distance slightly if there is a large height difference to ensure the angle of the eye contact is not too acute. Finally, there are differences between men and women. All the distances tend to reduce between two women and increase between two men.

Of course, sometimes we have to get closer to people in certain situations like a lift or a crowded train. We cope with people entering our 'intimate zone' by masking our emotions and pretending that the other people are inanimate. Pease (2004) gives us a list of rules that most cultures follow when faced with a crowded situation:

The rules of the crowded situation

1. There will be no talking.
2. Avoid eye contact with others at all times.
3. Maintain a poker face.
4. If we have a book or newspaper, pretend to be deeply engrossed in it.
5. In bigger crowds, no body movement is allowed.
6. In a lift, we must watch the floor numbers change.

I'd like to end this chapter with a quote from Julius Fast.

> We all, in one way or another, send our little messages out to the world... And rarely do we send our messages consciously. We act out our state of being with nonverbal body

language. We lift one eyebrow for disbelief. We rub our noses for puzzlement. We clasp our arms to isolate ourselves or to protect ourselves. We shrug our shoulders for indifference, wink one eye for intimacy, tap our fingers for impatience, slap our foreheads for forgetfulness. The gestures are numerous, and while some are deliberate . . . there are some . . . that are mostly unconscious.

(Julius Fast, 1971)

Key points from Chapter 2

When understanding and reading body language we should remember the following:

- 93% of our message is conveyed through nonverbal behaviours.
- We form impressions of people in 7 seconds.
- Always consider the context in which the behaviour is occurring.
- Then look at congruence - do the words match the actions?
- Gestures come in 'sentences' called clusters and like any language, we need at least three words before we can accurately understand the meaning.
- Check to see if the body language is open or closed.
- Look out for emotional leakage - the movements that tend to give away true emotions as they are usually unconscious.

Hands

- Our hands will be responsible for a great deal of our communication and our emotional leakage and will therefore influence how we are being perceived by others.
- Try to remember to keep our hands open or steepled if we want to appear confident and open.

Arms

- Our arms are our own portable defence mechanism. Whenever we experience anxiety or distress, we withdraw them and create a barrier across our body.

Feet

- The feet (and legs) are furthest from the brain and therefore there is less conscious thought involved in their movement.
- This means they are often the most honest parts of the body.
- Look at which direction someone's feet are pointing as that will give us an indication of how they are feeling.

Legs

- We will move towards things we want and move away from what we don't and the way someone uses their legs reveals where they want to go – to stay or leave a conversation.
- Open or uncrossed leg positions generally show an open or dominant attitude and crossed positions reveal closed or uncertainty.

Proximity

We all have a 'space bubble' that we use for protection and there are 4 identified zones:

- The intimate zone (15–46cm)
- The personal zone (46cm–1.2m)
- The social zone (1.2–3.6m)
- The public zone (over 3.6m)

Chapter 3

Eyes and faces

'Eye contact is way more intimate than words will ever be.'
Faraaz Kazi

I imagine it will not surprise anyone if I say that the face is the most important part of our body language. I look at your face and I see how you feel. The scientists agree too. The face not only discloses specific emotions but will tell us what matters most to that person. Borg (2008) states that people tend to believe what the face tells them rather than the words they hear. And the most important part of the face is the eyes. The eyes and facial tissue surrounding them can be the most eloquent part of our conversation and will reveal most information. Our eyes twinkle with happiness, become red and watery with sadness and glower with hostility. Our eyes convey important information on how our relationship with the other person is faring. They display affection and trust with one person, distance with another and disengagement with someone else. As Bolton says: 'In many cultures, warm eye contact is the purest form of reciprocity, the highest level of physical union' (1979) and maybe this is why the French novelist Victor Hugo (1802–1885) advised 'when a woman is speaking to you, listen to what she says with her eyes'.

So, as we communicate more with our eyes and our face than any other part of our anatomy, we are going to consider these two together in this chapter. They are of course part of our body language too so we could have included these in the previous chapter on body language. However, as eye contact and facial expression are so important in expressing ourselves non-verbally and there is so much to say about them, I decided to give them a chapter to themselves.

So in this chapter we will explore the face in more detail. We will consider the eyes and in particular how we use eye contact and eye movements in conversations and what that tells us. We will then consider facial expressions – both overt ones and those micro-expressions which reveal our true emotions!

Eye contact

There is no question that eye contact plays a significant role in our communication. As Borg (2008) says: 'It's not overstating it to suggest that the degree and level of effective eye contact, more than anything else, helps contribute to establishing that magical "holy grail" of positive interaction – rapport – a state that exists between people'.

We 'keep our eyes open' (or peeled), we 'see eye-to-eye' with some, but 'turn a blind eye' to others. Some people are 'more than meets the eye'; some are 'the apple of your eye', and some 'a sight for sore eyes'. We may prefer 'not to bat an eye' but be sure that no one can 'pull the wool over your eyes'. It would appear that eye contact and our eyes are hugely important. Why? Well, eye contact helps us to strike a rapport with the other person and to establish trust, and also helps us to read the other person. If we fail to make eye contact we generally come across as someone not to be trusted. In fact, eye contact is so important that we can accurately read emotions just from eye slits (Furnham 2014), which explains why it is so hard to talk to people with dark or mirrored glasses.

So how do we use our eye contact or our eye behaviour to communicate? Borg (2008) describes four main ways in which we use our eye contact:

Four ways we use eye contact

1. *Express liking or intimacy.* **We look at people more if we like them, so how much someone is looking at us will give us a sense of how the relationship is progressing.**
2. *Exercise control.* **We will increase our eye contact when trying to make a point or be persuasive.**
3. *Regulate interaction.* **We use our eyes to direct the conversation in terms of initiating it and turn taking.**
4. *Provide mood and character information.* **Our eyes will give information on aspects such as attentiveness, competence, credibility and liking.**

So, it is not straight forward. It is not just a case of looking at the other person's eyes. We need to understand about our eye behaviour: where we look, how much we look, when do we look, and how much we open and close our eyes. The amount and type of eye gaze imparts a great deal of information. Pupil dilation, blink rates, direction of gaze, widening of the eyes all send very clear messages. It is certainly more complicated than we ever imagined but is totally fascinating! We will start by examining the eye contact rule – where we should look – and we will then go on to look at all the other aspects of eye behaviour that influence our eye contact.

Where to look

Some people struggle with eye contact and are not as good as they could be and they will often say that they find it difficult to know which area of a person's face to look at. So what is 'normal' behaviour?

- In a formal or more serious setting, we should look within a triangle that goes from just above the eyebrows down to the nose.
- On a social level, with people we know well, we are able to gaze anywhere between the eyes and the mouth.

- On an intimate level, when men and women want to show they are interested in each other, their gaze will go from the eyes, to the mouth and then may briefly scan below the mouth to other parts of the body. Usually this is a discreet scan before quickly returning to the eyes.

Some writers use a triangle the other way up to explain this rule, i.e. with the apex at the top of the triangle and in the middle of the forehead. However, I have found that when teaching young people the rule of eye contact, it is much easier to describe the triangle with the flat side always just above the eyes and the apex at the bottom – either at the nose, the mouth or the chin, as the eyes are then both within the triangle in all three levels which makes more sense to the young person learning where to look.

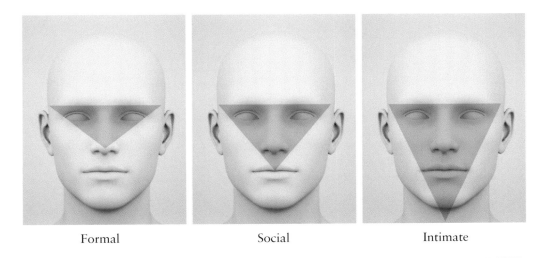

| Formal | Social | Intimate |

Figure 3.1 The eye contact rule

The rule is adapted for someone who has a hearing loss, as they need to look more at the other person's mouth to help lip read. Some people have also got into the bad habit of looking more at the mouth when talking to someone. In both scenarios it is important to be aware of the impact their eye contact has on the other person. In most everyday situations we interpret people (who are not very close to us) who look at our mouths as over-familiar or as flirting with us. So be warned! If we need to look at someone's mouth to help hear what they are saying, we may need to explain why we are doing it.

Eye behaviour

Now let's look at the eye behaviour we typically adopt when talking to someone in a normal conversation, as eye gaze plays a crucial role. Looking at another person is a way of getting feedback on particular points and we also use it as a synchronizing signal. Furnham (2014) describes the following eye behaviour in conversations: we look up at the end of utterances which hands over the conversational baton to the other person. We also look up more at the end of grammatical breaks, but look away when hesitating, talking non-fluently, or thinking. There is often mutual eye contact during attempted interruptions, laughing, and when answering short questions. Borg (2008) describes this eye behaviour as a 'dance' of gaze shifts:

> ### 'The eye dance'
>
> - I start my conversation and glance *towards* you.
> - When the momentum of my words takes hold, *I look away*.
> - As I come to the end of that particular point, *I glance back again* to check the impact of my statement.
> - You, as the listener, have been *watching me* and are now ready to take over as speaker, so you in turn begin your conversation, *look away*, and then *return* to check the impact of your words . . .

We may also try to start a conversation by staring at another person on the other side of a room. If the other person returns the eye gaze, then it is generally interpreted as acceptance of the invitation, whereas if they avert the eyes, we interpret this as a rejection of the request. So, in a typical interaction, this is the common pattern that we see – eyes are going back and forth to ensure we take turns smoothly and to check the listener's reaction to what we are saying. If we see the listener is looking at us, we know they are interested and understand what we are saying. If they are confused about something or they are not interested, they will use minimal eye contact. And if the listener is looking away all of the time, then we know we have done something seriously wrong!

One of the things we notice about this eye contact 'dance' is that the speaker will look away far more than the person who is listening. This is because we don't like people using too much eye contact when they are talking to us. So, as a speaker if we use too little, we appear nervous and untrustworthy and if we use too much eye contact, we appear aggressive or weird. In fact, an accomplished speaker with high emotional intelligence will spend on average around half the time or slightly less making intermittent eye contact (Borg 2008). So why do we look away when we are talking to someone?

We mostly look away to concentrate on our thoughts and to be free from the visual distraction of the person we are talking to. We give the other person 'space' from us and it also gives us fewer sensory stimuli to have to deal with. We will then bring our eye contact back to the listener to indicate that we are just about to finish.

We can be even more precise with this. Research shows us that during a typical interaction a speaker will look at the listener between 45–60% of the time. The listener will look at the speaker 70–80% of the conversation. Around 31% of time is spent in mutual gazing and the length of gaze is around 2.95 seconds and the average mutual gaze is only 1.8 seconds (Borg 2008, Pease and Pease 2004). Of course, this will vary depending on how much we like the person. As Furnham (2014) says: 'there is more mutual eye contact between friends than others. . . . Lovers really do gaze more into each other's eyes'.

Furnham (2014) also describes 10 factors that determine our amount of eye gaze and these are summarised in Table 3.1.

One thing that we may think is that we can tell if someone is lying by how much they avoid eye contact with us. We imagine the person with the shifty eyes looking away from us because they are lying. But, actually, the opposite is true. Rather than looking away, a liar may overcompensate and use excessive eye contact. Of course, there is no doubt that we will come across people who won't look us in the eye when they are telling a lie, but it is often the opposite. So that is why we must also look at other behaviours, such as the rest of their body language and also other aspects of their eye behaviour such as eye direction, blinking rate and the 'eye shuttle'.

Table 3.1 Ten factors that affect eye gaze

1.	Distance	For example, in a lift or an elevator, we turn to face the door because we are standing too close to the other person and reducing eye gaze helps reduce the discomfort of having our body zones invaded (see the previous chapter on proximity).
2.	Topic of conversation	It is easier to talk about embarrassing or intimate things if we are not looking directly at the other person. So it's no accident that Catholic confessionals and psychiatric couches are arranged to reduce the amount of eye contact between the priest or therapist and the confessor or patient. This may explain why it is often easier to talk to someone about something difficult when we are close to them but not looking at them. I can honestly say that all of my successful 'tricky' chats with my teenage children have been either in a car or on a walk!
3.	Conversation task	This is to do with what we are trying to achieve within a conversation. If we are trying to persuade someone, we look more at them. We look more at co-operators rather than at our competitors. And doctors look more at patients when talking about emotional rather than physical symptoms or conditions.
4.	Attention	We will look at people to get their attention. Consider the person who is hitchhiking or collecting for charity – they will try to look at us to get our attention.
5.	Interpersonal relationships	We look at those we like more than those we do not – and our pupils dilate more when we are looking at those we like.
6.	Co-operation	We will communicate that we are willing to co-operate rather than compete through our gaze patterns. The amount and type of gaze is important though – a high level of gaze usually means that the person is interested and attentive. However, if it is combined with certain expressions it could as easily indicate threat.
7.	Personality	According to Furnham (2014) 'extroverts look more often, and for longer, than introverts do. The confident, the bright, and the socially dominant look more, while it is the opposite for the socially anxious'. In addition, we know that women look more at those they are talking to than men do.
8.	Physical appearance	We generally look more at attractive people than less attractive individuals.
9.	Mental illness	'Many psychopathologies are associated with reduced and/or 'odd' gaze patterns, especially autism and paranoia. Schizophrenics and depressed people tend to avert eye gaze' (Furnham 2014).
10.	Ethnicity	Finally eye gaze alters according to the culture, so cultures like those in the near East look at each other more than some cultures in Europe.

Eye direction

We can also tell quite a lot about what a person may be thinking from their eyes and specifically the direction of their eye movements. When we are next listening to someone, try and notice where they are looking and we may see the following (Borg 2008, simplybodylanguage.com 2012, Pease and Pease 2004):

Up and to the right (your left)

If the eyes move upwards and to the right then they are trying to imagine something. So ask someone to 'imagine a purple buffalo', this would be the direction their eyes moved in while thinking about the question as they *visually constructed* a purple buffalo in their mind. We look to the right and up, if we're trying to remember a recent experience, or we're trying to assess if what the other person is saying is logical.

In short: up and right is about remembering recent experiences and thinking logically.

> **Figure 3.2 Eyes up and to the right: visually constructed images**

Up and to the left (your right)

If the eyes move upwards and to the left then they are trying to visualise something that happened before. If we asked someone 'what colour was the first house you lived in?', this would be the direction their eyes moved in while thinking about the question as they *visually remembered* the colour of their childhood home. Looking up is a sign of thinking. If we're looking to the left as well, we're processing information, and relating it to a past experience or an emotional feeling.

In short: Looking up is thinking, left and up is thinking about experiences and emotions.

> **Figure 3.3 Eyes up and to the left: visually remembered images**

Left (your right)

If they just move to the left then they are trying to remember sounds. So if we asked someone to 'remember what their mother's voice sounds like', this would be the direction their eyes moved in while thinking about the question as they *remembered* this sound.

   In short: Looking at the left ear, is remembering a sound.

Figure 3.4 **Eyes to the left: auditory remembered**

Right (your left)

If their eyes move across to the right then they are trying to reconstruct sounds. So if we asked someone to 'try and create the highest pitched sound possible in your head', this would be the direction their eyes moved in while thinking about the question as they *constructed* this sound that they have never heard of.

In short: Looking at the right ear, is constructing a sound.

Figure 3.5 **Eyes to the right: auditory constructed**

Down and to the left (your right)

If their eyes move to the left and down, then they are talking to themselves.

   In short: Looking down and left, is talking to themselves.

Figure 3.6 Eyes down and to the left: internal dialogue

Down and to the right (your left)

If a person's eyes move to the right and also down, then they are trying to access feelings. So, if we asked someone 'can you remember the smell of a campfire?', this would be the direction their eyes moved in while thinking about the question as they recalled a smell, feeling, or taste.

In short: Looking down and right, is remembering a smell, feeling or taste.

Figure 3.7 Eyes down and to the right: feeling/kinaesthetic

In simple terms, if a person is remembering something or thinking about something, their eyes will move upwards. If they are recalling something they heard, they look to the side and if they are recalling a feeling or emotion, they look down and to the right and when they are mentally talking to themselves, they look down and to the left.

Blinking

We can also look at someone's blinking rate to check for anxiety or discomfort. We blink at an average rate of 8–15 times per minute but when someone is anxious, this will go up to more like 30–40 times per minute. Someone is also more likely to blink more if they are lying. Some people may actually flutter their eyelids if they are struggling to explain a point or if they are embarrassed about something. Again, this is usually due to discomfort.

Another aspect to notice is the length of the blink – a person who blinks slightly slower than the normal rate is showing us that they feel themselves to be in a more superior position to the other person. This means that their eyes are closed for longer than they would normally be which blocks us out of the picture. And if they tip their head back slightly – then they are looking down on us as well. On the other hand, if the person reduces their rate of blinking, this can be due to boredom, disagreement or hostility. We may see this as the glazed eyes of listeners who want to escape.

Closed eye activity

Some people have a tendency to shut their eyes completely when they are talking to us or when they are answering a question. The eyes will close for a blink but will then stay closed for a few seconds. This can also indicate that a person is bored or feels superior to us. Closing the eyes denies both the speaker and the listener the opportunity to receive and give feedback, which can be frustrating. In some cases, it is the body effectively 'shutting up shop' to block an unpleasant encounter or a pressurised situation. So, we may also see this in someone who lacks self-confidence. In other cases, it is simply a person's way of blocking out sensory activity in order to concentrate fully on their thoughts. But the important thing to realise is that to the listener, this behaviour is irritating and sends the wrong message.

Eye blocking

Covering or shielding the eyes is a more extreme version of the closed eye activity and often seen when people literally do not like what they see. We see this when people feel threatened by something or are repulsed by what they are hearing or seeing and it is therefore an indicator of unhappy behaviour. We also see eye-blocking in the form of eye-rubbing or lots of blinking. It is a powerful display of consternation, disbelief or disagreement and is actually an innate behaviour; children who are born blind actually cover their eyes when they hear bad news (Van Edwards, scienceofpeople.com).

The eye shuttle

The eye shuttle is where the eyes move from side to side while the head remains still. This is essentially a 'flight' response – the darting eyes are scanning for an exit or some kind of help (as well as showing nervousness or discomfort). We see this regularly in television programmes that try to expose rogue traders when the presenter finally catches up with them and they are questioned on camera.

Widening and narrowing eyes

Finally let's consider the narrowing of the eyes. This usually indicates some kind of disapproval of something or a sign to show dominance and has been likened to the effect of 'looking through a visor' (Borg 2008). It often accompanies a lowering of the eyebrows and so can often be mistaken as anger. Squinting and closing or shielding our eyes are actions that have evolved to protect the brain from 'seeing' undesirable images and to communicate our disdain toward others (Navarro 2007). However, some people adopt this expression and it is actually caused by their personality type. Let's assume they are reading a report and while they are concentrating intently, they adopt a pensive or menacing look. This may not be them showing concern or annoyance. It may be a consequence of their personality type and their intenseness towards a situation. So always look for other signs as well – the clusters that will tell us the truth.

Conversely, if we want to show signs of incredulity or innocence, or that we are really paying attention and are really interested, we open our eyes wide and raise our eyebrows. We know that large eyes are appealing so raising our eyebrows and eyelids will help build rapport.

We should end this section on eyes with a note of caution. It can be tempting to want to rush out and try to analyse people using this knowledge, and in particular to detect whether someone is lying to us, but the first step is always to find their *baseline*. A baseline is how someone acts when they are under normal, non-threatening conditions, as we all behave slightly differently. We can easily establish this baseline by sitting down with the person and talking to them about neutral topics that they would have no reason to lie about, like the weather or what they want to have for dinner. Take note of how they act and in particular what their eyes do. Once we have established their baseline we can look for some of the typical eye behaviours outlined in this chapter, as well as some of the body language behaviours from the previous chapter. If we see some of these clues and it is different than their baseline behaviour we know we need to dig a little deeper. Just also remember the rule of looking for *clusters*. Don't be too quick to label someone a 'liar' with one eye movement!

So, who thought that such a small part of our bodies could reveal so much? There is a lot to be learnt about someone from simply looking at their face and in particular their eyes. But we will find out even more if we also look at their facial expression.

Facial expression

We have discussed the eyes and how revealing they can be. But combine them with the face – the nose, mouth, lips and jaw – and we see the true message. As the ancient Chinese Proverb goes: 'Watch out for the man whose stomach doesn't move when he laughs'. The face is the most expressive part of our body language and we give out more signals with our face than in any other part of the body. Not surprising when we think that there are 22 muscles coming together on each side of the face to create a running commentary of what we are thinking and feeling. So, in any interaction the face is the first thing we look at. The judgements we make and the impressions we form of other people are the most important forms of rapid cognition. In the presence of other people, we constantly form predictions and inferences about what that person is feeling and thinking. So, we see someone grinning with their eyes twinkling, we assume they are happy. We see them nod and smile exaggeratedly, with the corner of their lips tightened, we assume they have been teased and they are responding sarcastically. If they make eye contact with someone, give a small smile and then look away, we assume they are flirting. As Gladwell (2006) explains in his excellent book *Blink*:

> This practice of inferring the motivations and intentions of others is classic thin-slicing. It is picking up on subtle, fleeting cues in order to read someone's mind – and there is almost no other impulse so basic and so automatic and at which, most of the time, we so effortlessly excel.

Much research has been done on the face. It was Charles Darwin's research in the nineteenth century that highlighted the importance of studying facial expression, but it was Paul Ekman and Silvan Tomkins that really increased our understanding by devising the Facial Action Coding System (FACS) (Ekman 2005), which includes all the combinations of muscles moving and contracting that we generally recognise as emotion. They have effectively mapped all the expressions that we are able to produce and what they mean and which facial muscles produce which expression. Ekman says that the face is a gold mine of information and that the 'information on our face is not just a signal of what is going on inside our mind . . . it *is* what is going on inside our mind' (Gladwell, 2006).

This insight occurred during some work he was doing with a colleague on expressions of anger and distress. They discovered that making facial expressions alone was enough to create a marked change in the autonomic nervous system. As they lowered their brows, raised their upper eyelids, narrowed their eyelids and pressed their lips together to generate the facial expression of anger, their heart rate and body temperature increased. This means that emotion can also *start* on the face. As Gladwell (2006) puts it, 'the face is not a secondary billboard of our internal feelings; it is an equal partner in the emotional process'.

It was always thought that as the face is the barometer for our emotions, the facial expressions follow after an emotion has been felt. So, it was assumed that we first of all feel happy, or sad, and then the corresponding facial expression is displayed. Someone says something funny and we smile; something hurtful and we frown. But the research that Paul Ekman did revealed that the facial expression itself can create the emotion. This means that if we force ourselves to display a certain expression, the mind and body work together and physiologically recognise and process that emotion with appropriate biochemical changes. So, if we are feeling sad and we turn our 'frown upside down' and force ourselves to smile, this makes us feel better inside because of the feel-good hormones that are now working their way through our body. So, it's amazing . . . smile and we will feel happy. Frown and we will feel sad.

Of course, this may explain a problem with Botox. Botox procedures are often advertised as the solution to insecurities and negative emotions, but the changes aren't more than skin deep. A recent study shows that, although Botox can dilute certain insecurities, it also inhibits the ability to feel deep emotions and empathise with others (cited by Tatera 2015). Botox works by paralyzing the muscles involved in facial expressions. Although most of the toxins are temporary, research suggests that the facial muscles don't ever fully recover from the injections. Basically, Botox could prevent people from being able to feel deep emotions.

A modern study by Neal and Chartrand (2011) found that women with Botox were significantly less able to match the eyes to the appropriate human emotions than people who have not had Botox. So, while Botox can prevent wrinkles, it inhibits the genuine emotional experiences because people who have had Botox injections are physically unable to mimic the emotions of others. So, this failure to mirror the faces of those they are watching or talking to robs them of the ability to understand what people are feeling. So, what are the easily identifiable emotions?

The six universal emotions

It is universally accepted that there are six easily identifiable emotions: happiness, sadness, surprise, disgust, fear and anger. In daily life we are more used to exhibiting two 'shorthand' facial expressions – the two relating to happiness and sadness.

Happiness and smiling

Happiness is the only positive emotion and in research studies people seem hard-wired to rec-ognise when someone else is happy as there was 100% recognition of happiness (Ekman and Friesen 1982). Smiling is generally considered to be the easiest expression that we are able to display and it can be powerful. A smile will impact on other people's attitudes towards us and will encourage positive interaction. Consider how much we are affected by a smile. Do we go back to shops where the staff smile easily at us and avoid the places where they look grumpy? Or maybe we eat in the restaurant because the management and waiters have a positive friendly attitude, in favour of the place that serves better food. I certainly do! There are two kinds of smiles: the *real* smile and the *false* smile.

The real smile appears because of the action of two sets of muscles: the zygomatic major muscles and the orbicularis oculi muscles. The zygomatic major muscles run down the side of the face and are linked to the corners of the mouth. When we contract these muscles, they pull the mouth back, the corners of the mouth are pulled up, whilst giving the cheeks a pumped-up look. The orbicularis oculi muscles are the ones around the eyes and movement results in a narrowing of the eyes as the eyes are pulled back with 'crow's feet' appearing and a slight dipping of the eyebrows. These last muscles are not under our control and so are only present in a real smile.

So, the genuine smile is signified by the two corners of the mouth being forced upwards towards the eye with the outer edges of the eyes displaying that familiar crinkling. It also has a slow onset and decline and there is bilateral symmetry in the face. And finally, a real smile also has to be 'congruent' with the words or vocal content of our message.

The false smile is where we see the two corners of the mouth moving sideways towards the ears (there is no lift upwards) and no activity or emotion around the eyes. There is also an abrupt onset and decline and a bilateral asymmetry in the face. In addition, if we see a mismatch between the smile and the words, then we don't believe the message. So, when a politician is told to smile (because the public will warm to people who smile) but their smile does not match the content of what they are saying, then the meaning of the whole message is void. We also find people who do this irritating and believe them to be deceitful.

The false smile is also referred to as 'the social smile'. This is because it is an expression we sometimes have to adopt for social purposes. We are usually pleased that someone is smiling at us, whether it is genuine or not, because most of us use smiling to indicate friendliness as opposed to hostility. Consider the shop or restaurant again. People in jobs like these have been told to smile even when they don't feel inclined to. So, it's an expression that we have been used to from an early age. And it is very effective. Research has shown that waiters who smile more receive more tips!

I think the most fascinating aspect of facial expression though are the fleeting looks that cross our face that reveal our true emotion and these are called our micro expressions.

Micro expressions

Many facial expressions are made voluntarily – we change our facial muscles to look sym-pathetic, happy, worried. But our faces are also governed by a separate, involuntary system that makes expressions that we have no conscious control over. We can try to use our volun-tary muscular system to suppress those involuntary responses, but often, some little part of that suppressed emotion leaks out. So, it is our micro expressions that reveal our authentic feelings.

A few years ago, I asked to meet with one of my employees in my office. It was just before Christmas and I wanted to wish her a happy Christmas and to thank her for all her hard work that year, and also to offer her a pay rise. She said all the right things – she was happy, said thank you, she loved working for us – but her face very briefly said something else. I was confused and said to my partner afterwards that something wasn't right. Had she expected more of a pay rise? After Christmas, all was revealed. She came in and handed in her notice. I had in fact offered her a pay rise the day before she was attending a second interview for another job and the expression I saw cross her face fleetingly was guilt. She loved her job with us but needed to move for personal reasons and she felt guilty.

Our face will always 'leak out' what we truthfully feel as it is highly efficient in displaying our inner feelings. In a split second it registers a message after activating the appropriate facial muscles. An opposing message from the brain to hide an expression comes too late and so the true emotion leaks out for a second or two before being cancelled by the counter-expression. Since we try to suppress these lightening expressions in a split second, it takes a very astute and observant person, or sophisticated equipment and freeze framing, to detect them.

A perfect example might be at a job interview where we are asked about our relationship with our previous boss, one that we really hated. In the interview we insist that the relationship was great, and we only left the job because we wanted to have better options for our future, but our face will display a sneer, if only for a split second.

This kind of body language happens unconsciously and often goes unnoticed unless the person who is talking to us is highly perceptive to body language. If he is, he will see the contradiction between our verbal and nonverbal signals, and since nonverbal signals have five times more impact than the verbal ones, he is unlikely to believe us. Being highly perspective to reading these real emotions is not always about being trained to do it though. Reading people's faces is a skill but can be based on good genetics, better than average intuition, an intellectual gift, great social skills; or it can be due to the fact that the person has had extensive practice with their family or care givers. The best face readers are in fact those people who have had to pick up the subtle clues of explosive rage or violence in one or both of their parents, before danger erupts. Interviews with these adults who had alcoholic parents tell the tale: 'I knew when my dad turned his head a certain way and his eyes narrowed when he looked at me that he was about to lash out' or 'I saw the way my mum's mouth would tighten that she was going to start screaming and hitting me' (Albrecht, 2014).

We are now going to look at some specifics in interpreting facial expressions and we will break these down into the following: the lips, the forehead and the nose.

The lips

The lips can also be nicely revealing, quite independent from the smile. Just as with open body language, the more open the mouth, the more open we appear. Conversely, tense or tight lips show some kind of restraint of an emotion – usually a negative one. Here are some of the common things we do with our lips!

- *Disappearing lips and the upside-down U.* The most easily recognised is when the lips disappear as we press them together. This is often related to stress and it is as if our limbic brain is telling us to shut down and not allow anything into our bodies. It is a clear indicator that something is wrong. If the corner of the mouth turns down as well, giving the mouth an upside-down U look, then this is an indicator of high distress or stress.
- *The lip purse.* The lip purse usually means someone disagrees with us or they are thinking of an alternative idea. So, it can be useful to look out for in a conversation as it will indicate when someone is not agreeing with us or thinks we have got something wrong.

The lip purse is different from the *pout* which seems to cover a multitude of emotions. It may indicate sadness, anger, disgust and if we see it, we will need to look for clusters of behaviours to understand it. Of course, it might be just for effect. After all, the pout is popular in the acting and modelling world!

- *The sneer.* The sneer, like the eye rolling, is a universal expression of contempt. It is disrespectful and reflects a lack of caring or empathy. We may see it in someone who thinks we don't know what we are talking about or we lack knowledge. We may also see it in couples who are not getting on well, and it can accurately predict a break-up (Gottman, cited by Navarro, 2007).

- *Tongue displays.* Tongue behaviour can also provide us with insight into a person's thoughts or mood. When we are stressed, our mouth can get dry, so we lick our lips to moisten them. Also, when we feel discomfort, we tend to rub our tongues back and forth across our lips to calm ourselves. We may stick our tongue out to concentrate on a task or poke our tongues out to antagonise or show disgust. When someone shows other mouth cues such as lip biting, mouth touching, lip licking or object biting, it indicates that the person is insecure. And if someone touches or licks their lips while pondering their options, it can show insecurity. If the person shows *tongue jutting* behaviour, where the tongue pokes out between the teeth without touching the lips, this can mean 'I got caught, I am excited, I got away with something, I am naughty'. In business we may see this at the end of a dialogue to indicate that someone feels he has got away with something that the other person has failed to detect. So, if we see this, consider if we have been fooled or cheated; or if the other person has just made a mistake.

The forehead

A furrowed forehead usually occurs when someone is anxious, sad, concentrating, concerned, bewildered or angry (Navarro, 2006). Even though it can be an easy way to see discomfort or anxiety, it is important to see it within the context to determine its meaning. So, someone may frown as they concentrate on doing a difficult sum, but we will also see it on someone who has just been arrested. Frowning is so common and ancient that even dogs recognise it and can exhibit a similar expression when they are anxious or concentrating! As we get older, our foreheads develop deeper furrows that eventually become wrinkles so a person with a wrinkled brow has probably had a challenging life.

The nose

Flaring of the nostrils is a cue that signals that a person is aroused. This is seen in lovers and is probably a subconscious behaviour as they absorb each other's scents of sexual attraction (Givens, 2005). However, nose flaring can also indicate intention – an indicator of the intent to do something physical and not necessarily sexual. This is because as someone prepares to act physically, they will oxygenate which causes the nostrils to flare. This can be very useful to look out for, particularly if we are worried that someone may attack or run away. We also crinkle our nose to indicate dislike or disgust and in some cultures this is very pronounced.

The other thing we can see with 'nose behaviour' is people who hold their nose (and chin for that matter) high. Navarro (2006) describes this as 'a nose-up gravity-defying gesture' which indicates high confidence. It can also indicate an attitude of contempt as they literally look down their nose at the person talking to them.

Facial blushing or blanching

Being someone who grew up blushing furiously, this is something I can immediately relate to. In fact, I used to blush so badly, that I would have a rather alarming blotchy rash that would creep up my chest and neck as well as cover my face – quite unattractive! Luckily it has eased with age, but I am still able to surprise myself sometimes with a nice red face. A blush is a limbic reaction that is transmitted by the body – maybe someone gets too close, they are being looked at, they are caught doing something wrong, they like someone but don't want them to know. Conversely, blanching can take place when we are in the sustained limbic reaction known as shock. This can happen at an accident or when presented with overwhelming evidence of guilt. The involuntary nervous system hijacks all the surface vessels and channels the blood to our larger muscles to prepare for fight or flight. Although these behaviours are only skin deep, we should not ignore them as they indicate stress.

In body language terms, our face is the most expressive part of the anatomy and in any interaction is the first thing we look at. So, if someone is saying something, we look at their face to see if they mean it. We don't always say what we are really thinking but our faces reflect it anyway and the more we know how to read the signs, the better we will be at mind reading. Sometimes we see mixed messages in a face, maybe happiness cues mixed in with anxiety or pleasure alongside displeasure, or maybe the verbal message does not correspond to the nonverbal message. If this happens, side with the negative emotion as they tend to be the more honest of the two. Also notice the first emotion, especially if it is negative, as our initial reaction to anything or anyone is usually the most honest and accurate. Just don't forget to look for clusters. The face may be the most informative and fascinating part of someone's body language, but still put it into context and take note if the face agrees with the rest of their body.

Key points from Chapter 3

We communicate more with our eyes and our face than any other part of our anatomy.

Eyes

There is much to learn and notice about someone's eyes but the keys things to consider are:

- Where to look . . . learn the triangle rule and adapt it according to our relationship
- The eye dance . . . we need to alter our eye behaviour to show people we are listening, to hand over the conversation and to express our feelings
- Eye gaze . . . is affected by factors such as the situation, topic, personality and task
- Eye direction . . . tells us what they are thinking and what they are trying to access from their brain
- Blinking . . . different rates of blinking can indicate anxiety and discomfort or boredom or hostility
- Closed eye activity . . . can show boredom or superiority or insecurity

- Eye blocking . . . is a more extreme version of the closed eye activity and often seen when people literally do not like what they see
- The eye shuttle . . . is a 'flight' response, indicating nervousness or discomfort
- Widening or narrowing eyes . . . shows innocence and incredulity or disapproval or dominance

Facial expression

A face provides a running commentary on what someone is thinking or feeling and the more we are able to read these signals, the more we will know the true message behind the words. In particular remember the following:

- A facial expression can create an emotion as well as respond to an emotion. So smile and we will feel happy. Frown and we will feel sad
- There are six easily identifiable emotions and happiness is the only positive one
- A real smile and false smile can be detected by presence or absence of a narrowing of the eyes and 'crow's feet' appearing

Micro expressions

Micro expressions 'leak out' in a split second and reveal our true feelings before we are able to activate our muscles into a facial expression. These are small movements that are only noticeable to someone who is very observant or when the person is filmed and watched back frame by frame. We have no conscious control over these and so are very useful to look out for.

The lips

- Open versus closed . . . has the same effect as open versus closed body language. Tightly closed lips shows a restraint of an emotion, usually negative
- Disappearing lips . . . is related to stress or distress
- The lip purse . . . means they disagree with us or are thinking of an alternative
- The sneer . . . shows contempt
- The tongue . . . licking lips shows discomfort and poking the tongue out shows disgust. The tongue between the teeth means 'I got caught'
- Lip biting . . . shows insecurity

Other parts of the face

- The forehead . . . the furrowed forehead shows discomfort or anxiety
- The nose . . . flaring of nostrils can reveal that someone is either aroused or just about to do something physical like attack or run away
- Facial blushing . . . is a limbic reaction that is transmitted by the body, and facial blanching takes place when we are in the sustained limbic reaction known as shock, as all our blood is channelled to our larger muscles for 'fight or flight'

Chapter 4

Listening and paralanguage

'We have two ears and one mouth so that we can listen twice as much as we speak.'
Epictetus, Greek Philosopher

An introduction to conversation skills

In the next three chapters we are going to consider conversation skills and the art of a 'good conversation'. This is such an important part of our lives and something that many people struggle to get right.

Consider arguments or relationship problems. How many of them, whether big or small, start with a bad conversation? Probably all of them. Someone doesn't listen. Someone criticises us. Someone interrupts or advises us. We all long for effective communication with others, but time and time again, we fail, and this can have a devastating effect on our relationships and self-esteem. The most common reason that it goes wrong is that people typically inject what Bolton (1979) describes as 'communication barriers' or 'conversation spoilers'. We may also be too quick to judge. Carl Rogers (1961) says that he believes that the major barrier to interpersonal communication lies in our 'very natural tendency to judge' – to approve or disapprove of the statements of the other person. We criticise, name-call and label people, and we also diagnose – searching for a hidden motive behind what is being said. We often want to provide solutions with our advice or we bombard with questions. Finally we avoid other people's concerns by diverting away from what they are saying or reassuring them too quickly. All of these behaviours are likely to block a conversation and leave us feeling dissatisfied.

The other reason is of course gender. As we saw in Chapter 1, men and women are different and when communicating with each other, it can often go wrong. A man will instinctively try to help a woman who is upset by trying to fix the problem and offer solutions, thus invalidating her feelings (in her eyes). A woman will instinctively try to help the man improve the way he does things (in her eyes) by offering unsolicited advice or criticism. Neither sex like it and the conversation that ensues does not generally go well. John Gray in his book *Men are from Mars, Women are from Venus* (1992) says that men mistakenly expect women to think, *communicate* and react the way men do and women expect men to feel, *communicate* and respond the way women do. Both sexes need to relearn their conversational skills. Women need to stop giving advice or criticism and men need to stop talking and listen to how the woman is feeling rather than offering solutions. Simple.

So what skills are involved in conversations? There are eight verbal behaviours that are important within a conversation: listening, opening a conversation, maintaining the conversation through taking turns, asking questions, answering questions, being relevant, repairing, and ending a conversation. But before we focus on listening, we will consider the nonverbal elements of the words: paralinguistic skills, because the two areas are interlinked. As a listener, we must focus on listening to the person in the truest sense. This means we should not just listen to the words being spoken, but to the true meaning and the feelings behind them, and we do this by listening to the paralanguage.

Paralinguistic skills or prosody

Paralinguistic literally means 'beyond words' (from the Greek word 'para' which means beside or beyond) but they are also known as 'vocal cues' or 'prosody' or 'the way we talk'. It is commonly referred to as 'that which is left after subtracting the verbal content from speech' (Hargie et al., 1994). Paralinguistic skills are therefore nonverbal behaviours as they are not to do with the *verbal* content of the message but the feeling behind it, therefore they are best described here in this chapter as they affect the conversation very directly.

In a conversation, the listener hears far more than the speaker's words. They listen to the pitch, the rate of speech, the volume, clarity and fluency. Prosody will help us to know which words are the important ones to listen to and 'are there to direct us to the words that matter most' (Boyce, 2012). These cues give words their meaning and they will tune us into the message behind them, making up 38% of our communication according to Mehrabian's research (1971) which we discussed in Chapter 2.

That is why when we meet someone for the first time, we often don't remember their name or the details of what they said, because we are concentrating on 'listening' to the essential aspects of their nonverbal communication: their body language and the way they talk. It is this that tells us: this person is trustworthy or funny, arrogant or stressed. The psychotherapist Rollo May (1969) said 'I love to feel where words come from' and also that when someone enters his consulting room he asks himself, 'what does the voice say when I stop listening to the words and listen only to the tone?'

There are three levels to prosodic function according to Attwood (2016): grammatical, pragmatic and affective. The grammatical function is to communicate aspects such as a question (with a rising pitch), or a statement (with a falling pitch), or whether a word was intended as a noun or a verb. The pragmatic function is to provide social information to the listener such as our opinion, our thoughts or to emphasise what we want to draw the listener's attention to. The third function is the affective function which communicates feelings and attitudes. This tells the listener how we are feeling – are we happy and interested or anxious and needing reassurance – when we call out and say 'come here'.

At a basic level, we distinguish meaning by noticing differences in voice quality. For example, the sentence 'no-one told me you were coming over tonight' can have several different meanings depending on the tone of voice of the speaker. This ambiguous sentence might mean they are excited, but with different vocal qualities, the listener would assume they were annoyed or sad. If someone's voice was quiet, flat and dysfluent when they said 'I have left my boyfriend' it might indicate they are sad, angry or fearful. But if their voice was bright, clear and bouncy, then we would assume that they are happy about the situation.

The five paralinguistic qualities we listen to are: intonation, rate, volume, clarity and fluency.

Intonation

The intonation pattern not only helps to communicate our emotion but also helps the listener know which words to pay attention to. Intonation where there are 'up contours' is linked to happiness, interest, enthusiasm, surprise but also fear; and a flat intonation demonstrates a lack of interest or boredom. We also change our intonation to indicate that we are just about to finish speaking, which helps the listener know when it is their turn to speak. We also learn to use stress to emphasise a part of a word that is important and this again helps the listener to pay attention to what is significant. Sometimes it is just one word that can make the difference. Try altering which word you place the stress on in the sentence, 'I didn't say you had smelly feet'. You can end up with quite a few different meanings depending on which word you emphasise.

Volume and rate

Volume and rate are often dependent on the context, so we recognise that we need to raise our volume over the background noise to be heard or lower it when someone is trying to get to sleep. We also increase our rate if we see that someone is in a hurry to leave or we slow our rate if they have not understood us. In terms of emotions, volume and rate can be directly related to anger (Scherer, cited by Hargie et al., 1994). 'Hot' anger has a fast tempo and louder volume while 'cool' anger is more moderate in pace and volume. Feelings of boredom or depression tend to be accompanied by slower rate, lower volume and also a lower pitch; and in addition you may see dysfluency and mumbling (a lack of clarity).

Fluency and clarity

Fluency is how we connect the words without too much silence, hesitation or use of fillers such as 'um' or 'er'. It is linked to apprehension, so that the more apprehensive we are, the less fluent we tend to be, and silence is associated with discomfort and negative feelings. Clarity is associated with confidence and is affected by our use of all the other paralinguistic skills. For example, if we use low volume, fast rate and a monotonous intonation, our clarity of speech will be affected.

Dr Len Sperry, cited in Bolton (1979), suggests that the voice characteristics (paralanguage) described in the table over the page, are likely to have the meanings described in the right-hand column.

In addition to conveying meaning and emotions, changes in our vocal cues can be useful in gaining and maintaining the attention of others. It is certainly the first thing I tried to learn when I started public speaking – how to sound confident and interesting, even when feeling daunted and nervous! We have all experienced the public speaker who bores us because of the way they are delivering their message and the person who interests us with a potentially boring topic because they change the pitch, tone, speed and volume.

So we must learn to use our paralinguistic skills to communicate effectively with others, but equally we must listen to the paralinguistic skills of the other person, so that we can listen to how they are feeling and to the true meaning behind their words. And listening is the beginning of any good conversation.

Table 4.1 Paralanguage meanings	
Paralanguage	*Probable feeling/meaning*
Monotone voice	Boredom
Slow speed, low pitch	Depression
High voice, emphatic pitch	Enthusiasm
Ascending tone	Astonishment
Terse speech, loud tone	Anger
High pitch, drawn-out speech	Disbelief

Listening

'Speak in such a way that others love to listen to you. Listen in such a way that others love to speak to you.'

Anonymous

Every good conversation starts with good listening. We need to listen so that we can understand what is being said; to show interest and feelings about what is being said; to give feedback to the other person so that they know they are understood; and to give them reinforcement to continue the conversation. In 1953 Dale Carnegie said 'If you aspire to be a good conversationalist, be an attentive listener. To be interesting, be interested'.

This advice has not changed over the years and if you are at all typical, studies have regularly shown that 70% of our waking hours are spent in communication and of that time, 45% is spent listening (Nichols and Stevens, 1957). Unfortunately, most people are actually bad at listening. Even at a purely information level, researchers claim that 75% of oral communication is ignored, misunderstood or quickly forgotten. One reason that is given is the fact that when we are growing up, we receive a lot of training in non-listening. Parents say things like 'don't pay attention to her', or 'pretend you don't notice', and then they demonstrate poor listening by being inattentive or interrupting or saying 'but . . .' So, the average listener does not do it well – they interrupt and divert the other person by asking too many questions or making too many comments. Indeed, they may talk so much, that they end up monopolising the conversation! Nathan Miller is cited in Bolton's book (1979) as saying 'conversation in the United States is a competitive exercise in which the first person to draw breath is declared the listener'. I love this quote because it really does summarise what can be bad about so many conversations where there is very little effective listening going on – just two people talking at each other in a semblance of a 'conversation'.

Effective listening is so important in so many scenarios, in so many parts of our lives, and yet how many people really do it well? It has certainly long been recognised as a core skill in most fields of employment and effective listening techniques are often central to success in interactions with clients and other professionals. Indeed, for those in a counselling role, 'the capacity to be a good and understanding listener is perhaps the most fundamental skill of all' (Nelson-Jones, cited by Hargie et al., 1994). Listening is so important that many top employers provide listening skills training for their employees. This is not surprising when you consider that 'good listening skills can lead to: better customer satisfaction; greater productivity with fewer mistakes; and increased sharing of information, which in turn can lead to more creative and innovative work' (Skills You Need, 2016). Indeed, many successful leaders and entrepreneurs credit their success to effective listening skills. Richard Branson frequently says that listening is one of the main factors behind the success of Virgin, and it has also often been cited as crucial in, for example, medicine.

Sir William Osler, first Professor of Medicine at Johns Hopkins Hospital, is quoted as saying 'listen to your patient, he is telling you the diagnosis' (Skills You Need, 2016). And when we think about going to see a doctor, what do we hope for? When asked what we want to get out of the appointment, most people say that we want them to listen to us; and yet Armstrong concluded that 'although it would seem that listening is a medical skill more valued than previously, this does not necessarily mean that doctors have yet learnt always to hear what patients are saying' (cited by Hargie et al., 1994).

Listening is also an important skill in the earliest stages of development. The infant begins to respond to the world by hearing and listening and he has to listen before he can speak. In this sense, listening is a fundamental skill and the foundation for conversations.

A definition of listening

But what does the term 'listening' actually mean? At first sight, listening may be seen to be a simple process: someone talks, the other person listens, and then they talk while the other person listens. But of course, it is much more complicated than that. The word 'listen' is derived from two Anglo-Saxon words: *hylstan,* which means 'hearing', and *hlosnian,* which mean 'to wait in suspense' (Wolff et al., cited by Hargie et al., 1994). Listening can therefore be seen to have two parts to it: the auditory activity of 'hearing', and the process of converting spoken language into meaning. So listening can be defined as 'the complex, learned human process of sensing, interpreting, evaluating, storing and responding to oral messages' (Steil, cited by Hargie et al., 1994). We can also define listening in terms of 'active or passive' listening. Active listening is when someone displays behaviours which indicate that they are overtly paying attention (listening) and passive listening is when they do not display outward signs that they are doing so.

So, what is the purpose of listening? The skill of listening serves a number of purposes in social interaction and its functions are described by Hargie et al. (1994) as:

The purposes of listening

- To focus specifically on the message being communicated.
- To gain an accurate understanding from the other person.
- To convey interest, concern and attention.
- To encourage full, open and honest expression.
- To develop an 'other centred' approach during interactions.

Types of listening

How we listen does depend on external factors though and this means that there are different types of listening depending on the situation and purpose of the interaction. Different writers describe these in different ways with varying numbers of categories from just two (usually discriminative and comprehensive) to one website that suggests 27 (changingminds.org)!

These can probably best be grouped into four main types though:

> ## Table 4.2 Types of listening

1. Comprehension or informative listening	This is where the listener's primary concern is to understand the message. The emphasis is on listening for facts, ideas, and themes in order to comprehend the message.
2. Evaluative or critical listening	This is where the speaker may be trying to persuade or influence us and we listen in order to evaluate, criticise or otherwise pass judgment on what someone else says.
3. Appreciative listening	This is when we seek out ways to accept and appreciate other people through what they say. This may mean listening to something for pleasure, such as to music or poetry, or attending church and listening to a person preach.
4. Empathetic or therapeutic listening	This is when we demonstrate a willingness to attend to and understand the speaker's thoughts, beliefs and feelings.

Adapted from Hargie 2017

In the first three types, it is interesting to note that listening is intrinsic in that they are all for the benefit of the listener, but in empathetic listening, it is extrinsic in that the listener is seeking to help the speaker. This is the hardest to get right and will be the focus of the rest of the chapter, although the skills described below will also have some relevance to the other types of listening.

The process of listening

The process of listening during a conversation is not straightforward as it includes listening to the person, but also an ability to evaluate what is being said, plan what we could say in response and then rehearse our words in our head before speaking them. Listening therefore involves both nonverbal behaviour and verbal behaviour and can be divided into three clusters of skills: attending, following and reflecting skills.

Attending

Attending is giving our physical attention to someone. Bolton (1979) describes this as 'listening with your whole body' and these skills are particularly important to show to the other person that we are listening to them. This can work wonders. It shows the other person that we are interested in them and in what they have to say. It facilitates the expression of the most important matters of the mind and the heart. And for the person being attended to, it can be an impressive experience: to really feel that someone is directly and totally there for us. So how do we do it? Well we do this in several ways:

- First, we use a *posture of involvement*. We know from the previous chapters that body language often speaks louder than words and so changing our body language to 'invite' or 'facilitate' interpersonal relations is important. So a posture of involvement will mean that we lean our body towards the person, we face them squarely and at eye level, we maintain an open posture and we position ourselves at an appropriate distance. All of these will send the message that 'what you are telling me is important and I am listening to you' and will encourage the other person to continue.

- Second, we use *appropriate body motion*. A good listener won't sit rigidly and unmoving. He moves his body in response to the speaker and what is being said. A poor listener will move his body in response to stimuli that are unrelated to the other person, for example, fiddling with a pencil or swinging a leg up and down.
- Third, we use *eye contact*. We have already talked about the importance of this in the previous chapter, but just to reiterate, good eye contact and eye behaviour is essential for effective interpersonal communication and is one of the most effective of the listening skills.
- Finally, we need a *non-distracting environment*. An attentive listener needs to cut distractions such as the telephone, TV and computer screen and barriers like desks and tables.

Good attending in these ways will increase your observation of the other person's body language which is an essential part of listening.

Following

Bolton (1979) says that 'one of the primary tasks of a listener is to stay out of the other's way so that the listener can discover how the speaker views his situation'. Unfortunately most listeners don't do this – they interrupt and ask too many questions. We can use four 'following' skills to help with effective listening:

- First, we use a *door opener* which is an invitation to talk as opposed to the 'door closer', which doesn't encourage the person to talk, such as 'oh no, what did you do this time?' or 'cheer up'. A door opener may start with a description of the other person's body language – 'you look happy' or 'you look a bit down'. Then there is an invitation to talk – 'do you want to talk about it' or 'please go on'. Then there is silence – giving the person space to decide what to say. Finally we use our attending skills – in particular eye contact and a posture of involvement.
- Second, we use *minimal encouragers* which are brief verbal indicators that you are still listening without interrupting the flow of talk. The most common one is 'mmm' or 'oh' but you may also say things like 'right' or 'really' or 'no way'.
- Third, we use *questions*. But it is important to remember not to fall into the communication barrier we have already mentioned and question excessively. The best kind of questioning in this situation is to ask one question at a time and to use open questions as opposed to closed ones. A closed question only requires a yes/no answer – 'did you like the film?' Whereas an open question gives the person options and space to reply what they want – 'what did you think of the film?'
- Finally, we should use *attentive silence*. Attentive silence is one of the most important elements in following the listener. We live in a culture in which silence is not comfortable and most listeners talk too much and feel uncomfortable with too much silence. To help we should try to concentrate on the other person; observe them – their eyes, face, posture, tone of voice; and we should think about what they are saying and what they are feeling. If we make sure we are busy doing those three things, we may feel less anxious about the silence. As the Bible says 'There is a time to keep silent and a time to speak' (Ecclesiastes 3:7). And the effective listener can do both. They learn to speak when it is appropriate and can be silent when that is a suitable response.

Reflecting

John Powell (1974) a theologian summed up reflective listening beautifully:

> In true listening, we reach beyond the words, see through them, to find the person who is being revealed . . . [but] the words bear a different connotation for you than they do for me. Consequently, I can never tell you what you said, but only what I heard. I will have to rephrase what you have said, and check it out with you to make sure that what left your mind and heart arrived in my mind and heart intact and without distortion.

Reflective responses require the listener to restate the feeling or content of what the speaker has said. This should be done in a non-judgmental way and should be an accurate reflection of what the other person was experiencing. In this way we are providing a mirror to the speaker, but acknowledging what they are saying or feeling. There are four ways in which we can show good reflecting: paraphrasing, reflecting feelings, reflecting meanings and summative reflections.

- *Paraphrasing* means we provide a *concise* summary of the essence of the other person's content but in our own words. We should concentrate on the facts and ideas and paraphrase the message back to the speaker. When we get it right, the speaker will usually say 'yes' or 'right' or will nod their head. If we get it wrong, they can correct us.
- *Reflecting feelings* involves mirroring back the emotions which are being communicated. Listeners often miss the emotional dimension of a conversation as we focus on facts and figures. But if we don't encourage disclosures of feelings, we miss the personal reaction to the event. So, while they are talking, take note of their body language, focus on the feeling words, note the general content of the message and ask yourself how you would be feeling in that situation. Then reflect that back: 'so you're feeling pretty lonely at the moment'.
- *Reflecting meanings* involves joining the feeling to a fact. Try using the 'you feel . . . because. . .' or 'you are . . . by/about/that . . .' Again, the more succinct the better.
- *Summative reflections* try to tie together a number of comments by concisely recapping them. This can help the speaker to see the fragments of their utterances gathered together in a meaningful summary.

I have summarised all these skills into a table to help us to remember them and to develop our listening skills:

Table 4.3 The process of listening

The 3 stages	Means . . .	For example . . .
1. Attending	A posture of involvement	Lean your body towards the person Face them squarely and at eye level Maintain an open posture Appropriate distance
	Appropriate body motion	Move your body in response to the speaker and what is being said Do not fidget

	Eye contact	Use good eye contact Look within the eye contact triangle of their face
	Non-distracting environment	Cut out distractions such as the telephone, TV and computer screen Reduce barriers like desks and tables This will help with observation of the other person's body language
2. Following	A door opener	Start with a description of the other person's body language: 'you look happy' An invitation to talk: 'do you want to talk about it' or 'please go on' Use silence to give the person space to decide what to say Use the attending skills above
	Minimal encouragers	Use brief verbal indicators that show you are still listening such as 'mmm' or 'oh'
	Questions	Ask one question at a time Use open questions not closed ones
	Attentive silence	Use silence to observe the other person; their eyes, face, posture, tone of voice Think about what they are saying and what they are feeling
3. Reflecting	Paraphrasing	Provide a concise summary of what the other person said but in your own words Concentrate on the facts and ideas and paraphrase the message back
	Reflecting feelings	Mirror back the emotions which are being communicated Take note of their body language and focus on the feeling words Ask yourself how you would be feeling in that situation and reflect that back
	Reflecting meanings	Try joining the feeling to a fact using the 'you feel. . . because. . .' or 'you are. . . by/about/ that. . .'
	Summative reflections	Try to summarise by concisely recapping what has been said

Factors that affect listening

Communication often breaks down because of ineffective listening. Poor listening is, of course, a regular occurrence in most of us. We are listening to someone else speak, but busy thinking about our reply whilst the other person is still talking and therefore we are not really listening at all. We are often guilty of critically evaluating what is being said before we fully understand and therefore we make wrong assumptions and conclusions about the speaker's meaning. This and other types of ineffective listening lead to misunderstandings and a breakdown in communication. So, what affects our listening? Why is it that sometimes it is just hard to do it well?

There are actually four main ways in which the process of listening can be adversely affected (Hargie et al, 1994, Skills You Need Ltd, 2016): the listener, the speaker, the message and the environment. Not surprisingly, most are to do with the listener.

The listener

Sometimes the ability to listen is just down to the listener. Some people are naturally better listeners than others and some are affected by factors that are not always in their control. These include:

- *Linguistic ability*: people who have wider vocabularies are often thought to be better listeners as they can more easily understand and assimilate a greater range of concepts. However, higher IQ does not necessarily mean better listening. People with higher emotional intelligence (EQ), on the other hand, are more likely to be better listeners.
- *Motivation*: the more motivated we are to listen, the better we are at it!
- *Organisational ability*: this means the ability to identify the key parts of a message and then store them appropriately. People who are good at this, tend to be better listeners.
- *Concentration techniques*: some people are good at using memory aids to help with their listening or using self-questioning techniques such as 'why is he telling me this?' or 'what is the main idea here?' which have been found to help with listening.
- *Gender*: there is some research that shows that women are better at listening as they are more perceptive at recognising and interpreting nonverbal messages (see Chapter 1). However, without trying to stereotype, men and women also appear to value communication differently. Women tend to place a higher value on connection, cooperation and emotional messages, whereas men are generally more concerned with facts and may be uncomfortable talking about and listening to personal or emotional subjects. This doesn't necessarily mean that women are better listeners than men, but women will be better at recognising the nonverbal message and during a conversation, men and women are likely to ask different types of questions of the speaker to clarify the message and their final interpretation of the conversation may, therefore, be different.
- *Physical condition*: when we are tired or ill, or just needing the toilet, we find it harder to listen.
- *Disposition*: introverts tend to be better listeners than extroverts as they are happier to sit back and let the other person take centre stage. In addition, people who are highly anxious, self-conscious or easily distracted are not good listeners.
- *Attention*: not surprisingly, if we are not able to give someone our full attention for one reason or another, we tend to be poorer at listening. As most of us have a lot of internal self-dialogue, we spend a lot of time listening to our own thoughts and feeling, and it can be difficult to switch the focus from 'I' or 'me' to 'them' or 'you'.
- *State of mind or mental set*: sometimes the listener is adversely affected by a previous experience, or an attitude or feeling that then gets in the way of their ability to listen. It particularly affects our ability to be objective and non-judgemental.
- *Focus*: sometimes we end up focusing on some aspect of the speaker apart from what they are saying. We may, for example, find them attractive/unattractive and concentrate on that. Perhaps we simply don't like the speaker or their accent.
- *Individual bias*: this may be linked to the previous point but may also be because they don't hear (or don't want to hear) the whole message. They may only pick up on one part

of the message or they disregard the part they don't want to respond to. This can happen in politics where someone wants to get a particular point across and so they don't listen to the question and answer the question they wanted to answer!

- *Lack of interest*: and finally we may struggle to listen simply because we are bored by the topic.

Several of the above may result in the listener using the process of *blocking*. This means they will use a number of techniques to end or divert the conversation. Sometimes these are useful or legitimate, but sometimes they can be a serious obstacle to good listening. The common ones are shown in the table below:

Table 4.4 Blocking tactics to listening

Tactic	Example
Rejecting involvement	'I don't want to talk about it with you' 'This has nothing to do with me'
Denial of feelings	'You have nothing to worry about' 'You will be OK'
Selective responding	Focusing only on specific aspects of the message and ignoring others
Admitting insufficient knowledge	'I'm not really qualified to say' 'I'm only vaguely familiar with that subject'
Topic shift	Changing the topic away from that expressed by the speaker
Referring	'You should consult your doctor about that' 'Your teacher will help you with that'
Deferring	'Come back and see me if the problem continues' 'We can discuss that next week'
Pre-empting any communication	'I'm in a terrible rush. See you later?' 'I can't talk now. I'm late for a meeting'

Adapted from Hargie 2017

The speaker

Some people are actually harder to listen to and this can be for several reasons:

- *Speech rate*: information is actually cognitively processed quicker than it is spoken which gives us time to process what we are hearing but it can also give us time to get distracted. This is particularly true if someone's rate of speech drops below 125 words/minute (there is too much time to get distracted) or conversely if it goes above 300 words/minute (we can't handle the volume of information).
- *Speech delivery*: the speaker's clarity of speech and their intonation, volume and fluency will also affect how easy they are to listen to. We can all remember the teacher whose lesson was hard to stay awake in due to their monotonous tone of voice.

- *Emotionality*: if the speaker displays high levels of emotion, the listener may be distracted by this or may pay too much attention to it and will not be able to listen to the verbal message.
- *Status*: if the speaker is regarded as important or of higher status, then we tend to listen more attentively and attach more importance to what they are saying.

The message

The nature of the message can affect how well we listen, in particular the following:

- *Structure*: if the message is delivered in an unclear and unstructured way, it will be much harder to listen to. In these cases, we may need to interrupt the speaker to ask questions to clarify the message.
- *Significance*: we find things of significance to us easier to listen to. So when the message holds similar values or attitudes to the ones we hold, we are more likely to listen attentively. Conversely, we may also listen more if the message is unexpected or challenging.
- *Complexity*: and last, we naturally find it harder to listen to a message that is complex.

The environment

Finally, we should consider the environment and the effect it has on our ability to listen effectively. In particular, there are three elements that have an impact on us:

- Ventilation and temperature
- Noise
- Seating

All the above will affect our comfort levels and each can become an intrusion into our ability to concentrate and listen.

So, if someone is not listening to us, how will we know? What are the signs to look out for? Signs of poor listening include: a lack of eye contact; an inappropriate posture or movement; distracted actions such as fidgeting, doodling, looking at a watch, yawning; an inappropriate expression and a lack of head nods; a sudden change in topic; selective listening; daydreaming or a 'far-away' look; and starting to offer advice before they fully understand the problem or concerns of the speaker.

In summary, listening is fundamentally important to effective communication and I have summarised with ten top tips for listening:

Table 4.5 Ten top tips for effective listening

Top tip	Or in other words. . .	A description
1. Stop talking	Stop, just listen	When somebody else is talking, listen to what they are saying, do not interrupt, talk over them or finish their sentences.

2. Prepare yourself to listen	Relax	Focus on the speaker. Put other things out of your mind and concentrate on the messages that are being communicated.
3. Put the speaker at ease	Help the speaker to feel free to speak	Nod or use other gestures or words to encourage them to continue. Maintain eye contact and show you are listening and understanding what is being said.
4. Remove distractions	Focus on what is being said	Don't doodle, shuffle papers, look out the window, pick your fingernails or similar and avoid unnecessary interruptions. These behaviours disrupt the listening process and tell the speaker that you are bored or distracted.
5. Empathise	Try to understand the other person's point of view	Look at issues from their perspective. By having an open mind we can more fully empathise with the speaker.
6. Be patient	A pause, even a long pause, does not necessarily mean that the speaker has finished	Be patient and let the speaker continue in their own time, sometimes it takes time to formulate what to say and how to say it.
7. Avoid personal prejudice	Try to be impartial	Don't become irritated and don't let the person's habits or mannerisms distract you from what the speaker is really saying. Everybody has a different way of speaking so try to focus on what is being said and ignore styles of delivery.
8. Listen to the tone	Volume and tone both add to what someone is saying	Let these help you to understand the emphasis of what is being said.
9. Listen for ideas – not just words	You need to get the whole picture, not just isolated bits and pieces	Try to link together pieces of information to reveal the ideas of others.
10. Wait and watch for nonverbal communication	Gestures, facial expressions, and eye-movements can all be important	Watch and pick up the additional information being transmitted via nonverbal communication.

Adapted from the website www.skillsyouneed.com

Without the ability to listen effectively, messages are easily misunderstood, communication breaks down and the speaker can easily become frustrated or irritated. We could argue that if there was one communication skill we should aim to master above all, then it really should be the art of good listening. It is a skill that underpins all positive human relationships and has huge benefits in our personal lives, including friendships and relationships at work, improved self-esteem and confidence, and general well-being. In fact, studies have shown that, whereas speaking raises blood pressure, listening can bring it down.

Of course, in defining listening, we have also begun to explain some of the other skills of the conversation. And that is because a conversation is a two way process and is always reliant on the skills of both people involved. So in the next chapter we will consider some of the other skills involved in a conversation.

Key points from Chapter 4

If you aspire to be a good conversationalist, be an attentive listener.

There are eight verbal behaviours that are important within a conversation: listening, opening a conversation, maintaining the conversation through taking turns, asking questions, answering questions, being relevant, repairing, and ending a conversation.

Paralinguistic skills

Paralinguistic skills are nonverbal behaviours as they are not to do with the verbal content of the message but the feeling behind it.

- Listen to the rate, volume, intonation, fluency and clarity of speech
- These behaviours will indicate emotion far better than the words will

Listening

Every good conversation starts with good listening and we spend 45% of our waking hours doing it. Listening can be divided into three clusters of skills: attending, following and reflecting skills.

Attending

Attending is giving your physical attention to someone, 'listening with your whole body', and requires four skills:

1. We use appropriate body language – a *posture of involvement.*
2. We use *appropriate body motion* – we move our body in response to the speaker and what is being said.
3. We use *eye contact.*
4. We need a *non-distracting environment.*

Following

Following means we need to stay out of the speaker's way so that we can learn what they are saying. There are four ways in which we do this:

1. We use a *door opener* which is an invitation to talk, such as 'do you want to talk about it?', and then we use *silence.*

2. We use *minimal encouragers* such as 'mmm' to show that we are still listening.
3. We use open *questions,* one at a time.
4. We should use *attentive silence* – concentrate on the other person. Observe their eyes, face, posture, tone of voice, and think about what they are saying and what they are feeling.

Reflecting

This requires the listener to restate the feeling or content of what the speaker has said in a non-judgmental way. Again there are four ways in which we can do this:

1. *Paraphrasing* means we provide a *concise* summary of the essence of the other person's content but in our own words.
2. *Reflecting feelings* involves mirroring back the emotions which are being communicated.
3. *Reflecting meanings* involves joining the feeling to a fact with statements such as 'you feel . . . because . . .'
4. *Summative reflections* try to tie together a number of comments by concisely recapping them.

Factors that affect listening

Communication can break down because of ineffective listening which is adversely affected by:

- *The listener.* some people are naturally better listeners than others and some are affected by factors that are not always in their control
- *The speaker.* some people are actually harder to listen to
- *The message.* the nature of the message can affect how well we listen
- *The environment* and the effect it has on our ability to listen effectively

Chapter 5

Starting and ending conversations

'Don't knock the weather; nine-tenths of the people couldn't start a conversation if it didn't change once in a while.'

Kin Hubbard, American journalist (1868–1930)

In this chapter we will look at the skills involved in starting and ending a conversation. Beginnings and endings are equally important parameters within which a conversation takes place, in that they are 'structured, formalised sequences during which interactors have a greater opportunity to make important points or create an effective impact on others' (Hargie et al., 1994). How we greet and part from others has long been recognised as crucial in our development and maintenance of relationships (Roth, cited by Hargie et al., 1994). So, in this chapter we will focus on how to open and close a conversation as they have similar features and rituals and are actually complementary skills, and then in the following chapter we will look at the middle 'meaty' part of the conversation.

The greeting and parting phase

The similarity between how we greet and part from friends can be seen with the following phases (Kendon and Ferber, cited by Hargie et al., 1994):

The greeting and parting phases

A. *Distant phase*. When two friends are at a distance, but within sight, they will wave, raise their eyebrows, smile, toss their heads and make eye contact.

B. *Medium phase*. When they are closer, they avoid eye contact, smile, and engage in a range of grooming (self-touching) behaviours.

C. *Close phase*. When they are very close they will make eye contact, smile, make appropriate verbal comments and may touch one another (shake hands, kiss).

During greetings the sequence is ABC, while when parting the reverse sequence CBA happens and the skills we need for both are naturally similar. So, we need to consider both the non-verbal skills that we need to use, as well as the verbal skills of what we need to say in order to understand this sequence in more detail.

Starting or opening a conversation

To start a conversation we need 'a combination of friendliness, curiosity, authenticity and verve. This mix is an almost magical key which opens many doors in social interactions. And more open doors mean more options' (Ezeanu, 2012).

In athletics, competitors are instructed: 'On your marks. Get set. Go!' By telling the athletes to 'get set', they are being told to become both mentally and physically ready for the take-off which they know is about to follow. This analogy can be useful to help us think about conversation starters. We are using a set of skills to prepare us for the main event. It will involve getting someone's attention and arousing motivation or establishing a frame of reference, so that the conversation can begin. It can be a long or short process depending on the context and how well we know the other person. At a simple level, with someone we know, it may just involve a phrase such as 'wait until you hear this...' or 'have you heard the latest?' With people we don't know, the rules are more complex.

The way we open or greet someone will not only depend on the other person but also the context of the interaction and what we want to achieve. For example, if I am lecturing, I will start a conversation with someone in the audience one way, and during a coffee break, I may use a different strategy with the same person. If I am greeting a friend in a street, I will start the conversation one way, and then I will use a different way to greet the person with whom I am in a counselling session. We are also influenced by the subject matter to be discussed, the amount of time available, the time of day, the location of the encounter and the personality, experience and socioeconomic background of the other person. So, these should be taken into consideration when employing some of the skills or strategies described in this chapter. In brief, we need to consider two main aspects to opening a conversation: how to establish rapport and then what to say.

Establish rapport

The first golden rule for starting a conversation is to be, or at least appear, friendly. The goal is not to impress someone with a conversation starter, but it is to show that we are a relaxed and sociable person who wants to have an enjoyable chat. We should also try to assume a rapport with the other person. So that means when we start talking to someone, we should do it in more or less the same manner as if we were going up to someone we already know and are friendly with. The way we do this will depend on the situation but Kendon and Ferber (1973) point out that the way in which we approach the other person immediately signals our social status, degree of familiarity and liking, and what role we will play in the forthcoming conversation.

The exact way we greet and establish rapport with someone will depend on the context and factors such as the person's role, the function of the interaction, the location and the sex of the other person. Greenbaum and Rosenfeld (1980) observed 152 greetings at an airport and found that 83% involved bodily contact, but these varied from mutual lip kisses to handshakes to embracing to face kisses. The choice can be daunting. But if we focus on the following four aspects of our nonverbal communication, it will be an excellent start (adapted from Ezeanu, 2012):

1. Breathe and relax

Sometimes we rush too quickly into an interaction and it would be beneficial to stop and breathe before we do anything. This is especially important if we are nervous or anxious as we are usually at our most nervous when we're first talking to someone, and the anxiety can cause us, or them, to falter. So, it can help to take a moment to concentrate on our body. Notice how we are breathing and slow the rate down to help relax. This will help to create a relaxed appearance in our body language and our face, which we will cover in the following two points. If we are very nervous, it may help to spend a couple of minutes before we need to start the conversation doing a 'power pose' such as the 'Wonder Woman' pose (see Chapter 2 on body language) as this will have an effect on our hormone levels and our confidence.

2. Open body language

How we sit or stand, gesture or cross our arms, will contribute to how we are perceived by others. Remember that it is 55% of our communication and people are more affected by how we look than by what we say. Open body language is welcoming, relaxed and attentive. It signifies a lack of barriers – our body is open and exposed and we are suggesting that we are vulnerable to others and we're comfortable about it. Our hands are in view, with exposed palms, and our legs and posture are free and easy and eye contact is good. Everything indicates a positive attitude. If we appear self-assured, we are more likely to make a good impression and draw the other person into the conversation. Confidence is like a magnet and it's one of the best qualities someone can convey to others from the start. So, we should try to uncross our legs and arms and keep our hands in view, and this will help to establish rapport.

3. Facial expression

It is important to remember that the face is the most important part of body language. We immediately look at someone's face when we meet them, as it is the face that will hold clues as to what they are thinking about and how they are feeling. So, first, we need to *look at the other person*. We look at people more if we like them, and so holding eye contact will express liking and a sense of intimacy. We also know that large eyes are appealing so raising your eyebrows and eyelids will help build rapport. Second, *smile* as we generally warm more to people who smile at us. Ideally this will be a genuine smile, but even if we have to fake it, people will still warm to us more than not smiling at all. Smiling is generally considered to be the easiest expression that we are able to display, it can be powerful, and a smile will impact on other people's attitudes towards us and will encourage positive interaction.

4. The way you talk

Also, always keep in mind that when it comes to making conversation, the way we talk is often much more important (in fact 38%) than what we actually say. If we sound confident and at ease, people will love talking to us and what we say becomes secondary.

Opening line . . . or small talk

An opening line depends a lot on whether we know the person or whether we are starting a conversation with a stranger. The latter is interesting and will be discussed first. Morin and Sander (2012) describe a study by a team of scientists from Boston who wanted to understand what really happens when two strangers meet. They made a surprising discovery about the initial conversation between two people.

Small talk, or as some writers call it 'non-task comments', turned out to be more important than they first thought. Some scientists describe small talk as like a 'bonding ritual' – a ritual to ensure we have time to take note of all the important stuff, like the messages we are receiving from their body language and paralanguage, and to decide whether this person is OK or not OK. So, while we engage in small talk, really important things are happening subconsciously. We are forming an opinion or a picture of the other person so that we can begin to feel relaxed with them and move onto more interesting conversation.

This small talk serves therefore to signal recognition for, and acknowledgment of, the other person and is definitely not expected to produce anything too meaningful or revealing. For example, we regularly open an interaction with 'how are you?' or 'you OK?' but do not really want to know that the other person is worrying about their health or their marriage or their son who has run away with the neighbour's wife! It is interesting to note that these common openers change in different continents and can mean different things. In the UK it is common for us to say 'you OK?' as a general 'non-task' greeting, but I soon learned that in Australia they do not use this and they are more likely to say 'how are you?' or 'how are you going?' Indeed, if we do happen to say 'you OK?' to an Australian, this really does mean 'are you OK?' i.e. 'you don't look OK'! This did lead to a couple of confused beginnings to a couple of my conversations!

So, our opening line is often not that important as it serves as a 'bonding ritual'. Small talk conversation starters that work well all also share three key traits (Ezeanu, 2012). First, they are *personal but not too intrusive*. It is nice to use a conversation starter that relates to the other person but by its very nature, small talk should be light and social, and not intrusive. Second, they are *authentic*, so it's not a good idea to use starters that take a conversation in a direction we're not really interested in, even if it is just small talk. Third, they are *adapted*. That means we don't use the one conversation starter everywhere, we need to adapt our approach so it makes sense in the social context we're in.

So even though the opening line is not as important as what follows, we do need to say something. So what could we use as a conversation starter? The table below gives a few examples of common starters:

Table 5.1 Conversation starter examples

1. Introduce yourself	In formal situations only, we can introduce ourself. 'Hello I'm Alex from Speaking Space' but we should never do this in a less formal situation such as at a bus stop or in a queue. Sharing names generally comes much later.
2. Comment on the weather	The weather is a very useful opener – some people make fun of this and see it as a 'cop out' but everyone does it so in my opinion there is nothing wrong with it. As the American Journalist Kin Hubbard (1868-1930) said 'don't knock the weather; nine-tenths of the people couldn't start a conversation if it didn't change once in a while'.

3. Comment on something pleasant	It is much safer to say something positive as we may offend someone by being critical. So comments like 'this coffee is delicious' is better than 'this cake is horrible' as the person we are talking to may be the cousin of the person who baked it!
4. Ask for information	Ask someone where the nearest coffee shop is or when the next session starts. Even if we know the answer, it can be a good way to get talking to someone.
5. Ask for assistance	Everyone likes to feel helpful so asking someone for help can be a good way to start a conversation. Just make sure whatever we ask for is something the listener can provide or do without too much inconvenience.
6. Offer assistance	This may not happen often, but if we find ourselves in a situation where we can offer assistance to someone we would like to talk to, do it! For example, 'can I help you with that large box?' or 'do you need a programme?'
7. Ask for an opinion	Most people like feeling that others are interested in their opinions and will be happy to respond.
8. Mention a mutual acquaintance	Mentioning someone we both know will tell the listener we are part of his or her extended social circle and they may then consider us as someone they know or should know. This can backfire of course, if we mention someone they really don't like!
9. Bring up a shared experience	Any common ground is a good way to start someone talking so asking if someone comes from the same town or region as us might work well.
10. Praise the listener	This can work well if we want to talk to someone prominent or well known. We'll never insult someone by saying, 'I really love your work,' or 'I thought your last article was great.' We must be careful not to fawn and only offer praise if we genuinely mean it.
11. Compliment the person's apparel or accessories	Most people like it when others appreciate their taste, so they will likely want to engage with us. But we shouldn't comment on their physical appearance – having a stranger or near-stranger tell us that we have beautiful eyes is pretty creepy.

Adapted from Zetlin 2015

In some situations we are expected to be sociable and so most of these will be perfect for this kind of situation, but if we want to start a conversation when it's not explicitly a social setting, for example on the train or in a queue, then it is important to not be too direct and start asking people questions out of nowhere. Instead, we need to say something related to the situation first. So, a question about the time the train gets in, or if there is Wi-Fi, would be suitable in this setting.

The four most common mistakes when starting a conversation

Sometimes we do get it wrong though and Morin and Sander (2012) describe four mistakes that can be made:

> ## The four most common mistakes when starting a conversation
>
> 1. *Being too linear in the conversation.* Most conversations jump around among different subjects at the beginning so if we have a too linear approach to the conversation, we will struggle as soon as we are unable to come up with anything to say on the current subject.
> 2. *Asking too few or too many questions in relation to how much we share about ourselves.* It is important to remember that conversation is a process of give and take, so we need to keep a balance in how much we share in relation to how much the other person shares. This balance helps us to connect with people fast.
> 3. *Not being genuine when asking something.* Ask questions that we genuinely want to know about the person we are talking to.
> 4. *Asking a question and not showing enough interest to the answer.* However, if we are asking questions we are genuinely interested in, this shouldn't be an issue.

The door opener

Before we move on to discuss ending a conversation, it is worth exploring another way in which a conversation can start, and that is the use of the 'door opener' which was talked about briefly in the listening section (Chapter 4). A door opener is a 'non-coercive invitation to talk' (Bolton, 1979). This is where we sense that another person wants to talk but needs encouragement. Sometimes door openers are not necessary to get the conversation going but may be needed later in the conversation if the speaker does not seem to want to continue. Door openers don't have to be verbal cues, a good listener can also use his or her body to send the signal 'I am interested, you have my attention, please tell me more'.

People often do the exact opposite of a door opener which is not surprisingly called a door closer. They may make a judgmental statement to someone looking withdrawn such as 'what did you do this time?', or they try to reassure them with 'cheer up' or 'things will get better'. Or they may just give advice such as 'don't mope around. That won't help'. These all provide 'road blocks' to a conversation – they discourage the person from talking.

A door opener encourages conversation and they typically have four elements as described by Bolton (1979):

> ## The four elements of a door opener
>
> 1. *A description of the person's body language.* This is where we just comment on the other person's facial expression or general body language, for example 'your face is beaming today' or 'you look a bit fed up'.
> 2. *An invitation to talk or to continue talking.* We could say 'fancy talking about it?' or 'let's hear about it'.
> 3. *Silence.* This means giving the person time to decide whether to talk and what he wants to say.
> 4. *Attending.* Using eye contact and a posture of involvement (see the chapter on listening) to demonstrate interest and concern.

All four parts are not always present in every door opener as it will depend on the situation and the relationship between the two people, but they are powerful ways to get a conversation going and to really practise those listening skills described in the previous chapter.

Ending a conversation

Ending a conversation in many ways is a complementary skill to opening a conversation in that there is a sequence of actions or rituals that we go through. It is defined by Hargie (2017) as 'directing attention to the termination of social exchange by summarising the main issues which have been discussed, drawing attention to what will happen in the future and, finally, breaking interpersonal contact without making participants feel rejected or shunned'. This makes it sound possibly more complicated and problematic than we had realised. Can't we just say 'I've got to go, bye'? Another problem is that people often spend time thinking about how to start a conversation and may even plan their opening line but tend to spend less time considering how they will then end the conversation. And it is equally important as a skill as it may then determine to a large extent whether someone will want to talk to that person again.

So how do we do it? Well, the way in which we end a conversation will of course depend on many factors such as the situation and the person we are talking to. Also, it will depend on why we need to end the conversation.

The functions of ending a conversation

There are a few main reasons why we may want to finish a conversation: we have to get back to what we were doing; the conversation is starting to wind down and we want to wrap it up; we're just not in a chatty mood and want to keep things short; we don't want to talk to the other person and we want an exit strategy.

Hargie (2017) describes this slightly differently and gives us seven main reasons why we end a conversation:

> ### Seven reasons why we end a conversation
> 1. To indicate that a topic has been completed
> 2. To focus the other person's attention on the essential features of the material covered
> 3. To help in consolidating the facts, skills, concepts covered in the interaction
> 4. To give the person a sense of achievement
> 5. To indicate possibilities for future action
> 6. To assess the effectiveness of the interaction
> 7. To establish a conducive relationship so that they look forward to future conversations

Of course how we actually end the conversation depends not only on the reason, but also on the context and the people involved. For example, we may be talking to someone by the photocopier at work; or chatting to someone at a party; or on the phone. We may bump into someone on the street; or sit next to someone on the bus or on a train. All of these situations need to be handled slightly differently but Hargie (2017) describes four main types of 'closures': factual, motivational, social and perceptual and these can help us learn how to end a conversation and are summarised below.

Factual closure

A factual closure is used when the conversation has included a number of facts or ideas or problems. It is more common in more formal settings and can be used to highlight what has been discussed and draw it together in an ending. We can use these types of closures throughout a conversation as well as at the end, particularly where there is a 'topic shift'. There are three main ways in which we do this: summarising, using questions and finally making future plans.

A factual closure: three ways to do it

1. *Summary*. Summing up what someone has said is the most common way we do this and can be done during the conversation as well as at the end. It also shows them that we have been listening (see chapter 4). It is particularly useful in more formal or clinical situations such as a doctor's appointment as it can be used to check that both parties have understood each other.

2. *Questions*. This may seem like a strange way to draw a conversation to an end, as it could encourage someone to continue talking, but in this case, the person uses a question to check they have understood or the other person has understood and to indicate that they are coming to an end. An example could be 'Is there anything else you would like to ask before you go?' or 'Is that OK?' In this way, we are indicating that the end is drawing near.

3. *Future plans*. This can be used to not only summarise future actions, for example 'so I will phone Dave and let you know what he says', but also shows the person that there is a desire to continue talking at a later date, for example by saying 'I will see you tomorrow' or 'let's talk again next week'.

Motivational closure

A motivational closure is used when we want to encourage the other person in something. In this type of closure, we are not giving a sense of finality or completion, but to let the person know that our relationship and interactions are on-going and will happen again. So, we may want to encourage them to think about something a bit more or to go and do something, and again, we can do it in one of three ways:

A motivational closure: three ways to do it

1. *A motivating statement.* This is the most obvious and can include final statements, like 'let's show them what you can do' or 'give it everything you've got', or statements that encourage people to put something into practise, such as 'you should try these out for yourself . . .' or 'only you can make that decision'.
2. *A thought-provoking statement.* This can be used at the beginning and end of encounters when we want someone to go away to consider something further. Teachers often use this to encourage students to study in their own time, but we can also use them effectively in work conversations to encourage a colleague to consider something.
3. *Future orientation comments.* These are used to give people ideas or direction for the future, for example the teacher who says 'so when you get home, I want you to. . .' or the therapist who says 'between now and our next appointment, I would like you to. . .' or the nurse who says 'the next time you need to. . ., try using the method I have shown you'.

Social closure

A social closure is concerned with leaving the other person feeling glad that the conversation has happened and that we have enjoyed the interaction and we are willing to talk again at some point in the future. These can be task-related or non-task-related.

A social closure: two ways to do it

1. *Task-related.* These are comments that relate to what we have been talking about, and help the other person to gain a sense of satisfaction by commenting on what has been achieved as a result of the conversation. For example, 'That's great! Thank you for helping me with that' or 'Well done. I think you've earned a rest now!' or just 'Thank you for that.' These are all aimed at making the other person feel good about what they have been doing.
2. *Non-task-related.* These are often used when the main business of the conversation has ended and we then make a personal statement to show that we are a warm, friendly person. This is the 'human' aspect of ending a conversation and would include statements such as 'take it easy' or 'have a lovely holiday'. In more formal situations, we may say 'It's been nice talking to you. I hope we meet again'. These statements all help to 'round off' the conversation and signal that it has been a pleasurable experience.

Perceptual closure

These are all the physical movements and 'positionings' that we employ to indicate leaving (the nonverbal markers) and the verbal 'goodbyes' that we use in different situations (the verbal markers), and which occur sometimes separately but more often simultaneously:

> ### A perceptual closure: two ways to do it
>
> 1. *Verbal markers*. These are all the different ways in which we say 'good-bye' and which one we choose to use will depend on the situation and how well we know the other person. It will vary from 'good-bye' to 'see ya', from 'good night' to 'catch you later'. The other way we use verbal markers to indicate the ending is the use of words such as 'well . . .' or 'ok . . .' or 'right . . .' We need to accompany these with a downward intonation of the voice and this will signal that we are drawing things to a close.
> 2. *Nonverbal markers*. These are used to complement the verbal markers. We may start with subtle cues such as shifting our body posture, putting our hands on our legs or the arms of the chair, breaking eye contact, or looking towards the exit and then we may need to use more obvious signs such as looking at our watch. All of these communicate that we want the conversation to come to an end.

In summary, all of these techniques can be used together or on their own depending on the context in which they are being used, but are important in leaving people with a good feeling or impression of the interaction; something that is essential for building relationships and self-esteem.

Six top tips to ending a conversation

To simplify, Dean (2017) gives us three or four steps to ending a conversation and succeed-socially.com (2017) gives us seven, which I have amalgamated below in a summary of my six top tips:

1. Use nonverbal behaviour to show you're ready to end the conversation

Start adjusting your body language and your actions to indicate to the other person that it's time for them to wrap up the discussion, or that you're about to end it soon yourself. You could try: standing up if you've been sitting down; starting to move towards the door, or in the general direction you were originally heading. And if those don't work, actually getting back to the thing you needed to do, for example, starting to type at your computer at the same time you're talking.

2. Use verbal cues that show you're ready to end the conversation

The word 'anyway . . .' or 'well . . .' can work wonders here. Also try giving quicker, shorter responses, for example 'Yep, yep, yep. Totally' and then 'Anyway. . .'

3. Restate one or two of the main points you talked about

This is a good way to transition from the conversation to its conclusion. You comment on a recent statement, or generally sum up the discussion, before you start to close it down. Most people don't do this, but it makes the other person feel you actually listened during your talk, so can work really well and will make you stand out in their mind. For example, 'have a great time on holiday, I'd love to see the pictures when you get back' or 'Good luck with that new project – I hope it works out' or 'Yeah, that film's going to be great. I'm really looking forward to it. Anyway, I should get going. . .'

4. Say you have to leave

It really can sometimes be that simple. Even if the reason you give isn't entirely true, it's fine. It's all part of the 'dance' of conversation and social interaction. It's often fine to just say you've got to go without any explanation, especially if you know the person already. If they know and like you, they'll understand you've got things you need to do and won't be offended. So, you might say 'I have to run, good talking to you' or 'Well I'm going to go. I'll talk to you later'. Examples where you give a reason could include 'Well, look. I have to run because I'm meeting a friend in a bit . . .' or 'I need to get home, it's getting late and tomorrow I have to . . .' If these seem a bit too abrupt for the situation, begin first by saying 'I'm so sorry, but I have to go . . .' or 'it's been great talking to you, but . . .' Just remember to use a sincere tone of voice and a genuine facial expression and then they won't seem so harsh.

5. Be gracious

After giving a reason for leaving, express how much you enjoyed the conversation. This helps transition to leaving and ends things on a positive note. For example, 'it was really nice talking to you' or 'lovely meeting you.'

6. Suggest a future meeting (optional)

This is the perfect time to suggest a future meeting if you enjoyed talking to the person. It is better to be specific though, otherwise it can sound insincere. So don't just say, 'let's meet up sometime' say something like, 'I really enjoyed talking to you; how about we get together for a coffee next week? I'll give you a call'. And then of course you may need their phone number. So, if they seem positive to the suggestion of meeting next week, go ahead and ask for it.

And, finally, we can go back to the phases of greeting and parting from people which we discussed at the beginning of the chapter (Kendon and Ferber, cited by Hargie et al., 1994), and as we prepare to leave the conversation, we follow the phases from C to A:

C.   *Close phase*. We make eye contact, smile, make appropriate verbal comments to say goodbye and then may touch one another (shake hands, kiss).

B. *Medium phase.* As we walk away, we avoid eye contact, we smile, and we engage in a range of grooming (self-touching) behaviours.

A. *Distant phase.* At a distance, but within sight, we will wave goodbye, raise our eyebrows, smile, toss our heads and make eye contact.

Key points from Chapter 5

How we greet and part from others has long been recognised as crucial in our development and maintenance of relationships and the two skills are similar.

Opening a conversation

The way we open or greet someone will not only depend on the other person but also the context of the interaction and what you want to achieve, but two essential aspects to opening a conversation are: how to establish rapport and what to say.

Establish rapport

The first golden rule for starting a conversation is to be, or at least appear, friendly. Four things to remember are to: breathe and relax; use open body posture; smile; and use a friendly tone of voice.

Choose an opening line

An opening line depends a lot on whether we know the person or whether we are starting a conversation with a stranger and 'small talk' acts as a 'bonding ritual'. This is important so that we can form an opinion or a picture of the other person and begin to feel relaxed with them and move onto more interesting conversation. So it doesn't matter too much what we say, the important thing is to appear genuine and interested. A few examples of opening lines are given below:

Table 5.2 Starting a conversation

Strategy	A bit more information	Example
1. Introduce yourself	In formal situations only. Never do this at the bus stop.	'Hello I'm Alex from Speaking Space'
2. Comment on the weather	'Don't knock the weather; nine-tenths of the people couldn't start a conversation if it didn't change once in a while'.	'It's turned cold, hasn't it?'

3. Comment on something pleasant	Always safer to say something positive as you may offend someone by being critical.	'This coffee is delicious'
4. Ask for information	Even if you know the answer, it can be a good way to get talking to someone.	'Do you know where I can get a coffee?'
5. Ask for assistance	Everyone likes to feel helpful. Just make sure what you ask for is something reasonable!	'Would you mind giving me a hand with this?'
6. Offer assistance	If you find yourself in a situation where you can offer assistance to someone you would like to talk to, do it!	'Can I help you with that large box?'
7. Ask for an opinion	Most people like feeling that others are interested in their opinions.	'Which one do you think I should buy?'
8. Mention a mutual acquaintance	Mentioning someone you both know can backfire if you mention someone they really don't like!	'Do you work with Bob?'
9. Bring up a shared experience	Any common ground is a good way to start someone talking.	'Are you from the UK?'
10. Praise the listener	This can work well if you want to talk to someone prominent but be genuine and don't fawn.	'I really love your work'
11. Compliment the person's clothes or accessories	Most people like it when others appreciate their taste but not their physical appearance.	'That is a lovely necklace!'

Ending a conversation

The way we end a conversation is equally important as it may then determine to a large extent whether someone will want to talk to us again. There are four main types of conversation 'closures': factual, motivational, social and perceptual but in summary, here are a few general pointers:

Table 5.3 Ending a conversation

Strategy	Description	Examples
1. Use 'ending' nonverbals	Start adjusting your body language and your actions to indicate to the other person that it's time to end.	Stand up if you've been sitting down; break eye contact; increase fidgeting; start to move towards the door.

(Continued)

Table 5.3 (Continued)

2. Use verbal cues	These also show you're ready to end the conversation. Also give shorter responses.	'Anyway . . .' 'Well . . .' 'Yep, yep, yep. Totally'
3. Restate one or two main points from the conversation	Comment on a recent statement, or sum up the discussion, before you start to close it down.	'Have a great time on holiday, I'd love to see the pictures when you get back'
4. Say you have to leave	With people you know you might not even need to give a reason.	'I have to run, good talking to you' 'I'm so sorry, but I have to go . . .'
5. Be gracious	After giving a reason for leaving, express how much you enjoyed the conversation.	'It was really nice talking to you' 'Lovely meeting you.'
6. Suggest a future meeting	This is optional if you want to meet up, but better to be specific otherwise it can sound insincere.	'I really enjoyed talking to you; how about we get together for a coffee next week?'

Chapter 6

Maintaining a conversation

'The most fruitful and natural exercise for our mind is, in my opinion, conversation.'
Michel de Montaigne (1580)

The English word 'conversation' is made up of two Latin roots: 'con' which means 'with' and 'vers' which means 'to turn about in a given direction'. This means that to have a conversation literally means: 'to turn about with others'. So once a conversation has been initiated, it needs to be maintained and we do this by taking turns. Within this there are a number of skills though. In taking turns we ask questions, we answer questions, we make relevant comments and we repair when we need to. This chapter will address all these skills under the main headings of: turn taking, questions, repair, and relevance.

Turn taking

> Christine Cagney: I'm being quiet now. That means it's your turn to talk.
> Mary Beth Lacey: I'm trying to think of what to say.
> (Cagney and Lacey, cited by Nordquist, 2017)

The organisation of turn taking was first explored as a part of conversation analysis by Harvey Sacks, Emanuel Schegloff and Gail Jefferson in the late 1960s/early 1970s and they state that 'taking turns to talk is fundamental to conversations, as well as to other speech-exchange systems' (Sacks et al., 1974). Turn taking is developed and socialised from very early between a parent and a child, but it can still be thought of as a learned skill, rather than an innate ability and is not a straight forward process. Once a topic is chosen and a conversation started, conversational 'turn taking' happens and knowing when it is acceptable or obligatory to take a turn in the conversation is essential to the cooperative development of this interaction. We may think that it is merely a case of one person talks, then the other person talks and so on, and of course, this is how we may start to teach the skill to children. However, how do we know it's our turn to speak? How do we recognise the appropriate 'turn-exchange points' and how long should the pauses between turns be?

Sometimes it is obvious. We are asked a question 'are you hungry?' and we will know that it is then our turn to talk. But in conversations we will also look and listen out for clues. In general, we are looking out for a pause in the conversation and the speaker looking at us. In addition, the speaker may make a facial expression that says 'it's your turn', maybe opening their eyes wider, tilting their head or they may gesture by pointing at us. We may also recognise from the intonation pattern that the speaker is about to finish what they are saying which will alert us to listen out for the pause which will then be our cue to talk. However, since not all conversations follow all the rules for turn-taking, it is also necessary to sometimes 'repair' a conversation that has been thrown off course by a misunderstanding. We will examine that later, but let's look at the skills of taking turns in a bit more detail.

The turn taking dance

There are two guiding principles in conversations: one is that only one person should talk at a time; and the second one is that we cannot have silence. Dr Mary Shapiro, a professor of linguistics at Truman State University in Kirksville, Missouri, describes several processes on her website Social Communication (Shapiro, 2017), and we can summarise what she describes almost like a dance:

The turn taking dance

- The speaker 'has the floor'.
- They then signal they are coming to an end using 'ending signals'.
- They then 'select' the next speaker.
- The next speaker accepts the turn to speak.
- They then start their turn using an 'opener'.

David Langford (1994) also states that turn taking is an organisational system. He examined facial features, eye contact, and other gestures in order to prove that turn taking is signalled by many gestures, not only a break in speech. So, what does this 'dance' mean exactly?

Having the floor

In a typical conversation, we can immediately see who 'has the floor' at a given moment; that is, the person who is speaking and therefore who we should be listening to. Most of the time, only one person speaks at any one time, so this is pretty easy to recognise. The person who has the floor expects everyone else to listen, but also has the responsibility not to talk for too long and turn the conversation into a monologue. How long we can talk for will depend on factors such as power (where superiors have the right to talk more) and how much interest the other participants have in what we're saying. Knowing how much to say can be tricky. If we don't give people enough of the information they're looking for, we'll be seen as uncooperative, uninterested in the conversation, and even hostile. If we talk for too long, we will be seen as boring and self-centred. It's a tightrope and we will discuss this more in 'changing topic'. But one thing that can help us is to look out for some tell-tale signs from the other person(s):

> ### Signs that might indicate that we have talked for too long
>
> - The other person(s) in the conversation show signs of boredom or annoyance while we are speaking. They may, for example, look away, sigh, narrow their eyes, fidget, or change to a closed posture.
> - The other person may keep trying to cut us off, with false starts.
> - The other people drop out of the conversation, even though we wanted to keep going.

Ending signals

The transition between one speaker and the next must be as smooth as possible and without a pause or break in the flow. We usually send several signals that we are ready to hand over to someone else and that we've finished what we wanted to say. The most obvious sign is when we hand over 'the floor' to someone else, either by using the person's name or by looking at them (we will look at this in more detail next). Even if it is not so obvious, we will typically lower our pitch and/or volume as we come to the end of a sentence. Often, we trail off as we do this, so a sentence may actually not be completed. We may also use words such as 'so . . .' or 'anyway . . .' to mark the transition.

Selecting the speaker

In a friendly conversation among equals, whoever has the floor has the right to select the next speaker and in a two-person conversation, the next speaker is the other person. We use different strategies (Shapiro, 2017) to select the next person and some of these are still relevant in a two-person conversation:

1. *Select by name.* This is where we make it very clear who should speak next, for example, 'what do you think, Naomi?' or 'Amy, tell everyone that story . . .' This is often used in a school classroom or in a parent-child interaction if we want to force someone to say something. It is also useful if someone is shy and the speaker wants to encourage them to join in the conversation, and it can be used when it is clear that someone wants a turn to speak but has not been able to yet. So by using their name, this guarantees that they get a turn.

2. *Select by gaze.* For most of the time during a conversation, the eyes of the speaker and the listener do not meet. But when speakers are coming to the end of a turn, they will look up more frequently, finishing with a steady gaze. This is a sign to the listener that the turn is finishing and that he or she can then come in. Selecting the next speaker by eye gaze is the most common way in which we hand over the turn to speak. We simply concentrate our gaze on the person we want to talk next whilst using our ending signals. If the listeners are using their effective listening skills and are looking at us, they will

be able to see the direction of our eye gaze, and will understand it as a suggestion for who the next speaker should be. As Dr Mary Shapiro from Truman University states, it 'is possible to recognize and interpret [this], even for people who are aversive to eye contact, as you are following where the speaker is looking rather than trying to make eye contact with the speaker yourself' (2017).

If one of the listeners is keen to go next, they will try to catch our eye and show signs of interest such as making one or two quiet gasp-like sounds, as if they're starting to speak ('Ah . . . Ah . . .'). This will then hopefully mean that we respond to their cues and look at them as we end their sentence.

3. *No selection.* If the current speaker does not select anyone, but simply finishes their turn, any member of the group can jump in. In this situation, we may glance quickly around the group to see if anyone else is about to jump in but this is not essential. If no one jumps in to take a turn in the few seconds of silence following the last words from the speaker, the last speaker will often resume. This is usually a sign that there's a problem with the conversation. It is possible that the other speakers aren't interested or comfortable, or that they want the conversation to end.

Sometimes, several people will jump in at the same time and try to take a turn. This doesn't have to be an issue, as it may just show that the conversation is pretty lively and that people are interested and eager to contribute. However, if there are power differences in the people wanting to talk, the subordinate will tend to give way to the superior and allow them to continue. If they are relatively equal in status, one may simply allow the other to continue. In those cases, it is customary for the speaker who continues to not talk for too long as they know that others are waiting to speak, and also to then hand over to one of them to take their turn. If neither person backs down, they will often increase their volume to try to assert themselves as the next speaker, until eventually one gives way to the other.

Accepting the selection (or not)

To accept the selection, the person receiving the eye gaze simply returns it and smiles and/or nods slightly. The other listeners will see the eye contact between them and know that the next speaker has been decided, so someone who ignores this and tries to speak will be seen as rude. Usually, the selected speaker then starts speaking exactly as the current speaker ends, leaving no pause at all, or even slightly overlapping with the end of the current speaker's turn.

To refuse the selection, the person receiving the eye gaze does not return it, but instead looks quickly away or down. The others will see this and it is understood by all that they do not wish to take a turn. The current speaker may then either attempt to force the person to speak by using their name or will try to select someone else. This can be an issue for people who struggle with eye contact as they may appear to others to not want to take a turn.

Starting their turn using an opener

Having accepted the selection to speak, we will firstly use brief openers to connect our turn to the previous one, and to acknowledge that we have heard and understood the previous turn. These are very subtle but important to keep the flow of the conversation. Shapiro (2017) suggests that these openers can be divided into the following:

Table 6.1 Turn taking openers

Opener	A bit more information	Example
1. Minimal responses	We often use minimal responses to show that we are listening. We usually do these while the person is actually talking which then encourages them to continue. If we use these at the beginning of our turn, and we say them with a level or falling intonation and little or no stress, it means that we have heard and understood, but we have nothing more to add. If we start with a stressed minimal response and immediately continue with no pause, we are saying that we have heard and understood and are responding to the previous turn.	'Yes', 'Ok', 'Mm'
2. Expressing surprise	We may start our turn by expressing surprise and will then add our bit to the conversation. We can also use these as a conversation opener as well, because if we say one of these out loud in the vicinity of friends they feel obliged to ask 'What?'	'Oh!' or 'Wow'
3. Agreement	If we want to show that we really agree with someone, we will tend to start our turn with something more emphatic or we may repeat back a part of the speaker's previous sentence. We may also use them to show we are in agreement but have something else to add.	'Yes, absolutely!' or 'Definitely' 'Yes and . . .' or 'Not only that . . .'
4. Disagreement	Disagreeing can be a bit tricky as people can get defensive or angry when someone disagrees with them. For this reason, it can be a good idea to start a disagreeing turn with a positive response, so we may actually say 'yes' before saying why we disagree. We could also use responses to invite further conversation on the topic or if we feel more strongly, we may use a slightly stronger response.	'Yes, no' or 'Yes, but . . .' 'Yes, I'm not sure about that . . .' or 'Yes, ok, so are you saying . . .' 'Mm, I don't know . . .' or 'Gosh, I'm not sure about that . . .'
5. Changing topic	If we actually want to change the topic, then we will start our turn with a phrase or word that indicates this. We will discuss this in more detail later on in the chapter.	'Did you hear about . . .?' or 'Oh, I forgot to tell you' 'Anyway . . .'

Differences due to culture and gender

As we said earlier in the chapter, turn taking is developed and socialised from very early on between parent and child and so it is greatly affected by the culture that child is growing up in. Turn taking will vary in the type of responses used as openers and also in aspects such as time, overlap, and the perception of silence. Stivers et al. (2009) examined ten different languages across the world to see if there were any similarities in how people take turns and found that all ten had the same avoidance of wanting to overlap in conversation and wanting to minimise the silence between turns. However, depending on the culture, there was variation in the amount of time taken between turns.

Research has also shown that gender is a factor that influences how we take turns but there have been varying results. One study (Zimmerman and West, 1975) reported that men systematically interrupt women and tend to dominate conversations, but other studies (Kollock et al., 1985) suggest that the dominant participant of a conversation will interrupt the other regardless of the gender of the speakers. So, it may be more about dominance than gender, as that will certainly impact on turn taking.

Avoiding silence

Most people would agree that a good conversation should flow between different people and this usually means there is no extended period of silence within it. In fact, most people find any period of silence within a conversation incredibly awkward. So, what can we do to avoid them? Ezeanu (2010) has three tips for avoiding silence. He suggests that we should, first, *'Think less, talk more'*. He says that sometimes there is silence because we are trying too hard to say the perfect thing, and when we can't we don't say anything. There is always something we can say in a conversation and a way to continue it and sometimes it's just a matter of giving ourselves permission to talk. Second, we should *'Get excited and curious'* and this means basically getting curious and asking questions based on this. Finally, we should learn to *'Keep the silence, remove the awkward'* and learn to enjoy the presence of someone else instead of trying to gap every silence, every once in a while, to let it be instead and enjoy it.

It is the second point that I want to explore in more detail now, because a large part of maintaining a successful conversation will be our ability to use effective questioning.

Questions

'Judge a man by his questions rather than by his answers.'

Voltaire (1694 –1778)

When it's our turn to speak, and we want to continue the conversation, we have to say something that will cause the other person, or people, to keep talking. We have two options. We can either ask them a question, which directly places the responsibility on them to speak, or we can make a statement of our own, which will hopefully lead them to think of something they want to say in response. Both have their place but questions are really at the heart of any human interaction and at some point within the conversation we will need to use them. Indeed, to have a conversation without any questions is difficult, if not impossible. Hargie (2017) says that 'in the absence of questioning DNA, the communication organism becomes unstable and dies'. Questions are essential for learning, decision making and problem solving and, in most conversations, it is in the asking and the answering of questions that we encourage communication, and share information and knowledge with each other. Of course, asking and answering questions might seem pretty straightforward, but it is not. Morgan and Saxton

(2006) say that 'we all know how to ask questions – after all, we have been doing it since we could talk – but . . . becoming an *effective* questioner is hard. It takes time and vigilance'.

A question can be defined as 'a statement or nonverbal act that invites a response' (Stewart and Cash, cited by Hargie, 2017). So, we are able to ask a question simply with a directional nod of the head or an 'hmm?' or using a statement like 'tell me more'. However, most questions in social interaction are verbal in nature and are accompanied by appropriate nonverbal signals and paralinguistic cues that indicate a question is being asked and an answer is expected.

The purpose of asking questions

Questions serve a range of purposes within a conversation, depending on the context, but it is the response that determines whether that goal has been achieved. In this sense, the question is only as good as the answer we get. We tend to assume that we mostly ask questions to seek clarity about something, but they do not have to be used exclusively for clarity. There is much to be said for the saying that a person's favourite subject is himself. Most people love to talk about themselves, and asking questions is a great way to show interest and develop new relationships with people. And as we ask questions, most people will start to naturally ask us questions and will listen more attentively and most likely ask questions in the same manner that we did. Hargie (2017) suggests there are thirteen main goals of questioning and four main benefits to asking questions within a conversation:

The main goals served by questioning

- Obtain information
- Initiate interaction
- Maintain control of an interaction
- Arouse interest and curiosity in a topic
- Diagnose specific difficulties the listener may have
- Express an interest in the other person
- Find out the attitudes, feelings and opinions of others
- Encourage maximum participation from others
- Assess the extent of someone's knowledge
- Encourage critical thought and evaluation
- Communicate in group discussions, that involvement from all is expected
- Encourage people to comment on the responses of others
- Maintain the attention of others

The benefits of questions.

1. *Control the issues.* By asking the right questions, we can control the conversation. This means that we can focus the conversation on the things that we want to talk about and avoid the things we don't want to talk about.
2. *Set the mood.* Questions can have a powerful effect on someone's emotional state. Depending on the type of question we ask, we can alter the mood of the conversation in either a positive or negative way.

3. *Focus the discussion.* Asking someone about something can immediately focus their attention. This is particularly useful if the conversation has strayed from the central topic and we need it to get back on track. Asking more questions can also speed up the pace if it is becoming a bit drawn out. Conversely, we can use questions if a conversation is progressing too quickly by asking something that will mean the other person has to temporarily focus on something else.

4. *Persuading others.* People are much more susceptible to persuasion if they don't think we are trying to persuade them. Asking questions helps us to disguise the fact that we are trying to persuade them by asking them questions about the thing we want them to consider. So as a trainer, I may want to persuade someone that my training is very effective, but rather than telling them, it may be better to ask them the question 'do you know how many people were able to evidence the effectiveness of the social skills work after my training?' or 'would you like to know how many people rate my course as "excellent"?'

Types of questions

'I keep six honest serving men,
(they taught me all I knew);
their names are What and Why and When,
and How and Where and Who.'

(Rudyard Kipling, cited by Hargie, 2017)

This poem actually reflects in some ways the different classifications of questions. We mostly think of 'open' versus 'closed' questions, which we will explore in more detail in a minute, but there are other ways in which we can classify different types of questions: open/closed; recall/process; affective; leading; probing; rhetorical; and multiple questions. These are summarised below:

Table 6.2 Types of questions

Question type	A bit more information	Example
Closed	These require a short response to a specific nature. There are 3 types: selection; yes/no; and identification (e.g. 'where' and 'who' questions).	'Do you want pizza or pasta?' (selection) 'Did you go to the shops?' (yes/no) 'Where did you go on holiday?' (identification)
Open	These can't be answered in a few words and generally encourage a longer response. Often start with 'what', 'how' or 'why'.	'What did you do at the weekend?' 'How are you going to fit all that in to your weekend?' 'Why do you want to go there?'

(Continued)

Question type	A bit more information	Example
Recall	These involve the simple recall of information and are often used in school settings, interviews and medicine.	'When was the battle of Waterloo?' 'Where did you go to University?' 'Have you felt sick today?'
Process	These require the person to give an opinion or make a prediction. Often there is no correct answer and they assess someone's ability to formulate ideas on a topic.	'What can you offer us as a company?' 'How do you think you could improve your relationship with your team members?'
Affective	These relate to emotions, attitudes or preferences. They can be recall, process, open or closed questions.	'Who was your favourite teacher?' (recall) 'What made you hate school?' (process) 'How did you feel when you moved school?' (open) 'Do you mind talking about it?' (closed)
Leading	These are 'assumption-laden' in that there is an expected or assumed response. There can be pressure on the person to reply in the expected manner. They can be conversational, simple, implication, or subtle leads.	'Isn't it a lovely day?' (conversational) 'You do want to go to the gym don't you?' (simple) 'When did you stop beating your wife?' (implication) 'Are you enjoying your meal?' (subtle)
Probing	These are secondary, follow-up questions for example to clarify, justify or check something.	'What exactly do you mean?' (clarification) 'Why do you say that?' (justification) 'How is this relevant to what we talked about?' (relevance) 'Could you give me an example of that?' (exemplification) 'That's interesting, tell me more' (extension) 'Are you sure?' (accuracy)
Rhetorical	These do not expect a response and are used either as a statement or to gain interest.	'How could you?' 'Do I look like an idiot?' 'Who would not wish their children well?'
Multiple	These are 2 or more questions phrased as one.	'When and where will we meet and how will we get there?'

Closed versus open questions

This is the most common way we talk about questions and within any conversation, it is best to use a mixture, as both serve different functions within the interaction:

- *Closed questions*: typically only require a quick response of maybe just one or two words and are usually easier to answer. This can make them useful at the beginning of a conversation to encourage people to relax as they give a higher degree of control of the conversation to the questioner. We will also use closed questions at the end of a conversation as we try to bring the conversation to an end. Closed questions are also useful for structured situations where we ask lots of questions to give us information, for example to assess or diagnose something. They are also useful when we are pressured for time and we want to retain some control over the length of a conversation.
- *Open questions*: give more control and freedom to the other person so will encourage people to open up and reveal more about themselves. The control here is very much with the person being questioned and so can be time consuming, but it is the best way to get to know people well, as people give you lots of information about themselves. In social situations where we are trying to get to know someone, open questions are definitely preferable to closed; but in more structured or research situations, they are not so useful in gaining the right information.

Top tips for asking questions to get to know someone

If we are trying to get to know someone, it might be useful to try my top tips for questioning:

1. Ask open questions

When you ask a closed question, you will most often get incomplete information. Instead, after a bit of small talk, ask an open question. You are more likely to get insights and additional information you might not have known existed.

2. Find their interests

Having started your conversation with some brief small-talk, it is important to consider how you can encourage or motivate people to want to talk to you. Carnegie (2006, p.102) says 'talk in terms of other people's interests' and you won't go far wrong. Remember that people love talking about themselves and never underestimate a person's willingness to do this! If you can find something the other person is interested in, a simple question could have them talking for quite a while.

3. Dig deeper

Try then using follow-up questions such as, 'What makes you say that?' or 'Why do you think that?' Follow up questions will give you more insight and let you make your own opinions about things.

4. Use silence

Try to practise feeling comfortable with a bit of silence. Try asking a question, waiting for response, listening to the response and then waiting some more. Often the person being questioned has more information to give and will bring it out when you wait for it. Generally, people feel a need to fill silence in a conversation and so if you hold back and keep quiet, they will then tell you more about themselves. Of course, just remember all of your good listening skills and body language whilst keeping quiet!

5. Don't interrupt

Don't interrupt the person. First, it tells the person you don't value what they are saying and secondly it stops their train of thought and directs the conversation the way you want, not necessarily the way it should go. Ask your question, and then let the person answer it in full.

Answering questions/responding

We have focused so far on asking questions, but it is also important to give some thought to how we answer a question. Knowing how much to say is always a bit tricky. If our answers are too short and we don't give people enough information, we'll be seen as uncooperative, uninterested or unfriendly. If our answers are too long, we may be seen as annoying and self-centred. This is particularly true when we are asked an open question. This type of question might appear to be an invitation to go on as long as we like, but how much should we say? How much should we self-disclose?

Self-disclosure

Hargie (2017) talks at length about the importance of self-disclosure in a conversation. He says that a great deal of our interaction consists of people making statements, or disclosures, about a variety of issues. As we said previously, people have an intrinsic need to talk about themselves, 'with between 30 and 40 per cent of all our verbal communications involving the revelation of personal details about our actions, thoughts, feelings and beliefs' (Tamir and Mitchell, cited by Hargie 2017).

There are four main ways in which we self-disclose:

1. *Observations/factual*: telling people what we have done or experienced
2. *Thoughts*: revealing our judgements about what we have experienced
3. *Feelings*: expressing how we feel or felt about something
4. *Needs*: telling people what we need or want

We will use these in different situations and in different ways. For example, when meeting someone for the first time, we tend to focus on using more factual disclosures (I live in London) while keeping feeling disclosures at quite a superficial level (I love loud music). We are also more likely to disclose more positive aspects of ourselves (I'm really happy in my work) and leave the negative ones (I worry about my health) to when the relationship has been established. This is because negative self-disclosures are regarded as being more informative as they are generally more heartfelt and revealing. The purpose of self-disclosure also depends on our relationship with the other person. Between friends, the main reasons for self-disclosure are to maintain our relationship and to learn more about each other's thoughts and feelings. With strangers, they are used to facilitate a social exchange through reciprocation (we self-disclose something, they self-disclose something) and to impress and show ourselves in the best light.

However, even though self-disclosure is important within a conversation, it is essential to get the timing right. Stewart and Logan (cited by Hargie, 2017) describe three factors to consider before self-disclosing:

1.   *Emotional timing*: is the other person in the right frame of mind to hear your disclosure?
2.   *Relevance timing*: does the disclosure fit with the purpose and sequence of the conversation?
3.   *Situational timing*: is the environment suitable for discussion of this topic?

Shapiro (2017) describes on her 'Social Communication' website the importance of getting self-disclosure right when we first meet people. We need to consider how much someone wants to know about us personally. Typically, 'opening up' to someone (gradually disclosing more and more intimate things about ourselves) is key to developing a closer relationship, but it has to be reciprocal: we shouldn't ask a question that we wouldn't feel comfortable being asked, and we shouldn't tell someone something that is noticeably more personal and/or embarrassing than the sorts of things they tell us. If we are unsure how much to share when asked an open question, it is always best to err on the side of caution and to say a few things and then wait for the other person to ask us to elaborate: 'What else do you like?' or 'Tell me more!'

The importance in knowing whether we have got it right is essential to a successful interaction and the best way to do this is to observe the reactions of the other person and to repair when we have got it wrong.

Repairing a conversation

Sometimes conversations breakdown and we need to repair them. These breakdowns can occur in any interaction for many reasons, some of them can include: background noise means the other person hasn't heard the whole message; the listener was temporarily distracted and failed to attend to the whole message; or we may misjudge the other person's prior knowledge. Whatever the reason, when a breakdown occurs, there are several ways in which we may need to repair whilst taking our turn in a conversation. We may need to correct something that has been misunderstood; we may need to add more information if the person is confused by our answer; we may have told them something they already know; or we may need to stop talking or give certain information. As Volden (2004) says 'effective repair strategies consist of adjusting the message to accommodate the listener's needs so that the conversation can proceed'.

- *Correcting a mistake*. Sometimes it is a simple case of correcting something quickly. This can be something that was misheard or a mistake of another kind. One mistake I have to regularly correct is my name. People can call me 'Kelly' as opposed to 'Alex' and I have to quickly say (nicely!) 'Actually, my name is Alex, my surname is Kelly' and if they look embarrassed I will add 'please don't worry, it happens all the time!' The trouble is that if we don't correct mistakes immediately, it can get very embarrassing the longer it goes on.
- *Adding more information*. Sometimes we leave out information from our answer or story if we believe the other person already knows it. They may then look confused or say 'sorry, who are you talking about?' All we need to do to repair the conversation is

to provide them with the information that was missing 'oh sorry, I should have said, Sally'. Sometimes, the other person is embarrassed to ask us or to show confusion and may try to pretend to know what we are talking about. This can lead to all sorts of mis-communication down the line and so if we detect signs of confusion, we should backup and say 'sorry, do you know Sally?'

- *Telling them something they already know.* Sometimes we tell people something that they already know. This is not a problem usually if the information is fairly obscure, as it can be assumed that we would have no reason to have known that the other person would know it, so there is no need to repair the error. The other person will probably say 'Yes, I know,' but will not be upset or offended. If we tell someone something they already know and the knowledge is common knowledge or something we should have known that the other person knows, we will be perceived as being condescending or 'talking down' to them. The other person may say 'Yes, I know,' but with extra stress and an apology is needed to repair the interaction: 'I'm sorry, of course you know that!'
- *Going on for too long.* If we are talking and the other person begins to look distracted, bored, and/or uncomfortable while we're speaking, we've probably gone on too long. A quick apology, 'I'm sorry, that was probably more than you wanted to know', will repair the situation and reassure them that we do care about them and will give them the chance to redirect the conversation, if they would like to do so.

Relevance

Finally, when considering how to maintain a conversation, it is important to consider relevance. It is a commonly held view that conversations are not random, but that there are conventions, structure, and rules that dictate them. What we are trying to examine in this chapter is how we can adhere to the protocols of conversation, or more importantly, how we observe these rules in relation to participants and setting. There have been a number of proposed theories as to what actually constitutes our conversational rules, but one template, known as Grice's Maxims, is referred to often (Grice, 1975):

Grice's Maxims

- *Quantity. be informative*
  Make your contribution as informative as possible
  Do not make your contribution more informative than required
- *Quality. be truthful*
  Do not say that which you believe to be false
  Do not say that for which you lack adequate evidence
- *Relation. be relevant*
  Say things that are pertinent to the discussion
- *Manner. be perspicuous*
  Avoid obscurity of expression
  Avoid ambiguity
  Be brief
  Be orderly

So Grice would define 'relevance' as saying things that are pertinent to the discussion or the conversation. One dictionary defines relevance as that which 'has a bearing on, or connection with, the matter at hand'. Miller (1999) says that 'according to this definition, that which is relevant is that which is within reach, that which can be handled, that which has direct practical application to one's present state and needs'.

Relevance, however, is relative. When we engage in a conversation, we join together with others to discuss a topic within a particular setting, and this serves to define what is considered, for the period of the conversation, as relevant, as well as what is irrelevant. In a purposeful conversation, a 'remark is relevant if and only if, it is related to the purpose of the conversational goal' (Powers, cited by Miller, 1999). Likewise, when people gather to begin a conversation, they create a common ground, or set of common grounds which is affected by their topic and relationship to one another, and relevance can be seen as the relationship between the current proposition and the common ground.

Miller (1999) suggests that 'relevance, like love, is in the eye of the beholder'. However, just as individuals can try to make themselves seem lovely, one can try to make one's utterances seem relevant. But a relevant remark usually responds to something said in the speaker's last sentence or two or to an essential point made by the speaker. We are showing our attentiveness by staying on topic and being relevant, and we are allowing the speaker freedom to define the nature of the interaction and to maintain control over the conversational goal.

Relevance also means that we are constantly being engaged in 'topic management'. During a conversation, we must constantly decide if a response or question is connected and therefore relevant, or irrelevant and therefore should be rejected. Individuals and groups often put a great deal of effort into topic management and if someone says something that is considered irrelevant, it may produce anger or disorientation in others.

Of course, sometimes we want to change the topic. We can't talk about the same subject for hours or maybe the topic is one that we are not interested in. Friendly conversations do not have a set agenda: if they go on long enough, it is accepted that at some point we may want to change topics, perhaps multiple times, and that we may also circle back and visit a topic already discussed. But this is not done randomly or abruptly. So how should we change the topic without appearing rude or irrelevant?

Changing the topic

Changing topic can be a delicate operation, especially if the topic has not completely run its course, and we may want to do this for different reasons. Sometimes we want to change the topic because we are not really interested in it. In this scenario it is important not to try and change it immediately. We should try to be indirect and subtle, maybe making one or two contributions before we attempt to change it; otherwise, we can appear rude and self-centred. Subtle signs that we are not interested include reducing eye gaze and other active listening cues; using a fake (social) smile (see the chapter on the eyes and face); and displaying other signs of boredom, such as fidgeting and changing our posture. Of course, if we notice these signs in people *we* are talking to, we need to remember that they are showing us that they are not interested in our topic, and we should find a way to wrap it up. We could begin to use phrases like 'one last thing . . .' or just simply begin trailing off, to show that we, too, are finished with this topic.

When we wish to change the topic, we could use one of the following strategies:

- Wait for the current speaker to finish or trail off
- Wait for a longer-than-normal pause

- Try to 'wrap up' a topic by providing some sort of summary statement such as 'well, I suppose we may never know' followed by a shared pause
- Use one of the following: 'Soooo . . .' (with elongated vowel), 'ANYwaay . . .', 'Oh I forgot to tell you . . .', 'Oh! Did you hear about . . .?', 'Before I forget . . .'

Several of these may be used together, and if our conversation partner(s) feel that they have not yet finished with the old topic, they will typically cut off our transition phrase before we have got to the point of telling them our new topic. This allows the old topic to resume until it appears to die out again, at which point we can try another transition phrase to introduce a new topic.

In summary, conversation maintenance is not straight forward. If we are to aspire to be a good conversationalist we need to remember the need to take turns in a manner that will encourage reciprocity, through asking and answering questions effectively, and through good use of relevance and repair. And we must remember that success in most walks of life is predicated on communication ability, and being able to converse with others is a rather essential component.

Key points from Chapter 6

This chapter covered the skills of maintaining a conversation under the headings of: turn taking, questions, repair, and relevance.

Turn taking

The organisation of taking turns to talk is fundamental to conversations and it can be described almost like a dance:

1. The speaker 'has the floor'
2. They then signal they are coming to an end using 'ending signals'
3. They then 'select the next speaker': by name, by gaze or there is no selection
4. The next speaker accepts the turn to speak
5. They then start their turn using an 'opener': using minimal responses, expressing surprise, agreement, disagreement or changing the topic

Turn taking can be affected by culture, gender and dominance.

Questions

Questions are really at the heart of any human interaction and at some point within the conversation we will need to use them.

- *The purpose of asking questions.* The benefits of questions include: controlling the issues, setting the mood, focusing the discussion and persuading others.
- *The different types of questions.* We can classify different types of questions in the following way: open/closed; recall/process; affective; leading; probing; rhetorical; and multiple questions.

Top tips for asking questions to get to know someone

When trying to get to know someone, try the following five tips:

- Ask open questions
- Find their interests
- Dig deeper
- Use silence
- Don't interrupt

Answering questions

Knowing how much to say is tricky. If our answers are too short we'll be seen as uncooperative, uninterested or unfriendly. If our answers are too long, we may be seen as annoying and self-centred. People have an intrinsic need to talk about themselves, and there are four main ways in which we self-disclose:

1. *Observations/factual*: telling people what we have done or experienced
2. *Thoughts*: revealing our judgements about what we have experienced
3. *Feelings*: expressing how we feel or felt about something
4. *Needs*: telling people what we need or want

Repairing a conversation

There are several ways in which we may need to repair: we may need to *correct* something that has been misunderstood; we may need to *add more information* if the person is confused by our answer; we may have *told them something they already know*; or we may need to *stop talking* or giving certain information.

Relevance

We can define relevance as saying things that are pertinent to the discussion or the conversation. We are constantly being engaged in *topic management* where we must constantly decide if a response or question is connected and therefore relevant, or irrelevant and therefore should be rejected.

Changing a topic

When we wish to change the topic, we could use one of the following strategies:

- Wait for the current speaker to finish or trail off
- Wait for a longer-than-normal pause
- Try to 'wrap up' a topic by providing some sort of summary statement
- Use one of the following: 'Soooo . . .', 'ANYwaay . . .', 'Oh I forgot to tell you . . .'

Chapter 7

Assertiveness

'You teach people how to treat you by what you allow, what you stop, and what you reinforce.'

Tony Gaskins

Go into any library or book shop and we see the shelves are full of books on how to be assertive. OK, that is a slight exaggeration, but you will certainly find a few! This is because as a subject it does attract enormous interest and is something that most people say they aspire to. It would also explain the number of assertion training programmes that are out there for us to sign up for and attend. Bolton (1979) suggests that in fact 'less than 5 percent of the population can be expected to communicate assertively' and that often in conversations, we do not see much personal or interpersonal importance being communicated. It is also recognised that assertiveness is something that we learn and improve with age, as McKay et al. (2009) says: 'Assertiveness is a skill you can acquire, not a personality trait that some people are born with and others not.' So what do we mean by assertiveness and why does it have to be part of a book on social skills?

Defining assertiveness

Early definitions of assertiveness were fairly broad and all-encompassing. Lazarus (cited by Hargie, 2017) regarded assertiveness as comprising four main components, the ability to:

1. Refuse requests.
2. Ask for favours and make requests.
3. Express positive and negative feelings.
4. Initiate, continue and terminate conversations.

This means that much of our ability to be assertive lies in our ability to hold a conversation appropriately and as Kelly (cited by Hargie, 2017) also said: 'the terms "assertion training" and "social skills training" were often used in interchangeable fashion.' So, the importance of our conversation skills is inherently important in our ability to be assertive.

There are numerous definitions of what it means to be assertive but two are particularly helpful and are cited by Hargie (2017). Lange and Jakubowski (1976) state that 'Assertion involves standing up for personal rights and expressing thoughts, feelings and beliefs in direct, honest, and appropriate ways which respect the rights of other people'. Alberti and Emmons (2008) say that 'Assertiveness enables us to act in our own best interests, to stand up for ourselves without undue anxiety, to exercise personal rights without denying the rights of others, and to express our feelings. . . honestly and comfortably'. Both of these definitions recognise the need to not only express our feelings and rights but also to respect the rights of others. Bolton (1979) describes this as the 'yin and yang of communication'. The *yang* of assertion is the disclosure to another of what we feel, need and desire; and the *yin* of listening is the understanding and accepting of the other person's view.

In defining assertiveness, it is also helpful to see it within the context (or scale) of aggression and passivity as it is often seen as the 'balance point' between passive and aggressive behaviour. So, before we explore assertive behaviour in more detail, we will firstly consider passive behaviour and aggressive behaviour. Some writers see this as a triangle, but I prefer to view it as a scale or a continuum, with assertiveness forming the mid-point of this continuum:

$$\text{Passive} \rightarrow \text{Assertive} \rightarrow \text{Aggression}$$

Figure 7.1 The passive-assertive-aggression continuum

Passive behaviour

Passive behaviour is also described by some writers as 'submissive' or 'non-assertive' behaviour. I prefer the use of passive or submissive, as non-assertive behaviour to me implies a lack of action whereas passive or submissive indicates choice. It can be argued that people who behave passively demonstrate a lack of respect for their own needs and rights. They either do not express their true feelings, needs, values and concerns and allow others to make choices for them, or they express their needs in such a way that they are not taken seriously. They add qualifying phrases such as '. . . do whatever you want' or '. . . don't worry about me, I don't mind'. Passive responses typically involve expressing feelings and desires in a self-effacing, apologetic manner, which means that these responses are easily ignored by others. Responding in a passive or non-assertive way tends to mean compliance with the wishes of others and will undoubtedly undermine an individual's rights and self-esteem. The objective of passive behaviour is to appease others and avoid conflict at any cost. So passive individuals will typically avoid public attention and will be modest and self-deprecating. They are also often viewed as weak characters who can be easily manipulated, and as a result often express dissatisfaction with their lives as they are unable to attain their personal goals. They do not inspire confidence in others and are often seen as incompetent.

Hargie (2017) describes the following behaviours in someone who is responding passively:

The passive person

- Hesitates and prevaricates
- Speaks softly
- Looks away
- Tends to fidget nervously
- Avoids issues
- Agrees regardless of personal feelings
- Does not express opinions
- Values self below others
- Lacks confidence
- Suffers personal hurt to avoid any chance of hurting others

So we see that the nonverbal behaviours of paralanguage and body language play a large part in demonstrating passive behaviour and that self-esteem plays a part too (we will discuss this more in Chapter 8). Many people adopt a passive response because they have a strong need to be liked by others, and do not regard themselves as equals because they place greater weight on the rights, wishes and feelings of others. This can result in a failure to communicate their own thoughts or feelings and results in people doing things they really do not want to do in the hope that they might please others. It may also mean that they allow others to take responsibility and make decisions for them. So even though low self-esteem may be an underlying cause of passive behaviour, the passive responses can then further reduce feelings of self-worth, creating a vicious circle.

However, this type of behaviour can have *benefits* and is actually appealing to some people. As Bolton (1979) says 'just as "it takes two to tango", it takes two to tangle. Submission is a way of avoiding, postponing, or at least hiding the conflict that is so fearful to many submissive people'. The person who behaves passively has the comfort and security of maintaining a familiar pattern of behaviour and as we said earlier, is often a way of trying to please others. They also carry a smaller load of responsibility than the assertive person does as if things go wrong, people rarely blame the person who simply followed someone else's leadership. So there can be some benefits to being passive and in our culture, people who behave passively are often described as 'nice'.

However, there are *penalties* to being 'nice' or passive. Bolton (1979) describes three rather large prices for 'nice' behaviour:

1. The first is that the person 'lives an unlived life'. They do not choose their own course but the course is chosen by others.
2. The second is that their relationships are often less satisfying and psychologists have found that passive behaviour in a relationship ultimately generates pity, irritation and finally disgust towards the submissive person (Emmons and Alberti, 1975).
3. The third is the inability to control one's own emotions and as they tend to repress their negative emotions, this either results in an explosion at some point or an indirect expression of the emotion – by being indirectly hostile or destructive. This can cause illness including headaches, high blood pressure and other more serious illnesses (Butler, cited by Bolton, 1979).

Aggressive behaviour

Aggressive responses are the opposite of passive responses as they fail to consider the views or feelings of other individuals. The objective is to win, regardless of the other person. Those behaving aggressively will rarely show praise or appreciation of others and will put the other person down. They will use attacks on the other person's ability, character or appearance and will use demands, blunt directions or threats, which do not take into account the rights of the other person. Aggressive responses also encourage the other person to respond in a non-assertive way, either aggressively or passively. Using this style, the aggressor will show the following behaviours (Hargie, 2017):

The aggressive person

- Interrupts and answers before the other is finished speaking
- Talks loudly and abrasively
- Glares at the other person
- Speaks 'past' the issue (accusing, blaming, demeaning)
- Vehemently and arrogantly states feelings and opinions in a dogmatic fashion
- Values self above others
- Hurts others to avoid personal hurt

Aggressive individuals tend to be viewed by others as intransigent, coercive, overbearing and lacking in control. They may get their own way, but they are disliked and avoided by others. Aggression is mostly thought of in terms of the open, direct kind of aggression, but it can also take the form of passive, indirect aggression. In this case, the person will use a range of behaviours to get their own way including sulking, using emotional blackmail, pouting and being subtly manipulative. These are still aggressive behaviours even if they are less obviously aggressive in nature, as they are seen as negative to the other person and will often have negative consequences. This type of indirect aggression is seen as being coercive and using indirect expression, which is the opposite to assertion which is non-coercive and uses direct expression.

So are there any benefits from being aggressive? Well a sizeable proportion of the population is aggressive, and they probably are, at least partly, because their aggression pays off. First, they secure the material needs and objects they desire, often being wealthier than the passive person. Second, they tend to protect themselves and their own space as the aggressive person is less vulnerable in a society. So, they are more likely to succeed and survive better than the passive person. Thirdly, they retain more control over their own lives and the lives of others and this can make things go their own way.

The penalties of aggression are numerous though. They include 'fear, the provocation of counter-aggression, loss of control, guilt, dehumanization, alienation from people, ill health and the creation of a society that is too dangerous even for the aggressive to live in comfortably and safely' (Bolton, 1979).

Assertive behaviour

As we have said previously, assertive behaviour is the 'balance point' between aggressive behaviour and passive behaviour. The assertive person will use all their methods of nonverbal and verbal communication skills effectively and appropriately to 'maintain self-respect, pursue happiness and the satisfaction of her needs, and defend her rights and personal space without abusing or dominating other people. True assertiveness is a way of being in the world which confirms one's own individual worth and dignity while simultaneously confirming and maintaining the worth of others' (Bolton, 1979). So assertive responses involve standing up for oneself yet taking the other person into consideration. The objective here is to try and ensure fair play for everyone. So, in this style of response, we see the person using the following behaviours (Hargie 2017):

The assertive person

- Answering spontaneously
- Speaking with a conversational yet firm tone and volume
- Looking at the other person
- Addressing the main issue
- Openly and confidently expressing personal feelings and opinions
- Valuing oneself equal to others
- Being prepared to listen to the other's point of view
- Hurting neither oneself nor others

Types of assertive behaviour

There are five key types of assertive behaviour described by Hargie (2017): basic, empathetic, escalating, confronting, and I-language assertion. We can also consider direct and indirect assertion and protective assertion. These are summarised in the table below.

Table 7.1 Types of assertiveness

Type	A bit more information	Example
1. Basic assertion	This involves a simple expression of standing up for rights, beliefs, feelings or opinions.	'Excuse me, I'd like to finish what I was saying' (when interrupted)
2. Empathetic assertion	This conveys sensitivity by recognising the other person's situation or feelings before making the assertive statement.	'I know you are keen to get your views across, but I would like to finish what I was saying'
3. Escalating assertion	Here we start with a minimal assertive response but then gradually escalate the degree of assertiveness if the other person fails to respond.	'No, I don't want to buy anything' 'No, as I have already said, I'm not buying anything' 'Look, I've told you twice that the answer is no. I'm now going to have to ask you to leave'

(Continued)

Table 7.1 (Continued)

4. Confronting assertion	This is where someone has not done what they had previously agreed to do. We need to remind them of what was agreed and then state what needs to happen now.	'You said the report would be finished by Tuesday. It is now Thursday and you still haven't done it. I want you to have it finished by 4.00 today'
5. I-Language assertion	Here we describe the behaviour of the other person, how it affects us and why the other person should change. We can use we-language to appear less self-centred. You-language will appear more accusatory.	'You are annoying me because you are not paying your fair share of these expenses' (you-language) 'I feel annoyed because I believe I am paying more than my fair share of these expenses' (I-language) 'We need to talk about how we are both contributing to these expenses. It is important that neither of us feels annoyed about how we are currently sharing them' (we-language)
6. Direct and indirect assertion	A direct assertive style might not always be appropriate and a more ambiguous, indirect style of response might be better. Alternatively, the direct response can be embellished with an excuse to make it appear more palatable.	Request: 'Could you lend me that DVD?' 'No, I never lend my DVDs to anyone' (direct) 'You know I'm still trying to get a chance to sit down and watch it myself' (indirect) 'I know you'd look after it, but I've recently had two DVDs that I loaned damaged, so I have decided just not to lend my DVDs to anyone again. I'm sure you'll understand' (complex-direct)
7. Protective assertion	We use this type of assertive response when we are coming under pressure so we use them as a form of verbal defence against manipulation, nagging or rudeness. There are three types: the broken record (keep repeating the assertive statement); fogging (verbally accepts the criticism but has no intention of changing); metalevel assertion (attempts to widen the perspective of the other person).	'No, I am not going to give you any money'. . . 'No, I am not going to give you any money' (broken record) A: You look down in the dumps B: Yes I probably do A: Could you try to look a bit happier? B: I suppose I could A: You'd be nicer to be around B: Yes, I'm sure you're right (fogging) 'We are obviously not going to agree with this, and I think it is indicative of what is happening in our whole team' (metalevel)

The benefits of assertive behaviour

So what are the benefits of being assertive?

1. *Self-esteem.* One of the most striking things about assertive people is that they like themselves. Not surprisingly, there is a link here with self-esteem as people with low self-esteem find it hard to be assertive and someone who is assertive is in a much better position to feel good about themselves. Indeed, Lightsey and Barnes (2007) said that assertiveness is 'incompatible with or inversely related to many negative psychological symptoms' such as anxiety, depression and low self-esteem. And the therapist Herbert Fensterheim claimed that 'the extent to which you assert yourself determines the level of your self-esteem' (cited by Bolton, 1979).

2. *Relationships.* A second benefit to assertiveness is that it fosters fulfilling relationships. The assertive person is less preoccupied by self-consciousness and anxiety or self-protection and can therefore 'see', 'hear' and 'love' others more easily. So assertive people find it easier to be intimate and have healthier relationships. Bolton (1979) describes intimacy as 'the ability to express my deepest aspirations, hopes, fears, anxieties, and guilt to another significant person repeatedly' which is actually a description of assertive behaviour. There is a link also between assertiveness and how important relationships are to us, and so whether our behaviour is affiliative (Leaper, cited by Hargie 2017). This gives us a matrix that shows that people who are assertive and affiliative are *collaborative* as they place a high value on having good relationships with others. However, if they are non-affiliative, they are not concerned about being friendly and so will use their assertive behaviours to *control* others and get their own way. Those who are unassertive and affiliative will be *obliging* by nature and those who are both non-assertive and non-affiliative will *withdraw* from interactions and keep themselves to themselves.

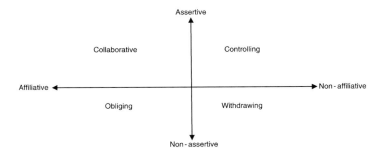

Figure 7.2 The assertion-affiliation matrix

Assertive people tend to 'feel more in control of their lives, derive more satisfaction from their relationships and achieve their goals more often' (Hargie 2017). They are also more likely to inspire confidence in others and are often respected and seen as strong characters that are not easily swayed.

3. *Living your life.* One of the biggest benefits of being assertive is that our chances of getting what we want out of life are improved greatly when we let others know what we want and when we stand up for our own rights and needs. Of course, sometimes this

doesn't work. But in most circumstances assertive behaviour is the most effective way to defend one's space and fulfil one's needs.

So is there a penalty or price for being assertive? We may think that there is no negative side to being assertive, but actually there is a price to be paid. It can be hard work or even painful to learn to be assertive, especially if we have to change a long pattern of submissive or aggressive habits and develop new ways of relating to others. And there can be negative outcomes. We may decide to constructively assert ourselves at work and then find ourselves fired for speaking out. Or in a relationship, our assertion may lead to some conflict and may make us feel vulnerable.

In addition, there is some evidence that tells us that, whereas assertiveness is rated positively in theory, when we are faced with the practical reality of assertive behaviour, we rate it less favourably than non-assertion (McCartan and Hargie, 2004) and whereas we respect assertive people, we do not like to have to deal with assertive responses (Dickson et al., 1997). So, assertiveness can provoke a number of adverse reactions in other people. These are described by Alberti and Emmons (2008) as:

- *Backbiting*: 'who does she think she is?'
- *Aggression*: e.g. hostile behaviour or sarcasm
- *Over-apologising*: which can be genuine or not
- *Emotionality*: e.g. temper tantrums, guilt-based accusations 'you don't love me anymore'
- *Revenge seeking*: hidden resentment leading to 'getting your own back'

When considering the difference between how a passive, assertive and aggressive person behaves, it can be helpful to identify aspects such as 'their style', 'what you see', 'what you hear', and 'what is the result' (see below, taken from Kelly and Sains 2009):

Table 7.2 The assertiveness scale

	Passive	Assertive	Aggressive
Their style	I lose, you win. Not expressing their needs or feelings. Puts self down, doesn't value self.	I win, you win. Honest, open and direct. Listens to others' opinions.	I win, you lose. Domineers and insists. Doesn't listen to others.
What you see	Small posture – hunched. Little eye contact. Voice is quiet and hesitant.	Upright and balanced posture. Steady eye contact. Voice is clear and easy to hear.	Tense posture. Pointing, clenched fists. Interrupts with loud voice.
What you hear	'Sorry . . .' 'I can't seem to . . .' 'I expect that's my fault' 'It's only my opinion . . .'	'I . . .' 'I believe/need/feel' 'No . . .' Open questions.	'You . . .' 'That's your problem, not mine' 'You can't be serious' 'You owe me'

	Passive	*Assertive*	*Aggressive*
What is the result?	They do not respond to hurtful situations. They allow problems to continue. They may have an explosive outburst when they can't take any more. They then feel guilty and confused so return to being passive.	They respect others' opinions and listen respectfully. They are confident about who they are. They realise it is important to speak honestly. They address issues as they arise. They take the responsibility for their own happiness.	They dominate others and control them by either abusing them or sabotaging a situation. They criticise and blame others to make themselves feel better. They become alienated from others. They never mature.

The purpose of assertiveness

The skill of being assertive helps us to achieve nine main goals in life. Most of these relate to the ability to respond to someone assertively but they are also linked to our rights, our self-esteem and our respect of others (Hargie 2017).

The goals of assertiveness

1. To protect our personal rights
2. To withstand unreasonable requests
3. To make reasonable requests
4. To deal effectively with unreasonable refusals
5. To recognise the personal rights of others
6. To change the behaviour of others
7. To avoid unnecessary conflicts
8. To communicate our real position on any issue confidently
9. To develop and maintain a personal sense of self-efficacy

This means that being assertive is not just about learning behaviours that will be seen as 'assertive' but it is also about understanding exactly what our rights are in that situation. Has this person got the right to ask me to do that? Do I mind doing it? Do I have the right to say something? The responses to these questions will vary according to the situation and so an assertive person needs to have a good awareness of these rights. Zuker (cited by Hargie 2017) produced a general Assertive Bill of Rights for individuals which included the right to:

Assertive Bill of Rights: the right to . . .

1. Be treated with respect
2. Have and express personal feelings and opinions
3. Be listened to and taken seriously

4. Set one's own priorities
5. Say no without feeling guilty
6. Ask for what one pays for
7. Make mistakes
8. Assert oneself even though it may inconvenience others
9. Choose not to assert oneself

The causes of unassertiveness

Before we start addressing how to teach assertiveness, it is important to consider why some people are unassertive as it may be necessary to address the cause either prior to the assertion training or as part of it. There are several reasons why people may act and respond in a non-assertive way and the four most common causes are:

1. *Low self-esteem.* As we have mentioned before, feelings of low self-esteem or self-worth often lead to individuals dealing with other people in a passive way. By not asserting their rights, expressing their feelings or stating clearly what they want, people with low self-esteem may invite others to treat them in the same way. Low self-esteem is therefore reinforced in a vicious circle of passive response and reduced self-confidence. If someone is experiencing low self-esteem, then I would work with that person on this prior to helping them learn assertive behaviours (see chapter on self-esteem).

2. *Roles and gender.* Certain roles are associated with non-assertive behaviour, for example low status work roles or the traditional role of women. Stereotypically, women are seen as passive, while men are expected to be more aggressive and Hargie (2017) quotes research that has revealed that men have significantly higher scores than women on tests of assertiveness. There can also be great pressure on people to conform to the roles that are placed upon them. We may be less likely to be assertive to our boss at work than we would be to a colleague or co-worker who we considered to be at an equal or lower level than us in the organisation.

3. *Past experience.* Many people learn to respond in a non-assertive way through experience or through modelling behaviour of others. Our parents behaved like that, so we behave in a similar way. Some people believe that people are born 'passive' or 'aggressive' because of their personality and past experience but this is not true. We can all learn to be more assertive with the right support.

4. *Stress.* When people are stressed they often feel like they have little or no control over the events in their lives and this will impact on their ability to be assertive. People who are stressed or anxious can often resort to passive or aggressive behaviour when expressing their thoughts and feelings. This can then increase the feelings of stress and potentially make others feel stressed or anxious as a result. This is another example of something that is worth exploring with an individual prior to working on their assertiveness.

Teaching assertiveness

In his book *People Skills* Bolton (1979) starts his chapter on assertiveness with a quote from two psychologists, Cotler and Guerra, who describe Assertion Training in the following way:

> Open honest communication. Learning how to relax and reduce anxiety. Getting more of your needs met. Learning social skills that form closer interpersonal relationships. Being able to verbally and nonverbally communicate your positive and negative feelings, thoughts, and emotions without experiencing undue amounts of anxiety or guilt and without violating the dignity of others. Taking responsibility for what happens to you in life. Making more decisions and free choices. Being a friend to yourself and maintaining your own dignity and self-respect. Recognizing that you have certain rights and a value system that need not be sacrificed. Being able to protect yourself from being victimized and taken advantage of by others. Discriminating as to when assertive behaviour may lead to negative as well as positive consequences. Essentially, that is what we believe assertion training is all about . . . assertion training . . . rests upon a foundation of respect – respect for yourself, respect for others, and respect for your own value system.

I love this quote because it not only describes the essence of what assertiveness training should be about but also shows how complex it is. It is not a straightforward task to help someone to become more assertive and we need to consider whether someone has the underlying skills to be successful at it – for example the nonverbal and verbal skills – and whether they have underlying difficulties with their self-esteem. This will be explored in depth in chapter eight but at this stage, it is important to recognise the complexity of this skill.

There are eight situations in which assertive behaviour is appropriate and which are useful to teach people. These are:

1. Expressing feelings
2. Standing up for yourself
3. Making suggestions
4. Refusing
5. Disagreeing
6. Complaining
7. Apologising
8. Requesting explanations

Before we deal with each of these individually, we will consider the three central components to an assertive response: content, process and nonverbal responses.

Content

The actual content of the assertive response will vary according to the situation but generally should include both an expression of rights and a statement placing this within the context of socially appropriate behaviour. Components that are often part of the assertive response include:

- A short *delay* or brief pause 'ahh' so that our response is not too abrupt
- An expression of *appreciation* or *praise*. It can be powerful to praise or compliment prior to a complaint for example, as it softens resentment 'I spoke to a lovely lady yesterday . . .'

- A *cushioning* in the way we refuse or disagree, for example by saying 'Much as I'd like to . . .'
- An *explanation* or *account* for why we need to assert ourselves, for example 'I can't come out to lunch with you because I'm going on holiday tomorrow so have to work through my lunch hour'. These can be an excuse or a justification.
- Showing *empathy* for the other person's situation 'I know you had been looking forward to it'.
- A short *apology* for any resulting consequence 'I'm sorry if this means . . .'
- An attempt to offer a *compromise* 'how about . . .'
- Finally, *humour* can be very effective in certain situations such as dealing with embarrassment. A well-formed joke can both express remorse and also put other people at ease.

Obviously two or more can be used at the same time, so an assertive response might involve giving an excuse (and account), apologising and at the same time employing some appropriate humour.

Process

The way in which assertive responses are carried out is crucial to their success, so it is not just a case of learning the right thing to say, it is also about the timing of the response and the environment we are in. The correct timing of vocalisations and nonverbal responses are essential, as in some situations a slight delay will be important, in other situations it will be important to have no delay. Long delays are almost always not appropriate. The environment will also have an effect on the success of the assertive response, for example by talking to someone in our office rather than in the corridor or by asking someone else's opinion (when we know they agree with us).

Nonverbal responses

Finally the nonverbal behaviour of the person will be essential. An assertive person will look and act strong, confident and fair. We will use appropriate nonverbal behaviours including: medium levels of eye contact; appropriate facial expressions; smooth use of gestures while speaking; minimal gesture or fidgeting while listening; upright posture; direct body orientation (face to face); medium proximity; and appropriate paralinguistic skills (good fluency, rate and clarity, medium volume, and increased intonation). All of these will give us an 'aura of assertiveness'.

These three central components are part of all of the situations that will be described below. However, we will address each individually and discuss any specifics that are pertinent to each one.

Expressing feelings

Expressing our feelings about something comes into many of the assertive responses and situations and so is the first area to teach. The beginning of assertion training in modern psychology is often traced to Andrew Salter's innovative approach to psychotherapy and to the emphasis he placed on the direct expression of feeling (1949). He discovered that the average person has a difficult time identifying and communicating his emotions. People seem to have three problems. First, they substitute a secondary emotion for the primary one, for example they will say they are angry when they were in fact frightened, and the fear led to anger. Second, they struggle to accurately state the degree of feeling they are experiencing, so they will say they are angry or furious when they are in fact annoyed, or they will say they are irritated when in fact they are seething with rage. Third, they choose words that are laden with judgement, such as feeling abused rather than feeling annoyed.

So the first step in expressing feelings assertively is to *understand* what we are feeling. We can help develop this ability in three ways:

1. *Listen to our emotions* without distorting or censoring them. Take note of how we are feeling.
2. *Listen to our body* – it will constantly be informing us of our inner feeling world.
3. *Express the feelings* we are experiencing, either silently or talking about them to others. The more we express our emotions, the more we sharpen our emotional awareness. Try to talk about how we are feeling at any time for any reason. Remember that we can express both negative and positive emotions. Sometimes we focus more on negative emotions, yet expressing positive emotions can be more powerful in motivating others. 'I feel really happy that you did that . . .'

Second, we need to learn to express our feelings in an assertive manner and done well, this can be very powerful. There are four steps and these are summarised below:

Table 7.3 Expressing feelings: four simple steps to follow

Step	A bit more information	Example
1. Name the emotion	A simple first step is to name the emotion, showing what we are feeling with just the word that best describes it. This makes it unambiguous and impossible for someone to deny. Only we can say how we feel.	'I am feeling angry'
2. Explain and describe	We should describe the emotion calmly, and this will demonstrate self-control, which has strong persuasive power over other people. Explain why we are feeling what we are feeling, and the cause. This makes the description even more rational and effective. A simple formula we can use is: 'I am feeling . . . about . . . because . . .' or even simpler 'I feel . . . because . . .'	'I feel annoyed about your lateness because this is the third time this week that you have arrived late' 'I feel annoyed because you are late again'
3. Use supporting body language	If we describe ourselves as angry, our face should mirror that and also say we are angry. But to show that we are in control of ourselves, this should be hinted at, not with appearances of extreme anger.	Angry face: redder complexion, less blinking, lowered eyebrows, narrowed eyes.
4. Use supporting paralinguistic skills	Think about how we say it – using clear, calm, measured speech will help people to listen to us and take us seriously.	Angry voice: medium rate, slightly louder volume (depending on situation), fluent and clear voice.

In all the following situations (standing up for self, making suggestions and so on) I would use a similar framework to teach the assertive behaviour:

1. Stop and think . . .
2. Use good body language . . .
3. Use good paralinguistic skills . . .
4. Try saying . . .

There are variations within each situation, but for example when teaching how to express feelings assertively to people with an intellectual disability or who are on the autistic spectrum, I would use the following four simple rules:

Expressing feelings . . . the rules

- Stop and think about what you are feeling and what you should do
- Remember to use good body language
- Use a calm voice and speak clearly
- Say how you feel and explain why you feel that way. Try saying 'I feel . . . because . . .'

Standing up for yourself

Standing up for ourselves also involves telling people how we feel and what we think so has many similarities to expressing our feelings. But it also includes saying what we believe in giving our opinions and sometimes defending our point of view. When standing up for ourselves in any particular circumstance it is particularly important to consider our opinion in the context of the other person and so we should try to consider the following before we use our assertive response:

- *The other person*. Where is the other person coming from? What do we think their thoughts and feelings might be? Could we begin simply by asking them? Or before we respond, take into account what at least we imagine might be going on with them?
- *Our point of view*. How much do we really need to justify, or explain, ourselves? Would it be enough simply to say that since our backgrounds and life experiences differ, it's only natural that we wouldn't see eye-to-eye on this matter? Think of how we can, without attacking, best clarify our perspective to them, that is, in a way that's neither self-righteous nor overly defensive.

At a simple level, we can try to use the following three step plan:

Standing up for ourselves. . . the rules

- Stop and think – do you agree with what is being said or done? Do you need to say something?
- Remember to use assertive body language to show you are confident in what you think
- Use a calm voice and speak clearly. Try saying 'I think . . . because . . .'

Making suggestions

Making suggestions is important within a conversation or within a relationship as we need to be able to give our ideas and opinions so that our voice is heard and our thoughts and feelings are listened to. At a simple level it may be a suggestion that will help someone out or will solve a problem or it may be a suggestion that centres around emotion – if we do this, it will affect how I/you/they feel. The context is important again. If we need to make a suggestion to the boss, then we must wait for a suitable time to speak to them. If we are talking to a group of friends, we must wait for a suitable moment in the conversation. Then once we have made our suggestion, we have to listen to their response and respond accordingly. So the rules will be:

Making suggestions . . . the rules

- Wait for a pause in the conversation to give your idea and explain it or arrange a time to speak to someone
- Use a calm voice and speak clearly, remember not to shout
- Try saying 'I think that . . .' or 'maybe we should . . .' or 'why don't we . . .'
- Remember to listen to the other person's suggestions and respond appropriately

Refusing

The word 'no' is important and yet the inability to say it is so widespread that there are whole books just dedicated to this subject! I can immediately think of several of my friends and colleagues who are not good at it. They say yes when they should have said no. Maybe it is because they find it difficult to be assertive but mostly I see it in people who want to please. They want to be liked. And they place their own feelings and needs below others. Of course, most of us are surrounded by people who ask too much of us but if we don't say no to them, we can lose control of our own lives.

There are different ways to say no and the context here is paramount to choosing the appropriate way. Sometimes we need to say no so that other people know what we think and feel. Sometimes we need to refuse because it is the safe or right thing to do. Sometimes we just can't do something and need to say no and then apologise. Bolton (1979) describes the many ways we can say no and these are summarised below. So the rules for refusing will be:

Table 7.4 Refusing: the different ways to say no

Saying no . . .	A description	An example
1. Reflective listening, then NO	We reflect on the content and feeling of the request, then reflect it back, and then say no. This would be used for a reasonable request.	'I can see that you really want me to help you with that project. I would love to but I just don't have the time so I will have to say no.'

(Continued)

Table 7.4 (Continued)

Saying no . . .	A description	An example
2. The reasoned NO	We say no and then give a succinct explanation of our reason. The reason should be sincere and not an excuse.	'No. Thanks anyway. I don't really enjoy being on the water.'
3. The raincheck NO	We say no to a request but then immediately suggest an alternative or that we are asked again.	'I'm afraid I can't today. What about tomorrow?'
4. The broken record NO	This is where we use a one-sentence refusal statement several times. We use this method when someone is repeatedly asking us something and won't take no for an answer. It can be helpful to maintain our self-control as well as to keep refusing. A friend of mine had to regularly use this with her hairdresser who was keen to cut her hair in a shorter style. The hairdresser eventually stopped!	'Your hair has got very long. Shall we cut it shorter this time?' 'No, I like it long' 'I think it would suit your face to have it shorter' 'No, I like it long' 'What about just taking it short at the front?' 'No, I like it long' 'OK, maybe next time'
5. The flat-out NO	A flat-out no is usually more appropriate when the request is not reasonable. We say no but offer no reason or rain-check. This is obviously a much blunter way of refusing and will be seen as aggressive if used when the request is reasonable.	'No'

Refusing . . . the rules

- Stop and think – do you agree with what is being asked? Do you have a choice?
- Remember to use assertive body language to show you are confident in what you say
- Use a calm voice and speak clearly
- Say 'no' and then if appropriate, give a reason or apology

Disagreeing

Once again the skill of disagreeing is important so that other people understand how we think and feel. We may want to express our opinion or we may have a better idea or a compromise that will make others happy as well as us. If we don't disagree or tell people our opinions we may not be able to do or get the things we would like. The rules for disagreeing are:

> ## Disagreeing . . . the rules
>
> - Stop and think – do you agree with what is being said or suggested?
> - Remember to listen and respect others' opinions, is there a compromise?
> - Use a calm voice and speak clearly, remember to use assertive body language
> - Try saying 'I'm sorry I disagree . . .' or 'Maybe we should . . . instead'

Complaining

It is sometimes important to complain if we feel something is not right or we have been misled or sold something faulty. However, complaining does have bad connotations. We look with distaste at people on holiday who are giving their holiday representatives a hard time and complaining endlessly. And how many times have we felt embarrassed to be in the presence of someone who seems to constantly complain about everything? But, of course, sometimes it is important to complain and if we do it well then we can all come away from it feeling OK about ourselves.

Here are a few suggestions to make complaining easier:

- *One complaint at a time.* If we have several complaints to make, try to consider what is most important to us and focus on that first.
- *Practice!* If we need to practise, we should start with easier complaints and work our way up to more meaningful ones.
- *What do we hope to gain?* Before we complain, we should think about what we hope to gain. What is our goal?
- *Breathe, relax, and get emotions under control.* Before we complain, we should also take a minute or two to get our anger under control.
- *Identify the right person to talk to.* Identify the person who has the power to make the changes we want and then complain to them. We should ask at the outset: 'Who do I need to talk to in order to . . .?'
- *Use a 'complaint sandwich'.* Starting with something nice will make them feel more sympathetic or warm towards us, for example 'I spoke to a lovely lady here yesterday'. Then add the complaint. Then finish it off with a few words that will increase the listener's motivation to help us: 'I'd really appreciate your help in sorting this out'.
- *Admit our part of the problem.* If we do have some culpability in the matter, we should admit it as our honesty will reflect positively on us and will make the claims more believable.
- *Don't complain too much.* Choose the issues carefully: some complaints are simply not worth our time and trouble.
- *Consider a compliment!* Sometimes compliments are called for too. If we give feedback about what we liked, we will hopefully get more of it in the future.

The simplified rules for complaining are:

> ## Complaining . . . the rules
>
> - Stop and think – who should you talk to? What are your rights?
> - Remember to use assertive body language to show you are confident in what you say
> - Use a calm voice and speak clearly
> - Explain why you are not happy. Try saying 'I am not happy . . . because . . .'

Apologising

It is important to apologise if we have made a mistake or upset someone and we should ideally do it quickly and with meaning so that people know we are really sorry. The way we apologise will be dependent on the situation. If we bump into someone in the corridor it just needs a 'little sorry' but if we reverse into our neighbour's car and then run over their cat we will need to use a 'big sorry'! Scher and Darley (1997) suggest there are four steps to apologising effectively:

> ## Table 7.5 Apologising: the four steps to saying sorry

The steps	A description	An example
Step 1. Express remorse	Every apology needs to start with two magic words: 'I'm sorry' or 'I apologise'. This is essential, because these words express remorse over our actions. Our words also need to be sincere and authentic so we need to be honest with ourselves and the other person, about why we want to apologise. Timeliness is also important here. Apologise as soon as we realise that we've wronged someone else. Do not offer excuses for our behaviour here as it dilutes the apology.	'I'm sorry that I snapped at you yesterday. I feel embarrassed by my behaviour.'
Step 2. Admit responsibility	Next, we should admit responsibility for our actions or behaviour and acknowledge what we did. We should empathise with the other person and demonstrate that we understand how we made them feel. However, we shouldn't make assumptions but simply try to put ourselves in that person's shoes and imagine how they felt.	'I know that I hurt your feelings yesterday when I snapped at you. I'm sure this embarrassed you, especially since all the team was there. I was wrong to treat you like that.'

| Step 3. Make amends | When we make amends, we take action to make the situation right. We should think carefully about this step. Token gestures or empty promises will do more harm than good. And because we feel guilty, we might also be tempted to give more than what's appropriate – so we should try to be proportionate in what we offer. | 'If there's anything that I can do to make this up to you, please just ask.' 'I'd like to pay for the damage on the car.' |
| Step 4. Promise that it won't happen again | Our last step is to say that we won't repeat the action or behaviour. This step is important because we need to reassure the other person that we are going to change. This helps rebuild trust and repair the relationship. | 'From now on, I'm going to manage my stress better, so that I don't snap at you. And, I want you to tell me if I do this again.' |

Apologising . . . the rules

- Stop and think – who should you apologise to? Does it need to be a big or little sorry?
- Remember to use assertive body language to show them you mean what you are saying
- Use a sincere tone of voice and express regret
- Take responsibility. Try saying 'I am sorry – that was my fault' and if appropriate do something to make up for it.

Requesting explanations

Finally, it is important to request explanations if we do not understand something or feel we need more information. It is important to do this clearly and appropriately so that other people can understand us and give us the right explanation and if we don't request explanations assertively, people may not know we need more information and we may not be able to complete tasks. The rules for requesting explanations are:

Requesting explanations . . . the rules

- Stop and think – do you understand what has been said or asked of you?
- Use a calm voice, speak clearly and remember to use assertive body language
- Ask a question or for an explanation. Try saying 'I'm sorry I don't understand, could you explain'
- Remember to say thank you

Summary

As we have seen in this chapter, assertive behaviour is certainly not easy but is necessary to maintain our self-respect, satisfy our needs, and defend our rights and personal space without abusing or dominating other people. It is a way of behaving which confirms one's own individual worth and dignity while maintaining the worth of others. It can be a daunting step for many people and it is important to break each skill down into small steps, and also to ensure that someone has enough foundation skills to be successful (more of this in the chapter on assessing social skills).

To summarise, here are a few small steps to take to help us on the road to assertiveness:

Assertiveness . . . a few small steps

- *Start small* – don't start with a scary situation, start small. Choose something where you can practise your assertive tone of voice, for example on the phone.
- *Learn it from the inside out* – practise using assertive body language whenever you can. Walk tall, use the power pose before any interaction, and practise your eye contact.
- *Take your time* – sometimes you should put off saying something until you have calmed down or thought about your response. Be honest and say you need a few minutes to think about what you want to say.
- *Fake it 'til you make it* – practise, practise, practise, and the more you say it, the more you will sound like you mean it. Fake your confidence until you are confident.
- *Accept the learning curve* – initially you may come on too strong or too wishy washy. Don't worry – take note of what went well and what you could do differently and praise yourself for trying. Keep trying and changing things until you find the way that works for you.

Key points from Chapter 7

This chapter covered assertive, passive and aggressive behaviour. We looked at the purpose of assertiveness, the cause of unassertiveness and at teaching assertiveness and the situations in which assertive behaviour is appropriate.

Defining assertiveness

Assertiveness is standing up for our personal rights and expressing our thoughts, feelings and beliefs in a direct, honest, and appropriate way which respect the rights of other people. It can be seen as a mid-point on the continuum of passive to aggressive behaviour.

Passive behaviour

Passive people will not express their own desires and wishes and will avoid conflict in order to please others. They lack self-confidence and show certain behaviours:

- Hesitates and prevaricates, speaks softly
- Looks away and tends to fidget nervously
- Avoids issues and does not express opinions, preferring to agree with others regardless of personal feelings

Aggressive behaviour

Aggressive behaviour is the opposite. They value their own opinion above others' and will want to win at all costs. They show the following behaviours:

- Talks loudly and abrasively
- Glares at the other person
- Interrupts and answers before the other is finished speaking

Assertive behaviour

Assertive behaviour is the 'balance point' between aggressive behaviour and passive behaviour and the assertive person will use all their nonverbal and verbal communication skills effectively and appropriately to get their message across. They will express their own opinion but will listen to others. They will also:

- Answer spontaneously and address the main issue
- Speak with a conversational yet firm tone and volume
- Look at the other person

Types of assertive behaviour

We described five key types of assertive behaviour: basic, empathetic, escalating, confronting, and I-language assertion. We also considered direct and indirect assertion and protective assertion.

The benefits of assertive behaviour

We described three main benefits to being assertive: self-esteem, relationships, and living your life, and these linked in with the *purpose* of assertiveness as it helps us to achieve nine main goals in life. Most of these relate to the ability to respond to someone assertively but are also linked to our rights, our self-esteem and our respect of others.

The causes of unassertiveness

We described the four main causes of unassertive behaviour: low self-esteem, roles and gender, past experience, and stress.

Teaching assertiveness

The three central components to an assertive response are: content, process and nonverbal responses. *Content* describes what we say; *process* is all about the timing of the response and the environment in which we deliver it; and *nonverbal responses* are how we use our body language and paralinguistic skills to give the aura of assertiveness.

There are eight situations in which assertive behaviour is appropriate:

- Expressing feelings
- Standing up for yourself
- Making suggestions
- Refusing
- Disagreeing
- Complaining
- Apologising
- Requesting explanations

Each one is described but a similar framework is used in most:

1. Stop and think
2. Use good body language
3. Use good paralinguistic skills
4. Try saying . . .

Chapter 8

Self-esteem

'Believe in yourself and all that you are. Know that there is something inside you that is greater than any obstacle.'

Christian Daa Larson (1874–1954)

Having addressed assertiveness in the previous chapter and remarked on the abundance of self-help books there are on that topic, there are possibly even more books on the subject of self-esteem! Fifty years ago, there was little written about self-esteem and it was not a subject for discussion in schools. However, interest began to build in the 1970s as people began to see the link between low self-esteem and social problems such as unemployment and academic achievement, and in the 1980s the movement was in full swing (Zeigler-Hill, 2013). It is still considered to be important today but has lost some of its status as the 'panacea for societal change' that it held 30 years ago. So, does it play an important part in our lives today? And is there a link between self-esteem and social skills? This chapter will focus on explaining what we mean by self-esteem and will then address the effect low self-esteem can have on developing effective interpersonal communication.

Defining self-esteem

Self-esteem is the value we place on ourselves. It is the feeling we have about all the things we see ourselves to be. It is the knowledge that we are lovable, we are capable, and we are unique. It is therefore made up of 'self-perception' – a collection of feelings and beliefs that we have about ourselves. It is also how we define ourselves in terms of our motivations, our attitudes and our behaviours and all of these affect our emotional well-being. Self-esteem can also be defined as feelings of capability combined with feelings of being loved. A person needs to feel as if he is capable of achieving success and also to feel loved in order to develop healthy self-esteem.

Self-esteem was first described in 1890 by a man called William James as the sense of positive regard that develops when individuals consistently meet or exceed the important goals in their lives. More recently, Zeigler-Hill (2013) gives a similar definition saying that self-esteem is considered to be 'the evaluative aspect of self-knowledge that reflects the extent to which people like themselves and believe they are important'. Trzesniewski et al. (2013) also define self-esteem as 'an individual's *subjective* evaluation of her or his worth as a person'. If they believe they are a person of worth and value, then they have high self-esteem, regardless of whether their self-evaluation is validated by others or corroborated by external criteria.

Indeed, the more we read about self-esteem, the more confusing it can seem. We think we know what it is all about, and yet the terminology can get in the way as people use different terms to mean the same (or a similar) concept. The three ways in which the term 'self-esteem' is used in the literature can be summed up in the following table:

Table 8.1 Defining self-esteem

The term	aka	What it means
Global self-esteem	Trait self-esteem	Refers to a personality variable that represents *the way we generally feel about ourselves*. It is relatively enduring over time and situations. Some writers assume it is a decision we make about our worth as a person, others as a feeling of affection for ourselves that is not derived from a rational or judgmental process. It is stable throughout adulthood and probably has a genetic component.
Feelings of self-worth	State self-esteem	This refers to *the emotions we are calling feelings of self-worth* and our self-evaluative reactions to events. So people talk about experiences that 'threaten self-esteem' (e.g. a divorce) or 'boost self-esteem' (e.g. getting a promotion). These are more temporary than global self-esteem.
Self-evaluations	Domain specific self-esteem *or* self-confidence *or* self-appraisals	Refers to how we evaluate various abilities and attributes such as academic ability and physical appearance. We therefore may rate ourselves highly in one domain but less in another.

Adapted from Brown and Marshall, 2006

Although different, it has been found that the three constructs are highly correlated so that the person with high self-esteem will evaluate themselves more positively and experience higher feelings of self-worth than the person with low self-esteem.

We will describe what we mean by 'high self-esteem' and 'low self-esteem' in more detail later, but first we should consider how self-esteem develops.

The development of self-esteem

The development of a healthy self-esteem is not straightforward and is affected by many factors. Sullivan (1953) believed that 'one's concept of self develops out of the reflected appraisals of significant others' (cited by Hargie, 2017). This means that positive, rewarding experiences with parents and significant others will lead to positive views of self, while negative experiences such as blame, constant reprimands and ridicule, lead to feelings of worthlessness. This is backed up by DeHart et al. (2013) who summarise the research in this area to state that 'people develop a sense of self on the basis of how other people treat them. . . . Self-esteem is a consequence of people's perceived social standing through their interaction with others'. This means that people who have developed a high self-esteem have experienced many subjectively successful and non-rejecting interpersonal relationships.

However, Trzesniewski et al. (2013) claim that there are other factors to be considered. They state that it emerges from 'complex transactions between a person's genetic make-up and his or her family, social, and cultural context'. This means that certain genetic differences in temperament, intelligence, physical attractiveness, health and so on, will influence and shape social interactions, the social contexts that they seek out, and the reactions they receive from significant others. These will also affect their capacity to experience success in forming friendships and later on in intimate relationships and employment. Collectively these will all influence someone's development of self-esteem. However, even though it is recognised that genetics is a component to self-esteem, psychologists generally agree that self-esteem is rooted in our interpersonal experience, reflected appraisal from others, relationships, social comparisons, and group comparisons, and from early interactions from our family.

This can also be shown through the 'cognitive model of self-esteem' (cited by Brown and Marshall, 2006) which shows that self-esteem starts with *evaluative feedback* (success or failure, interpersonal acceptance or rejection). This then influences our *self-evaluations* and these determine feelings of *self-worth* and *global self-esteem*. It is referred to as the 'bottom-up' model because it assumes that self-esteem is based on beliefs about our qualities. If we think we are intelligent, and if we think we are attractive and if we think we are popular, then we will have high self-esteem.

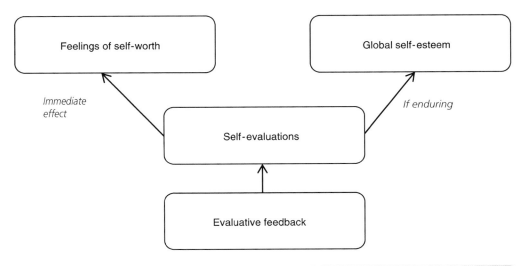

Figure 8.1 A cognitive model of self-esteem formation

The importance of self-esteem doesn't just lie in whether it is high or low but also in our pursuit of self-esteem throughout our lives and the ways in which we seek to protect, maintain and enhance our feelings of self-worth in different areas that motivate or are important to us.

Park and Crocker (2013) describe ten domains, or 'contingencies of self-worth' on which we base our self-evaluations:

Ten contingencies of self-worth:

1. Academic competence
2. Physical appearance
3. Virtue
4. Having God's love
5. Love and support from family
6. Outdoing others in competition
7. Others' approval
8. Friendships
9. Romantic relationships
10. Body weight

According to this model, people differ in the areas on which they base their self-worth and this means that the impact of life events on self-esteem will depend on which particular domain is affected. So, if someone strongly bases their self-worth on their academic competence, then they are more likely to experience a lower self-esteem and negative affects when they perform badly on an academic test, than the person whose self-esteem is less invested in this domain.

In addition, this model shows that people will pursue self-esteem in domains on which their self-esteem in based, to ensure boosts to their state of self-esteem. This means that the student who bases their self-worth on academic competence will spend more time studying whereas the student who bases their self-worth on their appearance will spend more time grooming, exercising, shopping, etc. These contingencies of self-worth are thought to originate in response to acute events and/or experiences in which our sense of safety was threatened, such as criticism, being rejected or abandoned. We internalise specific beliefs about what we need to do to be a person of worth and value, and in doing so, we feel protected from future harm. So, *if* we can succeed in 'x', we will feel safe and protected from 'y'.

The strategies we use to regulate these feelings of safety and self-worth are also affected by our attachment styles. According to attachment theory, 'attachment styles reflect individual differences in prototypical, internal working models of self and others formed in the context of the early caregiver-infant relationship' (Park and Crocker, 2013). The link with self-esteem can be seen in the table below:

Table 8.2 Attachment styles and self-esteem

Attachment style	A description	An important domain
Secure attachment style	They report feeling loved, cared for, and supported by their partners and believe that others will be responsive to their needs in times of stress. They base their self-esteem on having positive, supportive relationships with others.	Love and support from family.

Attachment style	A description	An important domain
Dismissive-avoidant attachment style	They feel uncomfortable with closeness and find it difficult to trust and depend on others. They are less emotionally dependent on others and are therefore less likely to base their self-worth on obtaining other's approval, having love and support from family, or having God's love (if religious).	Domains that don't depend on other people's approval. Possibly physical appearance or academic competence.
Anxious attachment style (preoccupied and fearful)	They seek emotional intimacy but worry that other people will not want to get close to them. They look to other people for validation and reassurance and are likely to base their self-worth on how they appear to others.	Physical appearance.

Finally, another factor in the development of self-esteem is the idea that once we have established a sense of high or low self-worth, that we then 'promote continuity' through the kinds of environments we seek out for ourselves. This is consistent with Swann's self-verification theory (cited by Trzesniewski et al., 2013). Swann proposes that we are motivated to confirm our pre-existing self-views. So the person with low self-esteem seeks out contexts that confirm and maintain their low self-regard and the person with high self-esteem seeks contexts that promote their high self-regard. This would explain why individuals with low self-esteem may seek out a relationship that involves negative feedback.

Self-esteem does also vary for an individual from day to day and year to year, but there are a few factors that are significant and that will affect us. Research has shown that there are age-related changes to self-esteem (cited in Zeigler-Hill, 2013) where we see relatively high self-esteem during childhood before it drops hugely at the beginning of adolescence. It then gradually increases during adolescence, young adulthood, and middle age, before reaching its peak at around 60, and then declines again in old age. Zeigler-Hill also describes a gender difference which emerges in adolescence and shows that women have a lower self-esteem compared to those of men and this difference continues until old age when the self-esteem difference reverses and men then drop significantly lower than women. The third significant factor is the difference between majority and minority group members. It has been found that minority groups are often targets for discrimination and prejudice and these have a direct impact on self-esteem as they internalise the negative views of their group (and society). Common stigmatised groups include individuals who are overweight, those who have physical abnormalities, and those who have a severe mental illness.

In summary, we could use the following model to help us understand what factors impact on our self-esteem. In addition, the darker arrows represent activities and experiences that we seek out to boost our self-esteem and promote continuity.

So what does 'high self-esteem' and 'low self-esteem' look like?

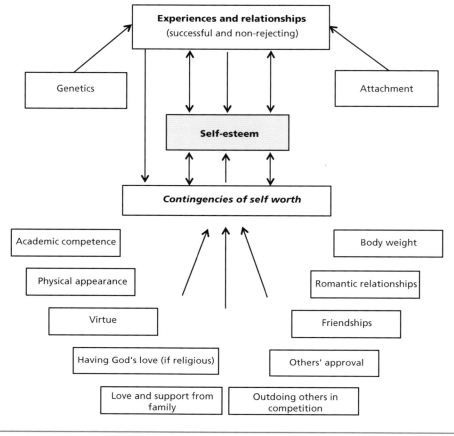

Figure 8.2 A model of self-esteem

High self-esteem

I particularly like Rosenberg's (1965) definition of high self-esteem:

> When we speak of high self-esteem, then we shall simply mean that the individual respects himself, considers himself worthy; he does not necessarily consider himself better than others, but he definitely does not consider himself worse; he does not feel that he is the ultimate in perfection but, on the contrary, recognises his limitations and expects to grow and improve.

So high self-esteem means having a favourable view of oneself that is not necessarily accurate or inaccurate but rather reflects our perception (rather than reality). This is important, as feelings of self-worth may have little to do with any objective view of the individual. Most people across the world seem to desire and aspire towards having high self-esteem and will adopt different strategies to maintain or enhance their feelings of self-worth according to their level of self-esteem. So people with high self-esteem will focus their energy on further increasing their feelings of self-worth through activities that will make them feel good about themselves, whereas people with low self-esteem will use self-protective strategies to protect what little they already have.

> ## High self-esteem means:
> - Having a healthy view of yourself
> - Having a sense of self-worth
> - Having a positive outlook
> - Feeling satisfied with yourself most of the time
> - Setting realistic goals

We can also recognise someone with high self-esteem through the signals they give off. Cameron (2013) says that 'self-esteem signals appear in many forms, from public appearance to body stance, and even email addresses'. So, we associate self-esteem with a healthier appearance (as opposed to a sickly appearance), a smiling face, an energetic stance (as opposed to a tired stance) and an open posture (as opposed to a closed one).

Children in particular need high self-esteem to feel good about themselves, their world, and the contributions they can make to it. It is their armour against the challenges of the world. A child must believe that he has the talents to achieve and more important than achievement, self-esteem is also crucial to a child's happiness. Only when he is comfortable with himself and believes that he is capable of success, will a child truly feel fulfilled. Children rely on good feelings to help them grow in confidence and emotional stature, and self-esteem for them is a mixture of feeling happy, confident, secure, important, and that they fit in. Children who therefore have a high level of self-esteem seem to have an easier time coping with the challenges of growing up.

Table 8.3 Identifying children with high or healthy self-esteem

1.	They tend to smile more and enjoy life
2.	They tend to enjoy interacting with others
3.	They are comfortable in social settings and enjoy group activities
4.	They are also happy to work independently
5.	They may welcome new challenges and can work towards finding a solution
6.	When they don't understand or can't succeed they may say 'I don't understand' *not* 'I'm an idiot'
7.	They will tolerate frustration
8.	They are able to take responsibility for unsuccessful ventures
9.	They are aware of their individual strengths and weaknesses and accept them
10.	They are generally realistic but also optimistic
11.	They feel loved and will love others in return

Low self-esteem

Rosenberg (1965) says low self-esteem 'implies self-rejection, self-dissatisfaction, self-contempt. The individual lacks respect for the self he observes'. In contrast to people with high self-esteem, they are either uncertain or negative about themselves and can find the challenges of life difficult to cope with. People with low self-esteem will use self-protective strategies to protect what little they already have. This means that the person with low self-esteem will be reluctant to be noticed (or their perceived bad qualities to be noticed) and will avoid certain situations as they do not want to call attention to themselves and risk failure or rejection. Low self-esteem has also been found to contribute to a number of maladaptive outcomes, including lower life satisfaction, depressive symptoms and suicidal impulses (Jordan et al., 2013).

Table 8.4 Identifying children with low self-esteem

---

1. They may not smile as readily
2. They may be easily influenced by others and by advertising
3. They may be reluctant to try new things and may become anxious in new situations
4. They may even avoid new challenges for fear of failure
5. They may easily become frustrated with setbacks – giving up all together or waiting for someone else to take over
6. They may find it difficult to find solutions to problems
7. They may frequently speak negatively about themselves e.g. 'I'm stupid'
8. They may be self-critical and are likely to feel disappointed in themselves and may say things like 'I'm no good at this' or 'I can't do this'
9. They may blame others when activities are unsuccessful
10. They may see temporary setbacks as permanent and intolerable
11. They are generally pessimistic about themselves and the future
12. They may not believe that they have any special qualities or talents
13. They may feel unloved
14. They may become passive, withdrawn or depressed

So why do people want to feel good about themselves? What are the benefits of high self-esteem?

The benefits of high self-esteem

'It is a universally acknowledged truth that people want to feel good about themselves' (Pyszczynski and Kesebir, 2013) and this desire can play an essential role in our lives. Self-esteem is often considered to be a fundamental human *need* and people will express a preference for self-esteem boosts over other pleasant activities (Zeigler-Hill, 2013). Park and Crocker (2013) state that 'the pursuit of self-esteem – the desire to protect, maintain, and enhance feelings of self-worth – is pervasive in Western societies in which the self and self-esteem are strongly emphasized and valued'.

But why do we *need* self-esteem? Partly this is due to the nature of being human. Unlike other animals, human beings are not only conscious but also self-conscious, so even though animals think, feel and behave, they do not think about the fact they are thinking, feeling and behaving. As Pyszczynski and Kesebir (2013) state: 'the human capacity for self-awareness is central to the processes through which members of our species control and regulate their behaviour. Life is weaved from an incessant thread of choices, decisions, and possible courses of action'. We use our capacity for self-consciousness and self-evaluation to help us reach our goals and increase our chance of survival. And viewing oneself as a good person (in other words, having good self-esteem) is the superior goal toward which other goals in life are oriented, which means that most of our specific goals in our lives are ultimately oriented towards being a valuable person.

There are also several benefits and positive life outcomes associated with self-esteem and the most common are:

1. *Status or social acceptance*

    In essence it can be argued that self-esteem allows an individual to monitor or measure the degree to which they believe they are valued by others. This means that self-esteem has a 'status-tracking property' (Zeigler-Hill, 2013) and that the feelings of self-worth depend on the level of status or social acceptance the person believes they possess. Self-esteem also influences how individuals present themselves to others and how they are perceived by their social environment. Those with higher self-esteem will generally be evaluated more positively than those with lower levels of self-esteem.

2. *Protection*

    Self-esteem can serve to protect people from potential threats such as rejection and failure, as people with high self-esteem appear to be more resilient and less affected by negative experiences and therefore recover more quickly than those with low self-esteem. This means that self-esteem and stress interact in such a way that 'high self-esteem protects the individual from . . . the consequences of stress, whereas low self-esteem increases their vulnerability to the effects of stress' (Zeigler-Hill, 2013). As a result, people with high self-esteem are more emotionally stable and less prone to psychological distress.

3. *Mental health*

    High self-esteem contributes to a greater psychological well-being (Jordan et al., 2013). This 'benefit' is linked to the previous point around protection in that people with low self-esteem are vulnerable to the effects of stress and are more prone to psychological distress. This means there is a link between self-esteem and mental health problems, as low self-esteem is included as a diagnostic criterion or an associated feature in a number of mental health problems such as depression, anxiety, social phobias and others. Self-esteem can act as a risk factor either because of someone's thought processes (e.g. a tendency to ruminate) or their coping strategies such as excessive reassurance seeking.

4. *Physical health*

    High self-esteem is also linked to health benefits as it is a psychological resource that protects people and supports good health. This is thought to be linked to cortisol reactivity following stress as well as cardiovascular responses to feedback, which all produce health benefits by protecting people from the effects of a negative experience. Conversely low self-esteem is a risk factor that leaves people vulnerable to poor health, including a higher body mass, cardiovascular problems, smoking and alcohol consumption.

5. *Relationships*

    The connection between self-esteem and relationships is well documented from the earliest writings on the nature of self (James, 1890). In brief, our interpersonal experiences are generally thought to have a huge impact on our self-esteem in that if someone feels valued and accepted by others, they will have a higher self-esteem than the person who struggles with relationships.

6. *Academic outcomes*

There is some evidence to suspect that people with high self-esteem do better academically and this is possibly because they may make more effort and persist in the face of failure (Wylie, cited by Zeigler-Hill, 2013). However, this is not consistent in the literature and some people argue that the link may be the other way round: academic achievement can result in higher self-esteem.

7. *Crime*

A number of studies have shown a link between low self-esteem and various criminal behaviours but other studies have failed to show an association, so it would appear that more research is needed in this area (Zeigler-Hill, 2013).

Assessing self-esteem

We have already defined self-esteem as 'an individual's *subjective* evaluation of her or his worth as a person' (Trzesniewski et al., 2013). This means that if they believe they are a person of worth and value, then they have high self-esteem, regardless of whether their self-evaluation is validated by others or corroborated by external criteria. Some authors have tried to focus on accuracy when defining self-esteem, talking about 'valid versus inflated' appraisals, and if there is ever a need to lower self-esteem in certain contexts. The trouble is that this leads to some difficult questions which are undoubtedly prejudiced against certain types of people. As Tangney and Leary (2003) ask 'is the suggestion here that the average college freshman, unemployed person, or mentally retarded individual *shouldn't* on the whole take a positive attitude toward themselves?'

The Rosenberg Self-Esteem Scale

By far the most common way to assess self-esteem is to use the self-report method and the most widely used assessment of global self-esteem is the Rosenberg Self-Esteem Scale (1965). This assessment is a ten-item scale that measures global self-worth by measuring both positive and negative feelings about the self. The scale is uni-dimensional and questions are answered using a four-point Likert scale format, ranging from strongly agree to strongly disagree. This then gives the person a score from 0–30 where scores between 15 and 25 are within normal range and scores below 15 suggest low self-esteem.

Questions in the Rosenberg Self-esteem Scale:

1. I feel that I am a person of worth, at least on an equal plane with others
2. I feel that I have a number of good qualities
3. All in all, I am inclined to feel that I am a failure
4. I am able to do things as well as most other people
5. I feel I do not have much to be proud of
6. I take a positive attitude toward myself
7. On the whole, I am satisfied with myself
8. I wish I could have more respect for myself
9. I certainly feel useless at times
10. At times I think I am no good at all

Despite being very brief and easy to administer, Koestner and Mageau (2006) state that the psychometric qualities of the Rosenberg scale are excellent. They explain that the scale has high internal consistency and correlates with peer reports and other self-esteem measures. It also functions well as a marker of positive mental health and life satisfaction and is negatively related to indicators of psychological distress. It has also been found to be unrelated to demographic factors such as gender, age and marital status.

The self-report measures of self-esteem have many strengths but also weaknesses in that they can be easily manipulated. It is also hard to assess a child's self-esteem if they do not have the language or concepts necessary to self-report and so we need to assess their self-esteem in a less direct manner.

Talkabout interview

Talkabout for Children: Developing Self-awareness and Self-esteem (Kelly, 2018) uses an informal interview with the child where questions are asked about friends, school, likes, strengths etc. and a judgment is made about that child's self-esteem based on their answers.

Table 8.5 *Talkabout* assessment of self-awareness and self-esteem

Main question	Prompt questions	What you are assessing
1. Tell me about your best friend	Why do you like them? What do they look like? What are they like?	Other awareness
2. Why do you think your friend likes you?		Awareness of qualities Self-esteem
3. Tell me about you. What do you like doing?	Do you have a favourite game or activity?	Awareness of likes
4. Anything you really don't like doing?		Awareness of dislikes
5. What do you think you are good at?	Can you think of something at school or home that you are good at?	Awareness of strengths Self-esteem
6. Can you think of something that you find difficult?	Can you think of something at school or home that you are not so good at?	Awareness of needs Self-esteem
7. How would you describe the way you look?	Can you tell me three things about the way you look?	Awareness of personal appearance Self-esteem
8. What kind of person do you think you are?	Can you think of three words to describe what kind of boy / girl you are?	Awareness of qualities Self-esteem

(Continued)

Table 8.5 (Continued)

Main question	Prompt questions	What you are assessing
9. Can you think of one good thing about being you?	Something that makes you feel special or really happy?	Awareness of qualities Self-esteem
10. Do you like talking to people?	Do you find it easy or difficult to talk to people?	Awareness of strengths Self-esteem

We are also able to assess how much support or prompting they required, which is useful when we come to look at evaluating the effectiveness of interventions.

Developing self-esteem

When considering how we can develop and change self-esteem, there are two critical questions. Can intervention increase self-esteem and does it improve the outcome for the individual? Research suggests that we can. Haney and Durlak (1998) say there is evidence that it is possible to 'significantly improve' levels of self-esteem and produce 'concomitant positive changes in other areas of adjustment'. This is good news, but how can we do it?

As we said earlier, the development of self-esteem is not straightforward and is an accumulation of a number of factors, some of which we can have no influence over, for example, genetics. However, if we consider Sullivan's (1953) belief that 'one's concept of self develops out of the reflected appraisals of significant others' (cited by Hargie, 2017) then this is something we can influence. This means that positive, rewarding experiences with parents and significant others will lead to positive views of self, while negative experiences such as blame, constant reprimands and ridicule, lead to feelings of worthlessness.

Trzesniewski et al. (2013) also talk about three important factors that will promote a change in self-esteem. Firstly, we know that people are responsive to *environmental feedback* so if a child is rewarded for certain behaviours at school and at home, then this will have a positive effect on their self-esteem. Second, that *self-reflection* can provide a useful tool to change self-esteem. Third, *perceptions by others* may shape someone's self-esteem. So, if we are viewed as competent and liked by peers, then this will promote a healthy self-esteem. Trzesniewski et al. also say that the ideal intervention should try to not only enhance global self-worth but should also try to enhance the domain-specific self-worth.

So, if we believe that a person develops the feelings that make up their self-esteem from the responses and behaviour of the people around them, then the ideal self-esteem intervention is in a group where people can receive feedback from others and develop that sense of self-worth that we have been talking about. Of course, we would ideally need to consider and involve all the significant people in that person's life, for example teachers at school, parents and siblings, but this is not often possible and we may need to rely on building self-esteem within one context and then supporting that person to take it into other parts of their life.

I have summarised in the following table ten key aspects to a self-esteem intervention that can be used in group work and adapted for one-to-one work or work at home:

Table 8.6 Developing self-esteem: ten key aspects

Area/skill	A bit more information	Things that will help
1. Create a safe space	We all need to feel safe in order to feel comfortable, to learn and open up. When working with children (or adults) we should ensure that they feel safe in the group setting as then they will be less likely to be afraid of failure and more likely to risk trying again when they fail.	Provide a safe physical environment Use a consistent format to the session so that they know the routine Set clear rules and limits Treat everyone the same Be realistic in your expectations of them Be consistent so they know what to expect
2. A sense of belonging	Everyone needs to feel they belong and to know that they are important to someone. When they feel accepted and loved by the important people in their lives, they feel comfortable, safe and secure. If children feel respected and secure within a family, they will find it easier to make friendships outside the family. So, if they feel respected and secure within the group setting, this will help them to make friends outside of the group.	Encourage them to develop friendships within the group Encourage pride in the group Display work (if appropriate) or share good news with others Encourage pride in who they are, for example their ethnic background Share photos
3. An awareness and understanding of emotions	It is also important to teach people to be able to recognise and express their feelings as this will help them to develop positive relationships. It is also helpful for people to see that others feel the same.	Accept what they are feeling as true Use pictures / symbols to support people to consider how they may be feeling and extend vocabulary Group members to show respect for other people's feelings by listening with interest and respect
4. A sense of respect	A person is more likely to develop respect for themselves and for others if they learn from us and from others that what they think, feel and do is important. Right from the start ensure there is a sense of respect within the sessions and that everyone adheres to this rule.	Listen to each other and respect each other's opinions Only allow positive language Do not allow use of demeaning names, criticism or punishment which is too harsh Say 'I feel' or 'I believe', not 'you are' if you do have to tell someone what they are doing is wrong

(Continued)

| Table 8.6 (Continued) | | |

Area/skill	A bit more information	Things that will help
5. Strengths and qualities	We are all special and feeling special is an important part of self-esteem. It is important for everyone to discover their own special talents and qualities and research indicates that one of the main factors that contribute to a child developing self-esteem is the presence of at least one adult who helps them to feel appreciated and focuses on their strengths.	Understanding that we are all different Consider everyday activities and rate on a 'very good' to 'never good' scale Increase understanding of different qualities Consider which ones describe each person Use compliments (see below)
6. Complimenting	Hearing from another person our strengths and positive qualities helps to build a more positive image of ourselves. And teaching people to be kinder towards each other is important because as a result, they will tend to treat and think of themselves in a kinder way too. Ask them to consider qualities, successes, hard work and teach them to give and receive compliments in a genuine manner.	Ask everyone to say something nice to someone else in the group See what we can do during the week to make others feel good or trigger them to smile Make sure everyone receives a compliment Encourage keeping a diary or list of things that they did well – we call it an 'it's good to be me' diary Create individual 'stars', posters or bookmarks to summarise what everyone likes about each other Write a list of what everyone likes about themselves
7. Self-identity and self-image	How we feel about what we look like is also an important part of self-esteem. It is important for everyone to look at what they look like and to find the good in it. It may also be important to address topics such as sleeping, eating and exercise, and to help them set realistic goals to feel more confident, for example, having a shower every day, going for a walk or getting a haircut.	Challenge some of the myths about beauty and what we see in advertising Focus on the good and use others in the group to help build up a positive self-image in everyone Create a plan that is realistic and motivating

8. Likes and motivations	At times it can be hard to find the motivation to set goals, especially when we don't feel confident or worry about what other people may think. But it doesn't have to be something big. Making small goals can help us to feel more positive. Regularly doing things that we are good at and enjoy reinforces our belief in our abilities and strengths. It will also make us feel happier. And when we really like doing something then the motivation to do that thing tends to come automatically.	Identify goals that are important to them Ask 'are they doing what they really want to do?' If not and if possible, then refocus and start working on that very important thing instead. What activities could they bring into their day that will make them feel happier? Find something they like doing and do more of it
9. Problem solving	Teaching someone to learn from their mistakes, to work towards a goal, and to have pride in their successes is important as high self-esteem is associated with solid problem-solving skills and so it is important to develop the ability to problem solve and make decisions.	If someone is having difficulty with something e.g. a friend, discuss ways to solve the situation Try role playing to see the steps involved in problem solving Teach them to make decisions and to set realistic goals Provide choices to encourage a feeling of control over their lives Help them recognise that there are things that are in their control and things that are not Give them opportunities to succeed
10. Positive visualisation	Use the power of imagination and ask everyone to create an image of themselves as the confident and self-assured person they aspire to become. Use this prior to challenging situations to help someone picture themselves acting confidently. Developing a skill in positive visualisation can also work in conjunction with teaching relaxation techniques and teaching power posing (see chapter on body language).	Create an image of a confident self: How will they feel? How will others perceive them? What does their body language look like? How will they talk? Feel the feelings, experience being and seeing things from that person's perspective Write a description of this person and all the attributes they have observed Use role play, relaxation and power posing to help

The link between self-esteem and social skills

When I started working as a speech and language therapist, I would not have considered that it was my role to work with children or adults on their self-esteem or their friendship skills and yet I did work on social skills. However, the more I worked with children and adults with social skills difficulties, the more I saw that the three areas are inextricably linked. To understand the link between the acquisition of social skills and someone's self-esteem we should reconsider the questions asked in Chapter 1: what causes social skills difficulties and what is the impact?

What causes social skills difficulties?

Social skills difficulties are caused by a number of factors such as social background, family life, or a diagnosis such as autism, intellectual disability, ADHD, or communication disorder. However, we are all socially unskilled at times and this is usually caused by one or more of the following: heightened emotions, other people's behaviour, not knowing the rules, previous experience, a lack of information, illness, alcohol and a lack of self-confidence or *low self-esteem*. This means that the person who has low self-esteem is more likely to struggle with their social skills.

What is the impact of social skills difficulties?

If we think back to times when we have been socially unskilled, then people will tell us that we came across as maybe 'rude, arrogant, boring, inept, aggressive, weird . . .' and the result can be that maybe:

- They didn't see us for who we are
- They didn't react to us in a way that we intended
- We affected their feelings in a way that we didn't intend
- *Our self-confidence took a knock*

Summary

So, self-esteem and social skills are linked and having a healthy self-esteem is important to developing social skills for the following four reasons. Firstly, the person who has low self-esteem is more likely to struggle with their social skills and their friendship skills, so developing someone's self-esteem will go some way to helping someone to improve social skills. Secondly, being socially unskilled can have a negative impact on our self-esteem and in turn affects how other people perceive us, which also affects our relationships. Thirdly, the benefits of high self-esteem include social acceptance which is also linked to our social competence. Finally, the connection between self-esteem and relationships is well documented. Our interpersonal experiences have a huge impact on our self-esteem in that if someone feels valued and accepted by others, they will have a higher self-esteem than the person who struggles with relationships. So self-esteem and social skills are linked and in turn, these are also linked to our relationships – the topic that will be discussed in the next chapter.

Key points from Chapter 8

This chapter covered what we mean by self-esteem and addressed the effect low self-esteem can have on developing effective interpersonal communication.

Defining self-esteem

Self-esteem is the value we place on ourselves and has three separate concepts: global self-esteem, feelings of self-worth and self-evaluations. Although different, they are highly correlated so that the person with high self-esteem will evaluate themselves more positively and will experience higher feelings of self-worth.

The development self-esteem

Self-esteem is affected by many different factors but most people agree that it is rooted in our experiences, our feedback from others, and on comparisons made with others. Other areas discussed were:

- *Contingencies of self-worth*: In addition, there are ten areas in which we judge our self-worth from academic competence to body weight and we actively pursue self-esteem in domains that are important to us.
- *Attachment styles*: A child's attachment style will have a long-lasting effect on which domain is important to their self-worth.
- *High self-esteem* means having a healthy view of oneself, a sense of self-worth, and a positive outlook on life. It also means feeling satisfied with oneself and an ability to set realistic goals.
- *Low self-esteem* implies rejection, dissatisfaction and contempt towards oneself and an uncertainty and negativity about the future. It is found to contribute to a number of poor life outcomes.

The benefits of high self-esteem

There is a link between self-esteem and the following seven outcomes, although the evidence for the last two is not conclusive: status or social acceptance; protection; mental health; physical health; relationships; academic outcomes; and crime.

Assessing self-esteem

The most common way to assess self-esteem is to use the self-report method and the most common assessment is the Rosenberg Self-esteem Scale (1965). The *Talkabout* self-awareness and self-esteem interview (Kelly, 2018) uses questions about the child's school life and friends to make judgements about their self-esteem.

Developing self-esteem

Ten key aspects to a self-esteem intervention are described:

- Create a safe space
- Create a sense of belonging
- Develop an awareness and understanding of emotions
- Develop a sense of respect
- Develop an awareness of strengths and qualities
- Giving and receiving of compliments
- Develop an awareness of self-identity and self-image
- Develop an awareness of likes and motivations and an ability to set realistic goals
- Develop an ability to problem solve
- Develop positive visualisation

The link between self-esteem and social skills

The person with low self-esteem is more likely to struggle with their social skills and one of the impacts of having social skills difficulties is that our self-esteem can be affected.

Chapter 9

Friendship skills

'There is nothing on this earth more to be prized than true friendship.'
Thomas Aquinas, Italian theologian (1225–1274)

It is hard to imagine a world where we do not have many, or even any, friendships or relationships. Far more than any other species, humans seem programmed to form relationships with others. So much of our self-identity and self-worth comes from being a mother, a husband, a lover, a friend, or a confidant. Who would we be, without our relationships? How would we feel about ourselves, if we did not have any friends? How would we know if we were funny, a good listener, kind or a good friend? We rely on our friends for support and assistance in times of trouble and to gain a sense of well-being from the relationships we create and cultivate. In the words of the gifted playwright Tony Kushner (cited by Schneider, 2016), 'the smallest individual human unit is two persons, not one'. Even children at a very early age show a 'biological preparedness to cooperate'. By the age of two, we see children 'coordinating interaction around a set goal, behaving reciprocally and communicating effectively', as well as showing 'cooperative problem solving' (Schneider, 2016). There is an innate need to belong and to relate to others and this drives us to seek rewarding bonds or friendships with others.

So, it is hard, if not impossible, to imagine a life without friends and loved ones. Yet this is the experience of a great number of people, particularly those who struggle with their social skills. They often live in a world that segregates or isolates them as they lack the skills to make and maintain friendships. As Rubin (2002) says, 'Social skills are central to making a child a good friend and well-liked'.

In this chapter, we will mainly consider friendships, but will also refer to other more intimate kinds of relationships. We will consider how to define friendships, the importance and benefits of friendships, how they develop, and finally the link with social competence.

Defining friendships

When considering the question 'What are *relationships* or *friendships*?' we tend to assume that they are simply made from the feelings two people have for one another. We like someone, so we become friends; we love someone, so we become intimate. More often we think the converse: we are friends with someone because we like them; we get romantically involved because we love someone. We all understand what we mean by 'friends' – we consider them precious and believe our lives are enhanced by them; we feel warmth when we call another person a friend; and we profit from friendship in more ways than we can count. Yet the term 'friend' is hard to define and measure and English dictionaries mirror the ambiguity of friendship. In common usage, someone attached by feelings of affection is a friend, someone who acts as a patron or benefactor is a friend, and someone who is not hostile is a friend. So maybe it is a bit more complicated!

Developmental psychologists define friendship as a 'dyadic relationship that is horizontal'. This means that a sense of *equality* is at the core of the definition and distinguishes from other close relationships, such as parent-child, which are vertical in nature. Rubin (2002) says that friendship is 'the one connection in a child's life in which both members have reasonably equal power'. Another defining feature of friendship is that it is *voluntary*, unlike family relationships. 'Friendship is a reciprocal, voluntary affair' Rubin (2002).

Friendship is also based on *mutual affection* or *reciprocity* of liking. Friends are friends because they like each other and want to spend time together. The underpinning connection is an emotional one and mutual affection is at the core of the matter. Hartup and Stevens (1997) also say that the essence of friendship is reciprocity and this exists relatively unchanged across the lifespan. In constrast, the actual exchanges and interactions that occur between friends change with age. So, whereas playing and sharing are the social exchanges which define friendship in young children, social exchanges in adolescents centre on intimacy.

Sociological definitions of friendship are usually quite broad and inclusive. Friends are often assumed to be the peers with whom a child frequently interacts, or they may leave it up to the children to label other children as 'friends' with no check on reciprocity. And with young children, friendship may be defined simply as the relative amount of time they are in physical proximity to one another compared to other peers (Bagwell and Schmidt, 2011). Anthropologists try to use a more universal definition of friendship by focusing more on how it emerges in particular social and cultural contexts, and not on imposing any specific criteria with which to define it. They are more likely to consider friendship an 'idiom of interaction' or 'an idiom of affinity and togetherness' (Bagwell and Schmidt, 2011).

Other writers define friendship in other ways. Amado (1993) identifies four aspects or *dimensions* of friendship that need to be present:

1. *Attraction* is the mystery that brings friends together, and recognises that friends feel some kind of unity that they can preserve, deepen and express by being together. Attraction refers to the 'something' that draws friends together, and keeps relationships alive.
2. *Embodiment* identifies the particular ways in which people physically enact friendship, which differ from person to person, and from relationship to relationship. People may embody a friendship by playing in the park; watching films; making music; running a business together; or meeting once a year to fish.
3. *Power* distinguishes the extent and the ways in which friends can make choices about their relationships, as well as the accommodations that friends make to the personal and structural constraints that affect their friendship. So, whereas most friendships are 'horizontal', there is an assumption that sometimes there is an *agreed* power imbalance.
4. *Community* recognises that friendships are situated within, and contribute to, the life of a community.

Newton et al. (1996) define friendships within the context of four kinds of relationships, or 'circles of friends':

- The *circle of intimacy*, which includes those who are closest to us, and who provide anchors for other aspects of our lives
- The *circle of friendship*, which is not quite as close, but provides good friends and allies
- The *circle of participation*, which includes associates and acquaintances, and people we see regularly in social or work settings
- The *circle of exchange*, which comprises those people who are paid to be in our lives, such as teachers or doctors

It is generally agreed that we experience a better quality of life if we have relationships in all four circles.

So, even though there appears to be some differences, there are three elements that are considered to be the basic criteria of friendship: they are reciprocal, voluntary and based on mutual affection. And what makes a friendship high quality? Well, in addition, we need to see 'affection, trust, self-validation, the wish and willingness to get beyond arguments and conflicts' (Rubin, 2002).

Why are friends important? What are the benefits?

At the most basic level, friendship is important because we value it, and children value it from a very young age. Children will go to great lengths to maintain friendships, and they value their friends as sources of fun, excitement, happiness and good ideas. Rubin (2002) clearly explains the importance of friends in his book *The Friendship Factor*:

> The bottom line is, we are social beings; we need to establish satisfactory and satisfying human connections. Figuring out how to get along with people, how to initiate friendship, how to walk away from relationships that are no longer pleasant and maintain the ones that are enjoyable and valuable – these are the challenges at the core of our emotional lives, and childhood is when we must begin to meet them.

Indeed, few people want to live their lives completely on their own. People need people. As Amado (1993) says:

> Some of the most noble activities in life include having friends and being a friend. Friendship should occupy a strong place in everyone's human development. They call up the best parts of people - sometimes the fun-loving side and sometimes the serious. The saddest thing a person can say about someone is possibly, 'He doesn't have any friends'.

There are also many benefits to having friends. Not only do we value having friends, but friendships can affect many aspects of our lives which we will describe briefly in the following table. We will then describe the impact that friendships can have on a child's development: their social, emotional and cognitive development, and also their psychosocial adjustment.

Table 9.1 The ten benefits of friendships

Benefit	A bit more information	A nice quote or two
1. Quality of life	Our quality of life is very dependent on our personal relationships and how rewarding they are, and most people consider being happy as their main priority. When asked about happiness or quality of life, most of us will mention friends, family or a lover or partner. For example, in a large-scale study of what gave them happiness, single women and men both ranked 'friends and social life' and 'being in love' within their first three most important items.	'Happiness has many meanings, ranging from pleasure and fun to quiet contentment' (Nelson-Jones, 1996) 'Social relationships are one of the most important aspects of most people's lives' (Ouvry, 1998) 'For almost everyone, with or without a disability, the relationships with the people with whom they live, together with other social relationships, are a major contribution to the quality of their lives' (Firth and Rapley, 1990)
2. Meaning	People require meaning in their lives, and throughout our lives we search for it. Though there are other sources of meaning, e.g. work and religion, relationships provide a central purpose in our lives and we may feel incomplete when not in a close relationship.	'Having friends and being with people defines us as human beings. Friends can play many roles in our lives, and without friends life can become increasingly lonely' (Jobling et al, 2000)
3. Belonging	Most people prefer to belong: we want to be part of a family; to be somebody's friend; to be part of a community, or a larger social network. We like to be part of larger units, rather than remain in isolation.	'Rather than be alone they may even remain in unrewarding relationships, since receiving some social recognition seems preferable to no recognition at all' (Nelson-Jones, 1996)
4. Intimacy	Most people prefer not only to be part of friendship networks, but also to have a few intimate relationships. The deepest meaning of friendship is a sense of rapport and intimate engagement - having someone with whom we can share private experiences and emotions. The key here is the feeling that a bond has been established, that someone cares. The resulting intimacy relies heavily on trust, involving discretion, loyalty, and an expectancy of continuity.	'On the most fundamental level, human beings are driven to engage in sexual cooperation' (Schneider, 2016) 'Everyone craves the reward of intimacy in their close relationships. . .each person has a polite or socialised self, and also a personal private self that is not available except in intimacy' (Nelson-Jones, 1996)

5. Success	Our ability to form appropriate relationships can have a direct impact on our ability to be in employment and be successful. For example, the better a child is able to form and maintain friendships, the more likely they are to be accepted and valued within their peer groups and the more likely they are to do well in school and later on in life, thus improving the chance for success.	'Eighty percent of people who fail at work do so for one reason: they do not relate well to other people' (Bolton, 1979) 'There are powerful connections between how well a child fares socially and how successful they are in other areas of their lives' (Rubin, 2002)
6. Healing	People enter close relationships in varying degrees of emotional deprivation based on prior experience. In healthy relationships, we feel free to reveal our fears, vulnerabilities and perceived weaknesses, safe in the knowledge of the underlying love and acceptance we have for one another.	'People who have not worked through rejection from destructive relationships in their past, will enter new relationships feeling and thinking that no one can love all of me. The core of me is dark and unlovable' (Nelson-Jones, 1996)
7. Identity and self-esteem	Throughout life, people can have their identity or sense of who they are developed and crystallised through their relationships. We may receive feedback that we are valuable and worthwhile, and we may try out roles and different ways of behaving. In healthy relationships, we encourage one another as we develop and change, and this helps us develop self-confidence and a belief in ourselves.	'The sense that someone else values you so highly as to be a good friend provides an important form of recognition. . . for it means that people's sense of themselves as valuable. . . is confirmed and strengthened' (Richardson and Ritchie, 1989) 'Without relationships. . . we cannot know what we are like, or what kind of people we would like to be' (Firth and Rapley, 1990)
8. Health	The presence and quality of people's relationships affects our health. The more strongly we are attached to others, the longer we are likely to live. People who are married are less likely to die from a range of illnesses than those who have stayed single. Single people, who have never married, also have higher rates of mental illness.	'Length of life, physical illness and mental illness are all affected positively by close relationships' (Argyle and Henderson, 1985)
9. Support	Relationships can provide people with social and emotional support. Supportive relationships enhance people's ability to cope with stress. Support can include such activities as listening, companionship, offering sympathy, providing information and practical support.	'Friends are people who listen, who understand, who provide the opportunity to share experiences and emotions, both happy and sad' (Richardson and Ritchie, 1989)
10. Development	Friendships are important in childhood as they contribute to a child's social, emotional and cognitive development and on a child's psychosocial adjustment. These are expanded on in the next section of the chapter.	'Friends help each other to think things through more clearly and competently, thus improving problem solving skills. They also learn about what is right and wrong, about loyalty, and what happens when you hurt someone's feelings or betray their trust, thus improving emotional intelligence' (Rubin, 2002)

Friendships and a child's development

As mentioned in the previous table (number 10), there are four areas of a child's development that are affected by friendships: their social development, emotional development, cognitive development, and finally psychosocial adjustment. We will briefly look at each area and how the act of friendship can contribute to their development.

Social development

One of the clearest ways in which friendships contribute to a child's development is that they provide a context for learning and practising social skills and competencies. Because even though friendships require a child to be socially competent, it is also true that children 'hone and develop their social competence in interactions with friends' (Bagwell and Schmidt, 2011). Three components that capture the essence of friendships that contribute in important ways to social competence are companionship, intimacy and conflict.

Companionship

This is one of the key functions of friendship: providing that special companionship that we experience from a friend, as opposed to a class of peers. Companionship involves simply spending time together, engaged in an activity and enjoying one another's company. It is the earliest manifestation of friendship and is mentioned at nearly every age as a centrally important feature of the relationship (Bagwell and Schmidt, 2011). Companionship changes with development and the two most significant factors are language development and play. The table below summarises these changes.

In terms of social development, the companionship of friends appears to promote social competencies that are a by-product of satisfying and effective interpersonal actions: offering and receiving help, sharing and co-operating, and maintaining a sense of reciprocity and equality.

Table 9.2 **Companionship changes**

Age	Play/Activity	Language
18–24 months old	Engaged in similar activities and imitating each other.	Very little spoken language. Laughing with each other.
24–30 months old	Cooperative play. Social play or fantasy.	Communicate about their pretend actions: 'I'm making spaghetti'. Offer direction to the other: 'drive the car to the house'.
Preschool years	Pretend play continues to increase in complexity.	The communication shows an increase in integration and coordination between the two children as they play.

Age	Play/Activity	Language
Middle childhood	Development of reciprocity and cooperation. Enjoying time together, sharing specific tasks and interests together across a variety of settings. Able to cope with give-and-take and understand that some things are enjoyable (or not) for the other person.	Much more complex language and includes being able to suggest activities and discuss topics at length.

Adapted from Bagwell and Schmidt, 2011

Intimacy

Intimacy has already been described as a benefit of a friendship and is easy to picture – the giggling over a shared joke; the sharing of fears and secret crushes; the elaborate games and rituals only known by two friends – these are all images of intimacy within friendships. Intimacy describes a range of behaviours and characteristics between friends; sometimes it refers only to self-disclosure, but sometimes it describes something broader – closeness, nurturance and trust.

Sullivan suggests that the need for intimacy arises between the ages of nine and twelve years and increases through adolescence, and that, whereas self-disclosure is the primary pathway to intimacy and emotional closeness for girls, shared activities *and* self-disclosure lead to closeness for boys. Indeed, asking children about their beliefs about friendships in general indicates that intimacy emerges as a salient expectation of friendships in early adolescence (Bagwell and Schmidt, 2011). They expect friends to trust one another, to confide in one another, to share feelings, ideas and concerns with one another, and to feel emotionally close. Intimacy in friendships in adolescence is also related to well-being and social competence. Buhrmester (cited by Bagwell and Schmidt, 2011) found that adolescents' reports of intimacy were more strongly associated with higher sociability, lower internalising distress and higher self-esteem.

In younger children, intimacy is not expressed as an expectation of friendships and this is probably not surprising, especially as self-disclosure requires more complex language and social skills. But we still see intimacy in friendships being expressed. Young children may enact situations through pretend play that involve fear and anxiety through fantasy play and this suggests that these are displays of disclosure that reflect intimacy in the same way as older children will share secrets and confide in one another. In addition, even sharing fairly mundane information, such as favourite colour or food, may be a precursor to the more intimate self-disclosure found in older children and their friends, therefore acting as a foundation for intimacy in later life.

Conflict

Disagreements are common in every relationship and so they can provide excellent opportunities to develop and practise skills in conflict management, from object disputes in toddlers, that often results in physical aggression (they both wanted the red truck), to interpersonal issues in adolescence that are settled by negotiation or disengagement. There are positive outcomes to these conflicts. Children learn to see the world from someone else's view (they also want to go first), and to consider another person's feelings (allowing their friend to go first will make them happy), and then to negotiate or compromise ('I will go first this time, and then you go first next time'). In this way, children learn effective strategies of handling disagreement that allows the relationship to continue and flourish.

Emotional development

There is a great deal of emotional learning that takes place in the first ten years of life. Children are surrounded by lots of emotional information that is communicated by others – a process that is often referred to as the 'socialisation of emotions' (Bagwell and Schmidt, 2011). This is an important developmental task where children learn to become emotionally competent through understanding the interpersonal consequences of emotion and emotional behaviour. In early childhood, the caregivers are the primary source of emotional information and feedback, showing approval, disapproval and modelling, but as children get older, their peers and friends play a valuable role and 'friendships certainly have the potential to provide unique contexts for emotional development' (Bagwell and Schmidt, 2011).

Bagwell and Schmidt (2011) use Saarni's framework to describe three ways in which friendships are important for emotional development:

1. They offer a *context for learning appropriate emotional expression* and response. For example, friends are more accepting of mild aggression than parents, and children therefore learn that it is socially acceptable to show different emotions with different people in different contexts.
2. They contribute to the *development of emotional knowledge*. For example, friendships can help children to understand that other children have different thoughts and feelings and that talking about their emotions not only helps their emotional knowledge but also their friendship.
3. They provide opportunities to improve *emotion regulation skills*. This is defined by Thompson (1994) as 'extrinsic and intrinsic processes responsible for monitoring, evaluating, and modifying emotional reactions, especially their intensive and temporal features, to accomplish one's goals'. Children learn through lots of people to improve emotional regulation but friends provide opportunities to negotiate conflict and to learn to cooperate which develops their emotion regulation skills, as it ultimately affects both the making and keeping of friends.

Cognitive development

It may seem more obvious that friendships would benefit social and emotional development, but there is good evidence to suggest that children's experiences with friends can also help with cognitive development, primarily through the process of play. Play is an integral part of friendships, especially in young children, and it has a significant role in many aspects of development, in particular providing opportunities for three aspects of cognitive development: language, theory of mind and problem solving.

Language

Play between friends provides an ideal environment for developing language and it can be seen to be associated with friendship in three ways:

1. *In understanding and participating in friendships*, language is used to guide play and allows children to talk about friendships: "We're friends, right?" (Corsaro, 2003).

2. *In conflict resolution,* language is used to explore feelings and resolutions. Friends develop better ways to resolve conflict than acquaintances because they learn to use more emotional and literate language (Pellegrini et al., 1998).
3. *In the development of intimacy,* as language abilities increase, children are better able to express their needs, feelings and preferences, which then has a positive impact on their friendships (Mashburn et al., 2009).

Theory of mind

Theory of mind refers to a person's ability to put themselves in someone else's shoes and to understand that other people have thoughts and feelings that will have an effect on their behaviour. Interactions between friends at play give children opportunity to develop this skill as they engage in cooperative play, which in turn is associated with better theory of mind skills (Cutting and Dunn, cited by Bagwell and Schmidt, 2011). Friends are also more likely to engage in fantasy play, which means that they need to imagine the emotions, thoughts and beliefs of the characters that they play and that their friends play. This kind of play, which encourages children to share and create narratives, is likely to contribute to the development of theory of mind.

Problem solving

Finally, friendships can provide an important context for cognitive development by promoting problem solving and creativity. Friends are better at problem solving as they are able to support one another and offer help that fits their individual strengths and needs. They are also used to cooperating and working together, which promotes effective collaboration. Finally, friends trust and rely on one another and this feeling of security gives them a sense of freedom to explore opinions and ideas between friends. In short, collaboration between friends results in better problem solving and creative outcomes for children.

Psychosocial adjustment

The final benefit of friendships is on a child's psychosocial adjustment and this is immediately appealing to us as adults as it fits in with our understanding of the supportive nature of relationships. Friendships play a significant role in helping children to cope, and in particular there are links with stress, loneliness and depression (Bagwell and Schmidt, 2011). Firstly, normal school transitions between year to year are potentially stressful experiences for children and friends help children to negotiate these. They provide emotional support and security and make school more welcoming and fun. Friends can also provide emotional support when a child is experiencing stress from an outside source and this may then act as a buffer that protects the child from possible feelings of rejection or lack of self-esteem. Finally, many aspects of friendship are associated with warding off feelings of loneliness and depression. Having a friend, spending time with a friend, sharing thoughts and feelings with a friend, these are all positive experiences that will decrease the potential of a child feeling lonely or depressed.

So, there appear to be many benefits from friendships. Not only do friendships affect many aspects of our lives and give us an increased chance of happiness, health, success and self-esteem, but they also have a positive impact on a child's social, emotional and cognitive development, and their psychosocial adjustment. So, how do these friendships start? Are there things we need before we can make friends? And once we have made a friend, how do we help this friendship to continue?

How do friendships develop?

Have you ever thought about how early you see friendships developing in children? We may think that because young children of two or three years don't have the vocabulary to communicate about friendships, that maybe they don't have 'real' friends, but observation of young children tells us different. By the time a child has reached two years of age, children who have the opportunity to play on a regular basis with peers do form specific relationships. They are able to select from among a group of peers an individual (or individuals) with whom they play more frequently. They also respond more positively to invitations to play, and observations of their play show that they act out elaborate play sequences from as early as thirteen to eighteen months (Schneider, 2016). Young children, like adults, seek to satisfy their needs for companionship, affection and intimacy in their play with others. They also respond to each other's distress which can be interpreted as early signs of what is considered the distinguishing feature of a relationship – mutual commitment. So, their relationships can be thought of as friendships.

Of course, friendships don't just occur in a vacuum. It can help to see it as part of the three levels of social connection. As Rubin (2002) explains, children bring to any social exchange certain individual, biologically based characteristics (their nature or temperament), as well as their social skills. These factors lead them to interact with another child in a particular way. The child's *interactions* in turn predict the kinds of *relationships* they will form. And these relationships finally occur within a larger *group* or network. So, if a child is struggling with their friendships, we need to not only understand their individual characteristics and interactional styles, but also the behaviour and norms of the group in which the friendship has been established.

Different friendships and relationships develop in different ways at different times of our lives. Some will not progress further from a casual acquaintance, some develop over time. Some relationships begin and stay in one area of our life and some spill over into different areas. Whatever the course of a relationship, it helps to start by addressing four things: motivation, self-confidence, opportunity and social skills.

Motivation

Motivation is one of the pre-requisites to forming friendships, as without motivation, a relationship is unlikely. As we said earlier, people need people and from a very early age, children are motivated to have friends. Later in life, our motivation is undoubtedly affected by our past experience and some children and adults develop protective ways of coping without friendships.

Where motivation appears to be an issue for someone, they may express this by appearing to be not motivated by friends and preferring to be or play on their own. If this is happening, it may be because of a negative past experience and they have developed protective ways of coping without friendships. In this scenario, lots of careful handling and reassurance is required and, if the child is at school, ideally they will support the child to experience small amounts of success.

However, some children are truly not motivated to have friends and it is important to consider this, even if we cannot understand it. I have worked with children who have communicated clearly to me, either verbally or through their behaviour, that they find being around other children stressful and they prefer to play on their own. We must listen to them and not force them into friendships that they do not want. Instead, we can help them to cope with being around other people by helping them to understand what people are doing and why. For example, we may explain it in a social story so that they know what to expect from others. We may also teach them strategies to be accepted by their peers so that life at school, and after school, is easier. We may suggest a circle of friends approach in their school, so that their peers understand and accept them for who they are. Or we may write some social rules to help them understand the complex world of relationships and socially acceptable behaviour. One autistic lady once said to me, 'You will never teach me to be sociable, but please help me to be socially appropriate and accepted'.

Self-confidence

Self-confidence is also important as we need to believe in our own value as a friend. Of course, self-confidence also comes from relationships and friendships, and one of the main purposes of friendship is to build and maintain self-esteem. A person's self-esteem will help them at every stage of developing a friendship: saying hello, asking someone to play, or inviting them to a sleep-over.

So, if a child is struggling with their friendships, it is always relevant to consider what their self-esteem is like. Do they like themselves? Do they struggle with their confidence? If this is the case, then this will be affecting their ability to make friends and this is where we may need to start work. We may try to help them to develop their self-identity so that they see themselves accurately and positively. Or help them to recognise their strengths and qualities. Or help them to develop their ability to talk about their feelings and learn ways to handle them.

Opportunity

Opportunity is a factor in making friends as we need to go out to meet people face-to-face and, as adults, we sometimes need to force ourselves to go to certain places to meet like-minded people. For most adults, such opportunities present themselves in the course of everyday activity/occupation, but for children, they are more dependent on their parents to create these opportunities. Of course, school does give them the ideal opportunity, but if school is not going so well for a child, it may be necessary for parents to consider clubs where a child could meet potential friends. A few years ago, I worked with a family where the mum created a Saturday play session for her child and invited a few other potential friends from her girl's class. She set up games for the girls that promoted social interaction and that, in turn, had a positive impact on their relationships at school.

Social skills

Social skills are also needed, as we need the skills to interact with each other appropriately and a lack of social skills may be a barrier to making relationships. As Rubin says, 'Social skills are central to making a child a good friend and well-liked' (2002). We need the skills to interact with others appropriately, to listen to them, to know what to say, and to talk about things that are interesting to the other person. We need the skills to behave appropriately, to not touch or stand too close to them. If a child is struggling with their social skills, then this is something that will fundamentally affect their ability to make friends. Of course, as we said earlier, it is also important to remember that friends also help us to become more socially skilled, so there is a two-way process here. However, a lack of social competence will always be a barrier in the first place.

So, having considered these four underpinning factors, what then helps friendships to form and be maintained? Some of these go back to the benefits we get from a friendship and some to what defines a friendship, and some are just about logistics. The following table outlines the main factors that help friendships to develop.

Table 9.3 What causes friendships to develop?

The key factors	A bit more information	A nice quote or two
1. Proximity	Being physically close not only increases the likelihood that a child will be become a friend, but it reduces the effort needed to maintain the relationships. Some writers call this community, as it infers that friendships are more likely to arise out of a neighbourhood or school.	'Children are more likely to form friendships with peers from their own neighbourhood or school' (Furfey, cited by Schneider, 2016)
2. Similarity	Similarity is important in that it helps the mutual enjoyment of shared activities (see below). Also children at all ages resemble their friends more than their non-friends, as do adults. Similarity not only brings people together, but predicts that friendships will remain stable.	'Similarity in values and attitudes can reduce dissonance in a friendship and increase the chance of agreement' (Schneider, 2016) 'Friends appear to be more similar in terms of age, sex, race and social status' (Berndt, 1982)
3. Shared activities	The sharing of activities is particularly important in young children but remains an element even in adult friendships.	'The substance of childhood friendship is usually considered to be the sharing of common pastimes' (Rubin et al., cited by Schneider, 2016)
4. Reciprocity	This is a core part of how we define friendship, as the connection between two people is an emotional one and mutual affection is at the core of the matter. Without this, friendships will not last.	'The essence of friendship is reciprocity and this exists relatively unchanged across the lifespan' (Hartup and Stevens, 1997)
5. Intimacy	Intimacy has already been described in terms of a benefit and in terms of the importance it plays in a child's development. As such, it is also a requirement to develop and maintain a friendship, particularly in older children and adolescents.	Intimacy is broadly defined as 'the outcome of a collaborative, affectively based relationship that is grounded in reciprocal caring, closeness and involvement between equals' (Sullivan, cited by Bagwell and Schmidt, 2011)
6. Sharing and support	Helping a friend by lending them something appears to be a key element of childhood friendship, and in early adolescence the ability of a friend to stand up for them and support them becomes more important than shared activities.	'Of all the features of friendship, it is the support that friends provide at times of stress that is considered the link between friendship and general well-being' (Schneider, 2016)

The key factors	A bit more information	A nice quote or two
7. Trust	Trust plays an important role in maintaining friendships, although the expectations change with age from guarding secrets in young children to honesty and genuineness in adolescents.	'Reciprocal, dyadic trust. . . has been found to be an important component, particularly in the friendships of school-aged girls' (Betts and Rotenberg, 2008)
8. Exclusivity	Most children like to enjoy the exclusive attention of their friends and will experience jealousy when they don't. So exclusivity can be a factor in the maintenance of a friendship.	'Both boys and girls with low self-esteem, poor social skills, and inadequate problem-solving abilities may be particularly vulnerable to feeling jealous' (Schneider, 2016)
9. Conflict and competition	As we said earlier, if children can learn effective strategies to handle a disagreement, the friendship is more likely to continue and flourish.	'Friends worked harder to find a compromise and they displayed greater sensitivity in their discussions than non-friends' (Fonzi, cited by Schneider, 2016)
10. Forgiveness and apologising	Apologising and forgiveness are part of resolving conflict within a relationship and will reduce the hurt that can follow.	'Seeking reconciliation is particularly common within relationships that are close and highly valued' (Schneider, 2016)

The table above summarises the key considerations in the development and maintenance of friends and we can see that they can be further divided into three subheadings:

- The factors that will help a friendship to develop in the first place: *proximity* and *similarity*
- The factors that need to be part of a friendship in order for it to develop: *shared activities*, *reciprocity and intimacy*, *sharing and support* and *trust*
- The skills that need to be there (or learnt) to maintain a friendship: *exclusivity (or handling jealousy)*, *handling conflict or competition*, and learning to *apologise and forgive*

Friendship skills and the link to social skills

I believe we have mentioned social skills enough in this chapter to confidently conclude that social skills are inextricably linked to our ability to make friends. But to summarise, there are two main ways in which social skills and friendships are linked:

1. Social skills are central to making a child a good friend and well-liked, and a lack of social skills will be a barrier to making friends. Being socially unskilled will affect how others react to us. If we look at the definition of social inadequacy by Trower et al. (1978), they say that

a person can be regarded as socially inadequate if he is unable to affect the behaviour and feelings of others in the way that he intends and society accepts. Such a person will appear annoying, unforthcoming, uninteresting, cold, destructive, bad-tempered, isolated or inept, *and will be generally unrewarding to others.*

2. In addition, even though friendships require a child to be socially competent, it is also true that children hone and develop their social competence in interactions with friends. This is one of the clearest ways in which friendships contribute to a child's development, in that they provide a context for learning and practising social skills and competencies.

So, social skills are both needed in order to make friends and be liked by others, and then friendships are needed to help children further develop their social skills.

Relating online

It is a question I get asked a lot: 'Is the internet to blame for the difficulties we are seeing in children these days?' Some writers talk about a recent decline in social interaction and intimacy, especially in boys, and that the most salient reason for this is a greater portion of social interaction is occurring by means of electronic communication (Schneider, 2016). They also argue that online 'friendships' bear little resemblance to the traditional notion of friendship and are in particular devoid of intimacy (Turkle, cited by Schneider, 2016). It is, of course, true that the world is a very different place to a few years ago, but if the interpersonal relationships of children and adolescents are becoming more superficial than in previous years – which is sometimes claimed but has not been proven – it is by no means clear that the new technology is at fault.

In fact, the research to date seems to indicate more benefit than harm in establishing and maintaining friendships online (Schneider, 2016). Some argue that the internet may facilitate close interpersonal relating by individuals who have trouble being intimate in face-to-face encounters. Relating to others competently online is a vital twenty-first-century social skill and maybe that is the issue. We need to adapt our way of thinking to include this aspect of social skills training.

I recently heard an autistic man (as he likes to be described) talk about his use of technology and how it improves the quality of his life. He talked about designing the environment so that it doesn't disable the autistic person. He talked about having more control and autonomy. But he also talked about communication. He uses technology to communicate more successfully with others and to give him a 'social life', and he said that some weeks he has most of his social interaction over the internet. Is this wrong? Does this disable him or help him? I know what he would say! So, I don't think there is a simple answer to this question. As with many things in life, we have to take a step back and look at the individual and their situation. Because sometimes it gets in the way and sometimes it helps.

Key points from Chapter 9

This chapter covered friendship skills – what a friend is, why they are important, how they develop and the link with social skills.

Defining friendship skills

There are some differences in the way that friendship can be defined, but there are three elements that are considered to be the basic criteria of friendship: that they are reciprocal, voluntary and based on mutual affection.

Why are friends important? What are the benefits?

There are ten benefits of having a friend that directly have an impact on our lives:

- Quality of life
- Meaning
- Belonging
- Intimacy
- Success
- Healing
- Identity and self esteem
- Health
- Support
- Development

There are also four areas of a child's development that are affected by friendships:

- Social development: and in particular companionship, intimacy and conflict
- Emotional development
- Cognitive development: and in particular language, theory of mind and problem solving
- Psychosocial adjustment

In each area, we explored how the act of friendship contributed to a child's development.

How do friendships develop?

There are four things that are necessary to assess initially:

- Motivation
- Self confidence
- Opportunity
- Social skills

In addition, there are other factors that will help a friendship to develop and then be maintained.

- Factors that help a friendship to develop in the first place include *proximity* and *similarity*

- The factors that need to be part of a friendship in order for it to develop: *shared activities, reciprocity and intimacy, sharing & support* and *trust*
- The skills that need to be there (or learnt) to maintain a friendship: *exclusivity (or handling jealousy), handling conflict or competition,* and learning to *apologise and forgive*

Friendship skills and the link to social skills

Social skills are inextricably linked to friendship skills in two ways:

1. Social skills are necessary to help a child make friends, and be accepted and liked by others.
2. Children use their friendships to hone and further develop their social skills.

Relating online

Currently research does not show that technology has an adverse effect on friendships and may indicate more benefit in some cases.

Chapter 10

The development of social skills

'The strength people need to proceed along the path of human development can come only from the spiritual worlds.'

Rudolf Steiner, Austrian philosopher (1861–1925)

All parents want their children to be socially competent. To have a child who makes friends, who is accepted and liked by others and who can meet the challenges of everyday life without being crushed by them. We want our child to be able to manoeuvre their way through life successfully, safely and happily through the sometimes complicated social world of the playground, dinner hall, classroom and a friend's home. And most children do learn to become socially competent. But how do they get there?

Some children seem to arrive at this goal of social competence with very little help from us. From an early age they happily head off to school, to meet friends, to talk to relatives in a cheerful and confident manner. For another child, though, this social competence does not come easily or effortlessly at all. They need support, help and patience from us and from those around us. The frustrating thing is that as parents, we may have two children who are very different and it can lead us to feel frustrated as to why Charlie is not as socially skilled as Sam. What has gone wrong?

Rubin (2002) says that children will tend to behave in one of three ways: children will naturally *move towards* others, *move away from* others or *move against* others, and that the first step to understanding how to help our child develop social competence is to understand what kind of person they are. We will discuss this later in the chapter on parents, but it also shows us that the development of social competence is maybe not as straightforward as we like to think.

It is often assumed that social competence is a skill that is purely learned. Indeed, we said in chapter one that *social skills are behaviours which can be learned* through imitation, modelling and reinforcement as a child is growing up. Children acquire social competence in a similar way to an understanding of mathematics or science – through exploring, problem solving, practising and gradually building up knowledge with the help of friends, parents and adults. We also know that children reared in isolation miss out on essential learning experiences and, as a result, display 'distorted, socially unacceptable forms of behaviour' (Newton, cited by Hargie, 2017). However, even though this is true, it doesn't completely explain the normal development of social skills and the remarkable variation in people's ability to be socially competent. There are factors that will influence a child's development of social skills. So, in this chapter we will explore some of the factors that affect a child's potential and ability to be socially skilled, including genetics, attachment, child rearing, reinforcement and observational learning from parents and peers. We will then talk about what can go wrong and summarise at what age certain behaviours would be expected to be seen.

Genetics and biology

I used to be fascinated by genetics. As one of six children, I used to regularly wonder how the six of us looked similar, but different. Some of us had my dad's distinctive nose and some had my mum's, but I had neither! And why did none of us have my mum's gorgeous thick red hair? More interesting was how we were so different in our temperaments. We are all pretty talkative (our house was quite noisy!), but some of us had heaps of confidence and some were anxious and emotional. Some of us liked to please others and some of us pushed at all the boundaries. And I saw my parents treat us differently as a result. They were careful with some of us and could be more direct and demanding with the others. As a result, my childhood was far from dull and one of the main reasons was my lovely, large, loving and noisy family. Of course, I now have children of my own and my interest continues. One has brown hair, one has fair and one has red. One sailed through school socially, one sailed through school academically and one had to fight the system at every step of the way. So how did their social skills develop and why are they so different, just like I am so different from my siblings?

Every child is born with a set of genes which determines their eye colour, hair colour and height, but genes will also affect how they will act around other people. These are the aspects of their personality or temperament which will affect whether they are outgoing and confident around others, or cautious and shy. This means that some of a child's core inclinations in terms of approaching other children will have nothing to do with their environment and their parents, but will be down to who they are biologically. In other words, they are hard-wired to behave in a certain way. Schneider (2016) says that there is now ample evidence to suggest a substantial genetic basis for shyness, aggressive behaviour and even for children being targets of aggression. He describes two genetic models: the direct and the indirect:

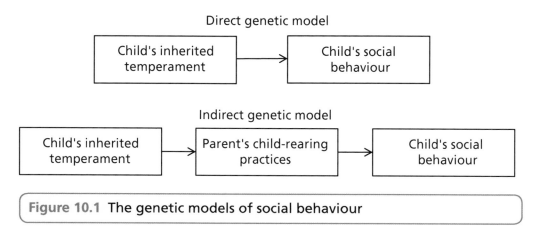

Figure 10.1 The genetic models of social behaviour

Many researchers who study brain activity also see biological differences in children. So, for example, they will see some who have excessive frontal brain activity, even at rest, and will say that this is a marker of an underlying disposition. These children will also have low vagal tone (a measurement of heart rate and the overall efficiency of the nervous system). This all means that they are more biologically predisposed to react to an unfamiliar situation with fear and anxiety, and tend to be more behaviourally inhibited (Rubin, 2002).

The other main difference to consider with biology is whether we are male or female and this was also discussed in chapter one. We know that the right hemisphere, which is the creative side, controls the left side of the body, while the left hemisphere controls logic, reason, speech and the body's right side. The left brain is where language and vocabulary is stored and the right brain stores and controls visual information (see Figure 1.1 in Chapter 1).

In 2001, researchers from Harvard found that certain parts of the brain were different sizes in males and females. They found that parts of the frontal lobe, responsible for problem-solving and decision-making, and the limbic cortex, responsible for regulating emotions, were larger in women. In men, the parietal cortex, which is involved in space perception, and the amygdala, which regulates sexual and social behaviour, were larger (Hoag, 2008). Baron-Cohen (2003) also says that male and female minds are different. Men tend to be better at analysing systems (better systemisers), while women tend to be better at reading the emotions of other people (better empathisers). Baron-Cohen shows that this distinction arises from biology, not culture. The main differences according to Baron-Cohen are summarised in the following table:

Table 10.1 The differences between male and female brains

Area	Female	Male
Cell numbers		Men have 4% more brain cells than women, and about 100 grams more of brain tissue.
Cellular connections	Women have more dendritic connections between brain cells	
Corpus callosum	A woman's brain has a larger corpus callosum, which means women can transfer data between the right and left hemisphere faster than men and they have greater access to both sides.	Men tend to be more left brained.
Language	Women seem to be able to use both sides for language. This gives them an advantage in reading nonverbal cues and the emotion of a message.	Language is most often just in the dominant hemisphere (usually the left side).
Limbic size	Women often have a larger deep limbic system than males. This means women are more in touch with their feelings; have an increased ability to bond and to be connected to others; and a more acute sense of smell. However, it also leaves a female more susceptible to depression, and suicide attempts.	

So how does this all link to the development of social skills? As we said in chapter one, boys find it harder to learn conversational skills and are slower to develop language. This would appear to be directly linked to a difference between the male and female brain. As we have also said, the corpus callosum (the neural fibres which connect the left and right hemispheres) is larger in the female brain. This means that messages travel faster between the two hemispheres, so the language part of the brain (Broca's area) on the left side can communicate more easily with the right side, which is where interpretation of nonverbal behaviour mainly occurs. This is backed up by Simon Baron-Cohen (2003) who found that women use both sides of their brains in language tasks and men just use the left hemisphere, with few connections bridging the two hemispheres.

So how much of children's social behaviour can be explained by *heredity* (genetics or biology) and how much can be explained by the *environment*? Behavioural geneticists have spent many years trying to tease out the effects of inborn dispositional influences and the effects of the human environment on the children's temperament and social behaviour. And there is now wide consensus that both genetic and environmental influences determine virtually every aspect of human development, including the development of social competence.

Geneticists talk about *gene-environment correlations* and *gene-environment interactions* when looking at a child's development. Gene-environment *correlations* refer to situations where heritable factors co-occur with specific situations. So a sporty child attends a sports club chosen by their parents to develop their athletic ability, or an aggressive child seeks out other aggressive children to play with. Their genetic make-up is influencing the situations in which they find themselves. Gene-environment *interactions* occur when the environment triggers or suppresses an inherited trait. So a child who is genetically predisposed to being aggressive is harassed by a peer group and becomes aggressive, and rejection by peers triggers depressive feelings in a child who has this in their genetic make-up. The environment is influencing their genetic make-up.

So indisputably it would appear that biology matters when considering the development of social skills. We can't make a shy, anxious child into a confident, gregarious child. But we *can* support the child who is inhibited to be happier and liked by their peers. We *can* help the child who is struggling with their social skills to be more socially competent. So, the environment also plays a part. There are many factors that are interlinked and impact on one another, but in particular we will discuss the development of joint attention and symbolic communication, and the impact of attachment, child-rearing, reinforcement and observational learning.

Joint attention and symbolic communication

By the end of the first year, most children are beginning to show the signs of social competence. They are able to coordinate attention between objects and people, engage in social exchanges and communicate intentionality, using gestures and sounds that have shared meanings. These skills of joint attention and symbolic communication are important to the development of social competence.

Joint attention contributes to social competence in children because it enables them to be 'active social partners in learning to talk' (Wetherby, 2006). There are three developmental achievements that contribute to this skill: sharing attention, sharing affect and sharing intentions, and these all develop within the first year of life. The ability to *share attention* starts at birth and continues to develop over the first year, from the child and adult sharing attention with the adult monitoring what the child is looking at, to the child actively observing others and shifting their gaze between objects and people to check the adult's focus of attention.

They are also able to follow an adult's attentional focus and this is the basis for the ability to be able to figure out another person's visual perspective and intentions.

Sharing affect is seen when children display pleasure or discomfort and then direct their gaze to the adult, to either share an experience or seek comfort. Children are also learning how to interpret the emotional states of others, as the adult then responds to their emotional expressions by mirroring the child's emotion. Finally, *sharing intentions* refers to being able to signal or direct behaviours in order to achieve a goal, or communicate intentionally. This could include holding out their arms to be picked up, or pointing at an object that they want picked up. Intentional communication develops from early gestures and sounds to the emergence of first words and symbolic communication, which is the ability to use words to refer to objects and events. The discovery that things have names begins to develop at about 12 months and, by their second birthday, most children can use and understand hundreds of words and can combine them into simple sentences.

The development of joint attention and symbolic communication enables children to become active partners in the intricate dance of reciprocal social communication. Children are learning to share experiences with others and to understand that other people have their own minds, and that thoughts and feelings can be shared with others through communication. As Wetherby (2006) says:

> These emerging capacities form the developmental underpinnings needed to engage in conversation, as children learn to consider the experience, knowledge and perspective of the social partner, to connect sentences in a cohesive manner, and to negotiate meaning. These capacities are essential to acquiring conversational competence, which entails knowing what to say, how to say it, how to interpret what others say, and how to participate in a reciprocal social exchange, depending on who you are talking to and what you are talking about.

Attachment

As we previously said in the chapter on self-esteem, 'attachment styles reflect individual differences in prototypical, internal working models of self and others formed in the context of the early caregiver-infant relationship' (Park and Crocker, 2013). However, we can also consider the impact that child-parent attachment, or the emotional connection between parent and child, has on the development of social competence. Attachment theorists claim that 'an attentive caregiver provides a secure base to support the child in its exploration of its objective and interpersonal environment' (Schneider, 2016). Bowlby (1980) suggested that infants create an 'internal working model' of themselves, their world and social contacts with their world. These are essentially mental pictures of relationships that the child uses to understand and predict other people's behaviour.

Secure attachment is believed to serve as a healthy foundation for exploring the world and the quirks of close personal relationships later on in life (Bowlby, 1980). The secure child becomes that way through responsive and sensitive attention from their parents, who from the start recognise their emotional signals and respond promptly and appropriately to their needs. The child then develops the belief that 'his parent is someone who can be relied on for protection, nurturance, and comfort. From that belief system or secure *internal working model*, in turn, grows his sense of trust in relationships in general' (Rubin, 2002).

The *anxious-resistant*, insecurely attached child, experiences a parenting style that is somewhat unpredictable and is usually characterised by intrusive control and over involvement in activities. As Rubin (2002) explains, biology and parenting work together here. Fearful babies mean that parents want to shield them more from danger and this well-intentioned effort to keep these children from feeling anxious and upset may lead to them being over-protective and controlling. This in turn intensifies and reinforces the child's biological tendencies.

Of course, this may lead us to have disconcerting thoughts like 'my son is clearly fearful and timid, so maybe I did something wrong back when he was a baby?' However, if we are thinking this, we should be reassured by the fact that mother-child attachment changes over time and other factors come into play. Indeed, the assumption that only security of attachment influences a child's adjustment has been challenged by a number of people (summarised by Schneider, 2016) and they state that we should be cautious when applying internal working models to developmental processes. They claim that attachment can be affected by many factors: the child's temperament, emotionality and sociability, and the parent's personality, sensitivity and responsiveness, and the stress under which they live. All will influence the security of the attachment between child and parent. Significantly, John Bowlby, the 'founding father of contemporary attachment theory' (Rubin, 2002) used the term 'internal *working* model' to indicate his belief that thoughts and feelings about relationships are subject to change – meaning that the child who doesn't feel very secure or confident can become more so over time. And this is where 'child-rearing' comes into play.

Child-rearing

Parents have a huge responsibility in the upbringing of their children, especially in the teaching of general values and interpersonal relationships. But for many years it was believed that children's behaviour was *only* caused by the way their parents raised them. University lecturers, religious leaders and psychologists, who all gave advice to parents, possessed a passionate need to believe in the nurture assumption. Our child's behaviour is a reflection on our parenting skills.

However, even though child-rearing does not have as causal a role as once thought, we should still explore it, especially when considering the development of social competence, because of all the various causes of children's social competence, parents' child-rearing is one of the easiest to change, as it is under their control. This has been evidenced by many systematic parent-training programmes that have been successful in managing the antisocial behaviours of pre-delinquent youths. So 'even if a trait is genetically determined to a considerable extent, an appropriate environment may mitigate the effects of the genetic pre-programming on the observable behaviour of the child' (Schneider, 2016). This is also called 'goodness of fit' (Chess and Thomas, 1996), which emphasises that children's overt behaviour and adjustment depend on the abilities of families and schools to provide them with an environment that 'fits' their temperaments. This means that the environment should offer the degree of structure, predictability and support needed by individuals of a particular temperament.

Parenting practises have been described in different ways, but Baumrind's (1989) classification system of parenting styles is most widely used. He distinguishes between authoritarian, permissive and authoritative. The *authoritarian* style involves strict limits enforced by punishment. The *permissive* style involves very few restrictions. And the *authoritative* style involves parental warmth and clear limits, backed up by reasoning rather than punishment.

The link between parenting styles and social competence can be seen if we look at the research into different types of children. This is shown in the following table which has been taken from Schneider's summary of the research into this area (2016):

Table 10.2 Child-rearing practices linked to social competence

The child who is . . .	The parents tend to be . . .
Socially competent	More child-centred, feelings-orientated, warmer. Involved with their children and encourage expressions of emotions. Explain their thinking and provide democratic households. Fair and consistent. Will actively initiate peer contacts and provide direct guidance or 'coaching' in how to make friends.
Aggressive	Punitive and excessively restrictive or controlling. They do not respond adequately to positive expressions of emotion.
Shy/withdrawn	Distant, cold, protective, restrictive, hostile and domineering.
Also . . .	*If* they have a shy girl and they demonstrate active and responsive problem solving, their child is less likely to be rejected by their peers, despite being shy. *If* they actively support the development of their child's social skills and their development of friendships at school, they are less likely to have children who are bullied.

In summary, what a large amount of research shows is that children who display competent and incompetent social behaviours receive very different treatment from their parents. But we can no longer put all the blame onto child-rearing and say that it *causes* social incompetence (or competence). We now know that genetics has much to offer us in terms of an explanation and that the child's temperament can affect the parents' behaviour as much as the child-rearing affects the child (as we saw in the indirect genetic model of social behaviour).

Indirect genetic model

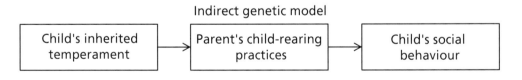

Figure 10.2 The indirect genetic model of social behaviour

Observational learning – parents

As well as their role in child-rearing, it is also vital for the child to learn their social skills from their parents. We know that social skills are behaviours which can be learned as a child is growing up, through imitation, modelling and reinforcement. Children acquire social competence through exploring, problem solving, practising and gradually building up knowledge with the help of friends, parents and adults. And parents are obviously well-placed to have the biggest impact on a child's learning, especially in the early years. We first experience the training process at an early age. Right from the beginning, parents and carers influence social skills development when they ascribe intentionality to the baby's behaviour ('you are hungry, aren't you?') and they treat them as a communicating being.

Parents also reward certain nonverbal behaviours, such as smiling, and communicate displeasure over other kinds of behaviour, such as throwing or shouting. When we have learnt to talk, they teach us to speak in a certain way. The child is taught that, even though they didn't want to go and see their elderly aunt, it is polite to smile at her and say 'it's lovely to see you'. They are also taught not to interrupt if two adults are talking and to say 'excuse me'. And the examples go on – 'sit up straight', 'look at me when I am talking to you', 'say please', and probably my favourite, 'don't use that tone of voice!' This is an important first step in their social development.

In addition to the admonitions they gave, these important people in the child's life are also modelling certain ways of behaving. Perhaps they rarely show their feelings. They may use sarcasm and put-downs regularly. And, as children, we learn by the example of the significant others in our lives as well as from their instructions, and as Bolton (1979) says, 'cultural norms in our society reinforce much of the training we received'.

The process of social learning involves primarily *modelling* and *imitation* of good social skills. Children will copy their parents and will learn to act and talk like them. In addition, a second major element in learning these social behaviours is the *reinforcing* of good skills and the *discouraging* of inappropriate ones. So, children learn to use behaviours that are encouraged, and they will tend to not use behaviours that are discouraged or ignored. This is such an important aspect to social development, that we will explore it in a bit more detail in the next section. Finally, parents will also sometimes use *direct teaching* of some skills e.g. good listening, and even *role-playing* certain situation and these will be discussed in more detail in the chapter on 'Teaching social skills: social skills interventions'.

Reinforcement

'From early childhood, the role of social rewards, in the form of verbal or nonverbal reinforcement, is crucial' (Hargie, 2017). Hargie goes on to explain that a fundamental principle governing behaviour is that people tend to do things associated with 'positively valued outcomes' and will not persist in doing things that have produced either little positive reward or an unwanted negative outcome. So, if all my friends laugh when I tell a joke, I am more likely to tell another one on another occasion. If my mother smiles at me when I say thank you to her, I am more likely to say thank you again. So, the key feature about reinforcement is that it increases the future probability of the behaviour that led to it. Hargie also talks about the research studies which have shown the benefits of reinforcement in teaching, to not only improve pupils' social behaviour but also their engagement and academic achievement. So, what gets rewarded, gets done.

Positive reinforcement can take many forms. It can be a verbal or nonverbal reward: 'Good job, Alex' (with a big smile and a pat on my back!). Or it can be a material object, money, a privilege or a valued activity. The important thing is that whatever is given as the positive reinforcement needs to be rewarding to that child. I have worked with children, for example, who would not like to be praised in front of other pupils and some who would love that. The reward or the reinforcement has to work for that person to be effective.

Negative reinforcement on the other hand is associated with 'the avoidance, termination or reduction of an adverse stimulus' (Hargie, 2017). We have a headache, we take a painkiller, the headache disappears, so we are more likely to take another painkiller next time we have a headache. We feel stressed, so we have an alcoholic drink or a smoke, we feel less stressed, so we are more likely to drink or smoke in the future to reduce our stress. In conversations we may be bored by someone else, so we bring the conversation to an end. We are questioned in a heated debate and we feel vulnerable, so we argue back. We break a rule, we apologise, and we feel better. In both positive and negative reinforcement, we are promoting or encouraging a targeted behaviour.

Finally, there is *punishment* and *extinction*. Punishment is where we take away something desired (the TV) or we introduce something unpleasant (a telling off). We are using punishment to suppress behaviour. Extinction is where nothing happens in response to behaviour and so the behaviour stops. In both punishment and extinction, we are suppressing or eliminating a targeted behaviour.

The following diagram shows an example of two behaviours – one positive and one negative and an example of how positive reinforcement and punishment might work for each.

Positive reinforcement has been found to be important in the development of social competence: children need positive reinforcement from others to learn how to be socially competent. However, they also need to experience it for another reason. Social encounters should be in themselves rewarding and we do need people to use positive reinforcement within any interaction. So, children not only need to experience it from others to help them learn how to be socially competent, but they also need to learn the importance of doing it themselves within any interaction, so that they can be accepted by their peers.

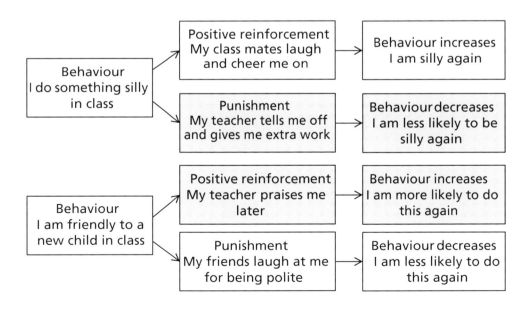

Figure 10.3 Positive reinforcement versus punishment

There are five core reinforcement categories:

> ### The five core reinforcement categories
>
> 1. Primary (what we depend on for survival, e.g. food)
> 2. Conditioned (e.g. tokens, stickers)
> 3. Social (behaviour of others)
> 4. Sensory (e.g. listening to music, watching sport)
> 5. Activity (e.g. the act of eating)

Social reinforcers are the main types of rewards that will govern or shape the social behaviour of others and are therefore the most important when considering the development of social competence. These are summarised below:

Table 10.3 Social reinforcers

Social process rewards	The mere presence of others, their attention and their responsiveness will be reinforcing to the other person and will encourage them to continue. *I sit with you. I listen to you. I smile at you. You continue.*
Social content rewards	The acts of showing praise, sympathy, approval, affection. *You do something good, I praise you. You do it again. You tell me something sad, I say how sorry I am and I offer you a hug. You confide in me again.*
Generalised reinforcers	The influence of their social setting and the reactions they get from their environment. *We do something that gets the respect of our peers. We do it again. We tell a joke and the class laughs. We do it again.*

In summary, reinforcement plays an important role in how social skills develop because what we do, the decisions we make and the feelings we have about ourselves and others can be shaped and moulded by the reactions of others.

Observational learning – peers and siblings

For some time, an accepted opinion of child development has been that children mostly learn how to act from their parents. However, more recently psychologists have been interested in how children learn from their peers and siblings. Researchers have found that children do indeed learn from other children and that the process of observation and imitation of peers influences individual patterns of behaviour (Schneider, 2016). Modelling their actions on other children, 'he repeats them, abandons them, or adjusts them according to the reception they get' (Rubin, 2002). Schneider (2016) also describes the process of 'group socialisation theory' which states that 'peers . . . are seen as the major socialising agents who determine the ways in which children relate to others'. He goes on to say that children are hard-wired to imitate other children, to seek out their company and to attempt to conform to the norms of their peer group. It is through the reinforcing and encouraging, or discouraging, from their peers that children learn when it is OK to be silly and the accepted (or cool) way to say hello. These peer friendships give children a safe place in which to test out behaviours and learn how to be socially successful.

Children also often spend a great deal of time in the presence of older children or siblings who are maybe taking responsibility for them, and who are therefore actually taking part in the child-rearing. Siblings in particular are important when it comes to coaching their younger brothers or sisters in social skills, especially when we consider the amount of time siblings often spend together. If we compare the interaction with siblings, we see that there are similarities to the skills needed to relate to peers and so siblings will undoubtedly influence a child's ability to relate to and be accepted by their peers.

Learning the 'why and when'

The final thing we need to consider in the development of social skills is the skill of learning why and when to behave in a certain way. As a child grows, they begin to be less influenced by their 'instructors' and are able to assess situations for themselves. They are more sensitive to situations and other people and are able to choose an appropriate course of action. They are then able to review their course of action and assess how effective they were. This is when children learn to use their knowledge of what other people think and feel to help them alter their behaviour accordingly.

Cameron (2000) says:

> A 'skilled' person does not only know how to do certain things, but also understands *why* those things are done the way they are. S/he is acquainted with the general principles of the activity s/he is skilled in, and so is able to modify what s/he does in response to the exigencies of any specific situation.

This means that the child has to learn *when* to use certain behaviours, as well as what behaviours to use and how to use them. This involves developing the appropriate thought processes necessary to consider the interpersonal encounter and the timing of certain skills. In short, this means that it can be as socially unskilled to say the right thing at the wrong time as to say the wrong thing at the right time.

The development of theory of mind

The development of a child's social skills is closely related to the child's development of theory of mind, as we have previously mentioned. Theory of mind covers two separate concepts: gaining the understanding that other people also have minds, with different and separate beliefs, desires, mental states and intentions; and being able to form theories as to what those beliefs, desires, mental states and intentions are. In brief, Baron-Cohen (2000) describes it as being able 'to reflect on the content of one's own and others' minds'. It is also often characterised as being able to 'put yourself into another's shoes'. Poor conversational skills or social skills can be interpreted as stemming from a lack of understanding that other people have access to different information or knowledge, and that communication occurs through the exchange of information. Hale and

Tager-Flusberg (2005) says that this lack of understanding, or theory of mind deficit, will result in difficulty engaging in reciprocal social discourse. The link between a child's development of theory of mind is therefore closely related to their social skill development.

This will be discussed more in the following chapter, but the normal development of theory of mind will have an impact on a child's ability to work out when to say something, as it is dependent on them being able to read the situation and how someone is feeling. An example would be a child who has learnt a joke, but knows it is not appropriate to tell it to her parents when she sees them talking very seriously to their neighbour. She does tell it later when they are relaxed and having a meal together.

Children need to learn this skill of when to say what, and Hargie (2017) describes a four-stage process in learning this skill:

Four stage process in learning when to say what

1. *Observation.* As we have described earlier, the child watches others perform the skill and pays attention to other dimensions such as motivations, values and how they vary with different audiences.
2. *Emulation.* The child emulates the behaviour but does not replicate it. For example, the style of praise may be similar but the actual words will differ.
3. *Self-control.* The child begins to master the skill and will practise it.
4. *Self-regulation.* Finally, the child learns to use the skill in different contexts and with different people.

Other factors that affect the development of social skills

Normal development of social skills can also be adversely affected by two other factors that have not yet been mentioned and which we will briefly discuss: attitudes to the environment and effects of deprivation.

Attitudes to the environment

People who struggle with their social skills are often affected by the attitudes of others and their environment, and are therefore less likely to be able to have control over and manage the situations they are in. They are more likely to experience feelings of powerlessness to control their environment and to experience situations where they are de-skilled by the attitudes of others. The implications for people with specific difficulties or disabilities are obvious. They are often treated as people with 'needs' as opposed to 'strengths', leading them to a belief that they are possibly 'incompetent'; they are often not given the opportunity to control their own environments, leading them to a possible state of 'learned helplessness'. All of these will have a negative impact on their ability to learn effective social skills.

Effects of deprivation

Deprivation or poverty of stimulation, such as that which can be found in child-care institutions, can have negative consequences for cognitive development, and deprivation involving family relationships seems to have negative consequences for emotional and behavioural adjustment. Significant factors are the lack of opportunities to develop attachments to other adults and the length of separations. Children who experience this kind of deprivation will often be less socially skilled than their peers and will be slower to develop effective use of social skills.

It has also been found that the socioeconomic background has an effect on social skills. Children from culturally rich home environments tend to develop more appropriate social skills than those from socially deprived backgrounds (Messer, 1995) and this is backed up by research on vocabulary development. By the age of four years, a child from a high socioeconomic background will have been exposed to around 42 million words and will enter school with a vocabulary of 20,000 words, as opposed to the child from a low socioeconomic family, who has only been exposed to 13 million words and will enter school with only 5,000 words (Hart and Risley, 2003; Marulis and Newman, 2010). This means that a parent's social skills and communicative ability is predictive of the child's communicative ability and will therefore have an effect on the development of social skills.

Stages of development for social skills

A question that I am often asked is when should we expect to see some of the social skills and friendship skills that I teach, and where does a child's self-awareness or self-identity fit in? I am also asked why I teach children nonverbal behaviours before verbal ones and why I leave friendship skills to later. We know that children develop and change a great deal in the first five years and that this is a critical time in their development, but when should we expect to see certain social skills and when should we worry if we don't?

In the past, it has been assumed that babies are born with the ability to communicate nonverbally, that is to read facial expression and body language, but in reality, babies are only born with a propensity to develop nonverbal skills. The development of nonverbal communication skills pre-dates the development of language and, without them, children cannot make full use of their verbal language (Boyce 2012). In the first few hours after birth, the new-born baby will be interested in faces and will copy facial movements. This process of looking at faces, and us looking back, is the start of interaction. Babies as young as three months are able to understand the meaning of hand gestures or signs long before they learn the words, and they can then use these signs to bridge the gap between the time until they can then be used.

By the age of four, children engage in actual social interaction and their personality becomes more defined, and then friendships begin to be an important part of their development as they begin to be interested in having friends. Then, in the school years, we see their social skills becoming more competent as they have better conversations and can assert themselves effectively and appropriately. Finally, we see a shift in self-identity and self-esteem as the child goes into adolescence and we see the importance of friendships change in nature.

The chart at the end of this chapter details the development of self and other awareness, social skills (nonverbal communication, verbal communication and assertiveness) and friendship skills. I have used a number of sources to collate this information, primarily Rochat (2003), McGrath (2013) and Feldman et al. (2004), as well as my own experience.

In summary, although we know a great deal about how social skills develop, it is also possible to see that there are many factors which will influence the development from genetics to the environment, from parents to peers, and from reinforcement to theory of mind. There is no single straight line to social competence, but the important thing to remember is that most children seem to develop social competence without too much difficulty. All the factors come together and they learn the skills without the need for specialist intervention.

Table 10.4 The stages of development for social skills

Age	Self and other awareness	Social skills	Friendship skills
Up to 3 months	Has a sense of their own bodily space in relation to other entities.	Gazes at faces. Copies facial expression. Makes eye contact.	
3–6 months	Reaches for objects so has a sense of where they are in space.	Watches face when someone talks. Will initiate social interaction e.g. peek-a-boo.	
6–12 months	Smiles at own reflection in a mirror. Will enjoy looking at another person's face.	Has developed shared attention. Will use sounds and gestures to communicate intentionally e.g. waving and pointing. Beginning to take turns using babble. Imitates facial expressions.	
12–18 months	Recognises themselves in pictures or the mirror and smile or make faces at themselves.	Is able to imitate a number of sounds at a later time and uses intonation, pitch and volume when 'talking'. Understands that things have names, but situation-specific. Can figure out someone else's visual perspective and intentions.	Plays alone Simple pretend play.
18 months–2 years	Can identify themselves in a mirror as 'me'. First signs of personal appearance and how others perceive them.	Follows adult body language, e.g. pointing, gesture, facial expression. Frequently asks questions. Learns to say 'no'.	Pretend play developing. Doesn't like to share.
2–3 years	Begins to demonstrate embarrassment. Can recognise distress in others. Starts to show awareness of own feelings and others' feelings. Shows awareness of gender identity. Begins to develop notions of themselves as good, bad, pretty etc.	Holds a conversation but jumps from topic to topic. Beginning to listen to people but easily distracted. Beginning to express basic emotions using words. Can use and understand hundreds of words in different combinations.	Interested in others' play and will join in. Plays next to others.

Age			
3–4 years	Begins to be able to simulate events and roles and take on the perspective of others (the beginnings of theory of mind). Able to answer if they are a boy or a girl. Can describe hair colour, likes & dislikes. Self-esteem based on what others tell him or her.	Initiates conversations. Listening is better but can't listen and do something else. Beginning to be able to disagree using words.	Becoming more interested in other children. Enjoys playing with peers. Beginning to understand about sharing and turn taking in play. Beginning to have friendships.
4–5 years	More aware of themselves as individuals. Compare themselves with others. Shows an awareness of other people's perspective and can infer feelings from another person.	Takes turns in longer conversations. Uses language to negotiate, discuss feelings and give opinions. Beginning to be assertive and asks people to stop if being annoying.	Chooses own friends. Co-operative play develops. Learns to play by rules. Can ask to join in.
6–8 years	Can clearly recognise others' perspectives. Can reflect upon self and attributes. Self-esteem based on ability to perform. Sensitive to others' opinions.	Learning to be a good listener and take turns well in a conversation. Able to be assertive when necessary, for example, say no, apologise, request an explanation.	Learning to give and receive compliments. Able to say no to peers when appropriate.
9–12 years	Recognises difference between behaviour and intent.		Learns to respect the opinions of others.
12–15 years	Self-conscious about physical appearance.		Social acceptance depends on conformity to observable traits or roles. Relies on peer group for support.
15–18 years	Forms identity by organizing perceptions of attitudes, behaviours, values into coherent 'whole'. Identity includes positive self-image comprised of cognitive and affective components.		Friendships based on loyalty, understanding, trust.

Key points from Chapter 10

This chapter covered the normal development of social skills and factors that affect its development.

Genetics/biology

Every child is born with a set of genes which determines their eye colour, hair colour and height, but these will also affect how they will act around other people – their temperament and personality. There are also differences between the male brain and the female brain which will affect the development of social skills and will mean that girls are better at some things than boys and visa-versa.

Joint attention and symbolic communication

The skills of joint attention and symbolic communication are important to the development of social competence.

Attachment

Child-parent attachment or the emotional connection between parent and child will also affect the development of social competence.

- Secure attachment serves as a healthy foundation for developing social skills
- Insecure attachment may mean that parents are over-protective and controlling

Child-rearing

There is a link between parenting styles and social competence, with more socially competent children coming from authoritative parents as opposed to authoritarian or permissive.

Observational learning – parents

Social skills are behaviours which can be learned through imitation, modelling and reinforcement as a child is growing up and parents are obviously well-placed to have the biggest impact on a child's learning, especially in the early years.

Reinforcement

People tend to do things associated with 'positively valued outcomes' and will not persist in doing things that have produced either little positive reward or an unwanted negative outcome. Positive reinforcement has been found to be important in the development of social competence: children need positive rein-forcement from others to learn how to be socially competent.

Observational learning – peers and siblings

Researchers have found that children do learn from other children and that the process of observation and imitation of peers influences individual patterns of behaviour. Siblings can also be very influential in helping children to develop skills needed to interact successfully with their peers.

Learning the why and the when

The child has to learn when to use certain behaviours as well as what behaviours to use and how to use them.

- *The development of theory of mind.* The development of a child's social skills is closely related to the child's development of theory of mind.

Other factors that affect the development of social skills

- *Attitudes to the environment.* People who struggle with their social skills are often affected by the attitudes of others and their environment and are therefore less likely to be able to have control over and manage the situations they are in. A key concept is 'learned helplessness'.
- *Effect of deprivation.* Significant factors are the lack of opportunities to develop attachments to other adults and the length of separations. Children who experience this kind of deprivation will be less socially skilled than their peers and will be slower to develop effective use of social skills. Children from culturally rich home environments also tend to develop more appropriate social skills than those from socially deprived backgrounds.

Stages of development for social skills

Table 10.4 details the development of self and other awareness, social skills (nonverbal communication, verbal communication, assertiveness) and friendship skills.

Chapter 11

Autism Spectrum Disorder and social skills

'What would happen if the autism gene was eliminated from the gene pool? You would have a bunch of people standing around in a cave, chatting and socializing and not getting anything done.'

Dr Temple Grandin

When planning a book about social skills, it seemed at least sensible, if not essential, to devote a whole chapter to autism. I certainly do not claim to be an expert on Autism Spectrum Disorder (ASD), so I suppose I come to this chapter with some trepidation as there are so many amazing text books out there on this subject and some much better qualified people than me to write about autism. But due to the nature of my work in social skills, I have naturally accrued many years of experience working with children and adults with a diagnosis of autism and so a book about social skills would be incomplete in my mind without us considering the specific difficulties that can occur in autism.

However, in attempting to describe Autism Spectrum Disorder, it is important to start by saying that this chapter will never be fully comprehensive. In fact, maybe we should not necessarily strive to understand 'what autism is'. Instead, as Dr Damian Milton says (www.autism-ducationtrust.org.uk), maybe we should strive to understand the 'autistic people' we work with as well as we can, and to see this as an ongoing process and mutually respectful interaction. We may also want to think about terminology. Most text books use 'autism spectrum disorder' and 'people with autism' but this can be unpopular with some people. Some autistic people say that 'they are not people who "just happen to have autism"; it is not an appendage that can be separated from who we are as people, nor is it something shameful that has to be reduced to a sub-clause' (Sainsbury, 2000, p. 12). But some don't want the label to precede them, so would prefer to be seen as a person first and having autism, second. In this chapter, I have chosen to use 'autistic people' rather than 'people with autism or ASD' simply because this is what my autistic friends prefer. I apologise if you would have preferred me to write it the other way.

In this chapter, I will briefly explain social skills difficulties in relation to autism and I will also look at some of the theories that explain why social interaction is more difficult for an autistic child or adult.

A diagnosis of Autism Spectrum Disorder

Autism used to be considered to be an extremely rare 'disorder' that only affected a tiny proportion of the population; however, in recent decades the numbers of those diagnosed as being somewhere on the wider 'autism spectrum' has massively increased. The National Autistic Society (www.autism.org.uk) quotes Brugha et al. (2012) in saying that there are around 700,000 people on the autism spectrum in the UK, that's more than 1 in 100, and if you include their families, autism is a part of daily life for 2.8 million people.

Autism is a relatively new 'disorder' and if you go back to the 1970s, the prevailing view was that autism was categorical: you either have it or you don't. It was Dr Lorna Wing, a social psychiatrist and parent of a daughter with autism, who first argued that autism lay on a spectrum, and was therefore much more common than previously thought. As Tony Attwood (2016) says, 'Autism is not achieved by personal choice, and does not come about as a response to a particular parenting style. The new-born infant who is subsequently diagnosed as having autism has a brain that is wired differently, not defectively'.

The first person to recognise that the child's development and abilities are different is usually the mother, or primary care giver. They may observe that their child has:

- A tendency to avoid, or be confused or overwhelmed in, social situations.
- A possible motivation to socialise, but difficulty reading body language or social cues.
- Intense emotions.
- An unusual profile of language skills that can include language delay.
- Different interests to other children of the same age.
- Difficulty coping with unanticipated changes in routines and expectations.
- Sensitivity to specific sensory experiences.

A diagnosis of autism is mostly carried out by a multidisciplinary team and in May 2013 we saw a change in this with the publication of the fifth edition of the *Diagnostic and Statistical Manual of Mental Disorders* (DSM-5, American Psychiatric Association 2013). Autism Spectrum Disorder (ASD) now replaces the term 'Pervasive Developmental Disorder' and the term 'Asperger's syndrome' has been replaced by the new diagnostic category of *Autism Spectrum Disorder Level 1, without accompanying intellectual or language impairment*. The rationale for this according to Attwood (2014) was that ASD should be 'conceptualised as a dimensional rather than categorical concept', although in reality, the term 'Asperger's syndrome' will probably continue to be used informally by both clinicians and the general public. Indeed Attwood (2014) says that he now uses the term *ASD Level 1 (Asperger's Syndrome)* so that everyone is clear.

In addition, this fifth edition of the DSM-5 has replaced the triad of impairment with only two essential features of ASD: firstly, the child (or adult) will experience '*persistent deficits in social communication and social interaction*', and secondly, 'restricted, repetitive patterns of behaviour, interests or activities' (DSM-5, 2013). So, having a diagnosis of ASD means that the person will struggle at some level with social communication and social interaction from requiring some support (Level 1) to requiring substantial support (Level 3). This is often the most common and prominent feature and the one that we will describe in more detail in this chapter.

The DSM-5 breaks down the deficits in social communication and social interaction into three areas or 'symptoms' which are summarised in the following table:

Table 11.1 Deficits in social communication and social interaction

Symptoms	Defined by the DSM-5, American Psychiatric Association, 2013
1. Deficits in social-emotional reciprocity	'Ranging . . . from abnormal social approach and failure of normal back-and-forth conversation; to reduced sharing of interests, emotions, or affect; to failure to initiate or respond to social interactions'.
2. Deficits in nonverbal communicative behaviours used for social interaction	'Ranging . . . from poorly integrated verbal and nonverbal communication; to abnormalities in eye contact and body language or deficits in understanding and use of gestures; to a total lack of facial expression and nonverbal communication'.
3. Deficits in developing, maintaining and understanding relationships	'Ranging . . . from difficulties adjusting behaviour to suit various social contexts; to difficulties in sharing imaginative play or in making friends; to absence of interest in peers'.

We therefore know that a diagnosis of ASD will mean that the person will have some difficulties in social communication and social interaction and that they will need a varying degree of support in this area. Wing (1996) describes four groups of individuals with ASD whose social interaction can be described as either 'aloof', 'passive', 'active but odd' or 'stilted and over-formal'. However, there is no single definition of the social impairment, rather there is a range of difficulties that varies from one individual to another. As the quote goes: 'If you've met one person with autism, you've met one person with autism' (Dr Stephen Shore).

So what are the specific difficulties? Simon Baron-Cohen (2008) summarises these potential social difficulties as follows:

Table 11.2 Social difficulties in autism

Extreme lack of interest in other people.
Atypical eye contact: either hardly making eye contact, or staring at you for too long.
Invading your personal space.
Lack of reciprocity (no turn taking, no dialogue, just monologue).
Preferring to be alone.
Difficulties anticipating how someone will feel or what they might think.
Difficulties knowing how to react to another person's behaviour.
Difficulty reading other people's emotional expressions, in their face or voice or posture.
Difficulty accepting that there may be other perspectives, not just a single correct perspective.

Areas of difficulty for the person with ASD

In the following sections, we will look at six areas of difficulties that autistic people experience that can all have a direct impact on their social skills: social use of language, conversational skills, literal understanding of language, body language, prosody and relationships.

Social use of language or 'pragmatics'

As we have seen in the previous chapters on nonverbal and verbal skills, our communication is much more complex than it seems at first glance. Most of our communication happens nonverbally (93%) and we have rules that govern our social use of language (often referred to as 'pragmatics'). These social rules are generally 'unwritten and unstated, complex, constantly changing, and affect most areas of social interaction' (Patrick, 2008). We see these rules in our conversations – how to greet and say goodbye, and how and when to take your turn. We see them in our body language – how close can we stand to someone and where do we look? And we see them in our voices – how a change in tone can mean the opposite to what the words actually mean. And to make things even more difficult, these rules change from person to person, from situation to situation and from age to gender to status.

So, communication happens within a social context. It is not just the words that people choose to speak, but all the other messages that are sent. Much of our communication is indirect, implied by a look, a nod, a smile, a gesture, which is understood by most of us, but is difficult for the autistic person to pick up on. So, it is understood by everyone at a meeting that when the boss said 'someone needs to do that today' (looking at Bob with a raised eyebrow) that she means Bob should do it. But this is not clear to the autistic person. They will understand it as 'someone needs to do that today' and if they happen to be that person (Bob) they will probably not do it!

So, the skill of effective communication is complex for the autistic person. As Powell (2016) says, it 'involves not only articulating one's own thoughts, but at the same time having an awareness of what the other person is thinking, feeling and saying, and then linking it all together. This requires multiple channels of attention to be processing at the same time'.

The autistic person may therefore struggle to follow these social rules of language for several reasons. First, it is harder to read the intentions of someone else (I will talk about this later in the section on theory of mind), so they may struggle to understand what the other person is thinking and feeling if it is not explicitly said. Second, they may not know the rule (think about the eye contact rule in the chapter on the eyes and face). Third, they may know the rule, but then not understand the purpose of it or the contextual side to it (who you can hug, why you might hug, where and when you can hug, etc.). Finally, they may not see the purpose of the rule (they don't need to say hello or goodbye, so don't see the point of doing it).

The underlying assumption with this area is that the autistic person has difficulty in 'reading' social situations and that this will affect the reciprocity and the quality of the conversations. Tony Attwood (2014) describes two main ways in which people may behave as a result of this. The most conspicuous is a tendency to be withdrawn, shy and introspective in social situations, avoiding or minimizing participation or conversations. Second, they may actively seek out social engagement, but be conspicuously intrusive and intense, dominating the interaction and being unaware of social conventions such as personal space. In each of these there is an imbalance of social reciprocity. However, Attwood suggests that there is a third strategy for coping with these difficulties that is mostly (but not exclusively) used by girls with Asperger's syndrome. They avidly observe and intellectually analyse social behaviour and will attempt to achieve reciprocal social interaction by imitation, using an observed and practised social 'script' which is based on intellectual analysis rather than intuition. In this way, they are able to express superficial social abilities that can make it harder to diagnose them with autism.

Conversational skills

'Smooth, reciprocal conversations are often difficult' (Powell, 2016). Conversations with an autistic person can include moments where there appears to be a breakdown in communication 'transmission' – they are deep in thought, deciding what to say, looking away – which can be disconcerting to the other person. There are also moments when the autistic person takes over the conversation, interrupts and talks over the other person, or changes the topic and speaks in monologues. They may fail to take notice of the listener and to allow them to join in – which can also naturally cause a communication breakdown. We may see difficulties at the following stages of a conversation:

Starting and ending a conversation

As we saw in Chapter 5 on conversational skills, there are quite complicated rules around greetings and farewells in a conversation and the autistic person may not follow these rules, either for starting or ending a conversation. They may initiate a conversation by not using any form of greeting, launching straight into a subject with a statement or a question. Or they may say 'hello' and then pause while wondering what to say next. They may start a conversation with what may seem to the listener as an irrelevant comment or question, failing to give the listener a 'lead in' to what they are thinking about. And they may also break a social or cultural code by striking up a conversation with a stranger in a supermarket by asking them a seemingly strange, personal or irrelevant question.

Similarly, they may struggle with ending a conversation. They may not use any closing statement at the end of a conversation, or they will say 'goodbye' and then stand awkwardly. They may also keep talking because either they want to finish what they needed to say, irrespective of the effect on the listener, or they will not know if the other person wants them to finish, so they carry on talking. This can all also apply to written correspondence, with emails being sent with no opening or closing remarks or even a signature (Patrick, 2008), or where there is no response at all, as they did not realise a response was expected or required by the other person.

Maintaining the conversation

Having started the conversation, the autistic person may struggle to maintain it for several reasons. Firstly, and maybe most importantly, they have difficulty in showing that they are listening. During a typical conversation, we like people to listen to us when we are speaking and there is an expectation that the person listening will show us they are listening by looking at us, nodding their head, and using appropriate facial expression and vocalisations. These signals are less apparent when in a conversation with an autistic person, which can lead them to appear rude or unsympathetic as we can assume they are not listening to us.

Once the conversation has begun, there can also appear to be no 'off-switch' and it only ends when the child or adult has finished their predetermined 'script'. The autistic person usually appears unaware of the effect of the monologue on the listener as they struggle to read the nonverbal responses and to alter their responses according to the social context. So, if the clues are all there that the listener is bored or needs to get away but the autistic person does not see these, then they may continue to speak. This difficulty to read people and the context means that they may give too much or too little information as they are unsure of what the other person wants. The friendly lady at the bus stop may ask the question 'how are you?', but she doesn't really want to know how you really are! During the conversation there can be 'a lack of recognition or appreciation of the context, social hierarchy and conventions, and little attempt to incorporate the other person's comments, feelings or knowledge in the conversation' (Attwood, 2007). This may also mean that some individuals may find it difficult to adapt their language for their audience, for example using lots of technical vocabulary that they use regularly but not having the awareness that the other person does not understand and/or is not interested. In contrast to engaging in a monologue, there can be times when the autistic person is reluctant to participate in a conversation at all, especially if the topic is not of interest.

They may also frequently change the topic, unaware that the logical link between the topics is not actually obvious to the listener. Such conversations or monologues can appear to be without any structure and lack coherence or relevance to the context. The listener is left wondering what the ultimate point of the story will be and also whether they will have an opportunity to contribute. With this type of conversation, there appears to be a 'conspicuous lack of inclusive comments such as 'what do you think of that suggestion?' or 'have you had a similar experience?" (Attwood, 2007), which can leave the listener feeling frustrated or bewildered.

Patrick (2008) also says that changing topics in the middle of a conversation happens because the autistic person may struggle to maintain a topic for more than a few reciprocal back-and-forth cycles, resulting in the need to abruptly change the topic so they can maintain the conversation. They may jump from topic to topic, with no obvious link or 'connecting comment' such as 'could I change the subject for a minute and tell you about . . .', which can leave the listener confused and unsure of how to contribute.

Another example of impaired conversational skills is the difficulty of repairing a conversation. As we talked about in the chapter on conversations, it is important to seek clarification when something is unclear or confusing. This can be difficult for the autistic person to do as they may lack the confidence to say 'I'm confused' and may prefer to just change the topic to an easier one. In addition, when the listener is confused and seeks clarification from the autistic person, they can struggle to provide an explanation using other words and may just repeat the same ones with no added clarity.

Finally, we may see children and some adults seemingly talking to themselves, commenting on their own actions or giving a monologue without the need for a listener. They may do this for several reasons: to help figure something out and express themselves, to keep themselves company (and feel less lonely), or to rehearse possible conversations for the following day (Attwood, 2007). This can be a problem the following day when the conversation that has been played out and rehearsed carefully does not go the way they had planned when the other person says something unexpected!

I spent a few years working with a young lady called Jessie who told me how sometimes conversations didn't go the way she had planned and gave me the following example:

A conversation between Jess and Dan as described by Jessie

How I predicted it would go. . .

Me: Hey, Danny, I got a new game today.

Danny: Awesome, what game was it?

Me: GTA which means grand theft auto.

Danny: Wow cool Jessie, I'll have to see it next time I'm over.

Danny: That's cool, Jessie, have you played it yet? What do you do on it? Is it good?

Me: Yes, I spent all day playing it and you can do loads of things from driving cars planes and helicopters around to doing missions. And yes it's amazing.

How it actually went. . .

Me: Hey Danny I got a new game today

Danny: Ah cool!

[Jessie thinks. . . 'Oh my God! What do I say now? Isn't he going to ask what one?]

Literal understanding of language

Language is used to send and receive messages that are both literal and figurative. The literal message uses words that are meant exactly as they are defined, so we say what we mean. These are nice and easy to understand for the autistic person, as there is no implied meaning or confusing imagery going on. Figurative messages, however, contain words that imply something else, not what the words necessarily mean, and we use these far more than we probably realise in everyday spoken language. We use figurative language to 'create emphasis, amplify meaning, draw a comparison or contrast, or to make a rhetorical point' (Sutcliffe, 2004). Examples of these are shown in the table below:

Table 11.3 Figurative language

	Defined as	Example
Similes	A comparison between two dissimilar objects, using the words 'like' or 'as'.	As light as a feather. As brave as a lion.
Metaphors	A figure of speech that is used to make a comparison between two things that aren't alike but do have something in common. They are meant to create an impact in the minds of readers.	A recipe for disaster. All the world's a stage. The light of my life. Broken heart. Bubbly personality.
Idioms	A group of words established by usage as having a meaning not deducible from those of the individual words.	Over the moon. Break a leg. Grab a bite.
Puns	The humorous use of a word or phrase so as to emphasise or suggest its different meanings or applications, or the use of words that are alike or nearly alike in sound but different in meaning; a play on words.	An elephant's opinion carries a lot of weight. 'On the contrary, Aunt Augusta, I've now realised for the first time in my life the vital Importance of Being Earnest.' (Oscar Wilde)
Paradoxes	It is a statement that appears to be self-contradictory or silly but may include a latent truth.	I am nobody. I can resist anything but temptation.

(Continued)

	Defined as	Example
Irony	The use of words to convey a meaning that is the opposite of its literal meaning.	(I had to work all weekend) 'How nice!' (But meant 'how horrible!').
Sarcasm	Is an ironic or satirical remark that seems to be praising someone or something but is really taunting or cutting. It often depends on the tone of voice.	Oh, I love you! (with tone of voice that would indicate that they don't love you). That's just what we need! (not).
Parables	A short story that uses familiar events to illustrate a religious or ethical point or conveys a meaning indirectly by the use of a comparison, or an analogy.	The boy who cried wolf.

Understanding figurative speech is often hard, especially for the autistic person, as it requires us to identify subtle relationships between words and phrases, and then understand the meaning from the message based on our prior experience (or knowledge) rather than direct observation, and then finally to take the perspective of the speaker. Sarcasm in particular requires us to know the speaker well enough to know if his message is reliable or not. How often have you said, 'are you joking?' So sometimes we get it wrong. So all of this can be very confusing for the autistic person and can lead to many misunderstandings within interactions as our language can appear illogical or untrue. It can also lead to the autistic person responding to something in an unexpected way. I work with a speech and language therapist (speech pathologist) who was once working with someone on recognising facial expression. She made her face look angry and asked the person how she looked and the response was 'ugly'. We still smile about that session!

Body language

This is another distinct characteristic of autism. As we saw in the DSM-5 criteria, a deficit in nonverbal communication is a symptom and is defined as 'ranging . . . from poorly integrated verbal and nonverbal communication; to abnormalities in eye contact and body language or deficits in understanding and use of gestures; to a total lack of facial expression and nonverbal communication' (American Psychiatric Association, 2013). A description of 'clumsy or gauche' body language is also included in the diagnostic criteria for Asperger's Syndrome by Christopher Gillberg (Gillberg and Gillberg, 1989). This means that we will often see difficulties in all aspects of body language, including use of eye contact, facial expression, gesture, distance, touch, posture and fidgeting.

Eye contact

It is common to see difficulties with eye contact in autistic people. They may avoid eye contact all together or stare. Or they may look at other parts of the face or body, such as the mouth. Research by Klin et al. (cited by Attwood, 2007) found that autistic adults tend to look less at the eyes and more at the mouth, body and objects. If you ask an autistic person why they find it difficult to look at the other person's eyes, some may describe an uncomfortable feeling, and even pain, when trying to make eye contact.

Facial expression

Hans Asperger noted that some of the children he saw had unusual facial expressions, sometimes 'sparse and rigid' (cited by Attwood, 2007). There can be a lack of variation in facial movements to express thoughts and feelings, which gives them a flat facial expression, which then can make them appear sad. Attwood also describes how, when asked to make a particular facial expression, he has even observed children and adults physically manipulating their face to try to resemble that emotion, for example pulling their mouth down or up. One explanation given was that they cannot express what they are not feeling at that moment in time.

Body positioning

The autistic person often has an unnatural posture or gait, which can vary from rigid to exaggerated. They may be unsure of how to position themselves so as to appear part of a group, or how to stand to show another person they are part of the conversation, interested and engaged. This can then result in them appearing on the outside of group and social situations. They may also struggle with the appropriate use of hand gesture – either using no gesture or at times exaggerated, theatrical gesture. They will often stand too close and may touch the other person inappropriately during the conversation – for example, by putting a hand on their shoulder. Finally, they may fidget or remain very still.

In addition to the autistic person having difficulties in body language themselves, they also struggle to accurately interpret nonverbal communication of others. This leads to constant misunderstandings as our body language accounts for as much as 55% of the meaning in face to face communication. We all give nonverbal signals that signify to our listener that we are interested or bored, that we are happy or sad. So, if our listener is not able to read the nonverbal signals that indicate 'I am bored now' or 'don't talk to me now', there is a lot that can go wrong that will seriously affect the success of social communication.

Prosody

As we saw in our previous chapter on listening and paralanguage, our communication is so much more than words alone and our paralanguage gives the listener important information about how we feel, what we want them to listen to, whether we are serious or joking, and whether we want them to answer us. When listening to the speech of an autistic person, we can often hear unusual patterns in their paralinguistic skills. Attwood (2007) cites research which has confirmed that the prosody of children and adults with ASD can be unusual, especially with regard to pragmatic prosody (where the change in speech draws attention to something – an opinion, thought, intention) and affective prosody (where it communicates feelings and attitudes). For some autistic people, there is a lack of variation in their intonation, volume and rate, which leaves the speech with a rather monotonous quality. For some people, their speech is too loud or has a high pitched nasal quality, which was first described by Hans Asperger. For some, their speech is dysfluent. And finally, some have adopted the accent of someone else, probably a character in a film, which may mean they speak in a foreign accent.

In addition to having difficulties with prosody, they may also have difficulty in understanding the relevance of paralanguage when listening to the speech of other people. This may mean that some individuals may misinterpret tone and think they are being shouted at when someone uses a firm voice. As we have said, these subtle clues are extremely important to establish intent, thoughts and emotions, and the autistic person will need support to understand these. So we can look at the different words that are emphasised in the following sentence and come up with seven different meanings!

> ### 'Stressed Eric'
>
> 'I didn't say you have smelly feet'
>
> **I** didn't say you have smelly feet (but someone said it)
>
> I **didn't** say you have smelly feet (I definitely didn't say it)
>
> I didn't **say** you have smelly feet (but I implied it)
>
> I didn't say **you** have smelly feet (but someone does)
>
> I didn't say you **have** smelly feet (but maybe you did)
>
> I didn't say you have **smelly** feet (but I did say something about your feet)
>
> I didn't say you have smelly **feet** (but you have something else that is smelly)
>
> ('Stressed Eric' taken from Kelly, 2018)

Relationships

Friendships and relationships are complicated, emotional and unpredictable, which makes them all very challenging for the autistic person. The DSM-5 defines deficits in developing, maintaining, and understanding relationships as one of the core symptoms of the persistent deficits in social communication and social interaction that someone with ASD experiences. This is defined in the DSM-5 as 'ranging . . . from difficulties adjusting behaviour to suit various social contexts; to difficulties in sharing imaginative play or in making friends; to absence of interest in peers' (American Psychiatric Association, 2013). There are a few issues that affect the autistic person from making and maintaining friends.

The need for friendship

The autistic person may not be motivated to make friends and may prefer the solitude of the library to the chaotic and noisy playground. And when they do want to 'socialise', they may seek out the company of adults to answer their questions rather than the other children who play games with incomprehensible rules. As Powell (2016) says, there is a 'clash of culture between the autistic and neurotypical world over socialising'. People in the neurotypical world prioritise socialising and friendship above most other things. We know that our friends are good for us; they help to lower our stress, increase our self-esteem and support us to solve problems. But in the autistic world this is often not the case. Socialising does not come naturally and is often an effort and can be tiring. This brings us to the capacity for socialising.

Capacity for socialising

We all have different capacities for socialising. I am happy to see friends at the weekend, but my husband finds too much socialising tiring and so we have to compromise so that we are both happy. As a rule, autistic people feel more comfortable if social interactions are 'brief, purposeful and have a fixed ending as they will need to go away and recharge their batteries'

(Powell, 2016). Solitude is often a natural state for autistic people and can be an effective way to calm down and restore emotionally. As Powell (2016) says, someone with ASD may describe their capacity for socialising as 'I fill up quickly . . . [and] after a while I'm used up, spent, I've said what I want to say and need a break, some restoration time, time on my own'. I have an autistic friend who I see once in a while. Our meetings are very enjoyable, but she likes to know at the beginning how long I am going to be there, and I have learnt that short meetings (usually no more than an hour) are just perfect. We chat, we laugh and then suddenly I am gone. And I know she is sat quietly in her flat, chilling out, restoring herself. Which bring us on to the next issue: two's company, three's a crowd.

Two's company, three's a crowd

Like my friend Jessie, autistic people can function reasonably well sometimes in a one-to-one social situation, but things get a lot more complicated when more people are around. The more people there are in a social situation, the more we have to try to understand and monitor an increasing number of relationships between those involved. For example, two people equals one relationship; three people equals three relationships; but four people equals six relationships. This means we are not just having to process the language and nonverbal communication of more people, but also each individual interaction and relationship.

This can all be made worse if the autistic person has slow processing and cannot keep up with the conversation. The other issue can be 'small talk'. Autistic adults often say that they are poor at 'small talk' or 'chit-chat', or they may say that they have learnt to do it but don't see the point. We usually engage in small talk to establish rapport or acknowledge the presence of someone, or simply for the pleasure of being friendly. We say 'hi, how are you?' to the person at the bus stop or the lady at the post office, but we don't really expect them to answer truthfully. We talk endlessly about the weather: 'bit chilly today isn't it?', but we don't really want to discuss the weather in detail. We are just being friendly. There is no real purpose or defined goal and it is often pretty spontaneous. And all of these things make this hard for the autistic person.

The motivation to have friends

Autistic people have certain qualities that make them good friends and partners and there may be a desire to establish friendships. But there also may be an unrealistic idea of what friendship entails. Attwood (2014) describes a particular developmental sequence that children who have Asperger's syndrome display.

- *In the early years*, the child may not be motivated to socialise with peers, having discovered that other aspects of life, such as collecting or reading about something, are more enjoyable than socialising. They may spend long periods of time in solitude, preferring to be engaged in their special interest.
- *In the early primary years*, the child may see other children having fun and will actively want to play with their peers. However, their level of social maturity is usually at least two years behind that of their peers, and they may have difficulties with the degree of reciprocal and cooperative play expected by other children. The play tends to be more active rather than conversational, with games that are simple and that have clear rules that must be followed. They may at this stage become acutely aware of being different and will want a friend to play with, as they long for social inclusion. But they are also not good in their judgements of which children are good to play with and which should

be avoided. For all these reasons, they are very vulnerable to ridicule, being bullied and being rejected by their peers.

- *In adolescence,* relationships are more about having someone to confide in rather than someone to play with, and the gap in social understanding becomes more apparent, as the young autistic adult can be overwhelmed by the increasingly complex nature of friendship, which can lead to isolation and loneliness. If they do achieve genuine friendships, they can have a tendency to be too dominant or rigid in their view of friendship, which can be an issue. But with a compassionate, sensitive child as a friend, or with a socially isolated child who shares some of the interests of the autistic child, friendships can be successful, if a bit functional and practical.

- *In adulthood,* some adults with Asperger's syndrome can succeed in achieving an intimate, and possibly life-long, relationship, although they may come to this several years later than their peers. Their partner usually has an understanding of ASD, either because they share some characteristics or they are naturally compassionate in understanding their autistic partner.

Theories of ASD and how they affect social communication

Having described the specific difficulties pertaining to autism, we will now briefly describe some of the key psychological theories that offer possible explanations for the social challenges in autism, and which may account for their different experiences of the social world. These are important to understand, especially when teaching social skills. My experience is that even though it may be relatively easy to teach someone a specific social skill, unless you teach it within a context and develop their social understanding, it will be difficult for them to put the skill into a social context appropriately and achieve social competence. To help us with this, we are going to look at four theories of autism: theory of mind (ToM), weak central coherence, empathising-systemising theory, and executive dysfunction theory.

Theory of mind

One of the most enduring psychological theories concerning autism has been the assertion that the key universal core 'deficit' found in autistic spectrum disorder is an impaired 'theory of mind' (Baron-Cohen et al. 1985). However, as we will see later, it is not a popular theory with everyone, especially with some autistic people, and it is certainly not helpful when we hear sweeping statements such as 'autistic people lack empathy because they have a lack of theory of mind'. However, it is well researched and documented and deserves a thorough description.

The term 'theory of mind' (ToM) means the ability to recognise and understand thoughts, beliefs, desires and intentions of other people in order to make sense of their behaviour and predict what they are going to do next. It is also sometimes referred to as 'mind reading' or 'mind blindness' (Baron-Cohen, 2008), or more colloquially, 'putting yourself in someone else's shoes'. A synonymous term is empathy (Gillberg, 2002). And as Attwood (2007) states: 'the child or adult with ASD does not recognise or understand the cues that indicate the thoughts or feelings of the other person at a level expected for someone of that age'.

So, when we see someone turn to look out of the window, we may infer that they have seen something of interest, and that they may know something that we cannot presently see. It might even be something that they want. Baron-Cohen (2008) says this is going beyond 'mere behaviour to imagine a whole set of *mental states* that link up in the other person's mind'. When we mind read, we can not only make sense of another person's behaviour (why did their head turn or their eyes move to the left?), but we can also predict what they might do next (if they like what they saw, they may move towards it or if not, move away).

We also use our ToM to identify someone's intentions behind their gestures and speech. If we see someone look at someone else and then look at their watch, we can infer that one person is communicating to the other that it is time to leave. They want the other person to understand that by looking at their watch, they are actually saying 'look at the time, it's late, we had better go'. The autistic person, however, may just wonder why they looked at their watch and may not infer the actual meaning behind the message.

It is in this sense that theory of mind can be thought of as a theory: it explains and predicts others' behaviour. The theory proposes that autistic children are delayed in the development of their ToM, leaving them with degrees of 'mind blindness'. As a result, they find it much harder to interpret or anticipate what others are doing or are going to do, and as a consequence will be puzzled, or even frightened, by the other person's 'unpredictable' behaviour.

Baron-Cohen (2008) identifies the key stages in the typical development of theory of mind which are summarised in the table below:

Table 11.4 Typical development of theory of mind

Age	A neurotypical child	An autistic child
14-month-old	Child shows *joint attention* (such as pointing or following another person's gaze) and pays attention to what the other person is interested in.	Child shows reduced frequency of *joint attention*. They point less, look at faces less and do not turn to follow another person's gaze as much as a neurotypical child.
24-month-old	Child can engage in *pretend play*. They begin to use their mind reading skills to understand that in the other person's mind, they are pretending.	Child shows less pretend play, or pretence is limited to more rule-based formats, such as a script from a film.
3-year-old	Can pass the *seeing leads to knowing test*. This means that when shown a picture of two children and a box, they identify the child looking in the box as the one who knows what is in a box (as opposed to the child touching the box).	The child is delayed in passing this test and is unable to do it at this age. They often need to be taught this specifically and will not pick it up naturally by interacting in the social world.
4-year-old	Can pass the *false belief* test where children are told the Sally and Anne story: Sally hides her marble in a box but when she goes out of the room, Anne moves the marble to the basket. The child is asked where Sally will look for the marble when she comes back in the room. The child will say that Sally will look for it in the box, since this is Sally's *false belief*.	Most children say that Sally will look where the marble actually is (in the basket), even though there is no way she could have known it had moved. In this way they demonstrate that they are unable to take another person's point of view.

(Continued)

Table 11.4 (Continued)		
5-year-old	*Deception* is easily understood at this age and they may attempt to deceive others. This is a sign of normal ToM, as it involves manipulating someone else's mind to make them believe that something is true when it is not.	Children are slow to understand deception and are at risk of being exploited for their gullibility. They tend to assume that everyone tells the truth.
6-year-old	The child is capable of understanding more complex *second-order* mindreading. For example, in the Sally-Anne test, Sally may peek through the keyhole and see where Anne has moved the marble (Anne *thinks* that Sally doesn't know she has moved the marble).	The autistic child is again delayed in reaching this milestone.
9-year-old	The child is capable of figuring out what might hurt someone else's feelings and what might be better left unspoken, i.e. they can recognise *faux pas*.	The autistic child is delayed by around three years in this skill and do not show this until they are 12.
	A 9-year-old can also interpret another person's expressions from their eyes to figure out what they may be thinking or feeling.	Autistic children find this much more difficult and even autistic adults score below average on this test.

The relevance of a delayed ToM on a person's social competence is significant. If someone has difficulty taking the perspective of another person, they are more likely to be puzzled by the actions of others, have difficulty recognising and working out the feelings of others and are likely to find people unpredictable. If someone is not able to 'read' someone else, they are more likely to encounter misunderstandings and may have more difficulties resolving conflict and showing empathy. A delayed ToM will also mean that autistic people will have 'a one-channel, single, literal perspective of the world' (Powell, 2016). So, they may take things very literally as they struggle to 'read between the lines'. All of the above will lead to difficulties with reciprocal interaction.

A further consequence of literal one-track thinking is that autistic people often have a strong sense of social justice, or moral code, and like to keep strictly to the rules. This in itself is not a bad thing. But it can cause problems, as they may lack negotiating skills and are likely to be rigid and confrontational in their approach. Finally, a delayed ToM will also mean that the autistic person is often remarkably honest and may not recognise the need to tell 'a little white lie' to avoid hurting someone's feelings or cause offence. I currently work with a delightful young autistic man called Joe. I introduced Joe to our new male speech and language therapist, Chris, and his first comment to Chris was 'you have very narrow shoulders for a man'. Of course, this is actually quite true – Chris has a narrow, slim build and therefore narrow shoulders, but it is not really what Chris wanted to hear on his first day at work!

This theory that autistic people have an impaired theory of mind has, however, been criticised. Eisenmajer and Prior (1991) state that failure on ToM tests could be due to difficulties in language processing or memory and DeGelder (1987) argues that it could be a lack of motivation to deceive. Some theorists question its applicability to all on the spectrum when 20% of children pass these tests, or its value for explaining all the aspects of what constitutes the autistic difference (Happe, 1994). It has also been argued that a deficit in 'social functioning' cannot be solely located within an individual, and that what is being seen as a 'theory of mind deficit' could be more to do with a breakdown in communication between two people who process information very differently. In this sense there exists a 'double empathy problem', as Damian Milton calls it, in that both autistic and neurotypical people have a severe difficulty in understanding each other, as neither shares the same frame of reference within social interactions (Milton, 2012). This is most evident by how empathetic autistic people seem to be if they share similarities with someone else. So, whereas this theory may help us to understand some of the underlying difficulties that an autistic person may experience, it is certainly not the whole picture.

Weak central coherence

This second theory suggests that 'people on the autistic spectrum have problems in integrating information to make a coherent, global picture. Instead, they are said to focus on the small, local details in a scene' (Baron-Cohen, 2008). This means that whereas the neurotypical mind has a strong central coherence and can attend to the gist of a scene rather than the nitty-gritty, the autistic mind is said to have weak central coherence and will attend to the detail and not see the whole picture.

This can mean that the autistic person is overwhelmed with the details of a scene: the sights, the sounds, the smells, the words that people are saying, and they may take longer to process the whole picture and make sense of what is happening. The autistic brain picks up on too many details, which is an advantage in maths or programming but, in everyday life, can be overwhelming. A common reaction to this overload is for the autistic person to try to control and order their lives: to systemise, break things down into categories, create a structure, routine and rituals, so that their world becomes more ordered and predictable. This sense of sameness generates a sense of safety and the establishment of a routine ensures that there is no opportunity for change, or the need to create a new coherence or framework to understand what is happening and what is expected of you.

This theory explains some of the aspects of autism that we have not discussed in this chapter, such as the *islets of ability* we may see in autism and the excellent attention to detail, memory and skills in a narrow topic. It can also explain why autistic people outperform non-autistic people in some visual tasks, such as 'embedded figure tests' and 'block design' tasks (Shah and Frith, 1993).

However, in relation to social contexts, this means that 'they may not 'see' the whole 'social picture' and this may lead to inappropriate behaviour' (Howley and Arnold, 2005) as they are missing some of the essential information. An example would be if an autistic person is sent to an office with a message for a colleague, but then does not 'read' their colleague's facial expressions and gestures, which are saying they want them to wait as they are on the telephone. The autistic person does not see the whole social picture and may deliver the message regardless of the signals. This theory also explains why they may remember details within a story but not the overall gist of the narrative, and may then give irrelevant information or struggle to summarise the important points.

Empathising-systemising (E-S) theory

This theory is linked to the theory of mind hypothesis, but adds in the dimension of a superior skill: 'systemising'. Professor Simon Baron-Cohen (2008) suggests that the two defining characteristics of autism are 'empathising' and 'systemising' and that these skills are opposite each other. The more empathy you have, the less systemising you have. Empathy encompasses not only ToM (cognitive empathy), but also the response element: having an appropriate emotional reaction to another person's thoughts and feelings (affective empathy). Systemising is the drive to analyse or construct systems; when we systemise, we are trying to identify the rules that govern the system in order to predict how that system will behave, for example, a numerical system like a train timetable, or a collectible system like a collection of stones or stamps. People who are systemisers ask questions and want to know how things work. They may collect things or take things apart. They may study numerical systems or make lists of capital cities. They prefer predictability, repeat patterns and they resist change.

Baron-Cohen (2008) states that:

> According to the empathising-systemising theory, autism and Asperger syndrome are best explained not just with reference to empathy (below average) but also with reference to a second psychological factor (systemising), which is either average or above average. So it is the discrepancy between E [empathy] and S [systemising] that determines if you are likely to develop autism or Asperger syndrome.

This is sometimes referred to as the 'extreme male brain theory', as Baron-Cohen's research found clear sex differences between male and female brains. In brief he found that the male brains are better at systemising and female brains are better at empathising, and autistic people score higher than average males and females on systemising traits and lower on empathising. Seen in this light, autism can be conceptualised as an extreme of the typical male profile which was first put forward by Hans Asperger in 1944 (cited by Baron-Cohen, 2008).

The strength of this theory is that it is a two-factor theory, which can explain both the social and non-social features in autism. The below-average empathy can explain the social communication difficulties, whilst average or above average systemising is a way of explaining the narrow interests, repetitive behaviour and resistance to change or need for sameness.

Executive dysfunction theory

The psychological term 'executive function' is defined as the 'ability to control actions' (Baron-Cohen, 2008). It refers to the 'ability to maintain an appropriate problem-solving strategy in order to attain a future goal' (Damian Milton, www.autismeducationtrust.org.uk) and, according to Attwood (2008), this includes:

Executive function

Organisational and planning abilities.

Working memory.

Inhibition and impulse control.

Self-reflection and self-monitoring.

Time management and prioritising.

Understanding complex or abstract concepts.

Using new strategies.

Executive dysfunction is characteristic of patients who have suffered damage in the prefrontal cortex, and whilst in autism there has not been any damage to the frontal lobe, developmentally the prefrontal cortex may not have matured in the typical way. According to this theory, some of the core features of autism are best explained by an inability to plan actions (executive control) and shift attention, such as transitioning. So, autistic people may have difficulties with switching attention and may have an adverse reaction to interference with attention (Tammet, 2006). They may also struggle to inhibit a response, have problems with working memory and using new strategies, and may also struggle with organising and prioritising work, and with abstract reasoning.

However, there is also evidence that some autistic people have performed well on executive functioning tests. Dawson et al. (2007) found that autistic people can often do very well at nonverbal IQ tests and problem-solving tasks that do not require verbal processing. Damian Milton (www.autismeducationtrust.org.uk) summarises that this suggests that executive planning for nonverbal tasks is separable in brain functioning from verbal tasks, or that this weakness in verbal response tests is not due to an executive functioning deficit.

In terms of understanding social competence, this theory is possibly the least useful. However, it may help to explain some aspects, such as a tendency to monologue or difficulties with turn taking, and some difficulties inhibiting their own beliefs and thoughts. Also, it helps to explain the fact that they may struggle to draw and reflect on past social experiences in order to problem-solve, anticipate and remember rules in social situations, and to change their behaviour. But, out of the four theories, it probably explains more about difficulties within the domains of cognition, motor and repetition than in social interaction.

Summary

In this chapter, I have only focused on social communication in autism and so I would also recommend that the reader explores the difficulties relating to the other main area of deficit relating to restricted, repetitive patterns of behaviour, as this will also guide your intervention in other practical ways. I have found that the more I understand about autism, the more I am able to be successful in supporting the young people I work with who have a diagnosis of autism, so I am hoping that this goes some way to increase your understanding of why autistic people struggle with their social skills.

I am also aware that in writing this chapter, I may have focused on the 'difficulties' and 'deficits' of autism and, whereas I know this knowledge has helped me in my work, I also know that I am in danger of putting autism into a medical model. It is true that autistic people struggle with social interaction, but I wonder what would happen if we all stopped seeing autistic people as having a 'disorder' or a condition that needed 'treatment' and starting seeing people who see the world from a different perspective, and who ultimately have to negotiate a social world that was not designed for them?

Jessie, the young autistic lady who I have had the pleasure to work with and become friends with, once wrote the following words to me after she had been coming to our day service for a couple of years following her late diagnosis: 'I now live in a world willing to adjust to me'. So, just like she says, I think we should all try to adjust our communication, our behaviour, our perspective, our intervention and our world. Because in doing that, Jessie (and other autistic people) can have more opportunities to experience success in how she lives her life, and how she interacts with others in this social world. How rewarding is that?

Key points from Chapter 11

This chapter covered social skills and the person with autism.

A diagnosis of ASD

There are two essential features of ASD: firstly, the child (or adult) will experience 'persistent deficits in social communication and social interaction', and secondly, 'restricted, repetitive patterns of behaviour, interests or activities' (DSM-5, 2013). Social skills deficits can be divided into three symptoms:

1. Deficits in social-emotional reciprocity
2. Deficits in nonverbal communicative behaviours used for social interaction
3. Deficits in developing, maintaining and understanding relationships

We looked at six areas of difficulty for the person with ASD:

Social use of language

Most of our communication happens nonverbally (93%) and we have rules that govern our social use of language (often referred to as 'pragmatics'). Communication also happens within a social context and so it is not just the words that people choose to speak, but all the other messages that are sent which are difficult for the autistic person to pick up on.

Conversational skills

Conversations with an autistic person can include moments where there appears to be a breakdown in communication 'transmission'. They may stop talking, take over the conversation, interrupt or change the topic and speak in monologues. We see difficulties with all stages: listening, starting, maintaining and ending a conversation.

Literal understanding of language

Understanding figurative speech is often hard, as it requires us to identify subtle relationships between words and phrases, understand the meaning based on our prior experience (or knowledge), and then to take the perspective of the speaker. Figurative messages include metaphors, idioms, sarcasm, puns and similes.

Body language

A deficit in nonverbal communication is a symptom of ASD and a description of 'clumsy or gauche' body language is also included in the diagnostic criteria for Asperger Syndrome. We will see difficulties in all aspects of body language, including use of eye contact, facial expression, gesture, distance, touch, posture and fidgeting.

Prosody

When listening to the speech of an autistic person, we can often hear unusual patterns in their paralinguistic skills.

Relationships

Friendships and relationships are complicated, emotional and unpredictable, which makes them all very challenging for the autistic person.

We looked at four theories of ASD and how they affect social communication:

1. *Theory of mind.* Theory of mind means the ability to recognise and understand thoughts, beliefs, desires and intentions of other people in order to make sense of their behaviour and predict what they are going to do next. Autistic people have a delayed ToM which leads to difficulties with reciprocal interaction.
2. *Weak central coherence.* This second theory suggests that autistic people have problems in integrating information to make a coherent, global picture. This means that they may not see the whole social picture and this may lead to inappropriate behaviour.
3. *Empathising-systemising.* According to the empathising-systemising theory, autism and Asperger syndrome are best explained not just with reference to empathy (below average) but also with reference to a second factor (systemising), which is either average or above average. It is sometimes referred to as the 'extreme male brain theory'.
4. *Executive dysfunction.* Some of the core features of autistic people are best explained by an inability to plan actions (executive control) and shift attention, such as transitioning.

Table 11.5 My top ten tips for working with an autistic child

Think about . . .	In particular . . .
1. The environment	Is there communication overload? Is there sensory overload? Is someone sensitive to a particular sense? Consider seating, colour/patterns, perfume, noise etc.
2. The task	One task at a time. Think about instructions. Think about routine. Think about the use of visuals or paper and pens.
3. Their anxiety	New situations will make them anxious. Prepare them in advance. Explain it clearly. Give the person a time and stick to it. Keep a routine as much as possible.
4. Their communication	How much do they understand? What is the best way to help them to express themselves? What are their specific difficulties?
5. Your verbal communication	Be clear and specific. Avoid abstract or ambiguous language. Repeat if necessary but keep same word order. Check that they have understood.
6. Your nonverbal communication	Use clear body language to back up what you are saying. Use a calm tone of voice.
7. Feedback	Encourage feedback. Give feedback on their performance. Get feedback on your performance.
8. Taking things personally	Communication can sometimes be blunt. Try not to take this personally. There is mostly no malice or forethought.
9. Time	Consider 'chill-out' spaces or 'alone time'. Bring in options for someone to take time away from others.
10. The 'why'	If the person behaves in an unexpected or challenging way, always ask why? What are they communicating? How can you help?

Chapter 12

Assessing social skills

The root of the word 'assessment' is from the Latin word 'assidere' which means 'to sit beside'.

For me, as a clinician, assessment is an essential first step to working with someone. We have to assess to know where to start. We have to know where to start so we set children up to succeed. Assessment should therefore enable us to adequately measure social skills competence so that we can firstly decide what to work on, then secondly to assess the effectiveness of our intervention through reassessment. Merrell (2001) sums it all up nicely saying:

> Screening and assessment are essential foundations for effective intervention in social-behavioural problems of children and youth. Without the careful identification, classification, and selection that should be part of good assessment, social behaviour interventions are likely to be haphazard at best and ineffective at worst.

The key questions for anyone assessing social skills are: How should we assess social skills? What should we assess? And how can we use the information to plan and measure the effectiveness of the intervention?

Methods of assessment

There are different methods of assessing social skills, and each one has its benefits, but the challenge with assessment is always to find meaningful ways to make the assessment results functional. Assessment is only useful if it can help us to identify the important skills for development.

There are six primary methods of assessment: behaviour observation, behaviour rating scales, interviewing, self-report tools, projective-expressive techniques (for example drawing), and socio-metric techniques (for example peer rating). In this chapter, we will focus on the first four as they are the most relevant to assessing social skills.

Observational methods

There are many advantages to observing people in the settings where they normally interact with others. Back in 1987, Elliott and Gresham proposed that 'analysing children's behaviour in natural settings . . . is the most ecologically valid method of assessing children's social skills'. Unlike other assessment methods, it does not require the use of specific tests or instruments, but relies on 'observer-constructed protocols, which are built on the basic empirical principles of naturalistic observation and which are designed specifically to meet the assessment needs of the situation' (Merrell, 2001). This means that they are hugely valuable because they are truly person-centred. According to Jones et al. (cited by Merrell, 2001), naturalistic behaviour observation includes three parts:

1. Observing and recording behaviours in a natural setting, for example the playground or other settings where interaction with peers occurs.
2. Using trained and objective observers.
3. A behavioural description system that requires minimal subjective inference from the observer.

Information needs to be gathered systematically to gain an overall picture of interaction and the following table sets out the three main categories of observation methods that can be used:

Table 12.1 Methods of observation

Method	Purpose	Method of recording	Benefits
Participant observation	Natural observation which takes place as part of ongoing work. Used to record behaviours identified as significant as they occur.	Informal narrative account written up immediately.	*Good* at capturing the quality of natural interactions. Requires no advance preparation. *But* relies on observer remembering details and can result in lots of information being recorded.
Event sampling	Used to record an event that has been identified as significant.	Formal recording using a schedule, recording how many times behaviour occurs, either during the whole length of the observation or by dividing up the period into time intervals.	Events that are similar can be compared over time. *But* observer needs to be present when the event occurs.

Method	Purpose	Method of recording	Benefits
Time sampling	Used to record the frequency of an event within a period of time.	Behaviour is recorded when it occurs or if it occurs and can also include how long it lasts.	Provides measurable information about social behaviour. *But* this may not be appropriate with some children, for example autistic children.

Adapted from Conn, 2016

Ideally, observations are done *in vivo*, which is naturally the most desirable way to observe social interaction but is also the least practical and most time-consuming. If this is not possible, we can also observe children using *naturalistic interactions*, where we use structured or staged interactions which are intended to parallel *in vivo* encounters. Finally, we can use *role play*, where we can present the child with a wide range of potentially relevant situations that cannot be easily replicated in the natural environment.

Despite the many advantages of using naturalistic behavioural observations to assess social skills, there are some potential problems.

Potential problems with naturalistic behavioural observations

1. *Time.* One of the most practical problems is the amount of time it takes to not only conduct the observation, but also to plan the appropriate recording system and train the observers to ensure that the observations are as useful as possible.
2. *Observational recording systems are either too vague or too cumbersome.* The categories of behaviour being observed have to be clearly defined otherwise it is impossible to compare one observation with another.
3. *Unreliability of observers.* Observers may drift from the original definition and may interpret behaviours differently, particularly borderline behaviours.
4. *Observer reactivity.* The child being observed is influenced by the presence of the observer and so does not behave naturally.
5. *Situation-specific.* The observations may not be representative of other situations and therefore they do not represent the bigger picture.

This all means that despite the quality of the information we can gain from completing observations, this comes at a cost. Conducting and coding observations is a slow and painstaking process and, at the end of the day, they only give us a snapshot of someone's social skills so should be used alongside other methods of assessment, such as behaviour rating scales.

Behaviour rating scales

Rating scales are an extremely useful measure of change and are one of the most widely used methods of assessment. Merrell (2001) states that:

> Assessment of social skills (and social behaviour in general) of children and adolescents is one area in which behaviour rating scales have made a particularly strong impact in recent years and in which an impressive body of supportive empirical evidence has accrued.

Using rating scales, information can be obtained about the person's behaviour through observing them in actual social interactions in their everyday environment (see earlier) and/or by talking to a number of people who know the child well. The information is then transferred onto a rating scale which may use either numbers or descriptions to rate each skill, and some use a combination of both.

There are several advantages to using rating scales and these are summarised below:

Advantages of rating scales

1. *Cost.* It is less expensive in terms of professional time involved and the amount of training required to be able to use an assessment rating system.
2. *Information on low-frequency behaviours.* Rating scales can provide information on behaviours that might not be seen in direct observational sessions.
3. *An objective method.* Provides more reliable data than interviews or projective-expressive techniques.
4. *Can assess people who cannot/will not provide information on themselves.* For example children with limited verbal skills or children who are uncooperative.
5. *Can assess over a period of time.* It can assess behaviours over several situations and over a period of time.
6. *Uses judgements of familiar people.* Rating scales capitalise on the judgements and observations of people who know the person well and are considered to be 'expert' informants.

So in short, they provide a 'big picture' of the assessment problem in a short amount of time, at moderate cost, and with a good deal of technical precision and practical use.

There are a few standardised social skills assessments available that use a rating scale. The most popular is the SSIS (Social Skills Improvement System) Rating Scales (Gresham and Elliot, 2008). This rating scale is designed to assess individuals in order to evaluate social skills, problem behaviours, and academic competence using a three- or five- point rating scale and is one of the few assessments that includes a comprehensive parent report version.

The assessment includes separate rating scales for teachers, parents and the student, and it includes 57 items divided into three scales:

- *Social skills*: communication, cooperation, assertion, responsibility, empathy, engagement, self-control
- *Competing problem behaviours*: externalizing, bullying, hyperactivity/inattention, internalizing, autism spectrum
- *Academic competence*: reading achievement, maths achievement, motivation to learn.

Other assessments, such as the '*Talkabout* Assessment Tool' (Kelly, 2010) use a four-point rating scale that is designed to be completed by a number of people who know the person well (including parents where possible or appropriate). Ratings go from 'never good' to 'not very good' to 'quite good' to 'very good' (with a description of what that would look like with each specific skill).

Interviewing

The interview is the traditional method of assessing social skills and assumes that the person we are assessing is potentially the richest source of information about themselves. The interviewee is usually the person being assessed, but it is also relevant to interview others as part of a social skills assessment, such as parents and teachers. One of the advantages of the interview method is that it is capable of providing relevant and functional information about the environment or situations in which the difficulties arise and can therefore be effectively linked to intervention. For example, we can ask about specific settings, or particular times, to gain insight into what is a priority for that individual or their parent/teacher.

Interviewing is an adaptable way of assessing social skills as it can range from the use of a highly structured interview schedule, such as the 'self-awareness interview' in *Talkabout* for Children (Kelly, 2011) or *Talkabout* for Teenagers (Kelly and Sains, 2009), to a free-flowing, unstructured interview. It is an opportunity to observe them interacting on a one-to-one basis and to assess their self-awareness and self-esteem, and to give them the opportunity to talk about those aspects of themselves which they think are the most important. As Rubin (2002) says, 'we can certainly learn a lot about a child's social life by simply asking him to tell us about it' and so I would always include an element of interviewing as part of my assessment process.

Self-reports

The fourth relevant assessment method is self-reports. Self-reports provide information about a person's subjective perceptions of his or her own social competence, but rely on the child being able to report their thoughts and opinions about his or her social behaviours, something which children with social skills difficulties can find hard. Self-reports or self-assessments are often found to be useful for evaluating internalising problems, such as depression and anxiety, but in the area of social skills, very little has been done to demonstrate the effectiveness of this.

As we mentioned earlier, the SSIS (Gresham and Elliot, 2008) uses a student self-report as part of the assessment, but there is 'a great deal of divergence between self-reported social skills of children and youth and more direct measures of social skills, such as behavioural observation and behaviour rating scales' (Merrell, 2001). Warnes et al. (2005) also state that:

> Although self-reports can provide unique information regarding a child's perceptions of his or her social behaviour, the subjective nature of this technique precludes

criterion-related validity and as such, is not often used as a stand-alone procedure for assessing social competence.

So it would appear that, whereas we may find self-reports interesting in assessing social skills, we should not use this as our main method of assessment.

In summary, there are primarily four ways in which we can assess social skills and Merrell (2001) places them (and the other two which are rarely used) in order of choice in terms of viability and reliability. He describes his 'first-line choices' as naturalistic behavioural observation and behaviour rating scales. His 'second-line choices' are interviewing (and socio-metric tools), and his 'third-line choices' are self-report assessments (and projective-expressive techniques). I agree with him, but would add that the ideal assessment should always include elements of the first three – observation, rating scales and interviewing – and then sometimes an element of the fourth – self-reports. So, for example, an assessment process may look like this:

Table 12.2 The assessment process

Age	Initial meeting	Second meeting	Methods used
Pre-school child	Meet with parents or care givers to discuss issues. Complete case history. Observe child. Start to complete rating scale with parents.	Observe child in another setting. Interview child if appropriate (e.g. self-awareness interview) Complete rating scale.	Interview Observation Rating scale Self-report
School-age child	Meet with teacher to discuss issues. Complete case history. Interview student. Start to complete rating scale with teachers.	Observe student either *in vivo* or as part of a session. Meet parents if possible. Complete rating scale jointly with teachers and parents.	Interview Self-report Observation Rating scale
Adult	Meet with adult (and others if relevant) to discuss issues and complete case history. Interview adult. Start to complete rating scale.	Meet adult in another setting if possible and observe. Complete rating scale and discuss priorities with adult and/or others.	Interview Self-report Observation Rating scale

What do we assess?

It is important to assess all social skills prior to intervention so that we can decide where we need to start work and also so that we have a baseline assessment from which to measure success. An assessment of social skills should initially include an assessment of body language, paralinguistic skills, conversational skills and assertiveness skills.

Assessment of body language

Our body language is made up of eight primary behaviours and, as we saw in Chapters 2 and 3, it accounts for up to 93% of our communication. We should assess the child or adult on the following skills:

Body language

Eye contact

Facial expression

Gestures/use of hands

Distance

Touch

Fidgeting

Posture

Personal appearance

The behaviours are rated using a consensus of opinions from a number of people who know the person well and who have ideally observed them in a number of different settings. We are also rating that person in terms of what is appropriate for them in terms of age and culture, so a child aged four will be rated differently from a person of 24 when considering appropriate use of touch and distance. It is also important to consider how other people are responding to these behaviours, so how appropriate they are to their environment.

As previously said, the *Talkabout* (Kelly 2010) rating scale uses a four-point rating scale where scores of a 1 or 2 indicate that this is a 'need' for the person and scores of a 3 or 4 indicate a relative strength. This means that any behaviours that have been scored 1 or 2 are highlighted as areas of concern (or behaviours that we will focus on for intervention) and those with a score of 3 or 4 are seen as relative strengths. These are then plotted onto a wheel (see end of section). So, for example, eye contact is rated using the following descriptions:

Table 12.3 Eye contact rating

	1 *Never good*	2 *Not very good*	3 *Quite good*	4 *Very good*
Eye contact	Avoids eye contact at all times or may continuously stare	Often will avoid eye contact or may regularly stare	Appropriate use of eye contact in most situations. May break down at times of stress.	Effective and appropriate use of eye contact in all situations

One problem that can occur when assessing people is the fact that a four-point rating scale can be quite narrow and does not always show subtle improvements when reassessing. This can lead to people over-assessing to show improvement, but in doing this, they mask a need. To help with this problem, I always recommend that when observing someone, we consider how much support they require to achieve the skill and I have devised a number of target forms to help us to complete the *Talkabout* Assessment wheel (see Table 12.12). We can then use these to set targets for intervention and measure effectiveness.

So, for example, the target for eye contact could be 'to be able to use appropriate eye contact for short periods of time' and we would assess their ability to do this using a six-point rating scale from 'skill not present' to 'skill present and consistent across most situations'. However, we also assess through observation how much support the child needs to achieve this. The following table shows how the target rating form could look.

Table 12.4 Target rating form for eye contact

Rating	*Talkabout Assessment rating*	*Eye contact* **Able to use appropriate eye contact for short periods of time**
1. *Skill not present* Child not able to do this even with lots of prompting and support from you	1	
2. *Skill emerging with prompting* Child can do this but only after lots of support from you	1	
3. *Skill emerging with occasional prompting* Child can do this with a bit of support	2	
4. *Skill present in a structured situation* Child can do this spontaneously in a structured setting only	2	
5. *Skill present in some other situations* The child is able to do this in some other settings	2	
6. *Skill present and consistent across most situations* The child is able to do this in any setting (and does not need intervention)	3 or 4	Achieved: . . . . (date)

In using this rating scale, we can extend out the ratings of 1 or 2 on the *Talkabout* Assessment Tool to ratings of 1–5 which enables us to show progress more easily, and we pay less attention to skills that are relative strengths for that person (a rating of 3 or 4 on the Talkabout Assessment Tool and a rating of 6 on the Target rating form).

Assessment of paralinguistic skills

Our paralinguistic skills are made up of five behaviours, so we should assess the child or adult on the following skills:

Paralinguistic skills

Volume
Rate
Clarity
Intonation
Fluency

As before, the behaviours are rated using a consensus of opinions from a number of people who know the person well and who have ideally observed them in a number of different settings. So, for example, volume is rated using the following descriptions:

Table 12.5 Volume rating

	1 *Never good*	2 *Not very good*	3 *Quite good*	4 *Very good*
Volume	Mostly uses inappropriate volume, e.g. voice is too quiet or loud for the situation	Regularly uses inappropriate volume, e.g. voice is too quiet or loud for the situation	Can mostly use and adapt their volume appropriately to the situation. May break down at times of stress.	Uses and adapts their volume appropriately to the situation

Assessment of conversation skills

Our conversational skills are made up of eight behaviours:

Conversational skills

Listening
Starting a conversation
Taking turns
Asking questions

Answering questions
Being relevant
Repairing
Ending a conversation

As before, the behaviours are rated using a consensus of opinions from a number of people. So, for example, relevance is rated using the following descriptions:

Table 12.6 Relevance rating

	1 *Never good*	2 *Not very good*	3 *Quite good*	4 *Very good*
Being relevant	Has difficulty in following a topic of conversation, e.g. regularly introduces unrelated ideas/topics	Has some difficulty in following a topic of conversation, e.g. will introduce unrelated ideas/topics	Can mostly maintain and develop a topic of conversation effectively and appropriately. May break down at times of stress.	Can maintain and develop a topic of conversation effectively and appropriately, e.g. asking relevant questions

Assessment of assertiveness

Finally in our social skills assessment, we will assess assertiveness. Our assertiveness skills are made up of eight behaviours so we should assess the child or adult on the following skills:

Assertiveness

Expressing feelings	Disagreeing
Standing up for yourself	Complaining
Making suggestions	Apologising
Refusing	Requesting explanations

As before, the behaviours are rated using a consensus of opinions from a number of people. So, for example, refusing is rated using the following descriptions:

Table 12.7 Refusing rating

	1 *Never good*	2 *Not very good*	3 *Quite good*	4 *Very good*
Refusing	Will either always comply with requests, even when against their will, or will refuse aggressively or continuously	Will often comply with requests, even when against their will, or will often refuse aggressively	Is mostly able to refuse appropriately and effectively to the situation. May break down at times of stress.	Able to refuse appropriately and effectively to the situation and using an explanation where appropriate

Having assessed all of the above skills, the ratings are then plotted onto the *Talkabout* wheel (see Figure 12.1), either manually if using the paper version of the assessment (Kelly, 2018b) or electronically if using the *Talkabout* Assessment Tool on CD (Kelly and Sains, 2010).

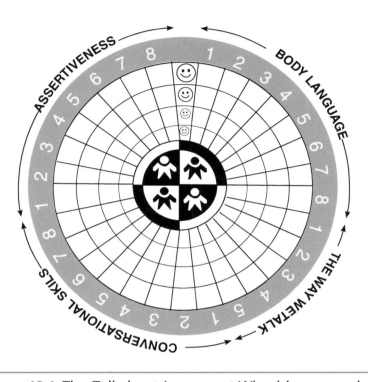

Social Skills Assessment Summary

Figure 12.1 The *Talkabout* Assessment Wheel (paper version)

Body language	The way we talk	Conversations	Assertiveness
Eye contact	Volume	Listening	Expressing feelings
Facial expression	Rate	Starting conversations	Standing up for self
Gesture	Clarity	Taking turns	Making suggestions
Distance	Intonation	Asking questions	Refusing
Touch	Fluency	Answering questions	Disagreeing
Fidgeting		Relevance	Complaining
Posture		Repairing	Apologising
Personal appearance		Ending conversations	Requesting explanations

Planning intervention

Following assessment, it is then necessary to choose the goal of intervention. Choosing the right skill to work on first has to be the most important part of intervention as it is the difference between potentially setting a child up to fail or succeed. Results from social skills work in the early nineties lead to the development of a hierarchy which is the basis of the *Talkabout* resources.

Talkabout was first developed in the early 1990s when I was working as a speech and language therapist in London, UK. I was particularly interested in social skills but was frustrated by two aspects of my work as a therapist. First, there was nothing in the literature to guide me on where to start intervention following assessment; and second, my experience showed me that I was not always successful in what I was trying to teach and I could not always predict which children were going to improve and which were not. I set about to answer these two questions over a period of four years.

I started my investigations at a college of further education where I was working with 60 students who had a mild to moderate intellectual disability. We assessed all of the young people I was working with using an adapted social skills assessment from the Personal Communication Plan by Hitchings and Spence – now published in Kelly, 2000. The students were involved in this assessment, which gave us some insight into their own awareness of their difficulties. From these initial results, we grouped students into their main area of need: body language, conversational skills, or assertiveness. We evaluated success through retesting on the original assessment and also compared students with poor and good awareness of their needs.

The results were fascinating. They showed that the students who had been working on their conversational skills progressed more if they had good existing nonverbal skills (i.e. body language), and students who had been working on their assertiveness progressed significantly more if they had good existing nonverbal and verbal skills. In addition, we found that students who had poor self and other awareness struggled with all aspects of the work. From this, we established a hierarchy which forms the basis of the *Talkabout* resources.

Over the next four years, we piloted this programme using different client groups and a group of willing therapists from all around the UK, and we all found consistently that the success of intervention increased if nonverbal behaviours were taught prior to verbal behaviours, and assertiveness was taught last (Kelly, 1996). This original hierarchy then formed the basis of the first *Talkabout* book and is shown in the following figure. In the following years, I became interested in the impact that self-esteem has on social skills and then also the relationship between social skills difficulties and friendship skills, and so the hierarchy was updated in 2000 to include these two additional areas.

Using this hierarchical approach, the clinician is able to start work with the person at a level that is appropriate to their needs and progress up the levels to enable them to reach their full potential, ensuring that basic skills are taught prior to more complex ones. So, it can be seen that someone who needs work on all areas of social skills would start work first on body language skills and then would progress onto working on paralinguistic skills, then conversational skills and finally assertiveness skills. If this person also had poor self-awareness and low self-esteem, they would need to work on this prior to working on their social skills. If they also had difficulties with friendship skills, they would only work on developing these skills if they had good self-awareness and good nonverbal and verbal skills.

This hierarchy is backed up by the normal development of self-awareness, social skills and friendship skills summarised in Chapter 10. But it can also be seen as three areas that have a

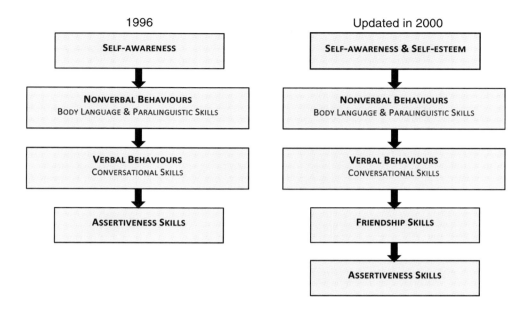

> ## Figure 12.2 The hierarchy of social skills
> *Source:* Original (Kelly 1996) and updated in 2000 to include self-esteem and friendship skills

direct effect on each other. As we saw in the self-esteem chapter, low self-esteem has a direct impact on social skills and friendship skills. We also saw in the friendship chapter that social skills are required to make friends and can be the cause of difficulties in this area. These relationships are shown by the black arrows in Figure 12.3. Of course, the opposite can also be true. Poor social skills and friendship skills can result in low self-esteem and poor friendship skills can make some social skills harder, but these are less common and are shown below as grey arrows.

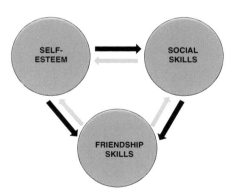

> ## Figure 12.3 The relationship between self-esteem, social skills and friendship skills

In summary, assessment is an essential first step to working with someone. We have to be able to assess someone so we know where to start. And we not only need to be able to assess social skills in an effective and measurable way, but we also need to consider the impact that self-awareness and self-esteem has on social skills, and sometimes we need to consider the impact that social skills have on friendship skills.

Interpreting a social skills assessment

As we have already said, choosing the right skill to work on first has to be the most important part of intervention, so in this next section I am going to talk through two examples of a young adult and a child I have assessed and what decisions I made regarding intervention.

Case example 1: 15-year-old young adult with Down's Syndrome

Mohammed, or Mo as he prefers to be called, was 15 years old when I first met him. He has Down's syndrome, a moderate intellectual disability and was just about to start a three-year life skills course for young adults with an intellectual disability within a mainstream college. His mother was concerned about his ability to cope within a more adult environment because of his poor social skills. I met him and his mother for an initial assessment at my house where I was able to interview both the mother and Mo, and also observe Mo in an informal setting, interacting with my own children and completing a few activities. I was then able to complete a social skills rating assessment jointly with his mother. The table below summarises my assessment:

Table 12.8 Initial assessment of Mo

Initial assessment	Method	Outcome
1. Informal observation	*Observation*/*video* Having a drink/ something to eat Talking to my children Playing a game	Mo has a good level of comprehension (approx. 3–4 word level) and good expressive skills. Mo is over-friendly – hugged me on arrival and linked arms with my 13-year-old son. Mo talks a lot about subjects he is interested in. Current interests include marriage, girlfriends, and several TV shows and Disney films. He can find it difficult to listen to others in a conversation when wanting to talk about his subject of interest.
2. Self-awareness/ self-esteem	*Self-awareness and self-esteem interview* from *Talkabout for Children* (2018) Watching a clip from the *Talkabout* DVD	Mo has a good self and other awareness (e.g. he has a good idea of what he looks like, his likes and dislikes, and was able to describe others on the DVD). Mo has a high self-esteem (e.g. he is able to think of things he is good at and why people like him).

Initial assessment	Method	Outcome
3. Social skills assessment	*Talkabout Assessment Tool* (2010) Completed jointly with mother	This showed that he had difficulties in all areas of social skills: body language, the way he talks (paralinguistic skills), conversational skills and assertiveness (see below). Skills that need work have been highlighted in bold and underlined.
4. Friendship skills assessment	Not assessed	n/a

Talkabout Assessment Summary

Name: Mohammed

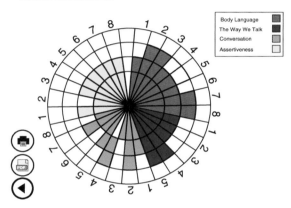

BODY LANGUAGE	THE WAY WE TALK	CONVERSATIONS	ASSERTIVENESS
1. **Eye contact** 2. Facial expression 3. Gesture 4. **Distance** 5. **Touch** 6. **Fidgeting** 7. Posture 8. Personal appearance	1. **Volume** 2. **Rate** 3. **Clarity** 4. Intonation 5. Fluency	1. **Listening** 2. Starting conversations 3. **Takingturns** 4. Asking questions 5. **Answering questions** 6. **Relevance** 7. **Repairing** 8. **Ending conversations**	1. **Expressing feelings** 2. **Standing up for self** 3. **Making suggestions** 4. **Refusing** 5. **Disagreeing** 6. **Complaining** 7. **Apologising** 8. **Requesting explanations**

Figure 12.4 *Talkabout* Assessment (CD version): assessment summary on Mo

Conclusion

Mo has good self-awareness and self-esteem and so, using the hierarchical approach, we need to start work on his *body language*. My initial goal for Mo was to teach him appropriate touch and distance, as it was felt that this will be a huge barrier to college life. Using the *Talkabout* Target Sheet (see Table 12.12), I rated him initially as follows:

Table 12.9 *Talkabout* Target Assessment summary on Mo

TARGET	1 Skill not present	2 Skill emerging with prompting	3 Skill emerging with occasional prompting	4 Skill present in structured situation	5 Skill present in some other situations	6 Skill present and consistent across most situations
Talkabout Assessment Rating	*1*	*1*	*2*	*2*	*2*	*3/4*
Distance Understands and uses good distance with other people			√ (date 1)			
Touch Understands and uses appropriate touch with other people			√ (date 1)			

This gives us a clear starting point for working with Mo on the two skills of distance and touch.

Interestingly, his mother was actually keen for me to work on his turn-taking and his relevance and had already tried to do this, with little success. Why is this? Well, it is logical. Conversational skills are more complex than the nonverbal behaviours. For example, consider relevance. In order to be relevant in a conversation, we need to listen. In order to listen we need to use appropriate eye contact, facial expression and posture to show we are listening. So, by choosing 'relevance', we are setting Mo up to fail as he doesn't have the underpinning skills necessary. By choosing 'distance' and 'touch' we are helping him to succeed, and this will immediately have an impact on his new course and his motivation to work with me. I will discuss his intervention in a subsequent chapter.

Case example 2: 9-year-old child

Thomas was nine years old when I first met him. He attends mainstream school where he is struggling to fit in. He is doing OK academically but he does not have many friends and he is getting bullied. Parents report that Thomas is obsessed by Pokemon and fantasy characters, and he is alienating his peers and his family by wanting to talk about this frequently. He does not have any formal diagnosis but his parents are beginning to question whether he may be autistic. I met him and his parents for an initial assessment at their house, where I was able to interview both the parents and Thomas, and also observe Thomas in a relaxed setting, completing a few activities with myself and his sister. I then visited him at school, where I was able to interview his teacher and observe Thomas in class and at break time. I completed a social skills rating assessment with input from both his teacher and his mother. The table below summarises my assessment.

Table 12.10 Initial assessment of Thomas

Initial assessment	Method	Outcome
Informal observation	*Observation / video* Chatting to his sister Playing a game School lesson (PSHE) School break time (playground)	Thomas is a shy, polite child who appears unsure of himself in company and not particularly happy. He has a stilted, formal way of talking and only seemed animated when talking about Pokemon. He was polite at school, if a little distant. He mainly played on his own in the playground, sometimes approaching another child and standing near to them, but neither child initiated any conversation or play.
Self-awareness/ self-esteem	*Self-awareness and self-esteem interview* and an activity 'It's good to be . . .' from *Talkabout* for Children 1 (2018)	Thomas has good self-awareness but appears to have low self-esteem. He described himself as 'not very happy most of the time' and identified a number of things he would like to change about himself.
Social skills assessment	*Talkabout* Assessment Tool (2010) Completed jointly with mother & teacher	This showed that he had some difficulties in all areas of social skills: body language, the way he talks (paralinguistic skills), conversational skills and assertiveness (see below). Skills that need work have been highlighted in bold and underlined.
Friendship skills assessment	*Interview (a few questions)* from *Talkabout* for Children 3 (2018)	Thomas does have a few friends at school that he wants to play with but he also recognises that sometimes they don't want to play with him. He thinks they are 'busy'.

Conclusion

Thomas has good self-awareness but low self-esteem. He also has some difficulties with his body language, but most of his social skills difficulties are with his conversations and assertiveness. He also has difficulties with his friendship skills which are being hampered by his social skills. Using the hierarchical approach, we need to help him to develop a higher

Talkabout Assessment Summary

Name: Thomas

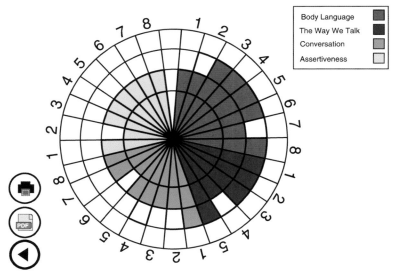

BODY LANGUAGE	THE WAY WE TALK	CONVERSATIONS	ASSERTIVENESS
1. **Eye contact**	1. Volume	1. Listening	1. **Expressing feelings**
2. **Facial expression**	2. Rate	2. **Starting conversations**	2. **Standing up for self**
3. Gesture	3. Clarity	3. **Takingturns**	3. **Making suggestions**
4. Distance	4. **Intonation**	4. **Asking questions**	4. **Refusing**
5. Touch	5. Fluency	5. **Answering questions**	5. **Disagreeing**
6. Fidgeting		6. **Relevance**	6. **Complaining**
7. **Posture**		7. **Repairing**	7. **Apologising**
8. Personal appearance		8. **Ending conversations**	8. **Requesting explanations**

Figure 12.5 *Talkabout* Assessment (CD version): assessment summary on Thomas

self-esteem, and then to help him to develop better conversational skills and then friendship skills. I did not think we needed to focus on his nonverbal behaviours, as the majority of these were appropriate and the few that were inappropriate (eye contact, facial expression, posture and intonation) were linked to his self-esteem or his possible autism.

Table 12.11 *Talkabout* Target Assessment summary on Thomas

Target	1 Skill not present	2 Skill emerging with prompting	3 Skill emerging with occasional prompting	4 Skill present in structured situation	5 Skill present in some other situations	6 Skill present & consistent across most situations
Talkabout Assessment Rating	1	1	2	2	2	3/4
Qualities To be able to say 3 qualities or strengths		√ (date 1)				
Self-esteem To be able to give 3 reasons why he likes himself	√ (date 1)					

Using the *Talkabout* Target system (see Table 12.12 at the end of the chapter), I rated his self-esteem using the target shown in Table 12.11.

My intervention included, over the year: group work at school, a social story about Pokemon and reward systems at home. These interventions will be discussed in the following chapters.

Summary

A good assessment is the beginning of any good intervention. We have to assess, to know where to start. Assessment should enable us to adequately measure social skills competence so that we can firstly decide what to work on, but then secondly to assess the effectiveness of our intervention through reassessment. In this chapter we have looked at the different methods of assessment and how to assess skills to help measure the effectiveness of our intervention. We will discuss how to do this second part of reassessment and evaluation in Chapter 17 but rating scales lend themselves ideally to this kind of quantitative analysis, both as a long-term measure, as in the four-point *Talkabout* (Kelly, 2010) rating and as a short-term measure, using specific targets and smaller scale points. So, to help with our baseline measure, I have included a framework at the end of this chapter (Table 12.12) for setting targets for all the social skills behaviours identified.

Table 12.12 Social skills targets

SOCIAL SKILLS Targets	1 Skill not present Child not able to do this even with lots of prompting and support from you	2 Skill emerging with prompting Child can do this but only after lots of support from you	3 Skill emerging with occasional prompting Child can do this with a bit of support	4 Skill present in a structured situation Child can do this spontaneously in a structured setting only	5 Skill present in some other situations The child is able to do this in some other settings	6 Skill present & consistent across most situations The child is able to do this in any setting
Talkabout Assessment Rating	1	1	2	2	2	3/4

BODY LANGUAGE

1. EYE CONTACT - Able to use appropriate eye contact for short periods of time

2. FACIAL EXPRESSION - Able to use a range of appropriate facial expressions

3. GESTURE - Able to use gesture to support what they are saying

4. DISTANCE - Understands and uses good distance with other people

5. TOUCH - Understands and uses appropriate touch with other people

6. FIDGETING - Sits still when appropriate and not fidget for short periods of time

7. POSTURE - Able to use appropriate posture for short periods of time

8. PERSONAL APPEARANCE - Able to maintain and adapt appearance to the situation

THE WAY WE TALK

1. VOLUME - Able to use and adapt their volume appropriately in different situations

2. RATE - Able to use and adapt their rate appropriately in different situations

3. CLARITY - Their speech is clear and easily understood

4. INTONATION - Uses and adapts intonation appropriately in different situations

5. FLUENCY - Able to speak fluently with few hesitations for short periods of time

CONVERSATIONAL SKILLS

1. LISTENING - Able to show good listening for short periods of time

2. STARTING A CONVERSATION – Able to start a conversation using a variety of appropriate openers

(Continued)

Table 12.12 (Continued)

SOCIAL SKILLS Targets	1 Skill not present Child not able to do this even with lots of prompting and support from you	2 Skill emerging with prompting Child can do this but only after lots of support from you	3 Skill emerging with occasional prompting Child can do this with a bit of support	4 Skill present in a structured situation Child can do this spontaneously in a structured setting only	5 Skill present in some other situations The child is able to do this in some other settings	6 Skill present & consistent across most situations The child is able to do this in any setting
Talkabout Assessment Rating	1	1	2	2	2	3/4
3. TAKING TURNS - Able to take turns appropriately in a conversation for short periods of time						
4. ASKING QUESTIONS - Able to ask a range of appropriate questions within a conversation						
5. ANSWERING QUESTIONS - Able to answer questions appropriately within a conversation						
6. RELEVANCE - Can maintain, develop and change topics appropriately						
7. REPAIRING - Able to maintain relevance by seeking clarification or correcting mistakes						
8. ENDING A CONVERSATION - Able to end a conversation using nonverbal & verbal behaviours						

ASSERTIVENESS SKILLS

1. EXPRESSING FEELINGS - Expresses feelings using appropriate nonverbal and verbal skills

2. STANDING UP FOR YOURSELF Stands up for self using nonverbal and verbal skills

3. MAKING SUGGESTIONS Makes suggestions and gives opinions appropriate to situation

4. REFUSING Able to refuse appropriately using good nonverbal and verbal skills

5. DISAGREEING Able to disagree using appropriate nonverbal and verbal skills

6. *COMPLAINING - Able to complain appropriately using good nonverbal and verbal skills*

7. *APOLOGISING - Able to apologise without prompting using good nonverbal and verbal skills*

8. *REQUESTING EXPLANATIONS - Able to request an explanation appropriately when needed*

Key points from Chapter 12

This chapter covered how to assess social skills.

Methods of assessment

There are four relevant methods of assessing social skills:

- *Observational methods*: observing and recording behaviours in a natural setting. This can also include staged interactions or role play.
- *Behaviour rating scales*: rating scales are an extremely useful measure of change and are one of the most widely used methods of assessment. They can be used in conjunction with observational methods.
- *Interviewing*: the interview is the traditional method of assessing social skills and assumes that the person we are assessing is potentially the richest source of information about themselves.
- *Self-reports*: self-reports provide information about a person's subjective perceptions of his or her own social competence, but rely on the child being able to report their thoughts and opinions about his or her social behaviours, something which children with social skills difficulties can find difficult.

What do we assess?

It is important to assess all social skills prior to intervention so that we can decide where we need to start work, and also so that we have a baseline assessment from which to measure success. An assessment of social skills should initially include an assessment of body language, paralinguistic skills, conversational skills and assertiveness skills.

Planning intervention

Choosing the right skill to work on first has to be the most important part of intervention. The hierarchy of intervention was developed in the 1990s and states that we should teach self-awareness and self-esteem, followed by non-verbal behaviours (body language and paralinguistic skills), followed by verbal behaviours, and finally friendship skills and assertiveness.

Interpreting a social skills assessment

Two cases are described in terms of a summary of their initial assessment (method and summary of findings), a summary of their social skills assessment (using the *Talkabout* Assessment Tool), my conclusion and decision for intervention, and a description of the targets set.

- Case 1: a 15-year-old young adult with Down's Syndrome
- Case 2: a 9-year-old boy in mainstream school

Chapter 13

Teaching social skills 1
Approaches to teaching social skills

'What I hear, I forget. What I see, I remember. What I do, I understand.'

Confucius

Now we come to the fun part! We have increased our knowledge of this fascinating subject; we have assessed the child who we want to teach; and now we can teach them! And the important thing to remember is that we *can* teach social skills. Even if a child has never learnt the skills to interact with others appropriately, we can help them to develop these skills. And even if someone has learned poor social skills at the beginning of their life, it is possible to unlearn those skills of relating to others that are not working well and to learn more effective skills.

People can be sceptical about this. Adults and older children are frequently fatalistic about their interpersonal skills and think that their way of talking and listening, like the colour of their eyes, is a 'given' in their lives. I have also heard people say that if you try to teach adults better interpersonal skills, the adults then come across as phony. Of course, this can be true. I can think of several politicians who have clearly received some social skills training and then came across as awkward as they attempt a different way of interacting. Years of bad habits will naturally have their toll and a new approach will appear awkward to begin with. But the more they practise the better they become and the more natural it appears. And I can also think of politicians who have had social skills training and it has worked wonders.

We can also think of children who appear to know (intellectually) what they should be doing in any particular situation, but they (physically) don't do it. This can be frustrating for parents and teachers alike. However, it is important to remember that we are often asking children to change a behaviour that they have not practised in that setting before. They have instead had lots of practice doing the 'inappropriate' behaviour and it is this that is ingrained in their memory and behavioural repertoire. It is hard to suddenly change a behaviour that we have been doing for years and the older we are, the harder it becomes. Imagine if I asked you to pronounce the sound 's' with a lisp (with your tongue protruding). Could you succeed immediately? Would it initially feel a bit uncomfortable and odd? And if I told you to 'pay attention' or 'just do it' and to 'not make that mistake again' or to 'revert back to your old ways', what might that do to your confidence to get it right? Would it help? Sometimes we are expecting children to immediately change a behaviour that is etched into their brains, feels 'comfortable', or has been 'assigned' to them by other adults who have labelled them as the person who 'does that thing'. So before we even start this chapter, it is worth having an appreciation for what we are sometimes asking children (or adults) to do. It is hard work for them and it is up to us to help.

The secret is to get your intervention right, not only in terms of *what* you are teaching, but *how*. The 'what' is easier in my opinion. The 'how' is the interesting one. And because it is so interesting, I am going to take four chapters to talk about it! In this chapter we will address the different approaches to teaching skills, what the research tells us and things you need to think about *before* you start the actual intervention. I call this my four-step plan. In the next chapter I will describe the most common methods of teaching social skills, and this is followed by chapters on developing skills at school, and at home. So, we will start by looking at the different approaches to social skills training and considering the evidence for whether it works.

Different approaches to intervention

Behavioural approach and Applied Behaviour Analysis (ABA)

I will start with this approach to intervention as social skills training was originally developed by psychologists trained within the behavioural model and so it makes sense to discuss it first, although I must admit that I am not trained in ABA and have never used it in my work. In its purest form, behaviourism defines overt behaviour and overt behaviour only, as the subject matter of psychology (Wolman, 1973) originating from Skinner's behavioural (stimulus-response) theories. Some behaviourally orientated practitioners then began applying the basic principles of behaviour modification to interpersonal skills and behaviours. One of the new slants on behavioural theory was the introduction of the notion of 'skill' where Phillips (1979) insisted that 'social skills were largely understandable by means of observable behaviours' (Schneider, 2016). In practise, this means that an environment is created where behaving appropriately leads to more rewards than behaving inappropriately, so 'learning takes place as a consequence of reinforcements following on from an action' (Conn, 2016).

The Lovaas model of Applied Behavioural Analysis (ABA) (Lovaas, 2003) is the most well-known behavioural approach to teaching social skills and is based on the principle that skills can be taught using positive reinforcement. Appropriate behaviour is rewarded, and inappropriate behaviour is redirected or ignored. An initial assessment will identify the 'target deficit skill area' and then intensive programmes are designed to teach this skill using a systematic progression through small-step 'treatment goals' based on normative frameworks. Each skill is broken down into its component parts and taught in a structured teaching environment. Skills are prompted, practised and reinforced and may require anywhere from 30–40 hours per week of one-to-one teaching. ABA is primarily used with autistic children and in my experience evokes strong feelings. There are many people who love this approach to teaching skills and possibly just as many people who feel as strongly against it, including some autistic adults I know who have described their experiences of ABA negatively. Whichever way, the feelings appear to be strong.

Social learning approach

Not all parents and teachers want to control the contingencies of reinforcement so carefully, so, without abandoning the principles of the behavioural movement totally, they wanted an alternative method of intervention. Bandura's (1978) model of 'reciprocal determinism' brought significant changes to the behavioural tradition and several elements inspired many of the techniques still in use with children. Most notably, one of the elements is 'observational learning' – the process in which children learn things by watching and imitating others. Cognitive abilities and beliefs also form an important part of reciprocal determinism. Children are helped to understand other people and their intentions, to consider their beliefs about what is right and wrong, to plan their own social behaviour, and to evaluate their own effectiveness.

Structured learning approach

The structured learning model came out of Bandura's social learning theory (1978) and 'observational learning'. It states that the best imitation of models happens when 'the observer pays attention to the model, understands the salient features that are to be imitated, encodes those features for future reference, and is convinced that there is some incentive for imitating the model' (Schneider, 2016). The key steps in this approach are:

1. Provide a rationale to motivate the child (or adult). This may include stories to illustrate why it is important to be socially skilled.
2. Select a skill that is appropriate to teach them and one that will be important for them to succeed socially.
3. Break the skill down into 'skill steps'.
4. Model the skill using live demonstration, video, puppets or peers.
5. Rehearse the skill using role play, video and feedback.
6. Reward, reinforce, praise.

Cognitive behavioural approach

Problem-solving interventions are used regularly for children and adults with various forms of psychological disorders, but can also be used to support children with social skills difficulties. This approach evolved from research into the problem-solving styles of aggressive children. They were found to believe that they had few alternatives to aggression and were more likely to interpret behaviours as hostile (Dodge and Tomlin, 1987). The problem-solving sequence starts with getting the child to recognise that they have a problem and the sequence that is typically taught is shown in Figure 13.1 (taken from Schneider, 2016). Then, through guided discussions, the children learn to recognise problems, either through role play or from their own experience and then to 'brainstorm' alternatives in solving the problem. Each solution is then discussed in terms of its consequences and they are then supported to implement the best solution.

Developmental approach

Whereas the behavioural approaches to learning emphasises the teacher or therapist imparting and reinforcing skills, the developmental approach sees the child as actively engaging in and shaping their learning in a two-way interaction between teaching and learning. In

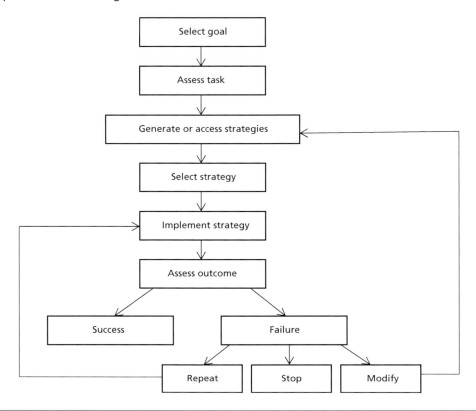

Figure 13.1 A social problem-solving model
Source: Rubin and Rose-Krasner, 1986

many theories of human development, play is seen to perform a key role. For Piaget, children's playful interaction with objects is 'an exploration of the environment that leads naturally to cognitive growth' and Vygotsky (1978) also stressed the importance of interactions with other people on human growth and that 'play is behaviour that precedes development' (Conn, 2016).

Vygotsky found that play was an optimum learning environment for children and that children showed greater motivation and self-control when engaged in playing. So a developmental approach to learning puts forward the idea that 'children are not passive learners, but participate actively in learning contexts, making sense of learning experiences, producing new learning and moving themselves forward in their understanding' (Conn, 2016). Therefore, it is not something that is 'done' to the child but something that occurs within the child, mediated through social interaction.

The evidence for social skills training

The effects of children's social skills training have been studied thoroughly over the years and many have been found to be effective. Even back in the 1970s, when social skills trainers focused on brief, verbal interventions, the evidence showed that these interventions do have a track record of some degree of success. However, many of the published studies demonstrated positive effects when effectiveness is measured immediately after treatment. Until recently, there were few long-term follow-up studies.

As social skills training expanded and enthusiasm grew, it became important to find out whether the improvement seen immediately after social skills work is maintained over time and generalised into other settings. Beidel et al. (2006) demonstrated that the gains of an enhanced social skills training programme for children experiencing social anxiety remained strong even five years after the intervention. O'Callaghan et al. (2003) showed that social skills training for children with attention deficit hyperactivity disorder (ADHD) generalises to other settings when specific generalisation techniques are used as part of the intervention. However, because we are asking more of the research, it is not always easy to find evidence that demonstrates both.

Most experts believe now that is it still worth doing, even if the evidence is not abundant. There have been ten review papers and meta-analyses of the effects of social skills training (cited by Schneider, 2016). These include the following conclusions: that social skills training for children with behavioural and emotional problems appears to be effective for about 65% of children, compared to 35% of children randomly assigned to treatment and control groups; that young children seem to respond better than older children; and that interventions in which there is active interaction between the group leaders and participants are typically more effective than didactic instruction alone.

In relation to working with autistic children, the evidence is similar to the children with emotional and behavioural difficulties, despite the differences in the social skills interventions. For example, the use of Social Stories™ to help children with autism to understand the subtleties of social interaction is a common and popular intervention. But a meta-analysis by Kokina and Kern (2010) indicated that results for the social narrative approach were no greater than those of other forms of social skills training with this population. More promising results came from interventions that were customised to the personal interests, skills, daily activities and social settings of each child and also where peers were involved, for example through peer mediation.

Schneider (2016) concludes by saying that, to date, research indicates that there are many techniques for improving social skills, and even though they may not work miracles, they are helpful, even in small ways, to many children. He goes on to say that the focus of research should now be on refining the techniques that have shown to be successful. Key aspects of success seem to be: ensuring the cooperation of other people in the child's life; adapting the content of the intervention to the setting, practitioner and child; and combining the programme with other techniques such as parental training. For example, Espada et al. (2012) found that the combination of social problem-solving and structured training of behavioural social skills is superior to either component by itself or to no treatment.

So, what can we take from all these theories and from what the research tells us? In my opinion, all the theories have something to offer and can be used at different times with different people, and the research, although not jaw-dropping, is encouraging. But there are some important themes coming through all of them. The importance of: motivation, role models and teachers, the environment, increased awareness and social understanding, reinforcement and praise. These will all be evident in some of the instructional approaches to teaching social skills that I will describe later, but let's not rush into them just yet. I want to start by suggesting that the first thing we should do is to stop and think about any intervention by using my four-step plan.

The four-step plan to intervention

I believe that sometimes we are too quick to jump into the intervention. We rush to write a story, set up a role play, or start a group. Actually, we should stop and think about the intervention and plan it carefully. So, I developed a four-step plan to help people to view the intervention as the final step.

The four-step plan to intervention

Step 1 Choose the behaviour
Step 2 Consider the motivation
Step 3 Consider the environment
Step 4 Choose the strategy

Step 1 The behaviour

There are four key words to think about in this first step: choose; why; describe; rules.

Choose

The first step to intervention is to choose the appropriate behaviour to start with. We need to assess the child and consider which behaviour is the most appropriate to work on; the behaviour that sets them up to succeed not fail. Remember Mohammed in Chapter 12? If we had chosen 'being relevant' like his mother wanted me to, we would not have been successful as he didn't have the underpinning skills necessary to be relevant. So, remember the hierarchy and choose a behaviour that is ready to be learnt.

Why

Before we go any further, it is sometimes important to consider why this specific behaviour might be happening? Is there an underlying reason why a child is struggling with a specific skill? Could they be reacting to a situation or a person? Are they compensating or telling us something else? Let me tell you about a little boy called Jonty. He is nearly five years old, has a speech and language impairment and is going through the diagnosis process for autism. He has just started school and is struggling to make friends. One of the problems is that he has been seen to push other children in the playground. His mum, who is a speech and language therapist, writes him a Social Story™ called 'friendly hands'. However, this story doesn't work and in fact, makes him cry. When she telephones me for advice, I suggest that she stops and looks at the behaviour again. Is there something else going on? It turns out, after an assessment by an occupational therapist, that Jonty has sensory difficulties and in particular proprioceptive difficulties which make it hard for him to feel physically safe. Pushing against his peers (and other objects) helps to ground Jonty. So, when the OT introduces some exercises for Jonty, his 'problem behaviour' goes away. So always consider if there is an underlying reason for the behaviour. Is there a simple fix within the environment?

Describe

It is important to be able to describe the behaviour to help the child to understand what is going wrong. It is not helpful to just say 'stop that' or 'don't be irritating'. What is 'that'? And what is it that is irritating? The more accurately we can describe the behaviour, the easier it is for children or adults to learn. I do always try to involve the person in this stage as it will help me to hear their language and the way they describe their behaviour may also give me insight. I remember working with a little boy who was quite a fidgety child. In talking to him about it, he described his legs as getting 'tweazy'. This was his language and made sense to him, so this is the language I needed to use to help him. It is then important to discuss and describe what other people may think and feel. This is particularly helpful for people who have not recognised the impact their behaviour has on others around them. Again, by doing this jointly with the person, they can think about what others are thinking and feeling, and for some people, this actually might be enough to make them want to change their behaviour.

Rules

Finally, describe what they should be doing instead. Again, the clearer we can be here, the better. If we can't describe it, it is going to be difficult to help them understand what they should be doing instead. In 2016, I was in Australia lecturing and in the first lunch break, one of the participants came up to talk to me. She introduced herself as being 38 years old and as someone with Asperger's syndrome. She had just heard me describe the eye contact rule and she wanted to ask me why no-one had taught her that? She told me she had always struggled with eye contact and felt it had taken her 37 years to learn to do it (and she did have relatively good eye contact). But why hadn't anyone explained the rule years ago to her? It made total sense to her and she said she was going to go home and tell her friend who also has autism and who still struggles with eye contact, as she knew it would help her too. So always be clear about what should be happening and why or what the child could be doing instead.

Step 2 The motivation

So now we are clear on what we are going to teach, we need to consider the motivation for the young person. What is the motivation? Are they motivated to change? And if not, is this a problem? If we get the motivation wrong, then we are not going to succeed. Motivation can happen in several different ways. We may use a description of the outcome of the behaviour, such as an *affirmative sentence*: 'this is the grown-up thing to do'. We may use *rewards*, such as 'a sticker for every time . . .' We may use a *life goal* to work towards such as 'being an adult'. We may use *increasing their awareness* into the impact of their behaviour. The important thing is to get it right for the individual, and the specific setting. I will give you a couple of examples.

Affirmative sentences

I often see sentences being used to motivate someone that are problematic, either because they may not be a motivator or they may not be in our control. For example, *'being friendly'* or *'this is the friendly thing to do'* will only work as a motivator if someone is motivated to be friendly. If they are not bothered by whether they appear or act in a friendly manner then this is not going to work. As we saw in the chapter on autism, this can be true for the autistic person, and so particularly unhelpful for them. Also *'your mum/teacher/friends will be happy . . .'*

or *'people will like me'* are never a good idea as we cannot promise something that is out of our control. Imagine a child who works hard to do his good listening or good eye contact, and one day he does really well but his teacher is frankly in a bad mood. She is not going to be happy whether little Max does his good listening or not. Even if Max is motivated by making his teacher happy, is he motivated to try it again tomorrow? Affirmative sentences therefore need to work for the person, be possible and accurate and should be motivating. Mo (from Chapter 12) was motivated by being a grown up. He had left school and was going on to college and wanted to act like a grown up so a better sentence to use for him when teaching him about good distance and use of touch was: 'this is the grown-up thing to do'.

Ros is an autistic adult who often lectures in the UK and she tells a story about when she was little and used to hit other children. She prefers to be on her own and says the hitting worked for her because then the other children went away. She says that it will never work if we tell her to stop hitting because it is 'the friendly thing to do' or 'people will like her'. She is not interested in that. She says it would have been better to motivate her with an activity such as going on the trampoline as she is more motivated by that than other people. In fact, her exact words when I heard her speak were: 'tell me if I hit people I can't go trampolining, because I value trampolining more so I won't hit them' (RB, at a presentation in 2011). So, this takes us to the second motivator: rewards.

Rewards

We all like our hard work to be noticed, praised, rewarded. So rewards can work well for both children and adults. The secret again is to get the reward right, otherwise it is meaningless. So, get to know your subject! Find out what it is that is motivating for them and work out how we could incorporate it into their social skills work. So, if it is going on the trampoline, then we could suggest that when Ros goes on the trampoline for five minutes at the end of the day, she gets an additional minute on the trampoline for every lesson she doesn't hit someone. She could have a reward chart with pictures of her favourite trampoline to represent each lesson.

When we introduce a reward chart, it is always important to make sure that the child succeeds initially so that they learn the benefit of the reward. So, it is important to ensure that the first few times or days the child uses the reward chart are a success. We have a young man who attends our day service who collects a portion of an iPad (created as a laminated puzzle) to give him 5 minutes per puzzle piece on his iPad at lunch time and at the end of the day. Another young lady has pictures of her shoes as her reward token as she just loves people complimenting and talking to her about her shoes! So, when she has a token, she can choose who gets to compliment her on her footwear! The point is that the motivator should work for that person. Just don't let anyone take the reward away when the behaviour deteriorates. I heard a story the other day from a mother who said her son has a reward chart at nursery, but when he is 'naughty', a member of staff will take away a star from his chart. This is not how reward charts should work and will be detrimental in motivating the child.

Life goals

Life goals can also work if you can put the social skill into a context that is meaningful and motivating to the person. Mohammed was motivated by the fact that he had recently left school and was an adult now so he wanted to be more like a grown up. So, using the motivator of 'being a grown up' helped him to learn the rules about distance and touch. I remember one young man I worked with several years ago and his main goal was to get a job. He wasn't particularly motivated to work with me, but when we put it into the context of the skills he needed to get through an interview and get a job, it made sense to him. Suddenly my sessions had a purpose and he was much more motivated to work with me!

Increasing awareness

This is linked to the previous step where we describe the behaviour and think about the consequences. As we said before, sometimes by doing this jointly with the person, this is enough of a motivation to make them want to work on changing their behaviour.

Step 3 The environment

Children also need the right support outside of therapy in which to practise and generalise skills and the more we involve significant others and peers, the better. So our third step is to consider the child in the context of their environment and to start thinking about *creating opportunities* across the child's environment for social skills to flourish and *involving peers* to support the use of social skills.

Creating opportunities

It is essential that any social skills intervention is supported by the child's environment and that skills that are being taught are encouraged throughout the day. It is often important to address this before you start work with the child, as you will want the environment to be supportive from the outset. So, I would start by assessing the social opportunities that exist within the child's routine, so that they can be used to support the generalisation and functional use of the newly acquired skill. As Shaked and Yirmiya (2003) state: 'it is important to evaluate the child's specific school environment and devise ways whereby the school setting can adjust to the child's needs and further enable social and emotional growth'. This will mean getting all staff on board and then creating opportunities across the day for the child to practise their emerging and newly acquired skills. It may also mean identifying aspects of their day that are not conducive to their development and then dealing with them. Involving families is also an essential part of this and parents should be encouraged to be as involved as possible. I will talk about both of these in more detail in the chapters on developing social skills within a school setting and at home.

Involving peers

Another consideration is how you are going to involve peers, as there is evidence to suggest that peer involvement will improve the outcome of the intervention. As Frea (2006) said: 'involved peers can accelerate the success of the programme. Lack of peer involvement can result in social behaviours that never truly become functional skills'. We will discuss this in more detail in the chapter on developing social skills in schools, but, in brief, Odom and Strain (1984) and Goldstein et al. (1992) have developed a number of successful peer-mediated strategies over the past 20 years and there is a large body of published work that focuses on peer-mediated interventions for improving social behaviour. Peers are taught to model targeted behaviours and reinforce new social skills through role play with adults, then through reinforcement and cueing which is gradually faded over a period of time. A targeted behaviour, such as maintaining attention, is subdivided into several steps, e.g. the peer moves in front of the child, the peer looks at him and the toys, the peer says his name and repeats if necessary. These strategies are powerful at increasing social interactions within the classroom and both generalisation and maintenance is good (Mastergeorge et al., 2003).

Another approach could be the 'circle of friends' method that involves using a group of six to eight peer volunteers to support the individual with social skills difficulties in a proactive manner. Volunteers can meet weekly and have three main tasks: to identify difficulties, to set goals and devise strategies for reaching them, and to offer encouragement and recognition for success and progress. Volunteers are encouraged to talk openly about the difficulties they encounter with the child's behaviour (Shaked and Yirmiya, 2003).

So, in summary, our first three steps to intervention are to choose the right behaviour to work on first; to consider the motivation and make sure you get it right for the person; and finally to ensure that any social skills intervention takes place and is supported within the whole environment. Then we can choose the right strategy to use.

Step 4 The strategy

Now finally we can start work! And it might not surprise you to find out that there are many different ways in which we can work with people to help develop social skills, and once again, we need to choose the right strategy for the individual. The different teaching interventions can be divided into four categories of therapeutic 1:1, therapeutic group, creative arts and technology. The most common ones are summarised briefly below, but this list is not intended to be exhaustive, as new approaches are being developed all the time.

Table 13.1 Different social skills interventions

Approach	Method	Description
Therapeutic 1:1 interventions	Social Story™	Social Stories™ are short descriptions of a particular situation, event or activity, which include specific information about what to expect in that situation and why.
	Comic Strip Conversation™	Comic Strip Conversations™ are simple visual representations of a conversation. They can show the things that are actually said in a conversation, how people might be feeling and what their intentions might be.
	Problem-solving/ discussion	Guided discussions to help individuals learn to recognise problems and then to 'brainstorm' alternatives in solving the problem, as described earlier in this chapter.
	Use of rewards/ visuals	This may include a reward chart or a visual prompt to support the child to make or remember the changes, as described earlier in this chapter.

Approach	Method	Description
Therapeutic group interventions	Social skills group	A group of peers or people with similar needs are supported to develop their social skills in a group setting. This is one of the most common methods of social skills intervention.
	Self-esteem group	A group of peers or people with similar needs are supported to improve their self-esteem in the safety of a group setting. This is often a pre-requisite to developing effective social skills and is best done in a group as opposed to a 1:1.
	Friendship/ relationship group	A group of peers or people with similar needs are supported to improve their friendship skills in the safety of a group setting.
	LEGO®-based therapy	Construction play is used to support the development of social interaction, using different 'roles' and a clear set of rules. This is popular as an approach with autistic children, as playing with LEGO® can harness their preferences and motivations for this type of play.
Creative arts interventions	Role play and drama	Drama and role play is used to help individuals to learn social skills and to practise new strategies in the safety of a group setting prior to trying it in real life situations.
	Modelling	Modelling of skills (both inappropriate and appropriate) is done preferably by two facilitators and observed by the individuals within a group setting (or 1:1 session). These can be videoed and replayed (see below).
	Puppets	Puppets can be used to model skills (both inappropriate and appropriate), to support children to practise skills and to talk through or to the puppets.
Technology interventions	Media clips	Video clips are used to teach skills either from a DVD that presents social skills clips, such as the *Talkabout* DVD, or from selected clips from the internet.
	Video modelling	Adults model skills (as described in Modelling) but these are also videoed and are presented in a video clip for the individuals to watch and learn from.

(Continued)

> ### Table 13.1 (Continued)

Approach	Method	Description
	Computer based software applications	Individuals can learn about social skills through creating 3D animated movies such as with the program 'Muvizu', which is a software application that enables you make animated cartoons on a home computer.
	Educational apps	There is now an abundance of applications to help individuals learn social skills through their iPad or smart phone. These vary from very simple tools to prompt to more complicated assistive technology devices. This is a fast-developing approach.

In the following chapter we will discuss most of these social skills interventions in more detail, because, as with most things in life, the more knowledge we have to do something, the better we will be at it.

> # Key points from Chapter 13
>
> This chapter is the first of four chapters on teaching social skills.
>
> ## The different approaches to intervention
>
> There are four main approaches to teaching social skills:
>
> - *The behavioural approach*: for example, Applied Behavioural Analysis (ABA) which is based on the principle that skills can be taught using positive reinforcement.
> - *Social learning approach*: for example, the observational method where children learn things by watching and imitating others.
> - *Structured learning approach*: that is, the child observes the model, understands why it is important, practises the skills and receives feedback and praise.
> - *Cognitive behavioural approach*: for example, problem-solving interventions where children learn to recognise problems, either through role play or from experience and then to 'brainstorm' alternatives in solving the problem.
> - *Developmental approach*: the children are actively engaging in and shaping their learning through play and social interaction.

The evidence for social skills training

Research indicates that there are many techniques for improving social skills, but the evidence to show both transference into other settings and long-term maintenance is limited. Key aspects of success in social skills training seem to be: ensuring the cooperation of other people in the child's life; adapting the content of the intervention to the setting, practitioner and child; and combining the programme with other techniques such as parental training.

The four-step plan to intervention

Step 1 The behaviour

There are four key words to think about in this first step:

- *Choose* the appropriate behaviour to start with
- *Why*? Consider if there is a reason for the behaviour
- *Describe* the behaviour including how it makes others feel
- *Rules* – what is the rule? What are you going to be asking the child to do instead?

Step 2 The motivation

Consider how you are going to motivate the child to change. Consider the use of:

- *Affirmative sentences*: 'this is the grown up thing to do'
- R*ewards* such as 'a sticker for every time. . .'
- A *life goal* to work towards such as 'being an adult'
- *Increasing their awareness* of the right thing to do

Step 3 The environment

Children need the right support outside of therapy in which to practise and generalise skills and the more we involve significant others and peers, the better. Consider:

- *Creating opportunities*
- *Involving peers*

Step 4 The strategy

Teaching interventions can be divided into four categories:

- *Therapeutic 1: 1*: for example, Social Stories™, Comic Strip Conversations™, problem solving, and use of rewards/visuals
- *Therapeutic group*: for example, groups to develop social skills, self-esteem, friendship skills, and LEGO®-based therapy
- *Creative arts*: for example, drama and role play, modelling and puppets
- *Technology*: for example, the use of media/DVDs, video modelling, computer-based software and apps

Chapter 14

Teaching social skills 2
Social skills interventions

'Learning is more than absorbing facts, it is acquiring understanding.'
William Arthur Ward (1921–1994)

Welcome to my book on social skills! I say this because I suspect that there are some people who have opened up this book and gone straight to this chapter. I am not surprised. I love teaching social skills and as I said before (although as a new reader, you won't know this!), this is the fun part. So, I know you are keen to get on with it, but I would encourage you to stop and think about the intervention and plan it carefully. In the previous chapter, we looked at the four-step plan for intervention and so, if you haven't done so, I would like to encourage you to read the final section of the last chapter. This is because choosing the right strategy is actually the *fourth* step in my four-step plan to intervention.

The four-step plan to intervention

Step 1 Choose the behaviour
Step 2 Consider the motivation
Step 3 Consider the environment
Step 4 Choose the strategy

In this chapter we will look at the main ways in which we can teach social skills under the four categories of: therapeutic 1:1, therapeutic group, creative arts, and technology. I will describe the common interventions under each heading but it is important to remember a couple of things:

- First, this chapter is not exhaustive of interventions. I will talk about the most common, but you may also need to read up about other ways to teach social skills.

- Second, it is all about the individual – their motivations, their environment and their needs, so choose the intervention that is right for the person and their setting.
- Third, it is also not often a question of *one* intervention, but a few. They often complement one another, so try to choose a few that will work well together.
- I will mostly use 'child' and 'children' in this chapter, but remember that most of these interventions will also be suitable for adults too.

Therapeutic 1:1 interventions

The use of 1:1 interventions is often appropriate to support children with social skills difficulties and will inevitably be a part of your intervention in some shape or form. We may use the 1:1 session to help children learn to recognise a problem through guided discussion and then to 'brainstorm' alternatives. Sometimes we use them to assess or reassess a child or to discuss progress with them; sometimes to try out different strategies with the child in a safe situation, for example through role play (see later in the chapter). However, the two strategies I use most that I would categorise under this heading are Comic Strip conversations™ and Social Stories™.

Comic Strip conversations™

Comic Strip conversations™ are my 'go to' strategy when I want to sit down and talk a problem through with one of the young people I work with. The active and visual nature of it helps them to 'see' the conversation and to then focus on a solution. They are simple to do, using 'stick figures' and symbols to represent social interactions and the abstract aspects of the conversation, and using colour to represent the emotional content. They were first developed by Carol Gray for use with autistic children and the technique is, at its simplest, a conversation between two people which involves the use of drawing. It involves drawing the relevant details and people in order to help a child visually work through a problem or situation. Speech bubbles are used to identify what key people said and thought bubbles are used to identify what people may have been thinking. So, for example, the following concepts may be represented in the following way:

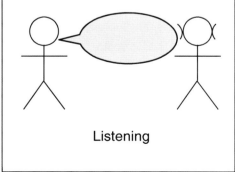

Figure 14.1 Concepts represented visually

In addition, colours can be used to represent emotions so that as the child or adult fills in the speech or thought bubble, they use a particular colour to represent how they think they are feeling, although this is not always necessary or appropriate for the child.

The colours in Comic Strip conversations™

Green	Good ideas, happy, friendly
Red	Bad ideas, anger, unfriendly
Blue	Sad, uncomfortable
Yellow	Frightened
Black	Facts, truth
Orange	Questions
Brown	Comfortable, cosy
Purple	Proud
Colour combination	Confusion

The actual drawing can be done by either the adult or the child (and you don't have to be an artist to be able to do it!). In this simple way, segments of conversations are visually presented in what each person said, thought, felt and did and can be used to illustrate the more abstract nature of the conversation by showing what someone's intention might be. By seeing the different elements of a conversation presented visually, some of the more abstract aspects of social communication (such as recognising the feelings of others) are made more 'concrete' and are therefore easier to understand.

How to use Comic Strip conversations™

We may feel that we need to introduce children to the idea of drawing first, especially if you think they will do the drawing. I tend to introduce it in the following way:

1. Have some nice paper and pens out on the table and explain that today we are going to draw as well as talk.
2. Start with some small talk, for example talking about the weather, and ask the child to draw their answers as well as speak. This will help them to get used to drawing whilst talking. If I am doing the drawing, I will ask the child to comment on my drawings to involve them in the process.
3. Then try talking about a specific situation that has occurred. Ask a range of questions about the situation or type of social interaction and then encourage the child to answer by speaking and drawing their response (see ideas for questions over).
4. Summarise the event or situation discussed using the drawings as a guide.
5. Think about how to address any problems or concerns that have been identified.
6. Develop an action plan for similar situations in the future.
7. The child may like to save their comic strips in a notebook or on their smartphone or tablet, so that they can refer to them as needed, and easily recall key concepts.

So if we are gathering information about a specific situation or event, we may ask:

Questions to ask	What we might draw
Where were you?	Draw a symbol to represent the place and a person to represent the child
Who else was there?	Draw a person/people
What were you doing?	Draw the relevant items or actions using simple symbols
What happened/what did others do?	Draw relevant items/actions
What did you say?	Use speech bubble
What did others say?	Use speech bubble
What did you think when you said that?	Use thought bubble
What did others think when you said/ did that?	Use thought bubble

A couple of issues may arise when drawing out a conversation.

First, the child may struggle to correctly identify the thoughts and motivations of other people. They don't know what someone could have been thinking or feeling and so will need help with this aspect. It is still important to involve them and to ideally give them some possible choices, for example, 'do you think they were thinking "I like Amy" or "Amy is being friendly today"'?

Second, the child may give an obviously incorrect answer to what someone may have been thinking. In this situation, it is important to suggest a correct answer without discrediting the child's answer, for example by saying 'I think your teacher was thinking . . .'

Finally, for complex situations, the child may have difficulty reporting events in the right sequence, so in this situation it is better to use 'comic strip boxes' or smaller pieces of paper for the drawings which can then be moved around and numbered in the sequence in which they occur.

The following figure is an example of when I used Comic Strip conversations™ with a teenager called Mo. We had been working on appropriate touch and distance and he was learning the rules and showing progress. We had been talking about being an adult and how he should behave when he started at College. However, in one session Mo was despondent with his progress and said 'he had hugged Eve' that week. His mother then described the situation that she had observed where a friend of the family 'encouraged' Mo to break his new rules by opening her arms up to hug him (after all she was used to getting a hug). Mo and I discussed what happened using drawings (see Figure 14.2) and then talked about what he could do differently in the future.

Using the drawings shown, it was easy for Mo to see what should happen and also to feel better about what had happened. We then added an extra page to Mo's social story about being an adult and used one of the drawings to describe what can happen when people want to hug him.

Figure 14.2 Using a Comic Strip conversation™ with Mo

Social Stories™

Social Stories™ were originally created by Carol Gray in 1991 for students with autism and have become increasingly popular as an instructional strategy (Barry and Burlew, 2004; Delano and Snell, 2006; Sansosti et al., 2004) but can also be used with children and adults who are not autistic. The terms 'Social Story™' and 'Social Stories™' are trademarks originated and owned by Carol Gray. A Social Story™ 'describes a situation, skill, or concept according to ten defining criteria' (Gray, 2010) and where the term 'social stories' are used with no capital letters, this would indicate that the story does not meet the criteria set out by Carol Gray.

What is a Social Story™?

A Social Story™ is a short story that has been written in a specific style and format. It describes a specific social situation and presents information in a structured and consistent manner. It gives information through pictures and text and each story provides clear, concise and accurate information about what is happening in a specific social situation. The story describes what people do, why they do it, and what the common responses are. So, they are intended to help a child to understand a small part of their social world and how to behave appropriately within it, without having to rely on 'telling them'.

Before we describe Social Stories™ in more detail, here is what a Social Story™ might look like. This one is taken from Smith (2003) and was written for Simon, aged 7, who became very agitated when his mother turned on the bath taps. As we can see, the story is short and straightforward and helps Simon understand what is expected in this situation.

> ## 'Why it is OK to run a bath' – a sample Social Story™
>
> In my bathroom there is a bath, a toilet and a basin.
> The bath and the basin have taps.
> It is important for people in my family to have a bath sometimes.
> Sometimes Mummy likes to have a bath.
> Sometimes Mummy likes Simon to have a bath.
> It is OK for Mummy to turn on the taps when she needs to run a bath.
> Mummy is safe when the taps are on.
> Simon is safe if Mummy turns on the taps.
> Simon's house is safe if Mummy turns on the taps.
> I will try to let Mummy run a bath.
> I will try to remember we are safe when Mummy runs a bath.

Why use a Social Story™?

Social Stories™ can be used for quite a few different reasons and these are summarised in the table below:

> ### Table 14.1 Reasons to use a Social Story™

Reason	Description
1. To learn a skill	This is probably what most people think of when they think about writing Social Stories™. For example, we think about teaching a self-care skill such as how to clean teeth, or a social skill such as how close to stand to someone or how to start a conversation.
2. To help someone to understand others	This kind of story will help the child to understand why people may behave or respond in a particular situation. Giving this information overtly will help them to have some perspective on the thoughts, emotions, and behaviours of others.
3. To help someone to understand an event	I have used Social Stories™ many times to support a child to cope with changes in routine or their situation, and unexpected or distressing events such as thunderstorms or a death.
4. To help understand the perspective of an autistic person	This kind of story will help others to understand the autistic child and why they may respond or behave in a particular way.
5. To provide positive feedback	It is important that some stories are positive ones about an area of strength or achievement in order to develop self-esteem.
6. As a behavioural strategy	For example, what to do when angry, how to cope with obsessions.

Despite a lack of evidence to show that Social Stories™ are an effective method to teach social skills in isolation, there is evidence to show that when they have been used as part of packaged interventions, some gains have been noted (Sansosti and Powell-Smith, 2008; Swaggart et al., 1995). They are certainly popular with teachers and parents and appear to work well for a number of children for a number of reasons.

The benefits of using Social Stories™ or why do they work?

My experience of using Social Stories™ with both children and adults is that they often work and when they don't work, it is possible to see why (more on that later). So what are the benefits and the main reasons why they work?

1. They present information in a literal, 'concrete' way, which may improve understanding of a previously difficult or ambiguous situation or activity.
2. They mostly use pictures to support the person to learn visually. As Temple Grandin (1995) says, 'I think in pictures'.
3. They can help with sequencing (what comes next in a series of activities) and 'executive functioning' (planning and organising).
4. They can increase structure in a person's life and thereby reduce anxiety by providing information about what might happen in a particular situation.
5. Social Stories™ also attempt to address the 'theory of mind' impairment by giving individuals some perspective on the thoughts, emotions, and behaviours of others. This may help autistic people to know how to act more appropriately in social situations because they understand that others might have a different opinion to them, or that others may want to do something different to what they want to do.
6. Social Stories™ can help the child better predict the actions and assumptions of others which can make social situations less unpredictable and confusing.
7. Social Stories™ also provide distance between teaching and the possible stresses of the social situation itself, giving the child a chance to practice the skills often and on his terms.
8. And finally, if we get it right, we will see results within two to three weeks.

So how do we write a 'good' Social Story™?

How to write a Social Story™

Social Stories™ can give the impression of being fairly simple to write. We read a well written short Social Story™ and think, 'there's not much to that. Simple!' However, actually this is deceptive. When we then sit down to write our first one, we see how difficult and daunting it can be to get it right. However, the more we write them, and the more we see how successful they can be, the more confidence we have to write another one!

The most important part of writing a Social Story™ is to gather information. It is intended to be written from the perspective of the child, so it is important that we try to get that perspective. When I am writing a Social Story™ for any reason (other than to explain an event such as a death), I will involve the child in the initial discussions. We may just talk about it, or brainstorm the problem, or use Comic Strip conversations™ to draw it all out. But I will try to get insight into the following: How do they see the situation? What are the difficulties? What words do they use? Certainly, with some higher functioning children and adults, they can help write the story, and this will give them more ownership on the story and they will be more motivated when it is written. It is also important to talk to other people and to observe the child. As Howley and Arnold (2005) state: 'this process is critical to the success of the approach'. They also state that in essence our aims are:

- To identify what is actually happening
- To look at consistency of factors surrounding the situation
- To consider the perspectives of those involved
- To identify which cues the child may be missing
- To observe how the child responds

In brief though, Carol Gray says that to write a Social Story™ we need to do three things: picture the goal, gather information, and tailor the text.

1. *Picture the goal*: Consider the purpose of the Social Story™ and what the child needs to understand to achieve this goal. For example, if we want to teach a child to cover their mouth when coughing, they need to understand why covering their mouth when coughing is important – that is, it stops germs from being spread which may make other people sick.
2. *Gather information*: Collect information about the situation. Where does it occur? Who is it with? How does it begin and end? How long does it last? What actually happens in the situation and why? If it is for a situation where a particular outcome is not guaranteed, use words like 'sometimes' and 'usually' in the story. Stories should also appeal to the interests of the person and should avoid using words that may cause the person anxiety, and should be appropriate to the person's age and level of understanding. So, we need to gather information about the person, including their age, interests, attention span, level of ability and understanding. So, with young children it may be appropriate to have a picture and one sentence per page, but with an older student, they may wish it to be more adult like in its presentation.
3. *Tailor the text*: A Social Story™ needs to have a title, introduction, body and conclusion and should use patient and supportive language. It should answer six questions: where, when, who, what, how and why?

As we have said earlier, Carol Gray has also devised ten criteria to ensure a story follows the rules of a Social Story™ and the following table summarises these:

Table 14.2 Carol Gray's ten criteria for a Social Story™

Criterion	Description
1. The goal	The goal is to share accurate information meaningfully and safely, using an overall patient and reassuring tone. The emphasis is on improving the child's understanding of events and expectations.

Criterion	Description
2. Two-step discovery	With the goal in mind, we need to firstly gather accurate information and then secondly identify the specific topics and types of information that will be shared in the story.
3. Three parts and a title	A Social Story™ has a title and introduction that clearly identifies the topic, a body that adds detail and a conclusion that reinforces and summarises the information.
4. FOURmat!	A Social Story™ has a format that clarifies content and enhances meaning for the child. The text is individualised and presented with the age and ability of the child in mind. Alter the length and vocabulary to suit the child, use pictures and illustrations if appropriate, and use repetition, rhythm and rhyme to help a child remember.
5. Five factors define voice and vocabulary	A Social Story™ has a patient and supportive 'voice' and vocabulary that are defined by 5 factors: First or third person perspective – think about what is most appropriate and who is going to read the story. Positive and patient tone – keep the self-esteem of the person safe. Past, present and/or future tense – it might be good to talk about references to the past or future. Literal accuracy – use literal language unless it is appropriate to use non-literal examples e.g. a metaphor or analogy. Accurate vocabulary – use clear language that is appropriate to the child.
6. Six questions guide story development	A Social Story™ answers relevant 'wh' questions, describing the context (where); time-related information (when); relevant people (who); important cues (what); basic activities, behaviours, or statements (how); and the reasons and/or rationale behind them (why).
7. Seven types of Social Story™ sentences	A Social Story™ is comprised of: Descriptive sentences: objective, often observable, fact. Perspective sentences: describe thoughts, feelings and beliefs of others. Sentences that coach: 3 types: Coach the child: 'I will try to. . .' Coach others: 'My mum will. . .' Self-coaching: 'I can think. . .' or 'I can use. . .' Affirmative sentences: enhance the meaning of surrounding statements, for example by saying 'this is OK' or 'this is important'. Partial sentences: used to 'fill in the blanks' to check comprehension or encourage the child to make guesses regarding the next step.
8. A gr-EIGHT formula	One formula and seven sentence types ensures that every Social Story™ describes more than directs. The number of sentences that DESCRIBE (descriptive + perspective + affirmative) should be divided by the number of sentences that COACH and the answer should be equal or greater than 2.

(Continued)

Table 14.2 (Continued)

Criterion	Description
9. Nine makes it mine	Whenever possible a Social Story™ is tailored to the individual preferences, talents, and interests of the child. This means that we should personalise the story to make it interesting to the child.
10. Ten guides to editing and implementation	Edit: carefully check the text for adherence to the criteria and ask others to check it too. Plan for Comprehension: look at the text and illustrations with comprehension in mind. Plan Story Support: consider resources and techniques to support the story as it is implemented. Would it be helpful to put the story on PowerPoint or to make a poster for the classroom with one important phrase from the story? Plan Story Review: consider when the story will be read and how often. Never read it as a consequence of bad behaviour. Plan a Positive Introduction: the key is to be calm and comfortable. Monitor! Consider how to monitor the impact. Organise Stories: one story leads to another, so keep them organised in a file. Mix and Match Stories to Build Concepts: copy stories of similar type into files to help with future stories. Story Re-Runs and Sequels: there is no such thing as a retired story. Keep them safe so we can reintroduce or update at a later stage. Recycle Instruction into Applause: stories can be recycled from an instruction one to one that applauds their new skill.

Source. Gray, 2010

What can go wrong?

As I said earlier though, some stories don't appear to work and for every Social Story™ that works well, I have seen another one that hasn't. Sometimes we know immediately. I always look at the child's reaction to the first reading of the story. Do they seem to understand? Sometimes I even see an 'aha' moment where you can see the person nodding and 'getting it'. Or are they confused or upset by the story? This would tell us immediately that something doesn't seem right. Do you remember Jonty in the previous chapter?

So, what can go wrong? In my experience it is usually one of seven reasons and we should check the following:

1.   Have we targeted the right behaviour? As we discussed in a previous chapter, it is important to teach certain skills prior to teaching more complex ones. So maybe we need to look at their assessment and check we have chosen the right behaviour to work on first.
2.   Have we written it in language that is too complex? Check for things like use of negatives or long complicated sentences.
3.   Are the directive sentences achievable and specific? Check to see if it is realistic.
4.   Have we included something that is not accurate? Check to see if we were accurate in our description and language.

5. Have we got the reason wrong? Maybe there is another reason for the behaviour that we have not considered. Go back and look again. (Think about Jonty)
6. Have we got more than one story on the go? It is best to work on one at a time.
7. Is it being used to tell the child off or being read in an unsupportive manner? Social stories should be read by someone who is empathetic and there should be some distance between the actual behaviour and the reading of the story.

Therapeutic group interventions

In this section we will consider setting up and running social skills groups (or self-esteem or friendship skill groups) as this has to be my favourite type of intervention. I love the energy of a group, the natural way we can encourage people to develop skills and of course the impact it can have on peer relationships. But even though the whole business of setting up and running a group is something that is fun and rewarding, it is also something that needs thought and skill. So, we will first consider the things that we need to think about prior to the group and then we will consider the actual running of the group. But first, why run a group? What are the benefits of this type of intervention?

The advantages of group interventions

Many people believe that social behaviour should be taught in groups rather than in a one-to-one situation and that the group forum, by its very nature, is an ideal one in which to learn about, change or practise any behaviour which is associated with social interaction and communication. The advantages of group interventions over one-to-one may include:

- Greater peer interaction and generalisation of skills
- Increased observational learning, as group members can offer additional models, reinforcement and feedback
- Increased opportunity to generate ideas in problem-solving, and to set up role plays and simulation games
- Opportunity to try out new skills in a safe environment
- Peer group pressure can motivate individuals
- A more relaxed and comfortable environment in which to learn new skills
- Opportunity to transfer skills to other staff, thus improving the chance of carryover into the person's everyday environment

However, there are a few things to be aware of that will affect the performance of an individual within your group.

Being in the presence of others

This may increase a child's motivation, but it may also have a socially-inhibiting effect. The presence of others can increase feelings of tension and excitement, which has the effect of increasing motivation and performance. On the other hand, the level of anxiety caused by 'performing' in front of others can have an opposite effect and can stop a child performing at all. So, watch out for the level of tension within the room and watch out for signs that a child is not performing due to this.

High task attractiveness

This means that children will want to participate and perform if there is 'high task attractiveness' – they understand why they are doing something and they want to do it. Where this is not the case, a child may choose not to participate and will let the others do the work. This is called 'social loafing'.

Group cohesiveness

Group cohesion will always help with performance. Children are much more likely to learn and perform if the group has gelled. Things that can help with cohesion are: interpersonal attraction and success in completing tasks. We will talk about this a bit more in the section on running a group.

The life cycle of the group

Whitaker (1989) identified three phases in the development of a group:

- The formative phase
- The established phase
- The termination phase

In the formative phase, members are establishing themselves as a group and individuals are finding a place and a role within the group. When this has occurred, the group is in the established phase. This means that learning does not really occur until the group has entered the established phase, as it is in this phase that the group will have gelled; they know what is expected of them and they are therefore ready to learn. The termination phase is the period during which members are preparing for the time when the group will finish so children are getting ready to let go. In this phase we may see a slight decrease in engagement or behaviour, as they protect themselves from the disappointment of the group ending.

Receiving feedback within the group

This is one of the advantages of the group intervention as children can get information about the impact of their behaviours on others which are not ordinarily available to them. However, we obviously need to ensure that all feedback is given in a constructive way. When giving feedback to children, it is always a good idea to try to use the sandwich approach: something good, something bad, then something good.

Setting up a social skills group

There are a few things to consider when setting up a group: who is going to be in the group, how big is the group going to be, who's going to run it with you, what are you going to do and where are you going to do it?

Who is going to be in the group?

This is usually the first question and the general rule is: the more homogenous the group the better. So, if we can match children for communicative strength and need, diagnosis, likes and dislikes, age and sex, then the chances are our group will gel quickly and be a huge success! Of course, in the real world, there are always compromises to be made. It is obviously important the children are matched for social skills, but I would also argue that it is even more important that the group members get on and like each other, because we need them to enjoy coming to the sessions and to relax enough to learn. Group membership should also ideally be closed, although it is sometimes necessary for children to drop out of groups, either for practical or therapeutic reasons.

How big should the group be?

The size of the group will depend on the age and ability of the children, but are usually four to eight, not including the group leaders. It is important to remember that some children find it difficult to communicate in larger groups, but it is important to have enough people within a group to make role plays and group discussions feasible and interesting. With adults, age is much less important, and we can easily run groups where there is a significant age difference.

Who's going to run it?

Social skills groups definitely run better with two leaders, especially as there is often a need to model behaviours (more on that later), work video cameras and facilitate group discussions. The co-facilitator should ideally be someone from the children's everyday environment and a good working relationship between the group leaders is often the key to a successful group. Of course, we live in the real world where often there are not enough teachers or staff to have two facilitators. This is obviously acceptable in some situations, but when this happens I would encourage people to consider how they are going to manage activities such as modelling and role play, and how they might use other staff to encourage the children to transfer skills outside of the group.

What are we going to do?

Setting realistic goals should be straightforward following assessment using the hierarchical approach described in a previous chapter. Defining goals and using a structured set of activities will also help with group cohesion and will give us something with which to evaluate success.

Where are we going to do it?

Sometimes being given a room in which to run a group can be a huge problem. Space is at a premium in some settings and we need to argue the case for an appropriate space to run our group. It is important to have a room that is large enough for the size and purpose of the group that is physically comfortable – for example, warm and quiet. It is also important to remember that children will not feel comfortable in a room where other people are coming in and out, or where they may be observed by others in their environment. On a practical note, it is also useful to have a means of displaying materials or writing up information – for example, a flip chart, wipe board or blackboard.

Do we need a contract?

Finally, it may be sensible to draw up a contract with a head teacher or an equivalent person, to include: how long the group will run and who will be in the group; on what day the group will run and the time it will start and finish; staff who will support the group and what will happen in the event of staff shortages; the aims of the group; and how the group will be evaluated.

Running a social skills group

In running a successful group, there are several factors that need to be considered: cohesiveness; group rules; format of the session; and evaluating the group.

Cohesiveness

Cohesiveness is essential in a group. As we said in the last section, children are much more likely to learn and perform if the group has gelled. Cohesiveness is more likely to occur when there is a good match between individual needs and the group goals. If this has been achieved, then it is hoped that there will be less work in ensuring ongoing group cohesion. However, it is important to ensure that the group gels initially and factors that can help cohesiveness are:

- Interpersonal attraction: people who like one another are more likely to gel
- Success in completing tasks: bring a group together by setting them a task that they work at and succeed at as a group
- Arrange the room prior to the group: a circle always works well as no-one feels left out
- Ensure that everyone feels valued in the group
- Ensure that everyone feels part of the group and has an equal 'say'
- Start each session with a relatively simple activity that is fun and stress-free and which cues each member into the group
- Finish each session with another activity that is fun and stress-free

Group rules

Group rules are also helpful to develop group cohesion and will hopefully instil a shared sense of responsibility for how the group functions. Asking the group questions such as 'what makes a group a good group or a bad group?' is a good basis for discussion around setting up group rules. These rules can then be used or referred to when problems arise that affect the cohesion or running of the group. At the same time as discussing group rules, it is also important to help the group members understand the group contract, for example, how long the group will last and what the aims are for the group. Both the rules and group contract could be done in a written or pictorial format and referred to in later sessions.

The format of the session

Careful time-tabling in a session is essential if it is going to run smoothly. Too slow a pace will lead to boredom and a low level of arousal, and too rapid a pace will mean that group members will not have enough time to process the information and respond.

The format of the session will vary from time to time but there are general guidelines which apply to most groups:

Table 14.3 The format of a social skills group session

1. A group cohesion activity	This is an essential beginning to the group. It brings the group together and helps them to focus on the other group members and the purpose of the group. The activity should be simple and stress-free and all members should participate.

2. Feelings board	Pass a 'feelings board' around the group and ask everyone to share how they are feeling and why. Ask them to ask the person sitting next to them to encourage peer interaction. Feelings can then be explored if appropriate or compensated for within the group.
3. Recap the previous session / introduce the theme for today	This is important to ensure cohesion between sessions. It may also be appropriate to recap on the aims and rules of the group and change the session plan if something has occurred that needs attention. The theme for that session is then introduced.
4. Main activity(s)	There may be several main activities, depending on the length of the session, and these may include: modelling of a new skill followed by role play by the children and feedback; brainstorming a problem; a group game; or a worksheet. It is during this part of the session that it is most important not to lose children's attention by allowing an activity to go on for too long, or for one person to dominate the conversation.
5. Summing up	The session is then summed up and may include setting home assignments if appropriate.
6. Finishing activity	Each session should end with a finishing activity to bring the group back together again and to reduce anxiety if the children have found any of the activities difficult. The activity should therefore be fun, simple and stress free.

Evaluation

Evaluation is obviously an essential aspect of any group. We will discuss this more in the chapter on evaluating effectiveness but, in terms of the group, questions that need to be asked are:

- Were the aims of the group met?
- How did the activities go and were they at an appropriate level?
- Did everyone take part?
- Did the children enjoy the session and are they improving and learning new skills?
- What needs to be addressed in the next session that has not been planned for?

Evaluation is therefore best done with well-structured session notes to evaluate the sessions and activities, rating scales to re-assess the children's skills and a format for assessing the children's views on whether they believe they have improved or not and if they have enjoyed the group, such as the ones used in the *Talkabout* programmes (Kelly, 2010–2018).

Running groups is, in my experience, the most popular way to teach social skills, but the effectiveness of the group will almost definitely be linked to the facilitator's ability to set up and run the group effectively. But with the essentials thought through, running social skills groups can be fun, rewarding *and* effective.

Creative arts interventions

The use of creative arts, for example, drama, movement, and music, is a common addition to any social skills intervention and certainly makes learning more fun and engaging for most children. As Conn (2016) says: 'the creative arts can be used to provide non-threatening, calming and socially accessible forms of communication and interaction, which in turn encourage personal expression, self-awareness, self-regulation and flexibility'. When used within a group setting, it can also encourage support for others and group cohesion.

There are three main ways in which we use the creative arts in social skills interventions: role play/drama; modelling; and puppets. In this chapter I will describe all three of these approaches.

Role play, drama and storytelling

The terms drama, role play and storytelling all mean and infer something different in the usual sense. However, in the context of the social skills group or intervention, I am going to use 'role play' to mean any activity that encourages children out of their chairs to act something out. So, for ease, I will use just the term 'role play' but in some sessions, this may look a lot more like drama or storytelling. But the rules generally remain the same.

Role play is something I like to regularly use in my social skills groups but it is important to have a good understanding of what you are doing to ensure that it goes down well. We all know that feeling when we are on a training course and the facilitator mentions 'role play'! I reckon it is a very small percentage of people who sit up and smile at that point . . . most of us have a slight sinking, sick feeling! However, it should not stop us using it to help children develop better social skills. It just means we have to be aware of what we should do to make the role plays safe and fun, and most importantly helpful.

First, let us consider the benefits of using role play. Role play is a very valuable tool for exploring issues, making learning memorable, and encouraging co-operation and empathy. Role play can give children the opportunity to voice their opinions, express their feeling and make genuine choices. It can allow children to step into someone else's shoes and consider 'what if?' The children can practise different social skills through acting out a scenario and they can take on different roles and pretend to be, for example, someone being bullied, which will give them new insights and sympathies. They may learn and practise new ways to communicate, how to be assertive with regard to their values, react under peer pressure, and find different ways to manage conflict, and so on.

Getting into role

When I first introduce role play in a group, I will introduce a way to signal children to 'go into role'. This can be something quite visual like a rug on the floor that is our 'magic carpet' and when we are on the carpet, we are in the role of someone else. Or I may use an action such as turning or twirling into role (like a superman twirl). Or I may use a prop like a hat or a clapper board: 'when I put on this hat, I will be the head teacher'. Or finally I may use a verbal prompt such as 'my name is . . . and I am . . .' It can feel embarrassing at first, but remember that children slip into role very easily and will accept it if you signal it clearly. The importance of these activities is for children to feel safe within the role play and that any mistakes or anxieties can be left within the role play. So, at the end we ask children to 'de-role' and return to being them. It can still be anxiety provoking, so it is also important to introduce the children gently by introducing drama games into the sessions regularly.

Role play games

There are many ways of using role play and these are some of the simplest and most flexible:

Table 14.4 Role play games

Game	Description
1. Hot seating	Hot seating is when one child pretends to be a character and the others ask them questions. It is great for thinking in depth about characters and their motivations, but also for taking on the character of someone else, for example Brad in the *Talkabout for Teenagers* book.
2. The empty chair	One non-threatening way into acting is to create a character using an empty chair. Arrange the group in a circle with one empty chair. Go around the circle and each person supplies one piece of information about the character that they are thinking about, e.g. He's 10 years old. He has a sister and likes football'. When everyone has contributed their idea we ask for a volunteer to sit on the chair and become that character.
3. Becoming the story	The children become the characters and the objects in a story as the facilitator tells it. It encourages the children to listen carefully to the storyteller and interact spontaneously with their peers. We can use pre-arranged actions or responses 'if you hear me say "monkey" make a monkey noise' or we can allow the children to make up their own responses. There are a couple of examples of this kind of storytelling in the *Talkabout for Children* books (Kelly, 2018).
4. Freeze-frame	When a group is performing a scene they have devised it is useful to freeze-frame at a decisive point in the story to involve the rest of the class in asking questions or predicting what will happen next.
5. Improvising in pairs	Ask the children to work in pairs to plan a conversation or a scene. They then stand up and act it out.
6. The story basket	Use a basket of props and have the children pick out one at a time and use it to add to the next part of a made-up story.
7. Create a scene	Ask the whole group to work together to create a scene from a TV show or a news item. They can use the whole classroom to create the scene.
8. The imagination game	Bring out a prop, which can be anything: a paper clip, a plastic plate, a basket or anything that can be transformed into something else using the power of the imagination. Pass it around the group and each child takes turns to come up with an idea of what it can be by demonstrating it or telling.
9. The mime mat	Use your magic carpet or a marked-out space on the floor and each child acts something or pretends to be something and allow the others to guess.
10. What's in the box?	Imagine a box and place it in the middle of the group, open it up and carefully mime taking something out and using it. The other children guess what it is. Carefully place it back in the box before passing it on to someone else to open.
11. Structures	The children work in groups to use their bodies to create an object or to spell out a word. For example, they may become a car, or spell the word 'love' using the shapes of their bodies.
12. Cut . . . action!	Use the teacher as a witness to an event (role play) and they say 'cut' to freeze a role play for everyone to explore the situation and 'action' to continue.

Role play will often happen after the group facilitators have modelled a social behaviour, so we will look at the rules for modelling next.

Modelling

Modelling is different to role play. Modelling is when the two facilitators model behaviours (both inappropriate and appropriate) through a short piece of drama (or role play) and the children watch and discuss what they have seen. The purpose here is different to role play. We are showing the children what happens when we get behaviours wrong and then when we get it right. Done well, this is not only an effective way to teach children but it can be funny and engaging. So, the process is as follows:

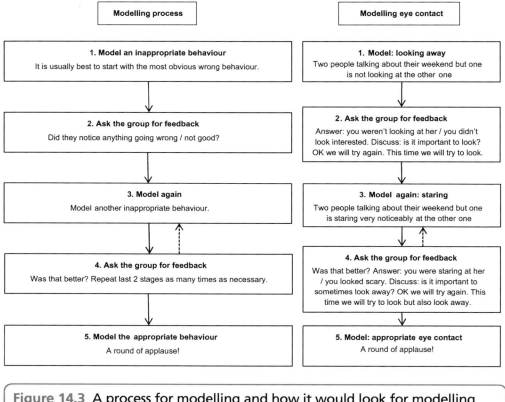

Figure 14.3 A process for modelling and how it would look for modelling eye contact

There are also some rules about modelling that will help the children to learn through modelling:

1. *Keep it simple*
   Try to only show one inappropriate skill and try to keep everything else appropriate. This is easier said than done and will probably take some practise! A helpful hint is to

think about what the children are going to *see* us doing, and therefore what they are going to *say*. So, for example, in the eye contact scenario above, if we exaggerate staring by also moving our body position forward, the children will see two things: staring, but also close proximity or aggressive posture, and so when asked what was wrong, they may just say, 'you got too close', or 'your posture was wrong or scary', when we actually want them to say 'you looked too much'.

2. *Don't pretend to be anyone else*
When we are modelling a behaviour it is important to be ourselves, so we may introduce it by saying 'I am going to have a conversation with Miss Green, let's see how I do'. If we take on another role, for example, a parent, shop assistant, child, teenager, or man, the children will be distracted by this (and our acting abilities!) and may stop noticing what we want them to. I remember seeing two male staff trying to model how to start a conversation with a woman and so one of them took the part of 'Sheila'. The young people (who had intellectual disabilities) thought it was very funny, but were not able to see past the fact that Tony was chatting up Tom!

3. *Don't pretend to be anywhere else*
This is similar to the above point. Don't pretend to be anywhere you are not, for example, a restaurant or bus stop. Again, this will be an unnecessary distraction.

4. *Keep it in the here and now*
Try to talk about something quite mundane – what we did last weekend or our plans for the holidays. This will help children to focus on what you want them to focus on and not be too distracted by the content of what you are saying (unless that is the topic for modelling of course).

5. *Start with the inappropriate, end with the appropriate*
We should plan out our modelling to logically work through the inappropriate behaviours so that we can end with the appropriate. Sometimes this is pretty simple: no eye contact, too much eye contact and finally good eye contact. Sometimes this is a bit more complicated and it can really help the children to see the skill being slowly improved and 'tweaked' until we get it right. To explain this, on the next page, I have shown the process I would use to model the assertive skill of apologising, which initially has five inappropriate scenarios and one appropriate.

6. *Use two facilitators to demonstrate a skill*
Modelling should be done by two group facilitators or, if the group only has one facilitator, then you will either need to find another adult to help you in that session or you will need to use a video clip or puppets (I will talk about this a bit later on in this chapter).

7. *Don't use the children to help you model a behaviour*
Modelling should only be done by group facilitators, so don't ever get one of the children to help model the behaviours. They are there to watch and learn and may be unpredictable in their response. We also cannot know what the other children will say in their feedback.

8. *Don't allow the children to then role play the inappropriate behaviour*
Once the modelling is finished, the children will often want to 'have a go'. They should be encouraged to only act out the appropriate version of the behaviour. I have talked to some teachers who say the children enjoy doing the inappropriate ones – they have found it funny watching them and want to make others laugh too. This is not a good

Modelling

Model 1: no apology

Two facilitators (Alex and Amy) having a talk about their weekend. Alex kicks Amy while talking. Amy says 'ooh that hurt' but Alex carries on talking.

↓

Ask the group for feedback 'What did you think?'

Answer: you kicked Amy / you should have said sorry. Discuss: is it important to say sorry (even if I didn't mean to kick her)? OK we will try again. This time I will try to remember to say sorry.

↓

Model 2: insincere apology

Alex and Amy continue their talk. Alex kicks Amy while talking. Amy says 'ooh that hurt' and Alex apologises but with an insincere tone of voice / facial expression / while laughing.

↓

Ask the group for feedback 'Was that better?'

Answer: no because you didn't sound like you meant it. Discuss: is it important to say sorry and sound like we mean it? OK we will try again. This time Alex will try to sound like she means it.

↓

Model 3: apology with blame (no responsibility)

Alex and Amy continue their talk. Alex kicks Amy while talking. Alex apologises but then blames Amy 'can you move back a little and then it won't happen again?'

↓

Ask the group for feedback 'Was that better?'

Answer: no because you blamed Amy. Discuss: is it important to say sorry and take responsibility? OK we will try again. This time Alex will say sorry, sound like she means it and won't blame Amy.

↓

Model 4: apology with repetition (no learning)

Alex and Amy continue their talk. Alex kicks Amy while talking. Alex apologises nicely 'I'm sorry, my fault' or 'Sorry Amy' but then continues to kick Amy

↓

Ask the group for feedback 'Was that better?'

Answer: no because you carried on kicking. Discuss: is it important to not do something again? OK we will try again. So Alex will sound like she means it, won't blame Amy and won't do it again.

↓

Model 5: over apologising

Alex and Amy continue their talk. Alex kicks Amy while talking. Alex then apologises excessively.

↓

Ask the group for feedback 'Was that better?'

Answer: no because went over the top. Discuss how apologising is complicated! Recap on all the things we have learnt and say Alex will get it right this time!

↓

Model 6: appropriate apology

A round of applause!

↓

Group discussion on apologising

Discuss how apologising will change according to the situation. Consider a 'big' versus 'little' sorry.

Figure 14.4 Modelling the skill of apologising

idea as we are then potentially reinforcing the inappropriate behaviours. Children should only get to act out and practise the appropriate behaviours.

Puppets

As I have said before in this book, having fun while teaching social skills is good as children are more willing to learn when they are having fun. And puppets can be fun. The art of puppetry has been around for centuries, and I, like many before me, enjoy using them with children and adults alike.

Christie Belfiore (2016) describes it well:

> Simple gestures with her hand bring life to the inert puppets, moving their little arms and mouths to animate a topic. Easy to operate, the children too can play with the puppets – bringing them to life and attributing personalities, characteristics, attitudes, and more. The puppet can become anyone or anything he or she wants. A best friend perhaps. Maybe even a sibling, teacher, or pet. It does not really matter because the world children create with puppets is entirely their own, a world without boundaries that they can freely explore. When used in the classroom, these puppets can help boost creativity and stimulate kids' imaginations, from the preschool age up to early teen years. The innate interactivity draws children in and encourages them to be actively involved in the learning process and share their thoughts and observations.

So, what do I mean by a 'puppet'? Well, to start with, I mean my gorgeous collection of animal hand puppets that I have collected over the years! I have a shy hedgehog (Harry), a noisy parrot (Mr Skittles), an aggressive lion (Roaring Richard), a passive mouse (Timid Timothy), an assertive owl (Wise William), and the list goes on. But I also have 'signing' boy and girl puppets that are much larger and sit on my lap with my hands in their hands, allowing me to use sign language through the puppet. I have also used finger puppets and, sometimes, just soft toys from my son's bedroom!

So why do I like using puppets? What are the advantages of using them to teach social skills?

1. *Puppets grab your attention*
   This is particularly true with younger children. I can introduce the group to my new friend (who is maybe a bit shy and is hiding behind my back) and suddenly I have their attention. For younger children, play is an important way to learn skills and when puppets are incorporated into sessions, children appear to retain knowledge more effectively as the puppets become tools for sharing or retelling what they have learned and observed.
2. *Two models are better that one*
   As we have just seen in the modelling section, we need two adults to model behaviours effectively. So, if we are the only facilitator, we can always use our puppet to help us model. Of course, some skills will be tricky – it is quite hard to interrupt and talk over your puppet! But a number of skills can be modelled with you and your puppet.
3. *Learning skills from the puppet*
   Puppets can help children to learn different communication and social skills. They get to practise skills in a fun and relaxed way using puppets, which they can then apply to regular conversations and situations. They may also learn skills by teaching the puppet or directing them in how to behave appropriately.

4. *A great introduction to role play*

    I usually find that children are happy to take a puppet and act out a scenario or a conversation, and this is a great way to build up confidence in one day using role play without the help of the puppets.

5. *Puppets help children to express themselves*

    Some children struggle to speak, either because they are shy or they find the attention intimidating. When puppets are provided, however, these children can often be encouraged to speak via the puppet, as it shifts the audience's attention away from them and onto the puppet and if they make a mistake, it is the puppet making the mistake, not the child. So, the puppet tells everyone how they feel, and then asks the child next to them. In such cases puppets can act as a psychological support for a child and these children can gradually grow more confident in communicating verbally. Similarly, I have also used puppets to help children to express themselves *to* the puppet. Let's tell the puppet how we are feeling or what happened today. Again, this takes the pressure off and allows some children to express themselves more easily.

6. *Talking about difficult issues*

    With older pupils it may be necessary to talk about difficult issues such as bullying, abuse, drugs, and cultural and physical differences. Many children are very uncomfortable with these personal topics and puppets can help break down barriers, to lighten the mood, and to encourage students to discuss these issues. As Belfiore (2016) says, 'Puppets also act as an outlet because students can use them to express things that may pain them, or share things without feeling vulnerable'.

My only word of caution is that some people react badly to puppets. This may be either due to a genuine fear of them, or to a belief that puppets are not age-appropriate. If it is the latter, then I tend to handle this by asking the young people if they would like me to use the puppets (or stop using them). Also, I would consider if the puppets are genuinely helping to develop skills.

I speak from experience, as I currently run a day service for adults with an intellectual disability in the UK called 'Speaking Space'. We run a number of social skills groups and we sometimes bring out the puppets. Is this OK? Are they age appropriate? Well, I suppose my opinion is that the world can sometimes just get a bit too serious and a bit too hung up on being 'PC' (politically correct) and my attitude is that 'if the young people I am working with are enjoying my sessions and learning skills (and I am doing it in a respectful manner), where's the harm and why shouldn't we?'

Technology interventions

Finally, we need to talk about technology and how it can be used to help teach social skills. The use of technology has unsurprisingly increased in the last few years. It has become so much easier to bring technology into our sessions by watching a video clip, recording a short conversation, downloading an educational Application, and even creating your own cartoon. Indeed, this is such a fast-moving area that I hesitate to write about it in this book because it is likely to be out of date before it is published! So, in this section I will briefly describe the main ways in which we can use technology to support our development of social skills and what the research says about using it, and hope that some of it remains relevant for a while yet! But I want to start with the three main reasons why I think using technology is a good idea and has benefits for teaching social skills: motivation, play, and relevance.

1. *Motivation*
   There will always be some children who are not motivated to work with us on their social skills, either in a group or in a 1:1 setting. As we have said before, motivation is critical to success. Singer-Califano (2008) says, 'In order to maximize effectiveness, social skills training programs must be motivating and personally relevant for students to want to use them'. This is where technology can play a part. Is the child interested in computers? Do they enjoy playing or creating things on their computer? Do they like videos? I usually find that the answer is 'yes' to all of these and so maybe using technology will be our 'way in' to working with them.

2. *Play*
   Children's play and technology have a strong link, whether adults like this or not. Technologies and media culture are a huge influence on what children play out in the playground and so if we are to think about making our social skills interventions fun, and playful, one sensible way is to consider how to introduce technology into them.

3. *Relevance*
   Finally, it is also worth considering how relevant technology is. Many writers have talked about the importance of access to digital technologies, particularly for autistic people. When using technologies, children may be 'more engaged, focused and able to follow instruction, and may be more able to self-regulate' (Conn, 2016). The mass media has also become one of the most prevalent ways in which children and adolescents gather information about their environment and 'that media, including television, movies, magazines and the internet, may be one of the key forces contributing to how young viewers' beliefs and behaviours are shaped' (Ward, 2005). With this in mind, technology should ideally play a part in our intervention, not only to make it motivating but also relevant.

In this section of the chapter I am going to mainly talk about three ways in which we can use technology: using media, video modelling and computer-based software applications.

Using media

Interventions involving videos (television, films and acted scenarios) have been used to successfully train new behaviours and eliminate old ones within children with a range of disabilities (Buggey, 2005). Not only does the media provide a means of learning through observation, but it also allows opportunities for children to look at different ways to behave and has the ability to affect their future behaviour, attitudes and emotional experiences.

Videos are also motivating. I just have to say 'let's watch a video' and most people (children and adults) sit up with interest. So not only are we using a strategy that is motivating and interesting, but if you are working with an autistic child, this type of intervention may also capitalise on their strengths. Very often, autistic children are drawn to the television or iPad more than they are to people and real-life interactions. So, in using videos to teach skills, we are using a medium that can be more manageable for them. Finally, if I am working without a co-facilitator, it can be an excellent alternative to modelling behaviours.

The *Talkabout* DVD (Kelly, 2009) was created exactly for these reasons. It has an acted scenario for all of the core social skills and each one demonstrates at least one inappropriate version of the behaviour and then one appropriate version. In a similar way to using modelling, children are asked to watch a scenario and comment on what they thought was good and not so good.

Video modelling

Video modelling is very similar to real life modelling, except for the obvious fact that the acted-out scenarios are videoed and replayed. The evidence for this intervention is also good. Research shows that video modelling has been used successfully in teaching a wide variety of skills, including building conversation skills and social skills and that many students with ASD are strong visual learners, enjoy watching videos, and attend well to a model presented in a video clip (Charlop and Milstein, 1989; Sherer et al., 2001; Ozonoff and Rogers, 2003). Video modelling has also been found to be effective in teaching social behaviours, particularly if followed by additional prompts and role playing (Apple et al., 2005).

In most cases, video modelling is done with an adult demonstrating the skill first (as in modelling) so that they can ensure that the important aspects of the target behaviour are highlighted, although in some cases, older peer tutors or mature peers can be used as models. Having observed a video clip of the behaviour, the children are then encouraged to practise these using role play or structured activities.

Another extension of video modelling is to video the children and then to give feedback on their performance, or to video them to help them visualise themselves getting something right. I have worked with teenagers and young adults who have had many years of getting a particular behaviour wrong so that they struggle to imagine themselves getting it right. Many years of wrong patterns of behaviour can be hard to change and certainly hard to imagine for some children, particularly those with autism. So, if we can manipulate the filming so that we video them with lots of prompting until they succeed, we can then replay it so that they can see for themselves that they are able to succeed. In teaching them social skills this way, the autistic child may feel that they have more control over what is happening than they experience in real life, with more opportunity to engage in repeated experiences that will build up their confidence and give them a sense of success. As Bandura (cited by Singer-Califano 2008) found, the advantage of seeing themselves perform successfully 'provides clear information on how best to perform skills' and will also 'strengthen beliefs' in their own capability.

Computer based software applications

The same kind of learning described above can also take place through computer-based applications. The two that I will describe briefly here are: a software package to create cartoons and virtual reality.

Software packages

Software programs to make 3D animations can be an excellent way to motivate children (mostly older children or teenagers) to work on their social skills. We can brainstorm ideas for scenarios, write scripts and create characters that they will relate to and enjoy learning from. I am not necessarily very 'computer clever', but I find that the children make up for any inadequacies on my part and all they need is some direction from me and they are off!

The software package I have used is called Muvizu. Muvizu comes pre-packed with a number of two-legged characters, objects, effects and pre-made animations which we can use to suit our own situation and stories. It also allows us to record a dialogue which it will lip-sync automatically. The main advantage to using it with children is the fact that we can produce relatively simple videos in as little as 20 minutes, which makes it incredibly rewarding within a social skills session. I have used Muvizu with children who have created cartoons to animate specific difficulties with certain situations and then possible alternatives. We have used it to explore all aspects of social skills: body language, the way we talk, conversation skills and assertiveness. And we have used it to consider how to make friends and cope with emotions such as high anxiety. I once received the following email from a mum who had been on one of my training courses:

> Thank you so very much for introducing me to the world of Muvizu! My 9-year-old Aspy [Asperger's] son has played around with this last night and this afternoon and is loving it! As a bonus on the side, when he has been creating the characters he has been using the words 'appearance' etc. and talking about body language and what head movements, eye movements are needed and if characters should be facing each other!! . . . Lots of awesome discussions have come from making it!

> (Debra, Australia, 2016)

Virtual reality

Virtual reality (VR) is also a fast-moving technology and will undoubtedly play a significant part in helping children to develop social skills in the future through computer generated simulations. VR technology provides a human-computer interaction paradigm in which the user is an active participant within a computer-generated scenario. The advantages of this approach include the fact that these experiences are immersive. They are multi-sensory, three dimensional and interactive, and have the ability to naturally transfer to real life. As Singer-Califano (2008) says, virtual reality provides 'a focused learning framework that is motivating, consistent, and able to be transferred to an actual environment'. So, the potential to teach children social skills and to help them transfer them into natural settings is huge. By using VR we are able to put people into social situations that they find difficult and coach them to think, feel and behave differently and more effectively in those situations. It enables the person to try things out in a safe environment that they wouldn't normally do. And all the scientific data shows that the learning we do in the VR environment does transfer into the real world.

There are obviously other ways in which we can use technology that we haven't discussed. For example, for the smart phone or iPad, there are an abundance of educational applications to help individuals learn social skills. These vary from very simple tools to prompt someone to say or do something, to more complicated assistive technology devices. This is a fast-developing approach and so it is always worth exploring what has been developed in the area in which you are working.

Summary

In this chapter we have described the most common social skills interventions, but it is important to remember that there are other strategies out there, so this is not an exhaustive list, and that mostly it is not a question of 'either, or', it is mostly a case of using a number that will complement one another. So, I may be running a social skills group, but I will also certainly be using some form of creative arts and technology interventions within the group and I may also use comic strips and stories as well. Finally, it is all about the individual. Consider their motivations, their environment and their needs, and then choose the intervention that is right for them.

In the following two chapters I will talk about developing social skills within a school setting and then at home.

Key points from Chapter 14

This chapter is the second of four chapters on teaching social skills and looked at developing social skills under four headings.

Therapeutic 1:1 interventions

Comic Strip conversations™

- The active and visual nature of Comic Strip conversations™ helps children to 'see' the conversation and to focus on a solution
- How to use comic strip conversations™

Social Stories™

- A Social Story™ is a short story that has been written in a specific style and format. It describes a specific social situation and presents information in a structured and consistent manner.
- Why use them?
- The benefits
- How to write a Social Story™
- Carol Gray's ten criteria for a Social Story™
- What can go wrong?

Therapeutic group interventions

The advantages of group interventions and performance in a group: being in the presence of others, high task attractiveness, group cohesiveness, the life cycle of a group, and feedback.

Setting up a social skills group

- Who is going to be in the group?
- How big should the group be?
- Who is going to run it?
- What are we going to do?
- Where are we going to do it?
- Do we need a contract?

Running a social skills group

- Cohesiveness
- Group rules
- The format of the session
- Evaluation

Creative arts interventions

Role play, drama and storytelling

- The benefits
- Getting into role
- Role play games

Modelling

- The process for modelling
- The rules for modelling

Puppets

- Why use them?

Technology interventions

Three main reasons why using technology has benefits for teaching social skills: motivation, play, and relevance.

Using media

- Video modelling
- Computer based software applications
- Software packages
- Virtual reality

Chapter 15

Teaching social skills 3
Teaching social skills in schools

'The roots of education are bitter, but the fruit is sweet.'

Aristotle, Greek philosopher (384–322 BC)

I wanted to dedicate a chapter to the specific challenges and advantages of teaching social skills within a school setting as this is what I spend most of my time doing – going into schools and helping them to find the best ways to support those pupils who are struggling with their social skills. Of course, every school is different and the needs of the pupils may also be different, but there are certain common factors or standards that we can apply to every school. So, in this chapter I will describe the different approaches to teaching social skills in schools and then the factors that make a difference. I will then describe some actual schools that have been very successful in their interventions and how they have achieved this. But first I will consider 'why'? Why is it so important to teach social skills within a school setting?

Why are social skills important to teach in school?

Let's start by going back to some of the reasons discussed in Chapter 1: quality of life, success and staying out of trouble.

Quality of life, success and staying out of trouble

First, our social competence contributes to our quality of life, as our lives are built on positive interactions and the relationships that we have with the people around us (Crawford and Goldstein, 2005). As John Bercow said in 2008, 'the ability to communicate effectively is the key life skill of the 21st century'. Most situations, including those at school, require us to interact with others and a great deal of our success within these social encounters depends on our ability to use and understand social skills. So social skills are central to helping a child to interact successfully in their social world, to have friends and to be a friend, and this in turn will contribute to their quality of life.

Second, social competence has been repeatedly demonstrated to be a critical variable in predicting success in future life (Denham et al., 2001) – the people who get jobs and then get promoted are the people with good social skills. Bolton (1979) also says that 80% of people who fail at work do so for one reason: they do not relate well to other people. Research has demonstrated powerful connections between how well a child does socially and how successful they are in other areas of their life (Rubin 2002).

Third, social skills appear to be important in staying out of trouble. A recent study showed that between 60% and 90% of the 7,000 young people who pass through young offender institutions have communication difficulties (Bryan et al., 2007) and this includes problems with social communication skills. This is backed up by Mash and Barkley, cited by Warnes et al. (2005), who say that 'social skills deficits are frequently associated with children exhibiting externalising disorders such as delinquency and conduct disorder'.

With all this evidence, it is interesting to consider what is important to us as a society and maybe as parents. Do we want our children to come out of schools with a handful of good academic qualifications? Of course, we do. But is it more important to us that our children have good social skills? After all, if we take note of the research, these skills will help our children to make friends, get through an interview, get a job, keep a job and stay out of trouble, and will have a better chance of giving them a good quality of life and higher self-esteem. So, if a child is struggling to learn good social skills, where is it best to teach them? I would like to argue in this chapter that the school setting has a vital role to play in teaching social skills and that as a society we should be enabling this to happen. Don't you wonder what would have happened if the 7,000 children in Bryan's research study (2007) had been taught social skills within school? What if social skills were on the curriculum of every school and teachers were trained to teach these skills effectively? Would we see a difference in youth offending in the years to come? I suspect we would.

Unfortunately, schools face pressure to teach academic subjects and mostly see their priority to be about maximising academic achievements, so don't have the time or the resources to teach social skills. Schneider (2016) describes this as the 'back to basics' position that gained some prominence in the 1980s, which 'brought a general conservatism to the field of education in many Western countries, resulting in an emphasis on the acquisition of facts and academic skills . . . [and that] social development was seen as the family's domain'. Supporters of the social role of education, like me, argue that the school should be responsible for teaching children social skills and encouraging social and emotional learning. Indeed, as Elias et al. (1997) maintained, the goal of the school is to produce 'knowledgeable, responsible, caring individuals'.

However, it is not really an 'either/or' situation, for as Schneider (2016) says 'research indicates that academic success and social competences are interdependent – that achievement may facilitate social development and vice versa'. There are academic gains to fostering social and emotional learning in children. As Elias et al. (1997) say, 'when schools attend systematically to students' social and emotional skills, the academic achievement of children increases, the incidence of problem behaviours decreases, and the quality of the relationships surrounding each child improves'. This is something we have also seen in the schools who have embraced the *Talkabout* programme and I will discuss our findings later on in this chapter and also in the final chapter which looks at evidencing the interventions.

Social skills and cognitive development and learning

There is a growing amount of research that looks at the link between social interaction and cognitive development, as well as academic achievement. Schneider (2016) says that 'numerous findings have illustrated the positive effects of social interaction on cognitive development'. It has also been suggested that social competence is a more accurate predictor of achievement than measured intellectual capacity (Wentzel, cited by Schneider, 2016). These all imply that the social forces within a school and a classroom are integral to a child's academic achievement. The findings of these research studies indicate that academic achievement is influenced by social competence and peer acceptance, which in turn is affected by levels of academic success – meaning there is a bidirectional relationship between social skills and academic success. This then also brings in the impact that friendships or peer relationships have on cognitive growth.

Schneider (2016) cites a number of influential studies in the United States that have demonstrated a correlation between positive peer relations and academic achievement, and between negative peer relations and poor academic progress. This has brought about speculation as to what it is that occurs during peer interactions for cognitive growth to occur. Piaget (1932) maintained that through interaction and conflict, children encounter disequilibrium which causes a restructuring of their logic and cognitive growth. This means that there may be some benefits to working with friends. Nelson and Aboud (1985) found that friends explained their opinions and criticised their partners more often than did non-friends and these higher levels of disagreement led to more cognitive change than did compliance. They also found that friends who experience conflict undergo more social development than non-friends do in conflict. It would appear that again, there is a bidirectional relationship between social skills and cognitive growth whilst learning with friends.

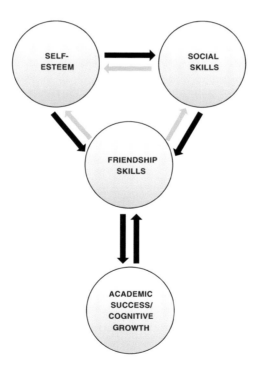

Figure 15.1 The relationship between self-esteem, social skills, friendship skills and academic success

With all this in mind, we could argue that the hierarchy of social skills explained in Chapter 12 is a prerequisite for cognitive growth. Children need social skills in order to make friends and be accepted by their peers, and friendship skills then enable them to learn more effectively. In addition, if we use social interaction with friends to help children learn, we see an improvement in academic achievement and social interaction with their friends. Finally, if we teach children using a more 'cooperative' approach, we not only see academic benefits but also improvement in self-esteem (Johnson and Johnson, 1989). Using this information, we could add to our previous illustration in Chapter 12 (Figure 12.2) to include the relationship of these skills with cognitive growth and academic competence.

We can summarise this section by agreeing that there is much evidence to support the teaching of social skills in schools and that this will benefit the children in many ways, including academic success. Howley and Arnold (2005) start their book by saying that 'the need to develop effective interaction should be reflected in any curriculum' and they go on to quote the English National Curriculum (Department of Education and Employment, 1999) which identifies 'working with others' as a key skill for all pupils and that 'if pupils are to work with others they must develop social skills and a growing awareness and understanding of others' needs'. I couldn't have put it better myself! So how can schools do this?

Different approaches to teaching social skills in school

A head teacher spoke to me recently at a conference and told me that the teachers at his school didn't need to teach their pupils social skills because the children learnt them 'by osmosis'. I would have liked to ask him more about his school, but as it was a passing comment at a busy stand, it was not appropriate or possible. But I suspect that whereas, for some of his pupils, this was true, for some of his pupils, it was probably not, and that they would have benefited from something additional. There are different approaches to teaching social skills within the school setting dependant on the needs of the children and the type of school. Some schools need a whole class approach to preventing future difficulties and encouraging social interaction, and some require a systematic targeted approach to support children who have more specific social skills difficulties. In both approaches though, we will firstly need to consider the school climate and the support from the management team.

School climate or culture: looking at the bigger picture

Private companies can spend a lot of money looking at the culture of their business. What does their brand say about them? What do they want the customer experience to be like? But we rarely hear about schools doing this. And yet school climate and culture does exist and is important in the pupils' development. We can all think about schools where we have walked in and known that the climate or culture is a positive, enabling one and that the pupils are generally happy. Equally we can think of schools where the opposite is true. But how do we define it? Schneider (2016) quotes an advocacy group in the United States that defines school climate as 'the quality and character of school life . . . based on patterns of students', parents' and school personnel's experience of school life and reflects norms, goals, values, interpersonal relationships, teaching and learning practices, and organizational structures'.

School climate is important because it is known to influence peer relations in schools in a number of ways. One of these is how much shy and withdrawn children participate socially. Several studies indicate that the warmth of the welcome by peers and teachers influence the extent to which shy, withdrawn children either withdraw further socially or increase their social participation (Gazelle, 2013). Another way in which school climate influences peer relations is on the rates of bullying. It has been shown that pupil perceptions of school climate influence decisions about their choice of action during a bully-victim confrontation – to 'upstand, bystand, or join in' the bullying (Ferrans and Selman, 2014) and it has been shown a number of times that it is possible to reduce bullying by improving the school environment (e.g. Kyriakides et al., 2014).

What does this all mean in terms of social skills? Well, in order to improve social skills, we do need to look at the wider context for a child as it is essential that any social skills work is supported by the person's environment and that skills that are being taught are encouraged throughout the day. So, if the school climate is one that is encouraging shy, withdrawn children to increase their social participation and that positively influences the rates of bullying, they are more likely to be indirectly helping children to develop good social skills.

It helps to do a basic assessment of the school's environment and in particular the social opportunities that exist within the child's routine, so that they can be used to support the generalisation and functional use of the newly acquired skill. As Shaked and Yirmiya (2003) state: 'it is important to evaluate the child's specific school environment and devise ways whereby the school setting can adjust to the child's needs and further enable social and emotional growth'. This will mean getting all staff on board and then creating opportunities across the day for the child to practise their emerging and newly acquired skills. It may also mean identifying aspects of their day that are not conducive to their development and then dealing with them. Involving families is also an essential part of this and parents should be encouraged to be as involved as possible. So, whether the climate is positive or not, it is often helpful to ask the following questions when working with a child on their social skills:

Questions to consider about the child's school environment

1. Consider the social opportunities that exist within the school. Can they be used to support the generalisation and functional use of any newly acquired skill?
2. Does the school (or home) environment need to be adjusted to promote new skills? Are there any aspects of their day that are not conducive to their development?
3. Are the teachers on board? Can the teachers create opportunities across their day for the child to practise their emerging and newly acquired skills?

Involving other teachers and parents in what is happening is clearly an essential part of any intervention but when considering the school environment, the climate or culture of the school will also have an effect on the outcome. So what happens when the odds are against us and it is the whole environment that really needs to change? What happens if there are children who really need social skills intervention but the school or the environment we find ourselves in is so poor that we're not sure where to start and the task seems too large and the numbers of staff willing to change too small? In these instances, it is important that we affect changes carefully. In summary, I try to follow four steps:

Table 15.1 Steps to affect change in a school	
Step 1 Get the support and permission from top-level management	Any intervention, especially if it requires any changes, requires support from management, otherwise at some point we will undoubtedly come across issues with staffing, curriculum, accommodation etc. Start by trying to sell the idea of change and if that doesn't work, try persuading them to agree to a short-term pilot. I often use the facts from the research into the additional benefits of developing social skills and also show how we can measure the effectiveness of the work (Chapter 16 covers this).
Step 2 Work with forces supportive of change and develop a critical mass of support	Start by working with the teachers who are interested and willing to implement any changes. It is essential that initially we work collaboratively with others who will support and motivate each other and prevent isolation.
Step 3 Identify the natural leaders amongst staff	Sometimes it is important for someone else to take a lead and it is useful to have someone who is a natural leader amongst your critical mass of support.
Step 4 Work within organisationally healthy parts of the system	Start any change in a part of the school that is already functioning well. Choose the class with the enthusiastic teacher and children who get on well. This will ensure initial work is as successful as possible and will influence and inspire others.

The whole class approach

The advantage of a whole class approach to teaching social skills is that it can be used before problems occur. Schneider (2016) says that 'social skills training can be implemented for primary prevention . . . [and that] the whole-class format avoids stigmatizing any individuals by assigning them to special groups'. This works very well in special schools where the size of the class tends to be much smaller and the needs of the children greater. I have worked with a number of special schools and units attached to mainstream schools that have put social skills onto the curriculum so that all pupils work through the stages over the years and I will describe this in more detail later on in this chapter. But I have also helped some mainstream schools to teach social skills within a class setting and I will also describe how we have achieved this.

The targeted group approach

The more common approach in schools is to use the targeted group approach where children are brought together with similar needs in a small group format where it is possible to provide more individualised attention. As we said in the previous chapter, the ideal group is one where children are matched for communicative strength and need, diagnosis, likes and dislikes, age and sex, but also that the group members get on and like each other, because we need them to enjoy coming to the sessions and to relax enough to learn. However, sometimes bringing students together with similar issues can backfire, for example in the case of children who are aggressive, but the research is mixed and, as Schneider (2016) states, 'if there is indeed any unintended harmful effect of aggregation, there is no reason to believe that this occurs any more or less in social skills training groups than in any other form of group counselling or therapy'. I will describe how this approach can work in more detail later on in the chapter.

The use of peers

Another approach to improving social skills is through the use of peers. As Frea (2006) says: 'involved peers can accelerate the success of the program [and a] lack of peer involvement can result in social behaviours that never truly become functional skills'. This can happen in a less structured way through the whole class approach as all children learn about the same skills in the same lesson. This has a natural benefit of not stigmatising the child with the social skills difficulties, but also helps the children to foster improved peer interaction with each other. But there are ways to use peers in a more structured way, using peer mediation or peer tutoring, where a competent peer tutors a child who needs help, and using the 'circle of friends' approach.

Peer mediation

There is a large body of published work that focuses on peer-mediated interventions for improving social behaviour. Odom and Strain (1986) and Goldstein et al. (1992) have developed a number of successful peer-mediated strategies over the past 20 years and Strain et al. (2008) found that having intervention mediated by classroom peers was successful in social skills training for autistic children.

Peer mediation started in schools as a process where students were trained in the skills of mediation to help resolve conflicts with their peers and younger children. In this scenario, peer mediators are taught to facilitate communication, negotiation, understanding and problem solving. However, even though the primary goal of peer mediation is to resolve disputes and conflicts, schools that have introduced this have also found an improvement generally in social behaviour so peer mediators are used to improve social skills. Importantly, it has also been shown that there are benefits not only to the child with social skills difficulties but also to the peer tutor. Gumpel and Frank (1999) examined the effects of peer tutoring on social interaction between two 12-year-old boys who acted as tutors to two five-year-old boys who were socially isolated and rejected. They found that there were benefits to the tutors as well as to the tutees as they saw maintained increase in socially skilled behaviours in all four boys and this reciprocal positive effect is seen throughout the literature (Schneider, 2016).

Introducing peer mediation into a school will depend on whether you are introducing it in a primary or secondary school. With younger children, volunteers can be taught to model targeted behaviours and reinforce new social skills through role play with adults. They are then encouraged to act these out with targeted children with reinforcement and cueing from the adult. This is gradually faded over a period of time. For example, a targeted behaviour, such as maintaining attention, is subdivided into several steps: the peer moves in front of the child, the peer looks at him and the toy the child is playing with, the peer says his name and repeats if necessary etc. These strategies can be powerful at increasing social interactions within the classroom and both generalisation and maintenance has been found to be good (Mastergeorge et al., 2003).

In secondary schools, they may use different models of intervention to facilitate the same outcome. For example, some schools have started a 'friendship bus stop' which is manned by peer volunteers who are trained to resolve difficulties other children may be experiencing, or a friendship bench and playground mentors/buddies. Volunteers will encourage appropriate social interaction and will model good social skills. In both settings, Schneider summarises the important requirements for peer tutoring to be effective: it should be highly structured; tutors must be trained; teachers must monitor and provide feedback; and students must know who their partner is, what material is to be taught, and how to correct their partner, prior to the tutoring session.

Circle of friends

'Circle of friends' is an approach that is used in mainstream settings to enhance the inclusion of any young person who is experiencing difficulties in school because of a disability, social skills difficulties, personal crisis, or because of their challenging behaviour towards others. The 'circle of friends' approach works through setting up a group of six to eight peers to provide practical support to the focus child.

Volunteers mostly meet weekly and have three main tasks:

1. To help identify difficulties that the child is having
2. To set goals and devise strategies for reaching them
3. To offer encouragement and recognition for success and progress

Volunteers are encouraged to talk openly about the difficulties they encounter with the child's behaviour, but the whole approach does obviously need to be well facilitated and it is important to ensure that from a hierarchical perspective that the focus child is not set up to fail by being encouraged to develop a skill that is too difficult (Shaked and Yirmiya, 2003). It is also important that the whole approach is seen to be supportive by the individual. This will hopefully be worked through with good facilitation, but one factor that might be important to consider is the name of the group. 'Circle of friends' may be inappropriate as it infers something that it is not and so it may be more appropriate to either call it 'Circle of support' or to allow the group to choose their own name.

One advantage of this approach to developing social skills is the fact that difficulties are shared and discussed with their peers and therefore the peers are involved in helping the focus child develop skills that are particularly relevant to them. They may also have interesting viewpoints as to why the focus child is having difficulties initiating conversations in the playground, for example, or is struggling at lunch time and this insight will be invaluable for the focus child. Another advantage of this approach is that it does not involve a major commitment of time from teachers or therapists. Teachers will need to facilitate the group and in particular their problem solving, but some groups end up becoming largely self-sufficient with only minimal input from teaching staff.

The use of play

Within education, play is seen as a valuable method of helping children to learn and to develop. For typically developing children, play supports learning and development across a number of areas: cognitive, social, communicative, linguistic and physical. It also has intrinsic value in that it supports emotional well-being, a healthy sense of self and feelings of safety, happiness and confidence, and supports social competency and participation (Conn, 2016). Play for children with autism is also seen as having value and is used to support the development of social skills. It can offer a platform for gentle experiences of social sharing and a starting point for engaging them in social interaction and communicating with another person.

Play is also an avenue through which social skills can develop. Children engage with other children through play, using play for the purpose of communication and shared meaning, and as a way of enjoying each other's company. Play is associated with feelings of safety and security and so supports personal growth and is used by children as a form of self-expression, emotional regulation and response to stress. It is therefore a useful means to help children develop effective social skills and friendship skills. For example, as children grow older, they learn about societal rules by making up games with rules, as well as about winning and losing and 'playing fair'. They also learn about controlling their impulses in order to do well at something and about space, negotiating and problem solving.

Despite the fact that play can help children learn and develop, it can be a challenge to incorporate it into a school-based curriculum, especially in secondary school. If it is incorporated in either setting, the role of the teacher is to create opportunities, supporting where necessary with suggestions or a comment or acting as a mediator when there are misunderstandings; or being an active play partner, following what the children are doing and responding accordingly. The following table gives some examples of the different types of play and how they can be used to develop social skills:

Table 15.2 Types of play to support social skills

Pretend play	Helps children to think about imaginary situations and roles that they can play. Can be used to help children learn about shared intentions and practise different social interactions.
Role play	More structured than pretend play, role play can be used to practise scenarios such as in the playground or at a party where the child does not know anybody. Model and create a list of different things you can say. To join others who are playing e.g. 'Can I play too?' (see previous chapter).
Puppets	Similar to role play, puppets can be used to talk to each other and role play different social situations. The children can help the puppet to learn different skills such as listening, making new friends (see previous chapter).
Board games	Turn taking games such as board games can be used to encourage a child to say whose turn it is in the game (e.g. 'My turn', 'Your turn'). They can also learn about winning and losing.
Construction play	Can be used to take turns, follow instructions and work collaboratively to achieve a goal. Lego® therapy is an example of this.
Rule-based play	Can help children to learn about rules and flexibility and negotiating with others.
Physical play	Can be used to develop self and other awareness and a social experience of another person. Can also be used for group gelling, turn taking, group negotiation and most other social skills.

(Continued)

> **Table 15.2** (Continued)

Technology play	Watching media or creating their own cartoons, images, presentations etc. can all be used to enhance social skills (see previous chapter).
Language play	Play can be around words, sounds, rhymes, nonsensical words, jokes etc. For example, call and response games where we repeat words with a rhythm can help children to learn to listen, take turns and cooperate in a group setting.

Examples of developing social skills in schools

I have spent the last ten years running my own business and, as part of this, I have been working in a number of different schools to support them to develop social skills and to evidence the impact of the intervention. In total I have collected evidence from over 1,000 schools, which I will talk about more in the final chapter, but it has given me a real sense of what works best and what schools should do to see most progress. In this section I will describe two main models of working within a school: the curriculum approach and the targeted approach and how these can work within different schools. I will end with my top tips for schools.

A whole school curriculum approach

The most important aspect of this approach is that all pupils are taught social skills as part of their school curriculum, so it is not only put onto their timetable, but it is seen as part of school life and reported on accordingly like any other subject. The main focus here is group work, so the focus of the intervention is on running social skills groups within the class. However, alongside this, it is often ideal to see schools using additional approaches, such as 1:1 therapeutic approaches discussed in the previous chapter.

The whole school curriculum approach to teaching social skills has worked well in a number of special schools I have worked in. In particular, I would like to credit two schools in the UK: a school in Lowestoft, Suffolk which is a school for pupils with an intellectual disability (7–16 years old) and a school in Southampton, Hampshire which is a school for pupils with social emotional and mental health difficulties (11–16 years old). Both schools have shown a commitment over a period of over five years to improving the way in which they teach their pupils social skills and develop their self-esteem and they have both progressed to a point now where they are seeing real progress in both social skills and self-esteem, but also behaviour difficulties and school attendance.

However, it can also work well in mainstream schools where there is an additional resource provision. These are sometimes specifically to support pupils with ASD or for pupils who are struggling with any aspect of their learning, for example dyslexia. These 'units' have many different names from the 'ASD unit' to the 'ARP' (additional resource provision) and others, and they also vary in how they work within the school, from occasional lessons or support for pupils, to full time provision for pupils. So how they implement their social skills lessons will also vary in terms of how long they spend working on each skill, but a whole curriculum approach can work within this kind of unit, and the structure will always follow the hierarchy.

The hierarchy of intervention

1. Self-awareness and self-esteem
2. Body language
3. Conversational skills
4. Friendship skills
5. Assertiveness

This can result in the following plans for different year groups:

Table 15.3 Different curriculum approaches to teaching social skills over five years

Year	Option 1	Option 2	Option 3
1	*Self-awareness and self-esteem* e.g. following the programme: *Talkabout* for Children developing self-awareness and self-esteem	*Self-awareness and self-esteem* e.g. following the programme: *Talkabout* for Children developing self-awareness and self-esteem	*Self-awareness and self-esteem* e.g. following the programme: *Talkabout* for Children developing self-awareness and self-esteem
2	*Body language* e.g. following level 1 in the programme: *Talkabout* for Children developing social skills + additional games/resources added in / slower pace	*Body language and conversational skills* e.g. following level 1 and 2 in the programme: *Talkabout* for Children developing social skills	*Body language and conversational skills* e.g. following level 1 and 2 in the programme: *Talkabout* for Children developing social skills
3	*Conversational skills* e.g. following level 2 in the programme: *Talkabout* for Children developing social skills + additional games/resources added in / slower pace	*Friendship skills* e.g. following the programme: *Talkabout* for Children developing friendship skills	*Friendship skills* e.g. following the programme: *Talkabout* for Children developing friendship skills
4	*Friendship skills* e.g. following the programme: *Talkabout* for Children developing friendship skills	*Assertiveness* e.g. following level 3 in the programme: *Talkabout* for Children developing social skills	*Targeted work on specific needs* e.g. assertiveness skills, or recapping on specific skills using *Talkabout* for Children or *Talkabout* 2e

(Continued)

Table 15.3 (Continued)

Year	Option 1	Option 2	Option 3
5	*Assertiveness* e.g. following level 3 in the programme: *Talkabout* for Children developing social skills	*Transition work or targeted work on specific needs* e.g. interviewing skills, or recapping on specific skills using *Talkabout* for Children or *Talkabout 2e*	*Targeted work on specific needs* e.g. interviewing skills, or recapping on specific skills using *Talkabout* for Children or *Talkabout 2e*

In all of these approaches the following are essential:

- Approval and sign up from the head teacher to make this work
- A core group of staff who are trained in delivering lessons in social skills
- A set of resources and plans, such as the *Talkabout* resources, to give teaching staff a scheme of work to follow
- A space on the timetable to add these lessons
- A way to assess pupils and measure the effectiveness so progress can be reported on (more on this in the last chapter)

In the school in Lowestoft, we have trained a core group of around eight staff who teach these lessons. These members of teaching staff are predominantly teaching assistants who are overseen by a teacher, and ultimately are driven by the head teacher. These members of staff work in year groups and co-facilitate all of the '*Talkabout* lessons' so that they are delivered in a consistent manner. They follow option 1 from age 11 onwards, but, in addition, they run a less structured *Talkabout* self-awareness group for their younger children (ages 7–11) as a lead into their secondary school curriculum. In addition to all of their *Talkabout* groups, the core group of staff have also received training in 1:1 therapeutic approaches and creative arts approaches, and these are used both during and outside of the lessons.

In the school in Southampton, there are two teaching assistants who have been trained to deliver social skills lessons and they teach all year groups. This means there is excellent consistency across the school and tracking progress is relatively simple as it is only reliant on these two members of staff. The lessons are called 'SEAL' (social and emotional aspects of learning) but they follow the *Talkabout* scheme of work and use Option 2 from 11 years old to 16.

In a few mainstream schools I am currently supporting, they have social skills on the timetable within their additional needs units and pupils come into their weekly '*Talkabout* lessons' in the same way as they come in for other lessons. They are all following a scheme of work similar to Option 3. All schools that I work in collect annual data on all the pupils using baseline assessments and targets to demonstrate progress in self-awareness, self-esteem, social skills and friendship skills. This will be described in detail in the chapter on 'measuring effectiveness'.

A targeted approach

The more common approach in schools is to use the targeted group approach where children are brought together with similar needs in small group format, where it is possible to provide more individualised attention. Most schools are familiar with this approach and to pupils being taken out of other lessons or break times to work on specific skills. Many schools adopt this approach therefore to develop social skills. The teaching staff identify those pupils who would benefit from this and create groups to teach them the skills. As with the whole school curriculum approach, the main focus here is group work, but, alongside this, it is also ideal to see schools using additional approaches such as 1:1 therapeutic approaches and technology.

As with the whole curriculum approach, how they implement their social skills lessons will vary, but the structure will always follow the hierarchy (as before). Most schools work with pupils over a term and will follow a topic, e.g. body language, so this might result in the following approaches:

Table 15.4 Different approaches to teaching social skills over 12 weeks

Requires work on . . .	Primary children aged 5–10	Secondary children aged 11–18
1. Self-awareness and self-esteem	Self-awareness and self-esteem e.g. following Talkabout for Children developing self-awareness and self-esteem (only covering relevant topics)	Self-awareness and self-esteem e.g. following Talkabout for Teenagers level 1 developing self-esteem
2. Body language	Body Language e.g. following level 1 in Talkabout for Children developing social skills	Body Language e.g. following Talkabout for Teenagers level 2 body language and Talkabout 2e level 1 (for pupils who need a more visual approach)
3. Conversation skills	Conversational skills e.g. following level 2 in Talkabout for Children developing social skills	Conversational skills e.g. following Talkabout for Teenagers level 3 (conversations) and Talkabout 2e level 2 (for pupils who need a more visual approach)
4. Friendship skills	Friendship skills e.g. following Talkabout for Children developing friendship skills	Friendship skills e.g. following Talkabout for Teenagers level 4 (Friendships)
5. Assertiveness skills	Assertiveness skills e.g. following level 3 in Talkabout for Children developing social skills	Assertiveness skills e.g. following Talkabout for Teenagers level 5 (assertiveness) and Talkabout 2e level 3 (for pupils who need a more visual approach)

Some schools are able to work with pupils for longer, for example over a three-year period, so this can mean the following approaches:

Table 15.5 Different approaches to teaching social skills over three years

Year	Primary children aged 5–10	Secondary children aged 11–18
1	Self-awareness and self-esteem e.g. following the programme: *Talkabout* for Children developing self-awareness and self-esteem	Self-awareness and self-esteem e.g. following the programme: *Talkabout* for Teenagers level 1 developing self-esteem
2	Social skills e.g. following level 1 and 2 in the programme: *Talkabout* for Children developing social skills	Body language and conversational skills e.g. following *Talkabout* for Teenagers levels 2 and 3 (body language and conversational skills) and *Talkabout 2e* levels 1 and 2 (for pupils who need a more visual approach
3	Assertiveness e.g. following level 3 in the programme: *Talkabout* for Children developing social skills	Transition work or targeted work on specific needs e.g. interviewing skills, or recapping on specific skills using *Talkabout* for Teenagers or *Talkabout 2e*

In all of these approaches the following are essential:

- A core group of staff who are trained in delivering lessons in social skills
- A set of resources and plans, such as the *Talkabout* resources, to give teaching staff a scheme of work to follow
- A way to assess pupils and measure the effectiveness so progress can be reported on (more on this in the last chapter)

Top tips for developing social skills in schools

I have supported many schools to develop social skills, self-esteem and friendship skills effectively and there are some core factors that will always influence the outcome, and I have summarised these below in my eight top tips:

Table 15.6 Top tips for developing social skills in schools

1.	Support from senior management It always helps to have support from the boss, so we may want to show them some evidence from other schools, talk about the research and the impact this work can have on quality of life, behaviour, learning etc. But sometimes their support will only come after they have seen progress, so we should be prepared to ask for a pilot group, then evidence our work and earn their support.

2. *Have one person who oversees the social skills work*
    We have found that it helps to have one person who is responsible for the social skills interventions and who can coordinate all of the work. If there are several people who are leading on the interventions but no one person is actually leading on it, then some aspects of the work will get missed, and usually this is the assessment and reassessment part!

3. *Training for the person leading on the interventions*
    Teaching social skills will always be more effective if the person leading on the interventions understands the theory behind why certain skills are taught before other skills and also knows how to teach skills in the most effective way. They also need to have good social skills themselves!

4. *Start small*
    We may have a long term vision for the school that involves lots of groups, lots of interventions and lots of resources, but it is best to start small. In this way we can build up our confidence and work hard to evidence the impact this work has on pupils' progress.

5. *A complete social skills package*
    Schools are hectic, busy places and we know that if the social skills interventions are going to work, we need to make it as easy as possible. Create resources that can be used again and again with session plans and activities all planned out, for example, the *Talkabout* resources.

6. *A space to work in*
    This is a luxury in most schools, but those who have been able to secure a 'nice' space in which to run groups report that pupils are happier to attend sessions and enjoy the fact that the space is special. We can also have resources to hand and maybe space to display work and information.

7. *Measure the effectiveness*
    No-one will take our work seriously if we can't show progress. Make sure there is a good baseline assessment with measurable targets that can be tracked and made into nice numerical data.

8. *Get others on board*
    The more that other staff and pupils are on board with what we are doing, the better. So this can be from ensuring other teaching staff know what we are working on with a specific pupil to involving all pupils in learning the rules around eye contact or how to handle peer pressure. We can also try to get parents on board by offering meetings, coffee mornings, workshops etc.

Summary

With all the evidence out there on the benefits of developing social skills, it is maybe surprising and certainly a shame that so many schools continue to be forced to focus on academic progress and qualifications. In 2010 I met the director of a charity in Wales that supports parents with children who have difficulties talking and understanding. She had a vision that all schools in Wales should have the skills and the resources to develop social skills and so she set about getting the funding to achieve this. Over the next seven years, I had the pleasure to train teachers in over 385 primary schools and 200 secondary schools and they were all given *Talkabout* resources and asked to run at least one social skills group for six pupils over twenty weeks and to evidence the progress. She collated all of this, along with case studies from each school and I will show the results in the final chapter. But this vision has clearly made a difference to so many children across Wales and so many schools have since decided to run these groups regularly or as part of their curriculum because they have seen the results for themselves. Maybe more importantly, the school inspectors have been taking note of the evidence too.

Key points from Chapter 15

This chapter is the third of four chapters on teaching social skills and looked at developing social skills in schools.

Why are social skills important to teach in school?

- *Quality of life, success and staying out of trouble*: Social skills are central to helping a child experience a better quality of life through their relationships, to be successful and to stay out of trouble.
- *Social skills and cognitive development and learning*: Improved social skills have a positive effect on learning and academic competence.

Different approaches to teaching social skills in school?

- *School climate or culture*: School climate is known to influence peer relations in terms of how much shy and withdrawn children participate socially and also the rates of bullying.
- *The whole class approach*: The advantage of a whole class approach to teaching social skills is that it can be used before problems occur.
- *The targeted group approach*: Children are brought together with similar needs in small group format where it is possible to provide more individualised attention.
- *The use of peers*: Involving peers can accelerate the success of any social skills programme and a lack of peer involvement can result in social behaviours that never truly become functional skills.

Examples of developing social skills in school

- *A whole school curriculum approach*: All pupils are taught social skills as part of their school curriculum, so it is not only put onto their timetable, but it is seen as part of school life and reported on accordingly like any other subject. The main focus here is group work.
- *A targeted approach*: Children are brought together with similar needs in small group format where it is possible to provide more individualised attention.
- *Top tips for developing social skills in schools*: Eight core factors that will always influence the outcome.

Chapter 16

Teaching social skills 4
The role of parents

'Be careful to leave your sons well instructed rather than rich, for the hopes of the instructed are better than the wealth of the ignorant.'

Epictetus, Greek Philosopher

In my fourth, and final, chapter on teaching social skills, I want to talk specifically about the role of parents. As I said in Chapter 1, social competence is a skill that is learned, and parents play a vital role in this. Children learn social competence in a similar way to learning science or mathematics – through exploring by trial and error, through working out problems and practising skills, and then building their knowledge with the support of friends and adults. We have said several times that social competence is central to making friends and 'peer relationships tend to be much like the relationships children have with their parents' (Rubin, 2002). So, if members of our family treat each other with respect, support, kindness, empathy and honesty, then these are the relationship qualities that our children will take into their other relationships and will expect from their friends.

However, it is not always easy to parent a child who is struggling with their social skills and parents can often feel frustrated by the day to day reality of their child's difficulties and the impact this can have on family life, and the occasional thoughtless comments from others. I have spent much of my working life talking to parents and trying to help them, and I have nothing but respect for them. It is also important to remember what I said in chapter 10. We cannot blame parents for their child's social skills difficulties. But we should be aware of the vital role that parents can play in helping their children to develop social skills.

In this chapter I am going to try to summarise a few ways in which parents can help to support their child who is struggling with social skills. Some of the suggestions may seem insultingly simple, so I apologise if you feel this way, but if you are a parent, I hope there will be something you can take away from this chapter. I will start with self-esteem as this is sometimes where it can all start going wrong and is also relevant to so many children at different times in their lives. I will then move onto how to develop social skills and specifically will consider the shy child and the aggressive child. You will notice some recurring themes throughout the chapter, so I will end by summarising these with my top tips for parents.

Developing self-esteem at home

As parents, we have the greatest influence in shaping our children's sense of self-worth. As we said in the chapter on self-esteem, psychologists generally agree that self-esteem is rooted in our interpersonal experience, reflected appraisal from others, relationships, social comparisons and group comparisons, and from early interactions from our family. Zeigler-Hill (2013) also cites many studies that argue that parents have a major influence on the psychological development of their children, and other studies from attachment theorists argue that people develop beliefs about the self on the basis of the responsiveness and sensitivity of their primary caregivers in childhood.

However, we also know that certain genetic differences in temperament, intelligence, physical attractiveness, health and so on, will influence and shape social interactions, the social contexts that they seek out, and the reactions they receive from significant others, and if the child has a disability, this may also have an impact on their self-esteem. So how do we recognise that our child has a low self-esteem? In short, there are fourteen signs that I would look out for:

Signs of low self-esteem

1. They may not smile as readily
2. They may be easily influenced by others and by advertising
3. They may be reluctant to try new things and may become anxious in new situations
4. They may even avoid new challenges for fear of failure
5. They may easily become frustrated with setbacks – giving up all together or waiting for someone else to take over
6. They may find it difficult to find solutions to problems
7. They may frequently speak negatively about themselves, e.g. 'I'm stupid'
8. They may be self-critical and are likely to feel disappointed in themselves and may say things like 'I'm no good at this' or 'I can't do this'
9. They may blame others when activities are unsuccessful
10. They may see temporary setbacks as permanent and intolerable
11. They are generally pessimistic about themselves and the future
12. They may not believe that they have any special qualities or talents
13. They may feel unloved
14. They may become passive, withdrawn or depressed

Ten ideas to develop self-esteem

So how do we help our child to develop a healthier self-esteem? Trzesniewski et al. (2013) say there are three important factors that will promote a change in self-esteem. First, we know that people are responsive to *environmental feedback*, so if a child is rewarded for certain behaviours, then this will have a positive effect on their self-esteem. Second, that *self-reflection* can provide a useful tool to change self-esteem, so helping a child to reflect on themselves is important. Thirdly, *perceptions by others* may shape someone's self-esteem. So, if we are viewed as competent and liked by others, then this will promote a healthy self-esteem. In the chapter on self-esteem I summarised ten key aspects to developing self-esteem, but in this chapter we will consider how these can be specifically achieved at home.

1. Creating a safe space

Children must have their basic needs met if they are to feel safe and comfortable. When children feel safe, they are less likely to be afraid of failure and more likely to risk trying again when they fail. A stable environment can also provide the child with a sense of security. Part of this stability is gained from knowing that their actions have consequences and that you can be relied on to be consistent.

Things that will help create a safe space

- Provide a safe physical environment
- Set and enforce clear rules and limits
- Be realistic in your expectations of them
- Be consistent so they know what to expect
- Treat each child fairly and don't compare siblings

2. A sense of belonging

Everyone needs to feel they belong and to know that they are important to someone. When they feel accepted and loved by the important people in their lives, they feel comfortable, safe and secure. If children feel respected and secure within a family, they will find it easier to make friendships outside the family.

Things that will help a sense of belonging

- Be spontaneous and affectionate with your child
- Give love with no strings attached
- Spend time together - play, work and relax together
- Show that you feel good about them by hugging them
- Tell them often that you like what they did/said and that you love them
- Encourage pride in who they are, for example their ethnic background
- Keep reminders of family events and family history around the home

3. An awareness and understanding of emotions

It is also important to teach people to be able to recognise and express their feelings as this will help them to develop positive relationships. It is also helpful for people to see that others feel the same. Some children respond better to tangible concepts so once you've come up with a list of feelings, you could categorise and colour code the list, for example by writing negative feelings in red and positive ones in green.

> ## Things that will help develop an understanding of emotions
>
> - Accept what they are feeling as true
> - Use pictures/symbols to support them to consider how they may be feeling and extend vocabulary
> - You could have a family 'feelings board' up in the kitchen where everyone can say or show how they are feeling

4. A sense of respect

A child will develop respect for themselves and for others if they learn from you that what they think, feel and do is important. If you put them down or call them demeaning names, your children will feel unworthy, and criticism or punishment which is too harsh will prevent children from developing self-confidence.

> ## Things that will help develop a sense of respect
>
> - Listen to each other and respect each other's opinions
> - Only allow positive language
> - Do not allow use of demeaning names, criticism or punishment which is too harsh
> - Say 'I feel' or 'I believe', not 'you are', if you do have to tell someone what they are doing is wrong

5. Strengths and qualities

We are all special and feeling special is an important part of self-esteem. It is important for everyone to discover their own special talents and qualities and research indicates that one of the main factors that contribute to a child developing self-esteem is the presence of at least one adult who helps them to feel appreciated and focuses on their strengths.

> ## Things that will help develop an awareness of strengths and qualities
>
> - Set aside a 'special time' during the week to be alone with your child
> - Focus on things that your child enjoys doing
> - Make a list of your child's 'islands of competence' or areas of strength
> - Find ways to reinforce or display these strengths
> - Provide opportunities for your child to help others
> - Value their uniqueness
> - Try things their own way
> - Help them to understand that trying your best is more important than winning
> - If your child has a disability, help them to understand the nature of their disability
> - Help them to understand that we are all different
> - Use compliments (see next point)

6. Complimenting

Hearing from another person our strengths and positive qualities helps to build a more positive image of ourselves. And teaching people to be kinder towards each other is important because, as a result, they will tend to treat and think of themselves in a kinder way too. Ask them to consider qualities, successes, hard work and teach them to give and receive compliments in a genuine manner.

Things that will help develop complimenting

- Try to give your child at least one compliment every day
- Make mealtimes a time when everyone talks about their day – their worries, their successes. Then ask every member of the family to say something nice to another member of the family.
- See what you all can do during the week to make others feel good or trigger them to smile
- Encourage your child to keep a diary or list of things that they did well – you could call it an 'it's good to be me' diary

7. Self-identity and self-image

How we feel about what we look like is also an important part of self-esteem. It is important for everyone to find the good in the way they look. It may also be important to address topics such as sleeping, eating and exercise, and to help them set realistic goals to feel more confident, for example, having a shower every day, going for a walk or getting a haircut.

Things that will help with self-identity and self-image

- Encourage your child to see the good in the way they look, but listen to their worries and don't brush them aside. Find out why they feel that way.
- Challenge some of the myths about beauty and what we see in advertising
- Focus on the good and use others in the family to help build up a positive self-image for your child
- If there is something realistic that your child wants to change about the way they look, help them to create a plan that is realistic and motivating

8. Likes and motivations

At times it can be hard to find the motivation to set goals, especially when we don't feel confident or worry about what other people may think. But it doesn't have to be something big. Making small goals can help us to feel more positive. Regularly doing things that we are good at and enjoy reinforces our belief in our abilities and strengths. It will also make us feel happier. And when we really like doing something then the motivation to do that thing tends to come automatically. It may be a good idea to read the section of the self-esteem chapter again on 'contingencies of self-worth' and to think about which are important to your child. Trying to find activities that match the important contingencies will help to boost their self-esteem quicker. So, if academic competence is important, find ways to boost this, for example with a trip to the library or to research a topic.

Things that will help with likes and motivations

- Identify goals that are important to them
- Ask 'are they doing what they really want to do?' If not, and if possible, then refocus and start working on that very important thing instead.
- What activities could they bring into their day that will make them feel happier?
- Find something they like doing and do more of it

9. Problem solving

Teaching someone to learn from their mistakes, to work towards a goal and to have pride in their successes is important, as high self-esteem is associated with solid problem-solving skills and so it is important to help your child to develop the ability to problem solve and make decisions.

Things that will help with likes and motivations

- If your child is having difficulty with something, e.g. a friend, discuss ways to solve the situation
- Try role playing to see the steps involved in problem solving
- Teach them to make decisions and to set realistic goals
- Provide choices to encourage a feeling of control over their lives
- Help them recognise that there are things that are in their control and things that are not
- Give them opportunities to succeed

10. Positive visualisation

Use the power of imagination and ask your child to create an image of themselves as the confident and self-assured person they aspire to become. Use this prior to challenging situations to help them picture themselves acting confidently. Developing a skill in positive visualisation can also work in conjunction with teaching relaxation techniques and power posing (see chapter on body language).

Things that will help with positive visualisation

- Help your child to create an image of a confident self: How will they feel?
- How will others perceive them? What does their body language look like?
- How will they talk?
- Feel the feelings, experience being and seeing things from that person's perspective
- Write a description of this person and all the attributes they have observed
- Use role play, relaxation and power posing to help
- Help your child to understand the power of 'fake it until you make it'

In summary, it is true to say that as parents, we can have a huge influence in shaping our children's sense of self-worth as self-esteem is rooted in interpersonal experiences, reflected appraisal from others, relationships, social comparisons and group comparisons, and also from early interactions from our family. Of course, we do need to remember that self-esteem does vary from child to child and from time to time, so some of these strategies may not be quick fixes and may need to be ongoing throughout a child's life.

Developing social skills at home

Some children seem to arrive at the goal of social competence with very little help from anyone, including us as parents. From an early age they happily head off to school, to meet friends, and to talk to relatives in a cheerful and confident manner. For another child though, this social competence does not come easily or effortlessly at all. They need support, help and patience from people around them and parents play a vital role.

We know that social skills are behaviours which can be learned as a child is growing up, through imitation, modelling and reinforcement and parents are obviously well-placed to have the biggest impact on a child's learning, especially in the early years. We first experience the training process at an early age. Right from the beginning, parents and carers influence social skills development when they ascribe intentionality to the baby's behaviour ('you are hungry, aren't you?') and reward certain nonverbal behaviours, such as smiling, and communicate displeasure over other kinds of behaviour such as throwing or shouting. When they have learnt to talk, we teach them to speak in a certain way. The child is taught that, even though they didn't want to go and see their elderly aunt, it is polite to smile at her and say 'it's lovely to see you'. They are also taught not to interrupt if two adults are talking and to say 'excuse me'. And the examples go on – 'sit up straight', 'look at me when I am talking to you', 'say please', and probably my favourite, 'don't use that tone of voice!' This process of social learning primarily involves modelling and imitation of good social skills. Children will copy their parents and will learn to act and talk like them, and will learn to use behaviours that are encouraged and to not use behaviours that are discouraged or ignored.

Of course, one child will vary from another and our parenting needs to change to suit that child. This is called 'goodness of fit' (Chess and Thomas, 1996) which emphasises that children's overt behaviour and adjustment depends on the abilities of families and schools to provide them with an environment that 'fits' their temperaments. This means that the environment should offer the degree of structure, predictability and support needed by individuals of one's particular temperament. So how we behave as parents will depend partly on how our child behaves and, when trying to help them, how our child behaves will certainly influence how we support and help them to develop. Rubin (2002) describes three main ways that children tend to behave:

- They will naturally move towards others – the socially competent child
- They will move away from others – the shy or withdrawn child
- They will move against others – the aggressive child

In this section of this chapter we will look at the last two and discuss the main ways in which we can help the shy, withdrawn child and the aggressive child. Finally, we will consider some general tips for developing social skills at home.

Helping a shy, withdrawn child

The child who is shy and withdrawn will typically have difficulty regulating their feelings of wariness or fearfulness and acting in a socially skilled manner. These children do need empathetic parental support, otherwise Rubin (2002) describes a spiralling cycle in which:

1. Anxiety and social wariness make the withdrawn child behave in a way that most other children find unappealing.
2. Those peers consequently ignore, avoid or actively rebuff the child.
3. Hurt by the peer rejection, the child backs away from further efforts to connect with others.
4. This withdrawal leads the child to miss out on experiences that might strengthen their social skills and make them feel more confident among their peers.
5. This in turn may cause the child to feel increasingly worse and to remain isolated.

Parental support is therefore essential to help your child to learn to deal more effectively with these situations that provoke fearfulness and withdrawal and the following ideas may help:

1. Consider how you are feeling

Rubin (2002) suggests that parents of shy, withdrawn children can help them by firstly 'looking in the mirror' and asking themselves if there is anything they are doing that might not be helping. Sometimes we try to shield our shy child from anything that might be anxiety provoking or encourage them to stay near us if we are feeling anxious. So ask yourself: do you feel stressed and tense when your child is going into a new situation or do you tell your child what to do, both at home and out with others? We may unintentionally be not helping, because what your child requires is gentle, consistent urging to venture forward and to gradually build the social confidence to move towards their peers, as opposed to away from them. So, try to give an encouraging nod or smile to your child to let them know that they will be OK when they go into a new situation.

> **Consider how you are feeling**
> - Work to overcome your own discomfort
> - Encourage your child with a smile and a nod and let them know that they are going to be OK

2. Be responsive to how they are feeling

Children who are socially withdrawn often have parents who keep close and are overly affectionate, making the child rely on their parents for comfort rather than their own techniques when faced with fear-related emotions. It is also important to not criticise or be impatient with the child's feelings. It can be easy to go from gentle encouragement to goading or teasing 'What happened, did the cat get your tongue?' or 'Don't be a baby'. What will help the child to cope better is sensitive and gentle reassurance that the world is 'knowable, manageable and really not so frightening' (Rubin, 2002). Try talking through an event in a reassuring manner or giving the child a 'trial run' to rehearse being in a new situation. This will then help them to self-regulate their emotions and may encourage them to use self-directed speech when in the situation, for example, 'those children are having fun, I can go over there. I can do this'.

Be responsive to how they are feeling

- Resist the urge to stay too close and be overly affectionate in social situations
- Resist the urge also to solve their problem or speak up for them
- Be sensitive and gentle in your reassurance
- Ease them into new activities by talking them through or rehearsing them

3. Encourage play

Research suggests that parents should encourage children to independently explore new play situations whilst monitoring from a distance, rather than controlling and restricting them by keeping them close by and repeatedly hugging them to reassure them. Play is the main activity of childhood and it is how children explore objects and people and how they begin to learn social lessons.

Encourage play

- Play with your child
- Allow them to lead the way
- Refrain from taking control or directing the action
- Encourage them to try new things or explore new objects
- Set up play-dates with other children and supervise from a distance

4. Encourage play with other children

Children who are shy and withdrawn will find it harder to play with other children, and especially hard to initiate play or conversation. Parents can help by initiating the conversation with other children and modelling friendly behaviours, hosting a play-date, and providing opportunities to foster a friendship with a younger child. This can give them confidence so that one day you can encourage them to go to someone else's house for a play-date. The important point here is to try to help your child to have peer experiences that are *non-stressful*, as research shows that shy children will then begin to develop social competence (Rubin, 2002).

> ## Encourage play with other children
>
> - Initiate conversations with other children in the presence of your child when out so that they can see you modelling friendly behaviours
> - Try to foster a friendship with another child, ideally a younger child who is socially competent
> - Host the play-dates

5. Teach good social skills

A child who is shy and withdrawn will also struggle with their social skills around other children. As we said before, anxiety and social wariness can make the child behave in a way that other children find unappealing. So, teaching them good body language, conversational skills and assertiveness will always help. Try practising tall, upright posture with a smile and good eye contact. Think about the saying 'fake it until you make it' and practise this at home. Use time at home to also practise conversations, about anything at all. Ask them for their opinion and respond with interest. When my boys were little, I started using the evening meal to take it in turns for everyone in the family to talk about their day. We then all asked questions and reflected on what had been good (or not so good) about the day. At first the boys looked at me as if I was mad and to begin with it was quite stilted and seemed quite formal. But 20 years on, we still do it and now it is only guests that might look surprised as we ask them about their day! The point here is to try to establish opportunities for your child to develop their conversation skills in a supportive environment and to make it just part of your everyday life.

> ## Teach good social skills
>
> - Practise good body language: standing tall, smiling and looking at the other person
> - Practise conversation skills with a clear voice
> - Encourage your child to give their opinion and tell you how they are feeling.

6. Problem solving

Children who are shy and withdrawn can sometimes find it difficult to problem solve a situation. Something went wrong and they can revert back into themselves and not want to explore options. Developing skills in problem solving can help the child to see that there is always another way. Try talking about 'what if . . .' situations to begin with and role playing or practising solutions. For example, 'what if a new child starts at school and they are looking sad, what could I do?' or 'what if someone tells me they don't want me to play with them, what should I do?'

> ### Problem solving
>
> - Think about real 'what if' situations and consider what they could do
> - Practise this until the child can hear themselves being assertive and saying or doing the right thing
> - If you are using meal times to talk about their day, try discussing things that happened that your child was unhappy about – 'what could they have done differently?'

In summary, parental support can really help a shy child to increase their social competence and social connections. Just remember that change will not happen overnight and it is better to take small steps over a longer period of time to help the child towards greater courage and confidence. Indeed, research shows us that 'a child's small successes . . . can have a wonderfully cumulative positive effect' (Rubin, 2002).

Helping an aggressive child

In the same way as parents can help a shy, withdrawn child, they are also essential in helping the child who is aggressive. These children often have difficulty in controlling their emotions and will act in a socially unskilled manner. They may quickly become angry and may show little awareness of what others are thinking, feeling or doing. This may have caused them to acquire a reputation that then fuels the behaviour, as other people expect them to be 'naughty, disruptive, or angry'. This can all lead to peer and adult rejection. The aggressive child is caught in a cycle of suspicion and reciprocal ill feeling that is similar to the cycle of rejection that the shy child will experience:

1. The aggressive child struggles to regulate their emotions and calm themselves down, and so is prone to anger outbursts and will behave in a way that most other children find unappealing.
2. Peers consequently reject the child and adults label him as a 'troublemaker'.
3. Hurt by the peer rejection, the child develops a chip-on-the-shoulder view of the world and will assume others are hostile towards them, even when they are not.
4. These in turn are strong predictors of future difficulties, including academic troubles and delinquency, both in adolescence and later in life.

The important thing to remember though is that if your child is stuck in this cycle or is only just beginning to show signs of aggressive behaviour, they will all benefit from parental support at any age and some of the following ideas may help.

1. Consider how you are feeling

As before with the shy, withdrawn child, it is helpful to firstly 'look in the mirror' and ask if there is anything we are doing that might not be helping. Sometimes we can have a positive effect by firstly changing some of our actions and behaviour. So ask yourself: do you feel annoyed, embarrassed, or guilty when your child is with other children? Do you hear yourself in the way your child talks to others? Do you become angry when they don't comply with a request? What is the atmosphere like in the house? We may unintentionally be not helping, because our child lives within an atmosphere where there is persistent suspicion or power struggles. It can be hard to face, but sometimes it is easier to start by looking at our own behaviour and resolving to help your child to change their behaviour by changing ours.

Consider how you are feeling

- How am I feeling?
- Remember that I am setting a model of the proper way to behave
- Remember to demonstrate self-control
- You are in control of your emotions and your behaviour should earn your child's respect

2. Teach them to recognise how they are feeling

Children who are quick to become angry sometimes are helped by learning more about their emotions and recognising the changes in their body that tell them they are getting angry or frightened. Try introducing a way for the family to talk about their feelings on a daily basis. Discuss or research the things that happen to our bodies when we get angry. What can we do to calm down? Try practicing a few strategies such as mindfulness, exercise, positive visualisation, self-talking or breathing. Work out which one will work for your child, and then teach them or give them opportunity to do it.

Teach them to recognise how they are feeling

- Introduce a feelings board
- Explore what happens to our bodies when we are angry
- Use the heart monitor on a fit-bit for older children
- Practise calming down strategies

3. Teach them that aggressive behaviour is not acceptable

It is possible that your child does not realise that what they are doing is unacceptable, so it is worth starting with that.

It is important to remember that anger is a normal emotion but that being aggressive is an unacceptable behaviour that usually follows feeling angry. Explore the behaviours and talk about how it makes people feel and think. Talk about the consequences of the behaviour, both for them and their peers. Help them to understand that aggressive behaviour pushes people away and will result in rejection and a lack of friends. Then talk about alternatives – how could the child have behaved differently? You could try practising different alternatives. You may also need to guide them in a situation where they are starting to be aggressive. Try telling them 'you're being a bit loud' or 'you need to stop pushing Tom because Tom may get hurt. If you can't calm down, Tom will need to go home'. You could then agree a signal with your child that you can use when he is with other children that will tell them that they need to stop and reconsider their behaviour. Just remember in all of this, to find fault with the behaviour and not the child. It is the behaviour that you don't like, not your child.

> ### Teach them that aggressive behaviour is not acceptable
> - Talk openly about aggressive or problem behaviours
> - What do other people think and feel? You could use comic strips to help.
> - Practise alternative behaviours in those situations
> - Work out a signal to use with your child if he needs to change his behaviour

4. Provide structure and support

Your child may also struggle to be compliant – they don't seem to listen to requests which can lead us to the inevitable 'just do it!' or 'because I said so!' What can be more helpful is the use of direction, a helping hand, and warm encouragement. So, you may try telling your child once and then if he doesn't respond, to model what it is you want them to do by saying something like, 'OK let's get this started together. You pick up the books and I will start with your action figures'. Then it is helpful to show the consequence of them not listening by saying something like, 'I'm afraid we haven't got time for a story tonight as it took too long to clear the toys away. Maybe tomorrow night we will have more time'.

> ### Provide structure and support
> - Support your child to listen to you, but offer direction and support
> - Encourage them to be compliant and to reap the rewards

5. Teach good social skills

A child who is aggressive will also benefit from learning appropriate social skills around other children. As we said before, they are behaving in a way that other children find unappealing and so teaching them good body language, conversational skills and assertiveness (not aggression) will always help. Try practising a tall, relaxed posture with a smile and good eye contact. Use time at home to also practise conversations, about anything at all. Try practising a friendly tone of voice. Use verbal prompts to encourage them to know how to behave and then praise them when they get it right. As part of this, teach your child to apologise. Ask your child to consider the positive impact of an apology, for example, your classmate might not think so badly about you. Practise it with them and praise them when they decide to say sorry.

> ### Teach good social skills
> - Practise good body language: smiling and looking at the other person
> - Practise conversation skills with a clear, calm voice
> - Encourage your child to give their opinion and tell you how they are feeling
> - Teach your child to say sorry and to understand why apologies are good

6. Problem solving

Children who are aggressive can also find it difficult to problem solve a situation. Something went wrong and they struggle to adjust their behaviour, possibly because they have not read the relevant social cues. Developing skills in problem solving can help the child to see that there is always another way and the fault is not always with the other person! Try talking about 'what if . . .' situations to begin with and role playing or practising solutions. For example, 'what if Tom takes the toy I want to play with, what could I do?' or 'what if someone calls me a horrible name and says they don't want me to play with them? What could I do?' When talking about real examples, talk about the context, then how it made them feel, what they then did and what the consequence was. Help the child to think of an alternative to their behaviour. What could they have done differently and what would the consequence have been then? Try the sentence 'what are all the things you could do . . .' to help explore difficult situations or things your child would like to achieve.

> ### Problem solving
>
> - Think about real 'what if' situations and consider what they could do differently
> - Practise this until the child can hear themselves saying or doing the right thing
> - Use the sentence 'what are all the things you could do . . .'

So, just as parental support can really help a shy child to increase their social competence and social connections, it is also essential to help the aggressive child. Uninhibited children have a lot going for them and have lots of potential. They have typically sociable, outgoing personalities and these can be a real positive if they can learn some critical social skills.

Summary

You will have certainly noticed some core themes in all of this, not only in what we teach but in how we should try to teach these skills. So to finish, I have firstly summarised this into my top five tips for how to develop social skills at home (see Table 16.1) through the use of modelling, direct teaching, reinforcing good behaviour, role play, and finally through problem solving. I have then created a list of a few activities that will help develop self-esteem (Table 16.2) and social skills (Table 16.3) at home.

> ### Table 16.1 My top five tips

Help your child through . . .	Remember . . .
1. Modelling	Children learn much of their skills and beliefs about themselves by watching their parents. Think about what you are doing and what you are saying and try to model the behaviour you want your child to learn.

2. Teaching	You may need to teach specific skills such as: emotions, body language, tone of voice, conversation skills, being assertive, or making friends.
	Prioritise one or two to begin with and then think about how you are going to teach the skill.
	You may need to do some background reading about it first. Explain the rules to them and help them to understand why these are important to learn.
	Try to use play and non-stressful experiences for your child to practise and learn these skills.
3. Reinforcing	Reinforce good behaviour through commenting on and praising the child.
	Discourage bad behaviour by teaching your child why the behaviour is unacceptable.
4. Role play	Role play different scenarios and help your child learn alternative ways to speak and behave.
	Practise until they feel confident to try it out for real.
	Remind your child of the saying 'fake it until you make it'.
5. Problem solving	When problems occur, use different strategies to problem solve what happened and what could have been done differently.
	You could use pen and paper to draw out what people said, what they were thinking and feeling and then what happened.
	Consider the 'what ifs' and the 'what are all the things you could do'.

In the next two tables I have created a list of a few activities that will help develop self-esteem and social skills at home. There are so many books out there with ideas for games, including my *Talkabout* books, so these lists are really just to get you started. Don't worry if your family initially reacts like mine did when I introduced the way we were going to talk about our days over our evening meal! They will soon accept it and may even grow to love it! So, have confidence in what needs to be done to help your child and believe in your ability to make a difference.

Table 16.2 Five activities to develop self-esteem

1. Feelings board	Create a feelings board in your kitchen and have a check-in with everyone in the morning and in the evening. You could use photos of all the family members and move your photo next to the feeling that best describes you.
	If your child does not want to tell you how they feel, encourage them to pick one of their toys to tell you how they feel.
	You could collect pictures of people that look happy, sad and others and then think about what they notice about their bodies, hands, faces.

(Continued)

	Table 16.2 (Continued)
2. 'This is me' book	Help your child to create a book or photo album all about them. You could have sections on what they look like now and what they looked like when they were a baby, what they like doing, their strengths and qualities, their close friends and family. It should be a celebration of who they are. You could also create a computer presentation using PowerPoint or write a story about their life and what makes them unique and amazing.
3. Bookmark	Design a bookmark with your child and decorate it with pictures and words that sum up their qualities. It could say 'Alex's bookmark. Alex is . . .' Laminate it so that your child can keep it safe and keep looking at it. A variation could be to make a poster that has all their qualities on it.
4. A 'Good to be me' diary	Help your child to keep a diary and to think of one thing every day that they did well. You could add in a feelings check-in each day where they tick the feelings they had that day and then complete a section that says 'the thing I feel proudest of today is . . .' If they are struggling to complete it, ask them if you can write something or suggest something to write.
5. Compliments	Ask everyone to say something nice to someone in the family once a day. Initially you may want to teach them to do it in a structured way, during a meal time, for example. You can then move on to asking them to do it spontaneously during the day. You could have a 'smiley' or 'sticker' chart to note down when you have given a compliment and made someone smile. Share the compliments you all received at the end of day.

	Table 16.3 Five activities to develop social skills
1. How was your day?	Take it in turns to talk about your day at your evening meal (or a time when the family are together). Encourage good listening and then think of one question each to ask them when they have finished. Make it part of your daily routine. If you are using a feelings board, you could check-in with how they are feeling at the end of their day.

2. How am I feeling? What am I thinking?	Play charades and act out different scenarios and feelings. You could collect ideas from your children first of different emotions and then situations that might make them feel like that, for example: angry – someone broke my toy; happy – my mum made my favourite dinner. Extend this to include 'what might I be thinking?' and 'what could I do now?' A variation would be the 'social detective' game: look at a person (on the TV or out in the park) and try to guess what they may be thinking or feeling. Why do you think that?
3. Board games	A lot of board games encourage turn taking, cooperation, listening and consideration of others. Explain the rules of the board game but also come up with some family rules, like 'good listening, good talking, good turn taking'. With younger children you could have a star chart for every time they remember the rule.
4. Tell a story	This is a good game to play in the car or around a table. Take it in turns to add one word (or a phrase) and try to make up a story. Start with 'once upon a time . . .' or a beginning of your choice. This encourages good listening, turn taking and cooperation. You could also use a 'talking stick' (you can only talk when you have the stick) or have a bag of objects that have to be taken out and added somehow to the story.
5. Talk it, draw it, act it	Talk about something that has happened or is going to happen. Draw the situation out using stick men and speech bubbles. Then act it out. Try changing roles and different endings. You can make this as light-hearted or as serious as necessary to suit your child and the situation. Use difficult situations that have happened to you where you have had to consider other people and your actions. Help your child to see how you made a decision or made a mistake and learnt from your actions.

Key points from Chapter 16

This chapter considered how we can develop social skills at home, but firstly we looked at how to develop self-esteem.

Developing self-esteem at home

As parents, we have the greatest influence in shaping our children's sense of self-worth.

Signs of low self-esteem

Ten ideas to develop self-esteem

1. Creating a safe space
2. A sense of belonging
3. An awareness and understanding of emotions
4. A sense of respect
5. Strengths and qualities
6. Complimenting
7. Self-identity and self-image
8. Likes and motivations
9. Problem solving
10. Positive visualisation

Developing social skills at home

We know that social skills are behaviours which can be learned as a child is growing up, through imitation, modelling and reinforcement and parents are obviously well-placed to have the biggest impact on a child's learning, especially in the early years.

There are three main ways that children tend to behave:

- They will naturally move towards others – the socially competent child
- They will move away from others – the shy or withdrawn child
- They will move against others – the aggressive child

Helping the shy withdrawn child

1. Consider how you are feeling
2. Be responsive to how they are feeling
3. Encourage play
4. Encourage play with other children
5. Teach good social skills
6. Problem solving

Helping the aggressive child

1. Consider how you are feeling
2. Teach them to recognise how they are feeling
3. Teach them that aggressive behaviour is not acceptable
4. Provide structure and support
5. Teach good social skills
6. Problem solving

Summary

My five top tips

- Modelling
- Teaching
- Reinforcing
- Role play
- Problem solving

Five activities to develop self-esteem

- Feelings board
- 'This is me' book
- Bookmark
- A 'Good to be me' diary
- Complimenting

Five activities to develop social skills

- How was your day?
- How am I feeling? What am I thinking?
- Board games
- Tell a story
- Talk it, draw it, act it

Chapter 17

Evaluation
Measuring the effectiveness of social skills interventions

'If my tongue were trained to measures, I would sing a stirring song.'

Paul Laurence Dunbar

In the final chapter I want to talk about the importance of evaluation. Developing social skills is mostly something that happens over time and with a lot of assessing, reassessing, evaluating and questioning. We will regularly ask ourselves: What do we need to work on? What method of intervention will work? Then we will ask: Has it worked? What do we need to do now? What could make this easier, better, or more successful? But how do we define 'evaluation' and why is it so important?

Defining evaluation and why it is important

Evaluation is a process that critically examines something. It involves collecting and analysing information about activities, characteristics, and outcomes. The purpose of evaluation is to make judgments about the intervention and to improve its effectiveness, and/or to inform future decisions. Evaluation can also be defined as the making of a judgement about the amount, number, or value of something. We are investigating the merit, worth, or significance of something and synonyms of the word 'evaluation' include: assessment, appraisal, judgement, gauging, rating, estimation, ranking, weighing up, summing up, consideration and analysis. So, evaluation is closely linked to assessment (see Chapter 12) and so a great deal of what we talk about in this chapter will refer back to this previous chapter on assessment.

Evaluations fall into one of two broad categories: formative and summative. Formative evaluations are conducted during interventions and are useful if we want direction on how to best achieve our goals or improve our intervention. Summative evaluations are completed at the end of an intervention and will tell us to what extent the intervention is achieving its goals. So, there are two main reasons why we evaluate the effectiveness of what we have done: to improve the quality of what we are doing and to demonstrate the impact of the intervention.

1. *To improve the quality of what we are doing*: First, we use the evidence to help us improve and shape the quality of our teaching and it is important to periodically assess and adapt our interventions to ensure they are as effective as they can be. Evaluation can help us identify areas for improvement and ultimately help us realise our goals more efficiently. This is sometimes referred to as making 'formative' decisions following evaluation – for example, 'how are we doing so far; what can we do to make this more successful for this person?' So, monitoring and evaluating any programme or intervention is essential to determine whether it works, to help refine delivery of the programme, and to determine whether the social skills intervention is appropriate for the person.

2. *To demonstrate the impact of the intervention*: Second, we use the evidence to 'sum up' the person's overall performance and to make 'summative' decisions – for example, to show to our manager or head teacher the progress that has been achieved over a period of time. Evaluation enables us to demonstrate the success of the intervention or the progress someone has made. It will not only provide feedback on the effectiveness of a programme but will also help to assess whether there are any problems with its implementation and support, and whether there are any ongoing concerns that need to be resolved as the programme is implemented. The information we collect allows us to better communicate the impact of the intervention to others, which is critical for continuing support of the programme.

So following evaluation, we make formative decisions to plan and revise our teaching, and summative decisions to evidence our work. We use our evaluation to improve what we are doing and positively affect the student, and to gain insight into our work and determine the effects of the social skills intervention.

What makes a good evaluation?

The best way to make the evaluation work for us is to plan to evaluate before you even start working with someone. Too many times I have asked someone if they have any evidence for the amazing progress they have seen with someone and the response has been: 'actually I just started working with them and I didn't bother with any assessment'. This is such a shame for so many reasons. But there are two essential points here. First, evaluation should be planned into any intervention. Secondly, we have to assess someone if we want to evaluate. So, what makes a good evaluation? Well, I think there are five rules to evaluating well:

1. *Good evaluation is well planned*: So, my first point is that you should plan to evaluate before you even start seeing someone for social skills intervention. Think about your assessment – what are you going to assess and how are you going to do it and think about how you will be able to evidence progress.

2. *Good evaluation is tailored to your intervention*: Your evaluation should be designed to address the specific goals and objectives of your intervention. So, if you are going to be working on body language then your evaluation tool should measure progress in body language.

3. *Good evaluation is inclusive*: Try to make your evaluation as inclusive of other people's viewpoints as possible. Input should be sought from all those involved, such as students, parents, teachers and others. This will mean that the results are much less likely to be biased.
4. *Good evaluation is honest*: Evaluation will show that your intervention has had some positive effect but it may also show some limitations. Evidence that your intervention is not working can be hard, but it can also help you learn what you can do differently.
5. *Good evaluation is replicable*: A good evaluation is one that is likely to be replicable, meaning that someone else should be able to conduct the same evaluation and get the same results. However, this is not easy with social skills as a student's behaviour may change from one day to the next, so the best way to make sure our evaluations are replicable is to ensure as much as possible that the method of assessment is replicable. This will give others confidence in your findings.

So, how do we do it? How do we know we have made a difference? Well, we do it in many ways. Sometimes we work with someone and they seem happier or they tell us they are happier. Sometimes a parent or a teacher remarks on the difference our intervention has made. Sometimes we are given hard evidence that shows the impact our work has had – maybe they are attending school more or they have not had an incidence of challenging behaviour for a while. These are all valid ways to assess the effectiveness of our work, but it is not enough. We live in a world where people need data and hard facts, so the more we can evidence our work using actual numbers and percentages, the more likely it is to be seen as important.

I speak from experience. In 2011 I was commissioned by a charity called Afasic Cymru to be involved in a three-year project across the whole of Wales. The plan was to offer social skills training and *Talkabout* social skills resources to every secondary school across Wales to improve social skills and reduce social isolation in teenagers. We trained two teachers from each school (200 schools in total) and asked them to run a *Talkabout* social skills group with six students for 20 weeks. They also had to assess each student using the *Talkabout* Assessment Tool (Kelly, 2010) before and after the intervention and this data was then sent to Afasic to collate. The schools loved the intervention side of this project but on the whole were not keen on the assessment side and the data collection. However, as the three years progressed, we saw that the data was getting noticed. Schools were showing it to their school inspectors and school governors and suddenly these interventions carried more weight. In the end it was this data that enabled us to roll out the project to nearly 450 primary schools across Wales over the following three years. This is surely the way to change the world! Tell someone a success story and they will sit up and smile. Show them a graph as well and they really start listening!

As I said in Chapter 12, assessment is an essential first step to working with someone. We have to assess to know where to start. We have to know where to start so we set someone up to succeed. Assessment should enable us to adequately measure social skills competence so that we can first decide what to work on, but then second to assess the effectiveness of our intervention through reassessment. So, a good assessment is the beginning of any good intervention and should ideally be used to then measure the effectiveness of work. This final evaluation or measurement is essential; however, as we have already said, measuring the effectiveness of what we do is not just something we do at the end of our intervention. Evaluation should be a fundamental part of any intervention. We need to be constantly assessing the effectiveness of what we are doing and adapting it to make it easier, better, and more successful. We can describe this as a model of constant evaluation: our assessment leads onto our target, which leads onto our intervention, which leads onto (re)assessment, and so on. We can also see it as a process that means that we review or reassess targets throughout intervention and then reassess and measure the effectiveness of the whole intervention at the end. I have summarised this in Figure 17.1.

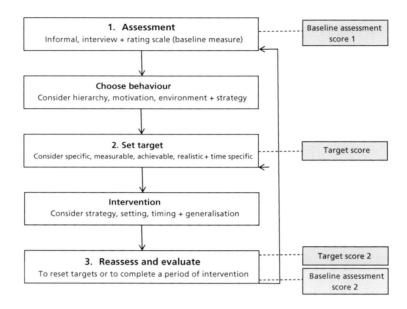

Figure 17.1 A model of intervention to measure effectiveness

This shows that there are three main stages where we can use information and scores to measure the effectiveness of what we are doing: at the assessment stage; the setting of targets; and the reassessment stage. This should enable us to show short term progress through our target scores and longer-term progress through our baseline assessment scores. In this chapter I will explain how we can do this.

Step 1 The initial assessment and the baseline score

In Chapter 12 we looked at the different methods of assessing social skills and their benefits, but the challenge with assessment is always to find meaningful ways to make the assessment results functional. We need assessment data that not only helps us to identify the important skills for development but also gives us an initial baseline from which to measure change.

Rating scales are an extremely useful measure of change and are one of the most widely used methods of assessment. Merrell (2001) states that 'assessment of social skills (and social behaviour in general) of children and adolescents is one area in which behaviour rating scales have made a particularly strong impact in recent years and in which an impressive body of supportive empirical evidence has accrued'. Using rating scales, information about the person's behaviour is transferred onto a rating scale which may use either numbers or descriptions to rate each skill, and some use a combination of both.

In the *Talkabout* Assessment Tool (Kelly, 2010), we use a four-point rating scale from 'never good' to 'not very good' to 'quite good' to 'very good' (with a description of what that would look like with each specific skill). The behaviours are rated using a consensus of opinions from a number of people who know the person well and who have ideally observed them in a number of different settings. We are also rating that person in terms of what is appropriate for their age and culture, so a child aged four will be rated differently from a person aged 24 when considering appropriate use of touch and distance. It is also important to consider how other people are responding to these behaviours, so how appropriate they are to their environment. A rating in the *Talkabout* Assessment of a 1 or 2 indicates that this is a 'need' for the person and rating of a 3 or 4 indicates a relative 'strength'. This means that any behaviour that has been scored 1 or 2 is highlighted as an area of concern (or behaviour that we will focus on in intervention).

This initial assessment is where we gain our baseline score. We can quantify this assessment easily by giving each area a score and then having a total score for the whole wheel. So, from Mohammed's assessment wheel we can calculate his scores to be:

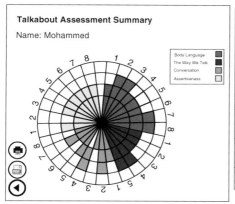

Summary of Scores		
Area	Score	Percentage
Body language	20/32	62.5%
The way we talk	12/25	48%
Conversations	15/32	46.9%
Assertiveness	15/32	46.9%
TOTAL	62/116	53.4%

Figure 17.2 Quantifying assessment data on Mohammed

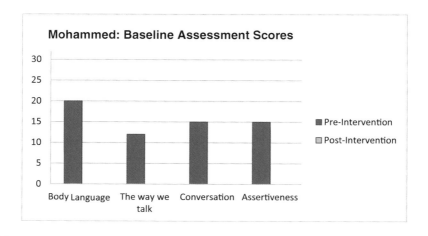

Figure 17.3 Mohammed's baseline scores shown with an Excel graph

I have also created a number of spreadsheets to enable us to easily analyse and present assessment data in a graph format (see over). However, the real benefit of this will be shown in more detail a bit later on in this chapter.

Step 2 Setting targets

The second stage of evaluation is setting targets. In order to set targets, we will need to complete a fuller assessment on the areas we are working on, as described in Chapter 12. As mentioned in this previous chapter, we need a bigger rating scale to evidence progress as it can take a while for someone to move from a 'not very good' to a 'quite good', so a four-point rating scale can be quite narrow as a method of evaluating ongoing intervention as it does not show subtle improvements. This can lead to people over-assessing to show improvement, but in doing this, they mask a need. To solve this problem, it is recommended that we assess skills and consider how much support they require to achieve that specific skill. We then assess their ability to do this using a six-point rating scale from 'skill not present' to 'skill present and consistent across most situations' (as described in Chapter 12).

The figure below shows this for the area of body language. In using this rating scale, we are able to extend out the ratings of 1 or 2 on the *Talkabout* Assessment Tool to

TALKABOUT ASSESSMENT & TARGET RECORD SHEET   Name   *Mohammed*   .... 1.

BODY LANGUAGE	1 Skill not present Child not able to do this even with lots of prompting and support from you	2 Skill emerging with prompting Child can do this but only after lots of support from you	3 Skill emerging with occasional prompting Child can do this with a bit of support	4 Skill present in a structured situation Child can do this spontaneously in a structured setting only	5 Skill present in some other situations The Child can to do this in some other settings	6 Skill present & consistent across most situations The child is be able to do this in any setting
Talk about Assessment Rating	1	1	2	2	2	3/4
1. EYE CONTACT - Able to use appropriate eye contact for short periods of time			Date 1			
2. FACIAL EXPRESSION - Able to use a range of appropriate facial expressions						Date 1
3. GESTURE - Able to use gesture to support what they are saying						Date 1
4. DISTANCE - Understands and uses good distance with other people			Date 1			
5. TOUCH- Understands and uses appropriate touch with other people			Date 1			
6. FIDGETING - Able to sit still when appropriate and not fidget for short periods of time			Date 1			
7. POSTURE- Able to use appropriate posture for short periods of time						Date 1
8. PERSONAL APPEARANCE- Able to maintain and adopt appearance to the situation						Date 1

Figure 17.4 A target record sheet for body language completed for Mohammed

ratings from 1–5 which enables us to show smaller amounts of progress more easily for the areas that we are working on, and we pay less attention to skills that are strengths (a rating of 6).

We can then enter this data onto a spreadsheet to enable us to easily analyse and present assessment data in a graph format.

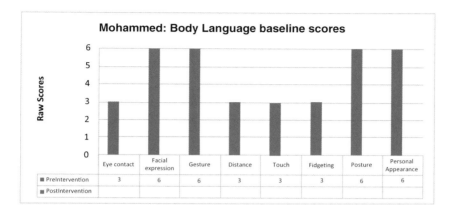

> **Figure 17.5** Body language baseline scores for Mohammed

Having identified the need to start work with Mohammed on his body language, we can identify the four skills that are 'needs' for him (eye contact, distance, touch and fidgeting) and we can then set him an appropriate initial target, such as: 'To be able to use appropriate distance and touch with other people with no prompting in a structured situation'. This can be reassessed over the period of intervention and will be described in the following section.

Step 3 Reassessment of targets and baseline assessment

At the end of any period of intervention, it is important to reassess and measure the effectiveness of our work. So here we reassess the targets, and if enough time has elapsed since the initial baseline assessment (usually a minimum of six months), we can also reassess using our initial rating scale, for example, the *Talkabout* Assessment Tool.

Reassessment of targets

Reassessment of the target rating scale may happen more regularly and so we can track progress in the following way:

* A target record sheet and an excel spreadsheet showing all of these scores (Figure 17.6)
* A spreadsheet highlighting the skills that need intervention, showing evidence after one review and then to show evidence with three assessment points (Figure 17.7)

TALKABOUT ASSESSMENT & TARGET RECORD SHEET   Name   *Mohammed*   .... 1.

BODY LANGUAGE	1 Skill not present Child not able to do this even with lots of prompting and support from you	2 Skill emerging with prompting Child can do this but only after lots of support from you	3 Skill emerging with occasional prompting Child can do with a bit of support	4 Skill present in a structured situation Child can do this spontaneously in a structured setting only	5 Skill present in some other situations The Child can to do this in some other settings	6 Skill present & consistent across most situations The child is be able to do this in any setting
Talk abourt Assessment Rating	1	1	2	2	2	3/4
1. **EYE CONTACT** - Able to use appropriate eye contact for short periods of time			*Date 1*			
2. **FACIAL EXPRESSION** - Able to use a range of appropriate facial expressions						*Date 1+2*
3. **GESTURE** - Able to use gesture to support what they are saying						*Date 1+2*
4. **DISTANCE** - Understands and uses good distance with other people			*Date 1*		*Date 2*	
5. **TOUCH**- Understands and uses appropriate touch with other people			*Date 1*		*Date 2*	
6. **FIDGETING** - Able to sit still when appropriate and not fidget for short periods of time			*Date 1*			
7. **POSTURE**- Able to use appropriate posture for short periods of time						*Date 1+2*
8. **PERSONAL APPEARANCE**- Able to maintain and adopt appearance to the situation						*Date 1+2*

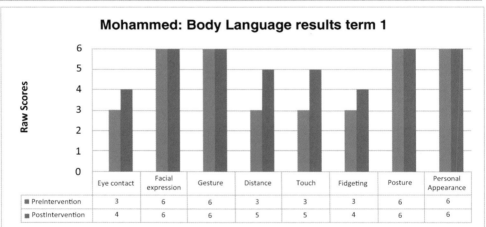

	Eye contact	Facial expression	Gesture	Distance	Touch	Fidgeting	Posture	Personal Appearance
■ PreIntervention	3	6	6	3	3	3	6	6
■ PostIntervention	4	6	6	5	5	4	6	6

Figure 17.6 A target record sheet for body language for Mohammed – first review

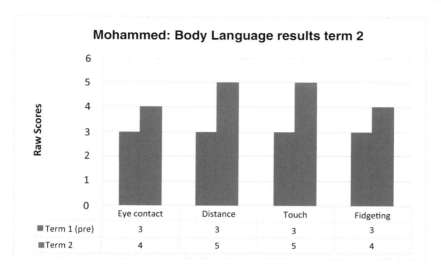

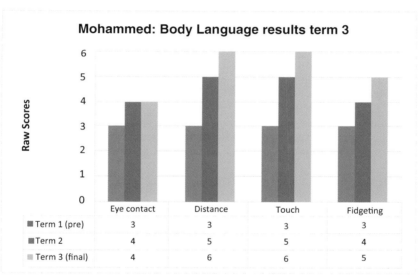

Figure 17.7 An evaluation of body language targets for Mohammed – first and second review (showing only the four skills being worked on)

Reassessment of baseline assessment

At the end of work, or after a longer period of time has elapsed, we can then reassess on our baseline rating scale. So for Mohammed his *Talkabout* Assessment wheel was re-done and his results were then put onto his spreadsheet to show the progress.

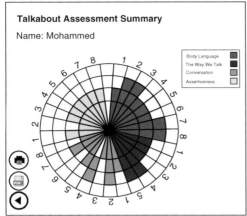

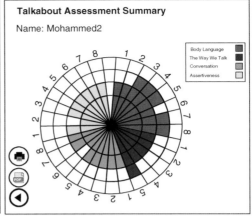

Body language	The way we talk	Conversations	Assertiveness
1. Eye contact 2. Facial expression 3. Gesture 4. Distance 5. Touch 6. Fidgeting 7. Posture 8. Personal appearance	1. Volume 2. Rate 3. Clarity 4. Intonation 5. Fluency	1. Listening 2. Starting conversations 3. Taking turns 4. Asking questions 5. Answering questions 6. Relevance 7. Repairing 8. Ending conversations	1. Expressing feelings 2. Standing up for self 3. Making suggestions 4. Refusing 5. Disagreeing 6. Complaining 7. Apologising 8. Requesting explanations

Figure 17.8 Mohammed's *Talkabout* Assessment Wheel before and after

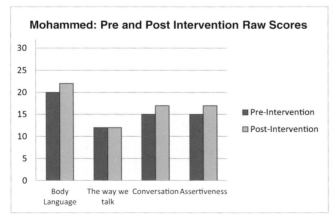

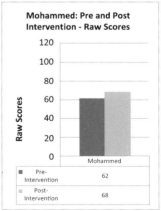

Figure 17.9 Mohammed's *Talkabout* Assessment data

In addition to analysing results for individuals, it is often useful to look at the results from a group or class – something that schools are very enthusiastic about! In these cases, it is possible to take the same data from both the target forms and the assessment wheels and then to enter the details for all the children in your group onto a spreadsheet to evidence improvements. The following three examples are from two projects in which I have been involved and a school in which I have worked.

Examples of evidence

1. The Afasic Project: secondary schools

Two hundred schools took part in this project and data was collected for 507 students over a period of three years (2011–2014). Students were taught social skills within a *Talkabout* group that ran for 20 weeks and assessments were done prior to the group starting and at the end of the intervention or the academic year (six to nine months later). The chart shows their pre and post *Talkabout* Assessments. It is interesting to note the shape of the graph which confirms the hierarchical model (body language is easier to teach/earlier to develop than assertiveness).

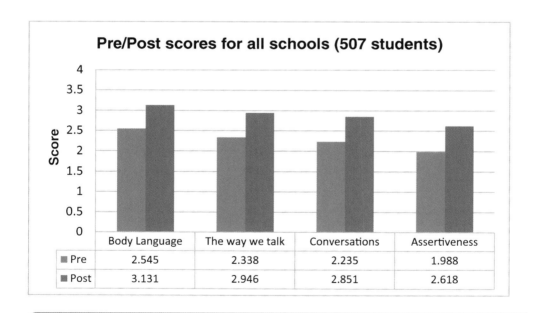

Pre/Post scores for all schools (507 students)

	Body Language	The way we talk	Conversations	Assertiveness
Pre	2.545	2.338	2.235	1.988
Post	3.131	2.946	2.851	2.618

Figure 17.10 Final results from Afasic secondary school project 2011–2014

2. The Afasic Project: primary schools

435 schools took part in this project and data was collected for 661 students over a period of three years (2014–2017). Students attended a self-awareness and self-esteem *Talkabout* group that ran for 20 weeks, and interviews were done prior to the group starting and at the end of the intervention or the academic year (six to nine months later). The chart shows their pre and post target scores from their self-awareness and self-esteem interviews. The target forms were simplified for this project from a 1-6 rating to a 1-4 and the final two ratings were not included.

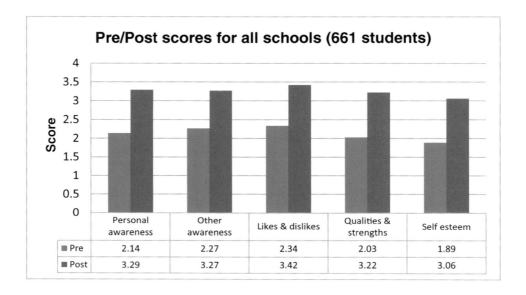

	Personal awareness	Other awareness	Likes & dislikes	Qualities & strengths	Self esteem
■ Pre	2.14	2.27	2.34	2.03	1.89
■ Post	3.29	3.27	3.42	3.22	3.06

Figure 17.11 Final results from Afasic primary school project 2014–2017

3. The Ashley School Academy Trust in Lowestoft

The Ashley School in Lowestoft is a special school for children with an intellectual disability aged 7–16. In 2014 we set up a pilot scheme in their school to evidence the progress that students made when placed in *Talkabout* groups with teachers that have been trained to teach social skills. As a result, the school saw huge progress in these children who were part of the pilot and so social skills was put on the curriculum, and now all students at Ashley School have one *Talkabout* lesson a week. The school evidences progress in two ways:

- A *Talkabout* Assessment wheel is completed when a student arrives in the school and this is repeated at the end of each Key Stage (approximately at ages 11, 13 and 16). So, for any student they could end up having up to 4 assessment wheels if they start at age seven and leave the school at age 16. This is the long-term measure.
- A target form is completed annually for each student on the topic of work being completed. For example, younger students will be working on the self-awareness

and self-esteem and so will have targets around this. Older students will have targets around other areas of social skills such as conversations or body language. These are then reassessed at the end of the academic year. The school also collects some qualitative data, such as examples of answers given during a *Talkabout* self-awareness interview.

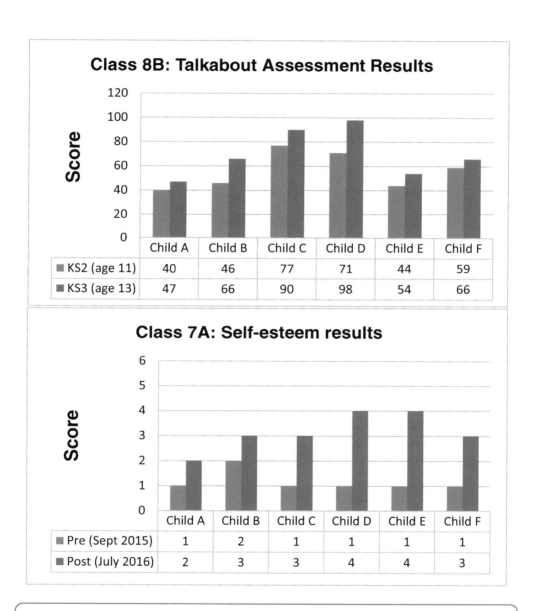

Class 8B: Talkabout Assessment Results

	Child A	Child B	Child C	Child D	Child E	Child F
KS2 (age 11)	40	46	77	71	44	59
KS3 (age 13)	47	66	90	98	54	66

Class 7A: Self-esteem results

	Child A	Child B	Child C	Child D	Child E	Child F
Pre (Sept 2015)	1	2	1	1	1	1
Post (July 2016)	2	3	3	4	4	3

Figure 17.12 Class evidence from Ashley School in 2016

Child	Question	Pre (Sept 2015)	Post (July 2016)
A	How would you describe the way you look?	Prompted *'Blondish'* Prompted *'Blue'*	*'White shirt, black trousers, multi-coloured shoes, a human being, white skin, hair, a boy'*
B		*'Red hair'* (incorrect response)	*'Curly hair, dark hair, girl, tall'*
C		*'My hair's funny, my teeth are funny, my voice is funny'*	*'Blue eyes, messy hair, I look cool'*

Mostly this evidence is encouraging and validating. I have heard many teaching staff reporting that their head teacher values the work they do on social skills much more now they can provide evidence like this. And, of course, our reports look more professional and impressive! But what happens if the evidence shows that someone has not made any progress or has actually got worse? Then, of course, we must investigate and we must ask ourselves a few questions to work out why.

Why hasn't it worked? Questions to ask yourself

Sometimes we are not successful. We may not need our assessment, our targets, or our evaluations to tell us that. We just know. We can see. The important thing to do at this point is to ask some questions and to work out why. There is always an answer and we can then change our intervention accordingly. So here are the most important questions to ask and the most common reasons why the intervention hasn't worked:

1. Is there something happening in the child's life that may explain this?

There may be a simple explanation for the fact that a student hasn't improved that has nothing to do with the intervention. I have worked with children who have had a traumatic year due to health, family, bereavement, and unsurprisingly this has an impact on their self-esteem and their social skills.

2. Did we choose the right behaviour?

As we said in Chapter 13, the first step to intervention is to choose the appropriate behaviour with which to start work. Remember the hierarchy that was described in Chapter 12? If we have chosen a skill to teach that is too difficult, and the person does not have the underpinning skills to support that (harder) skill, then we may have set them up to fail.

3. Is there another reason why a behaviour is happening? Consider the 'why?'

Sometimes we have not accurately understood the underlying reason why a particular behaviour is occurring and this is why our intervention has not worked. Remember Jonty in Chapter 13? Sometimes it is about *how* you need to teach a skill or it is not about teaching the skill at all, but understanding the context or the reason why it is happening and maybe changing something in their environment.

4. Is the person motivated to improve or change?

Sometimes I hear teachers saying that the intervention is not working because the students don't see the point. The students may complain that the work is 'boring' or 'babyish'. In almost all of these cases, I have found that the problem was in the students not being motivated because they did not see the relevance of what was being taught. We do need students to see the relevance not only to motivate them but also in order to then see generalisation of skills. Maag (2006) says that 'generalization will be enhanced when students . . . see the relevance of using targeted skills in everyday life'. The other reason that the person may not be motivated is because we are trying to teach something that is not important to them or we are motivating them with something that is not important!

5. Is the environment conducive?

Consider if there is more that can be done to make the environment more conducive. We know from research that if there is to be an increase in generalisation of the skill then the intervention must reach beyond the student to include his or her peer group (Maag, 2005). So how can we involve their peers and other staff to make it easier for the student to be more successful? This is particularly relevant if the student is able to achieve a skill within a social skills session, but is unable to take that skill out of the session into their everyday life.

6. Is the intervention strategy right?

Consider if the person enjoys the intervention. Sometimes we try to make the person fit the intervention that is on offer or that is easiest for us or the school, and we need to stop and consider what would work best for that person. We should always try to match the intervention with the person and the behaviour we are teaching. So consider their anxiety levels, their motivation to engage with the intervention, and their understanding of what is being asked of them. Also, if they are part of a group, what their relationship is like with others in the group and how well the group has gelled.

7. Is the intervention setting right?

Duncan (2001) says that 'the weak outcomes of social skills interventions can be attributed to the fact that these interventions often take place in contrived, restricted, and decontextualized' settings. Would it be better to implement something within the classroom or at home? We need to consider how easy it is for the person to learn the skill but also to generalise the skill into other contexts.

8. Are the duration and frequency right?

I sometimes hear clinicians complaining that they only have six sessions to work with someone on their social skills. Is this enough? Mostly I would say no. Maag (2006) theorises that teaching social skills to students with emotional and behavioural difficulties (EBD) is equivalent to teaching academics. He says that reading or mathematics instruction would not be terminated after a brief, three- to six-week long unit, so nor should the teaching of social skills. In fact, he feels that social skills training should be a standard portion of the curricula for students with EBD. So maybe we have not been successful because we need to give it more time.

Summary

Over the last 30 years, I have worked with many people who struggle with their social skills, their social confidence or competence, their self-esteem or their friendship skills. I have seen many people improve and many people's lives change for the better as a result. I feel proud of the things I have achieved with some of the amazing people I have worked with and I feel privileged to have been part of their success stories. However, without the evidence, these experiences I have had become just stories – the stories I can tell about the times I worked with Mohammed, Jessie, Jonty and many others, and how we made a difference. Don't get me wrong – everyone loves a story and I am no exception! But if we only tell stories, we lose a large part of the work and we lose a large part of our audience. The evidence is where we refine our work and demonstrate our effectiveness, but also how we ensure that social skills is given the status it requires and deserves, particularly in education.

As I said in Chapter 1, we live in a world where social skills are essential for our quality of life and our self-esteem. We need social skills to make friends, to get a job, to succeed at school and to stay out of trouble, and then we are more likely to feel good about ourselves and have a higher self-esteem. So, this is pretty important in the whole scheme of things. If we want to help someone to develop their social skills, we need to get it right. We need to know where to start. We need to know what to do. And we need to know how to evidence what we have done. This is still what gets me up in the morning and keeps me going through the days, weeks, months and years. We have to get it right because it's too important not to. I'm still working on it, but I feel proud of how far I have come and to feel that after 30 years, I have enough information to write a book about it. I hope it has helped. Thank you for reading it!

Key points from Chapter 17

This chapter covered how to evaluate and measure the effectiveness of social skills interventions.

Defining evaluation and why it is important

There are two reasons why we evaluate the effectiveness of what we have done: to improve the quality of what we are doing, and to demonstrate the impact of the intervention.

What makes a good evaluation?

There are five rules:

- Good evaluation is well planned
- Good evaluation is tailored to your intervention
- Good evaluation is inclusive
- Good evaluation is honest
- Good evaluation is replicable

A model of good evaluation is a process that means that we review or reassess targets throughout intervention and then reassess and measure the effectiveness of the whole intervention at the end.

Step 1 The initial assessment and the baseline score

Using rating scales, information about the person's behaviour is transferred onto a rating scale which may use either numbers or descriptions to rate each skill. This is then quantified ready for reassessment and evaluation.

Step 2 Setting targets

We set targets by considering how much support they require to achieve a specific skill and assessing their ability to do this using a 6 point rating scale from 'skill not present' to 'skill present and consistent across most situations'. This information is then quantified ready for reassessment and evaluation.

Step 3 Reassessment of targets and baseline assessment

- Target reassessment: reassessment of the target rating scale happens more regularly so we can track progress during intervention and evidence smaller steps of success.
- Baseline reassessment: at the end of work, or after a longer period of time has elapsed, we reassess using our baseline rating scale.

Examples of evidence

- The Afasic Project: secondary schools
- The Afasic Project: primary schools
- Ashley School in Lowestoft

Why hasn't it worked? Questions to ask yourself

- Is there something happening in the child's life that may explain this?
- Did we choose the right behaviour?
- Is there another reason why a behaviour is happening? Consider the 'why?'
- Is the person motivated to improve or change?
- Is the environment conducive?
- Is the intervention strategy right?
- Is the intervention setting right?
- Are the duration and frequency right?

Summary

A few last thoughts about this book from the author.

References

Alberti R and Emmons M (2008) *Your Perfect Right: Assertiveness and Equality in Your Life and Relationships,* 9th edition. Atascadero, CA: Impact.

Albrecht S (2014) 'Reading dangerous faces: small cues, intuition, and the children of violent alcoholics'. *www.psychologytoday.com*

Amado AN (1993) *Friendships and Community Connections between People with and without Developmental Disabilities.* Baltimore: Paul H Brookes.

American Psychiatric Association (2013) *Diagnostic and Statistical Manual of Mental Disorders,* 5th edition (DSM-5). Washington, DC: American Psychiatric Association.

Angelo DS (2000) 'Learning disability community nursing: addressing emotional and sexual health needs'. Astor R and Jeffereys K (eds) (2000) *Positive Initiatives for People with Learning Difficulties.* London: Macmillan.

Apple AL, Billingsley F and Schwartz IS (2005) 'Effects of video modeling alone and with self-management on compliment-giving behaviors of children with high functioning ASD'. *Journal of Positive Behavior Interventions* 7(1), 33–46.

Argyle M and Henderson M (1985) *The Anatomy of Relationships.* London: Heinemann.

Attwood T (2007) *The Complete Guide to Asperger's Syndrome.* London and Philadelphia: Jessica Kingsley Publishers.

Attwood T (2014) 'New Introduction 2014: The DSM-5 Diagnostic Criteria for Autism Spectrum Disorder', in Attwood T (2007) *The Complete Guide to Asperger's Syndrome.* London and Philadelphia: Jessica Kingsley Publishers.

Attwood T (2016) 'Introduction', in Wylie P, Lawson W and Beardon L *The Nine Degrees of Autism: A Developmental Model.* London and New York: Routledge.

Bagwell CL and Schmidt ME (2011) *Friendships in Childhood and Adolescence.* New York and London: The Guildford Press.

Bandura A (1978) 'The self-system in reciprocal determination'. *American Psychologist 33,* 344–358.

Baron-Cohen S (2000) *Understanding Other Minds.* Oxford University Press.

Baron-Cohen S (2003) *The Essential Difference: Men, Women and the Extreme Make Brain.* London: Allen Lane.

Baron-Cohen S (2008) *The Facts*: *Autism and Asperger Syndrome.* Oxford University Press.

Baron-Cohen S, Leslie A and Frith U (1985) 'Does the autistic child have a "theory of mind"?' *Cognition 21,* 37–46.

Barry LM and Burlew SB (2004) 'Using social stories to teach choice and play skills to children with autism'. *Focus on Autism and Other Developmental Disabilities* 19(1), 45–51.

Baumrind D (1989) 'Rearing competent children', in Damon W (ed.) *Child development today and tomorrow*. San Francisco, CA: Jossey-Bass.

Beidel DC, Turner SM and Young BJ (2006) 'Social effectiveness therapy for children: Five years later'. *Behavior Therapy 37*, 416–425.

Belfiore C (2016) 'Puppets Talk, Children Listen'. *www.teachmag.com/archives/5618*

Bercow J, Beardshaw V and Kerwin-Nye A (2008) 'How speech, language and communication are linked to social disadvantage', in *Getting in Early: Primary Schools and Early Intervention*. The Smith Institute and the Centre for Social Justice November 2008.

Berndt TJ (1982) 'The features and effects of friendship in early adolescence'. *Child Development 53*, 1447–60.

Betts LR and Rotenberg KJ (2008) 'A social relations analysis of children's trust in their peers across the early years of school'. *Social Development 17*, 1039–55.

Bolton R (1979) *People Skills: How to Assert Yourself, Listen to Others and Resolve Conflicts*. London: Simon & Schuster.

Borg J (2008) *Body Language*. Harlow: Pearson Education Ltd.

Bowlby J (1980) *Attachment and Loss*, vol. 3. New York: Basic Books.

Boyce S (2012) *Not Just Talking: Identifying Non-Verbal Communication Difficulties – A Life Changing Approach*. Milton Keynes: Speechmark Publishing Ltd.

Brown JD and Marshall MA (2006) 'The three faces of self-esteem', in Michael Kernis (ed.) *Self-Esteem: Issues and Answers*. New York and Hove: Psychology Press.

Brugha T, Cooper SA, McManus S, Purdon S, Smith J, Scott FJ, Spiers N and Tyrer F (2012) *Estimating the Prevalence of Autism Spectrum Conditions in Adults: Extending the 2007 Adult Psychiatric Morbidity Survey*. Leeds: NHS Information Centre for Health and Social Care.

Bryan K, Freer J and Furlong C (2007) 'Language and communication difficulties in juvenile offenders'. *International Journal of Communication and Language Disorders 42*.

Buggey T (2005) 'Video self-modelling applications with students with autism spectrum disorder in a small private school setting'. *Focus on Autism and Other Developmental Disabilities 20(1)*, 52.

Cameron D (2000) *Good to Talk? Living and Working in a Communication Culture*. London: Sage.

Cameron J, MacGregor J and Kwang T (2013) 'Badge of honour or mark of shame: self-esteem as an interpersonal signal', in Zeigler-Hill V (ed.) *Self-Esteem: Current Issues in Social Psychology*. London and New York: Psychology Press.

Carnegie Dale (2006) *How to Win Friends and Influence People*. London: Vermilion (first published in 1953).

Carney DR, Cuddy AJC and Yap AJ (2010) 'Power posing: Brief nonverbal displays affect neuroendocrine levels and risk tolerance'. *Psychological Science 21(10)*, 1363–1368.

Charlop MH and Milstein JP (1989) 'Teaching autistic children conversational speech using video modeling'. *Journal of Applied Behavior Analysis 22*, 275–285.

Chess S and Thomas A (1996) *Temperament: Theory and Practice*, vol. 12. New York: Brunner-Mazel

Conn C (2016) *Play and Friendship in Inclusive Autism Education*. London and New York: Routledge.

Corsaro WA (2003) *We're Friends, Right? Inside Kids' Culture*. Washington, DC: Joseph Henry Press.

Crawford K and Goldstein H (2005) 'Supporting social skill development in students with emotional/behavioural disorders'. *Impact 18(2)*.

Dawson M, Soulieres I, Gernsbacher M and Mottron L (2007) 'The level and nature of autistic intelligence'. *Psychological Science 18(8)*: 657–662.

Dean J (2017) 'How to End a Conversation Positively' www.conversation-skills-core.com/how-to-end-conversation-positively

DeGelder B (1987) 'On not having a theory of mind.' *Cognition 27*, 285–290.

DeHart T, Pena R and Tennen H (2013) 'The development of explicit and implicit self-esteem and their role in psychological adjustment', in Zeigler-Hill V (ed.) *Self-Esteem: Current Issues in Social Psychology*. London and New York: Psychology Press.

Delano M and Snell M (2006) 'The effects of social stories on the social engagement of children with autism'. *Journal of Positive Behavior Interventions 8*(1), 29–42.

De Montaigne M (1994) *The Essays: A Collection*. London: Penguin Classics (first published 1580).

Denham S, Mason T, Caverly S, Schmidt M, Hackney R, Caswell C and Demulder E (2001) 'Preschoolers at play: Co-socialisers of emotional and social competence'. *International Journal of Behavioral Development 4*, 290–301.

Department for Education and Employment/Qualifications and Curriculum Authority (1999) *The National Curriculum: A Handbook for Primary Teachers in England*. London: DfEE/QCA.

Dickson D and McCartan P (2005) 'Communication, skill and health care delivery', in Sines D, Appleby F and Frost M (eds) *Community Health Care Nursing,* 3rd edition. Oxford: Blackwell Publishing.

Dickson D, Hargie O and Morrow N (1997) *Communication Skills Training for Health Professionals,* 2nd edition. London: Chapman and Hall.

Dodge KA and Tomlin AM (1987) 'Utilization of self-schemas as a mechanism of interpretational bias in aggressive children'. *Social Cognition 5*, 280–300.

Duncan S (2001) 'Development, implementation, and evaluation of a social skills training intervention in a rural special school setting for students with mild/moderate disabilities'. Logan, UT: Utah State University Press.

Eisenmajer R and Prior M (1991) 'Cognitive linguistic correlates of "theory of mind" ability in autistic children.' *British Journal of Developmental Psychology 9*, 351–364.

Ekman P (2001) *Telling Lies*. London: WW Norton.

Ekman P (2004) *Emotions Revealed: Understanding Faces and Feelings*. London: WW Norton.

Ekman P and Friesen WV (1982) 'Felt, false, and miserable smiles.' *Journal of Nonverbal Behavior 6*(4), 238–252.

Ekman P and Rosenberg E (2005) *What the Face Reveals: Basic and Applied Studies of Spontaneous Expression Using the Facial Action Coding System (Facs),* 2nd edition. Oxford: Oxford University Press.

Elias MJ, Zins JE, Wessberg RP, Frey KS, Greenberg MT, Haynes NM, Kesler R, Schwab-Stone ME and Shriver TP (1997) *Promoting Social and Emotional Learning: Guidelines for Educators*. Alexandria, VA: Association for Supervision and Curriculum Development.

Elliott SN and Gresham FM (1987) 'Children's social skills: Assessment and classification practices'. *Journal of Counseling and Development 66*, 96–99.

Emmons M and Alberti R (1975) *Stand Up, Speak Out, Talk Back*. New York: Pocket Books.

Espada JP, Griffin KW, Pereira JR, Orgiles M and Garcia-Fernandez JM (2012) 'Component analysis of a school-based substance use prevention program in Spain: contributions of problem solving and social skills training content'. *Prevention Science 13*, 86–95.

Ezeanu E (2010) 'How to avoid awkward silences'. http://www.peopleskillsdecoded.com/how-to-avoid-awkward-silences/

Ezeanu E (2012) 'The best conversation starters'. http://conversation-starters.com/author/conversationstarters/

References

Fast J (1971) *Body Language.* New York: Pocket Books.

Feldman R, Olds S and Papalia D (2004) *Human Development,* 9th edition. New Delhi, India: Tata McGraw-Hill.

Ferrans SD and Selman RL (2014) 'How students' perceptions of the school climate influence their choice to upstand, bystand, or join perpetrators of bullying'. *Harvard Educational Review 84,* 162–187.

Firth H and Rapley M (1990) *From Acquaintance to Friendship.* Kidderminster: BIMH Publications.

Ford L, Dinen J and Hall J (1984) 'Is there a life after placement?' *Education and Training of the Mentally Retarded 26,* 258–270.

Frea WD (2006) 'Teaching social skills to students on the autism spectrum'. *Impact, 19*(3), 20–21.

Furnham A (2014) 'The secrets of eye contact revealed'. www.psychologytoday.com

Gazelle H (2013) 'Is social anxiety in the child or in the anxiety-provoking nature of the child's interpersonal environment?' *Child Development Perspectives 7,* 221–226.

Gillberg C and Gillberg IC (1989) 'Asperger Syndrome – some epidemiological considerations: A research note.' *Journal of Child Psychology and Psychiatry 30,* 631–638.

Givens DB (2005) *Love Signals: A Practical Guide to the Body Language of Courtship.* New York: St Martin's Press.

Gladwell M (2006) *Blink: The Power of Thinking without Thinking.* London: Penguin Books.

Goffman E (1955/2010) 'On Face-Work', in *Social Theory: The Multicultural Readings,* Lemert C (ed.). Philadelphia: Westview Press.

Goldstein HL, Kaczmarek R, Pennington R and Shafer K (1992) 'Peer-mediated intervention: Attending to, commenting on, and acknowledging the behaviour of preschoolers with autism'. *Journal of Applied Behavior Analysis 25,* 289–305.

Grandin, T (1995) *Thinking in Pictures and Other Reports from my Life with Autism.* New York: Doubleday.

Gray C (1998) 'Social stories and comic strip conversations with students with Asperger syndrome and high-functioning autism', in Schopler E, Mesibov GB and Kunce LJ (eds) *Asperger Syndrome or High-Functioning Autism?* New York: Plenum.

Gray C (2010) *The New Social Story™ Book.* Arlington, Texas: Future Horizons.

Gray J (1992) *Men are from Mars, Women are from Venus.* London: Element.

Greenbaum P and Rosenfeld H (1980) 'Varieties of touching in greetings: Sequential structure and sex-related differences'. *Journal of Nonverbal Behavior 5,* 13–25.

Gresham FM and Elliott SN (2008) *SSIS Social Skills Improvement System.* New York: NCS Pearson.

Grice HP (1975) 'Logic and conversation', in *Syntax and Semantics,* vol. 3, *Speech Acts.* New York: Academic Press.

Gross J (2008) 'Why we need to target four to eight year olds', in Gross J (ed.) *Getting in Early: Primary Schools and Early Intervention.* The Smith Institute and the Centre for Social Justice.

Gumpel T and Frank R (1999) 'An expansion of the peer paradigm; cross-age peer tutoring of social skills among socially rejected boys'. *Journal of Applied Behaviour Analysis 32,* 115–118.

Hale CM and Tager-Flusberg H (2005) 'Social communication in children with autism'. *Autism, 9*(2) 157–178.

Hall ET (1966) *The Hidden Dimension.* New York: Doubleday & Co.

Hamilton C (2014) *Communicating for Results: A Guide for Business and the Professions,* 10th edition. Boston, MA: Wadsworth.

Haney P and Durlak JA (1998) 'Changing self-esteem in children and adolescents: A meta-analytic review'. *Journal of Clinical Child Psychology 27*, 423–433.

Happe FGE (1994) 'Annotation: psychological theories of autism: The 'theory of mind' account and rival theories.' *Journal of Child Psychology and Psychiatry 35*, 215–229.

Hargie O (2017) *Skilled Interpersonal Communication: Research, Theory and Practise*, 6th edition. London: Routledge.

Hargie O and Dickson D (2004) *Skilled Interpersonal Communication Research, Theory and Practice*, 4th edition. London and New York: Routledge.

Hargie O, Saunders C and Dickson D (1994) *Social Skills in Interpersonal Communication*, 3rd edition. London: Routledge.

Hart B and Risley T (2003) 'The early catastrophe: The 30 million word gap'. *American Educator 27*, 4–9.

Hartup WW and Stevens N (1997) 'Friendships and adaptation in the life course'. *Psychological Bulletin 121*, 355–370.

Hoag H (2008) 'Sex on the brain'. *New Scientist 199*(2665), 28–31.

Howley M and Arnold E (2005) *Revealing the Hidden Social Code*. London and Philadelphia: Jessica Kingsley Publishers.

Hubbard K (1868–1930) https://www.brainyquote.com/quotes/authors/k/kin_hubbard.html

James W (1890) *The Principles of Psychology*. Cambridge, MA: Harvard University Press.

Jaspers K (1951) *The Way to Wisdom*. New Haven: Yale University Press.

Johnson DW and Johnson R (1989) *Co-operation and Competition: Theory and Research*. Edina, MN: Interaction.

Jordan CH and Zeigler-Hill V (2013) 'Fragile self-esteem: The perils and pitfalls of (some) high self-esteem', in Zeigler-Hill V (ed.) *Self-Esteem: Current Issues in Social Psychology*. London and New York: Psychology Press.

Kelly J (1982) *Social Skills Training: A Practical Guide for Interventions*. New York: Springer.

Kelly A (1996) *Talkabout*. London: Speechmark.

Kelly A (2000) *Working with Adults with a Learning Disability*. London: Speechmark.

Kelly A and Sains B (2009) *Talkabout for Teenagers*. London: Speechmark.

Kelly A and Sains B (2010) *Talkabout Assessment Tool*. London: Speechmark.

Kelly A (2011, 2018a) *Talkabout for Children Developing Self-Awareness and Self-Esteem*. London: Speechmark.

Kelly A (2011, 2018b) *Talkabout for Children Developing Social Skills*. London: Speechmark.

Kelly A (2013) *Talkabout for Children Developing Friendship Skills*. London: Speechmark.

Kelly A (2016) *Talkabout*, 2nd edition. London: Speechmark.

Kendon A and Ferber A (1973) 'A description of some human greetings', in Michael R and Crooks J (eds) *Comparative Ecology and Behaviour of Primates*. London: Academic Press.

Koestner R and Mageau G (2006) 'The assessment of implicit and explicit self-esteem: Lessons from motive research', in Kernis M (ed.) *Self-Esteem: Issues and Answers*. New York and Hove: Psychology Press.

Kokina A and Kern L (2010) 'Social story interventions for students with autism spectrum disorders: A meta-analysis'. *Journal of Autism and Developmental Disorders 40*, 812–826.

Kollock P, Blumstein P and Schwartz P (1985) 'Sex and power in interaction: Conversational privileges and duties'. *American Sociological Review 50*(1), 34–46.

Kyriakides L, Creemers BPM, Papastylianou D and Papadatou-Pastou M (2014) 'Improving the school learning environment to reduce bullying: An experimental study'. *Scandinavian Journal of Educational Research 5*, 453–478.

Lange AJ and Jakubowski P (1976) *Responsible Assertive Behavior*. Champaign, IL: Research Press.

References

Langford D (1994) *Analysing Talk: Investigating Verbal Interaction in English*. London: Macmillan Press.

Lightsey OR and Barnes PW (2007) 'Discrimination, attributional tendencies, generalized self-efficacy, and assertiveness as predictors of psychological distress among African Americans'. *Journal of Black Psychology 33*, 27–50.

Lovaas OI (2003) *Teaching Individuals with Developmental Delays: Basic Intervention Techniques*. Austin, TX: Pro-Ed.

Maag JW (2005) 'Social skills training for youth with emotional and behavior disorders and learning disabilities: Problems, conclusions, and suggestions'. *Exceptionality 13*, 155–172.

Maag JW (2006) 'Social skills training for students with emotional and behavioural disorders: A review of reviews'. *Behavioral Disorders 32*(1), 5–17.

Marulis L and Newman S (2010) 'The effects of vocabulary intervention on young children's word learning: A met-analysis'. *Review of Educational Research 80*, 300–335.

Mash FJ and Barkley RA (1996) *Child Psychopathology*. New York: Guildford Press.

Mashburn AJ, Justice LM, Downer JT and Pianta RC (2009) 'Peer effects on children's language achievement during pre-kindergarten'. *Child Development 80*(3), 686–702.

Mastergeorge A, Rogers S, Corbett B and Solomon M (2003) 'Nonmedical interventions for Autism Spectrum Disorders', in Ozonoff, Rogers and Hendren (eds) *Autism Spectrum Disorders*. Washington: American Psychiatric Publishing Inc.

May R (1969) *Love and Will*. New York: WW Norton.

McCartan P and Hargie O (2004) 'Assertiveness and caring: Are they compatible?' *Journal of Clinical Nursing 13*, 707–713.

McGrath J (2013) 'Development of Social Skills During Early Childhood' *Yahoo! Voices* http://voices.yahoo.com/the-development-social-skills-during-early-childhood-3356640.html

McKay M, Davis M and Fanning P (2009) *Messages: The Communication Skills Book*. Oakland, CA: New Harbinger.

Mehrabian A (1971) *Silent Messages*. Wadsworth, California: Belmont.

Merrell K (2001) 'Assessment of children's social skills: Recent developments, best practices, and new directions'. *Exceptionality 9*(1 and 2), 3–18. Lawrence Erlbaum Associates Inc.

Messer D (1995) *The Development of Communication: From Social Interaction to Language*. Chichester: Wiley.

Miller E (1999) 'Turn-Taking and Relevance in Conversation' published for the course: Ways of Speaking at the University of Pennsylvania. www.storytellingandvideoconferencing.com

Milton D (n.d.) 'So what exactly is autism?' www.autismeducationtrust.org.uk

Milton D (2012) 'On the ontological status of autism: The 'double empathy problem'. *Disability and Society, 27*(6), 885–887.

Morgan N and Saxton J (2006) *Asking Better Questions*, 2nd edition. Markham, ON: Pembroke Publishers.

Morin D and Sander V (2012) 'How to start a conversation with anyone'. www.socialpronow.com/start-conversation

Myers D and Diener E (1995) 'Who Is happy?' *Psychological Science 6*(1), 10–19.

Navarro J (2007) *What every BODY is saying*. HarperCollins e-books.

Neal DT and Chartrand TL (2011) 'Embodied emotion perception: Amplifying and dampening facial feedback modulates emotional perception accuracy'. *Social Psychological and Personality Science 2*(6), 673–678.

Nelson J and Aboud FE (1985) 'The resolution of social conflict between friends'. *Child Development 53*, 1009–1017.

Nelson-Jones R (1996) *Relating Skills: A Practical Guide to Effective Personal Relationships*. London: Cassell.

Newton C, Taylor G and Wilson D (1996) 'Circles of friends: An inclusive approach to meeting emotional and behavioural needs'. *Educational Psychology in Practice 11*, 41–48.

Newton M (2002) *Savage Girls and Wild Boys: A History of Feral Children*. London: Faber.

Nichols RG and Stevens LA (1957) *Are You Listening?* New York: McGraw-Hill.

Nordquist R (2017) 'Turn-taking in conversation analysis'. www.thoughtco.com/turn-taking-conversation-1692569

O'Callaghan PM, Reitman D, Northup J, Hupp SDA and Murphy MA (2003) 'Promoting social skills generalization with ADHD-diagnosed children in a sports setting'. *Behavior Therapy 34*, 313–330.

Odom S and Strain PS (1984) 'Peer mediated approaches to promoting children's social interaction: A review'. *American Journal of Orthopsychiatry 54*, 544–557.

Ouvry C (1998) 'Making relationships', in Lacey P and Ouvry C (eds) *People with Profound and Multiple Learning Disabilities: A Collaborative Approach to Meeting Complex Needs*. London: David Fulton Publishers.

Ozonoff S and Rogers S (2003) 'From Kanner to the millennium', in Ozonoff S, Rogers SJ and Hendren RL (eds) *Autism Spectrum Disorders: A Research Review for Practitioners*. Washington, DC: American Psychiatric Press.

Park LE and Crocker J (2013) 'Pursuing self-esteem: Implications for self-regulation and relationships', in Zeigler-Hill V (ed.) *Self-Esteem: Current Issues in Social Psychology*. London and New York: Psychology Press.

Patrick N (2008) *Social Skills for Teenagers and Adults with Asperger Syndrome*. London and Philadelphia: Jessica Kingsley Publishers.

Pease A (2001) *Why Men Don't Listen and Women Can't Read Maps*. London: Orion.

Pease A and B (2004) *The Definitive Book of Body Language*. London: Orion

Pellegrini DS, Galda L, Bartini M and Charak D (1998) 'Oral language and literacy language in context: The role of social relationships'. *Merrill-Palmer Quarterly 44*, 38–54.

Piaget J (1932) *The Language and Thought of the Child*. New York: Harcourt Brace and Company.

Pickering M (2006) 'The dance of dialogue'. *The Psychologist 19*, 734–737.

Phillips EL (1979) *The Social Skills Basis of Psychopathology*. New York: Grune and Stratton.

Powell J (1974) *The Secret of Staying in Love*. Boston: Argus Communications.

Powell T (2016) *Recognising Asperger's Syndrome (Autism Spectrum Disorder)*. London: Speechmark.

Powers R (1979) 'The organization of purposeful dialogues'. *Linguistics 17*, 107–152.

Pyszczynski T and Kesebir P (2013) 'An existential perspective on the need for self-esteem', in Zeigler-Hill V (ed.) *Self-Esteem: Current Issues in Social Psychology*. London and New York: Psychology Press.

Richardson A and Ritchie J (1989) *Developing Friendships: Enabling People with Learning Difficulties to Make and Maintain Friends*. London: Policy Studies Institute.

Robbins S and Hunsaker P (2014) *Training in Interpersonal Skills: TIPS for Managing People at Work*, 6th edition. Harlow, Essex: Pearson Education.

Rochat P (2003) 'Five levels of self-awareness as they unfold early in life'. *Consciousness and Cognition 12*, 717–731.

Rogers C (1961) *On Becoming a Person*. Boston: Houghton Mifflin Co.

Rosenberg M (1965) *Society and the Adolescent Self-Image*. Princeton, NJ: Princeton.

Rubin K (2002) *The Friendship Factor: Helping Our Children to Navigate Their Social World And Why It Matters for Their Success and Happiness*. New York: Penguin Books.

Rubin KH and Rose-Krasnor L (1986) 'Social-cognitive and social behaviour perspectives on problem-solving', in Perlmutter M (ed.) *Minnesota Symposium on Child Psychology.* Hillsdale, NJ: Erlbaum.

Sacks H, Schegloff EA and Jefferson G (1974) 'A simplest systematics for the organization of turn-taking for conversation'. *Language 50*(4), 696–735.

Sainsbury C (2000) *Martian in the Playground: Understanding the Schoolchild with Asperger's Syndrome.* Bristol: Lucky Duck.

Salter A (1949) *Conditioned Reflex Therapy: The Direct Approach to the Reconstruction of Personality.* New York: Capricorn Books.

Sansosti FJ and Powell-Smith KA (2008) 'Using computer-presented Social Stories and video models to increase the social communication skills of children with high-functioning autism spectrum disorders'. *Journal of Positive Behavior Interventions 10*(3), 162–178.

Sansosti FJ, Powell-Smith KA and Kincaid D (2004) 'A research synthesis of Social Story interventions for children with autism spectrum disorders'. *Focus on Autism and Other Developmental Disabilities 19*(4), 194–204.

Schalock RL (2000) 'Three decades of quality of life'. *Focus on Autism and Other Developmental Disabilities 15*(2), 116–127.

Scher SJ and Darley JM (1997) 'How effective are the things people say to apologize? Effects of the realization of the apology speech act'. *Journal of Psycholinguistic Research 26*(1), 127–140.

Schlundt D and McFall R (1985) 'New directions in the assessment of social competence and social skills', in L'Abate L and Milan M (eds) *Handbook of Social Skills Training and Research.* New York: Wiley.

Schneider BH (2016) *Childhood Friendships and Peer Relations: Friends and Enemies.* New York and London: Routledge.

Schumaker J and Hazel J (1984) 'Social skills assessment and training for the learning disabled: Who's on first and what's on second? Part 1'. *Journal of Learning Disabilities 17,* 422–430.

Shah A and Frith U (1983) 'An islet of ability in autistic children: A research note'. *Journal of Child Psychology and Psychiatry 24,* 613–620.

Shaked M and Yirmiya N (2003) 'Understanding Social Difficulties', in Prior M (ed.) *Learning and Behaviour Problems in Asperger Syndrome.* Guildford: Guildford Press.

Shapiro M (2017) www.socialcommunication.truman.edu

Sherer M, Pierce K, Paredes S, Kisacky KL, Ingersoll B and Schreibman L (2001) 'Enhancing conversation skills in children with Autism via video technology: which is better, "self" or "other" as a model?' *Behavior Modification 25*(1), 140–158.

Sheridan SM and Walker D (1999) 'Social skills in context: Considerations for assessment, intervention, and generalisation', in Reynolds CR and Gutkin TB (eds) *The Handbook of School Psychology,* 3rd edition. New York: Wiley.

Singer-Califano A (2008) 'The use of technology in enhancing social skills'. *i-manager's Journal on Educational Psychology 1*(4), 1–8.

Skills You Need Ltd (2016) 'An Introduction to Communication Skills' www.skillsyouneed.com

Smith C (2003) *Writing and Developing Social Stories: Practical Interventions in Autism.* Milton Keynes: Speechmark.

Stewart N (1985) *Winning Friends at Work.* New York: Ballantine Books.

Stivers T, Enfield NJ, Brown P, Englert C, Hayashi M, Heinemann T and Levinson S (2009) 'Universals and cultural variation in turn-taking in conversation'. Proceedings of the *National Academy of Sciences 106*(26).

Strain PS, Schwartz IS and Bovey E (2008) 'Social competence interventions for young children with autism', in Brown WH, Odom SL and McConnell SR (eds) *Social Competence of Young Children: Risk, Disability, and Intervention.* Baltimore MD: Paul H Brookes Publishing.

Sullivan HS (1953) *The Interpersonal Theory of Psychiatry.* New York: Norton.

Sutcliffe R (2004) 'Figure of Speech Dictionary'. www.opundo.com

Swaggart B, Gangon E, Bock SJ, Earles TL, Quinn C and Myles BS, et al. (1995) 'Using social stories to teach social and behavioral skills to children with autism'. *Focus on Autistic Behavior* 10(1), 1–16.

Tammet D (2006) *Born on a Blue Day.* London: Hodder and Stoughton.

Tangney JP and Leary MR (2003) 'The next generation of self research', in Leary MR and Tangney J (eds) *Handbook of Self and Identity.* New York, NY: Wiley.

Tatera K (2015) 'Botox Inhibits Deep Emotions and the Ability to Empathize'. www.thescienceexplorer.com

Thompson RA (1994) 'Emotion regulation: A theme in search of definition', in Fox NA (ed.) The development of emotion regulation: Biological and behavioral considerations. *Monographs of the Society for Research in Child Development* 59(2/3), 25–52.

Trower P, Bryant B and Argyle M (1978) *Social Skills and Mental Health.* York: Methuen & Co. Ltd.

Trzesniewski KH, Donnellan MB and Robins RW (2013) 'Development of self-esteem', in Zeigler-Hill V (ed.) *Self-Esteem: Current Issues in Social Psychology.* London and New York: Psychology Press.

Volden J (2004) 'Conversational repair in speakers with autism spectrum disorder'. *International Journal of Language and Communication Disorders* 39(2), 171–189.

Vygotsky LS (1978) *Mind in Society.* Cambridge, MA: Harvard University Press.

Ward ML (2005) 'Children, adolescents, and the media: The moulding of minds, bodies and deeds'. *New Directions for Child and Adolescent Development* 109, 63–71.

Ward WA (1970) *Fountains of Faith.* Droke House.

Warnes E, Sheridan S, Geske J and Warnes W (2005) 'A contextual approach to the assessment of social skills: identifying meaningful behaviors for social competence'. *Psychology in the Schools* 42(2), 173–187.

Wetherby A (2006) 'Understanding and measuring social communication in children with autism spectrum disorders', in Charman T and Stone W (eds) *Social and Communication Development in Autism Spectrum Disorders.* London and New York: The Guildford Press.

Whitaker DS (1989) *Using Groups to Help People.* London: Routledge.

Wing L (1996) *The Autistic Spectrum: A Guide for Parents and Professionals.* London: Constable.

Wolman BB (1973) *Dictionary of Behavioural Science.* New York: Van Nostrand Reinhold.

Zeigler-Hill V (2013) 'The importance of self-esteem', in Zeigler-Hill V (ed.) *Self-Esteem: Current Issues in Social Psychology.* London and New York: Psychology Press.

Zetlin M (2015) '11 Foolproof Ways to Start a Conversation with Absolutely Anyone'. www.inc.com/minda-zetlin/10-foolproof-ways-to-start-a-conversation-with-absolutely-anyone.html

Zimmerman DH and West C (1975) 'Sex roles, interruptions, and silences in conversation'. *Language and Sex: Difference and Dominance*, 105–129.

Index

Printed in Great Britain
by Amazon